W9-BAG-024

Jane
on the
BRAIN

Jane
on the
BRAIN

EXPLORING THE SCIENCE
OF SOCIAL INTELLIGENCE
with Jane Austen

WENDY JONES

PEGASUS BOOKS
NEW YORK LONDON

JANE ON THE BRAIN

Pegasus Books Ltd.
148 W. 37th Street, 13th Floor
New York, NY 10018

First Pegasus Books edition December 2017

Interior design by Maria Fernandez

Illustrations by Jocelyn Sawyer

Library of Congress Cataloging-in-Publication Data is available.

ISBN: 978-1-68177-554-8

10 9 8 7 6 5 4 3 2 1

Printed in the United States of America
Distributed by W. W. Norton & Company, Inc.
www.pegasusbooks.us

For my mother, Vicki Singer,

and in memory of my father, Iz Singer

CONTENTS

INTRODUCTION

Empathic Austen

I blame my first marriage on Jane Austen. Elizabeth Bennet married for gratitude and esteem, and these were exactly the feelings I had for my first husband. If they were good enough for Elizabeth, why wouldn't they be good enough for me? But I wasn't Elizabeth; I was much more like Emma, a far more flawed heroine. The romantic Emma would never have been satisfied with gratitude and esteem, and neither was I. To be fair, I know my husband felt the same way, although I don't think he blamed Austen for his mistake.

For better or worse, my hasty marriage was simple to undo—at least with respect to its legal and social aspects. For my next chapter, I returned to graduate school, pursuing a doctorate in English literature and specializing in Austen and other novelists of her time. Had I been a more daring scholar, I might have realized that my youthful folly had posed some interesting questions: Why did I look to Austen and her characters for guidance about how to live my own life? And I'm not, by far, the only one to do this. Surely this trust couldn't be separated from the great love I had for Austen. Why do so many people love Austen so intensely, and in such a personal way?

Austen certainly isn't the only literary celebrity among Anglo-American authors whose work inspires interest in her life. Captivated by the dark drama of *Wuthering Heights*, we visit Haworth, home of the famous Brontë family; drawn into Emily Dickinson's poetic vision, we tour the unassuming clapboard farmhouse where she slowly retreated to a life of solitude and poetry. Nor is Austen the only author who's created realistic characters. Nathaniel Hawthorne said that Anthony Trollope's novels were "just as real as if some giant had hewn a great lump out of the earth and put it under a glass case, with all its inhabitants going about their daily business, and not suspecting that they were made a show of." Indeed, readers tend to think of characters as real people when they read, especially when they read novels. One reason we read for the plot is that we want to find out what happens to people we've come to know and care about.

Nevertheless, Austen exerts a power above and beyond that of most other authors: She has a fandom rather than a following, readers whose devotion goes well beyond literary appreciation to infuse many aspects of their lives. "Janeites," the term for Austen devotees, are more like Trekkies than Brontë enthusiasts; many are willing to dress in Regency fashion at the annual meeting of the Jane Austen Society as easily as a Trekkie dons the Federation uniform at a *Star Trek* convention. Many, like myself, find guidance about how to live their lives in Austen's work. But unlike Trekkies, who are more absorbed by the *Star Trek* world itself than by the writers who created it, Austen fans idolize the author as well as her works. Austen is our beloved wise cousin, our ally in the quest for the good life.

Alas, the puzzle of Austen's influence didn't dictate the path of my scholarly research. In fact, musings of this kind were actively discouraged by the intellectual climate in many English departments of the time. At the elite institution I attended, thinking about characters as real people was strictly taboo, the sign of naïveté and ignorance. Doctoral candidates were expected to be professional readers who realized that every "text" (we didn't call them books or novels) consisted of words on a page and nothing more. We were being trained to decode, not to read. Many of us still harbored a "naïve" love of literature and authors, but this was our shameful secret, the madwoman who lived in hidden rooms in the attic.

It would take another twenty years and a late-flowering passion for psychology to prompt me to search for the reasons for Austen's allure. At this point, I was reading book after book on psychology and neuroscience while also taking courses in the mind-brain sciences. I began to publish essays on the connections between literature, psychology, and the brain, and to teach on that subject as well. Thinking about Austen in the context of the mind and the brain, I was now able to find an answer to my question: So many of us love and trust Austen because she possessed extraordinary powers of empathy.

Empathy means seeing the world from a different perspective, walking a mile, or even a moment, in someone else's shoes. It means actually experiencing, although in a weaker form, another person's state of mind, while also maintaining your own perspective. So if a friend is panicking, becoming anxious yourself wouldn't be true empathy but rather emotional contagion. Empathy means understanding your friend's panic while at the same time realizing that the anxiety of the moment is hers, not yours.

Such perspective-taking involves thinking and feeling. Empathy's cognitive aspect requires theory of mind (ToM)—also known as mentalizing, or a reflective capacity—which refers to the ability to infer other people's beliefs and intentions from their behavior. This includes facial expression, body language, actions, and speech. If you see someone come into a room, look around, move papers and books, look under the desk, and then leave with a puzzled expression on his face, you're likely to think that he was looking for something that he didn't find.

Theory of mind also includes the ability to recognize feelings, but in a dispassionate, knowledge-based sense. If you see your boss frowning, you realize that he's displeased about something and that this isn't the time to ask for a raise. You don't necessarily enter into his feelings; it's enough to know what they are. Many sociopaths can often read other people's feelings accurately, yet they possess zero empathy. Instead of empathizing with pain or sadness or even anger, they use their mentalizing powers to manipulate others.

Empathy is much better known for its emotional qualities. The first of these involves emotional resonance, feeling what someone else is feeling in an intuitive, subliminal mode. Empathy further involves knowing that you're conscious of another's feelings, that these are not your own. In everyday usage, the word *empathy* is used to include sympathy, which means responding in an emotionally appropriate manner—for instance, with compassion for suffering and delight at happiness. A more technical definition of empathy refers to taking another's perspective and feeling what someone is feeling. True empathy includes both emotional resonance, the pure feeling part, and theory of mind, which includes your awareness that you're grasping someone's thoughts and emotions.

Of course, when I say that Jane Austen had empathy, I'm inferring the mental powers of the living, breathing woman who's no longer with us from the evidence of the written record she left behind. But how else to explain Austen's array of such differently minded and totally believable characters? For Austen to have created such a variety of convincing imaginary people, she must have been a profoundly astute mindreader of real people. And no one familiar with her work can doubt her compassion for the unfortunate, or her glad participation in the happiness of others. She knew loss and thwarted love in her own life, which enabled her to portray the sufferings of disappointed love. But she could also show the joy of love's fulfillment. I can think of no other novel in which the happy ending is rendered so poignantly meaningful as it is in *Persuasion*. Yes, Austen must have possessed a high degree of empathy.

Yet it's not an abstract appreciation of empathy that draws us to Austen, but the experience of empathy itself. Austen's uncanny ability to convey what others think and feel allows two kinds of empathy to take place for the reader. The first is the empathy we experience for her characters. Countless people have shared the feelings of these fictional people: Elizabeth's humiliation on reading Darcy's reproachful letter, which shows how greatly she's misinterpreted events (*Pride and Prejudice*); Marianne's pain on being rejected by Willoughby, the man she loves with all her heart (*Sense and Sensibility*); Emma's sudden realization that no one must marry Mr. Knightley but herself (*Emma*).

The second experience of empathy is even more crucial: Because Austen understands human nature so thoroughly, we have the sense that she empathizes with *us*, her readers. To put this in the apt phrase of psychiatrist Daniel Siegel, when we read Austen, we have the feeling of "feeling felt," of having our innermost feelings understood and resonated with.* This is inherently gratifying because as a species, humans crave such understanding. We have a profound need for empathy, to know that we're not alone with our joys and sorrows.

These two kinds of empathy, of recognizing and feeling recognized, are two sides of the same coin. Austen conveys her understanding of us, her readers, precisely by creating characters that we identify with. And we're able to identify with Austen's characters because they mirror our ways of thinking and feeling. In fact, mirroring is an important way that empathy and other forms of resonance are communicated. In person, this happens through facial expressions and body language that imitate, and through speech that restates, one person's perception of another's state of mind. You're likely to convey empathy for a friend's distress by mirroring her facial expression—a furrowed brow, for instance—and telling her that you're sorry she's so upset. You reflect her feelings verbally, with the word *upset*, and nonverbally, with a furrowed brow.

In telling your friend that you're sorry she's feeling bad, you also express sympathy. But this is almost unnecessary because mirroring behaviors do more than simply reflect content; they convey caring. This is because humans automatically perceive mirroring as positive and, in the case of distress, comforting. And the brain knows how to tell the difference between mirroring and simply reacting. So vital is mirroring to conveying understanding and support that counselors who specialize in crisis management and suicide prevention are trained to restate the feelings of the person at risk as a major strategy for alleviating distress; this is known as "reflective listening."

And so, when we see ourselves reflected in Austen's work through characters who resemble us and others we know, it's like peering closely into a two-way mirror: We see Austen behind the glass,

---

* Daniel J. Siegel, *The Developing Mind, Second Edition: How Relationships and the Brain Interact to Shape Who We Are* (New York: The Guilford Press, 2015), 176.

watching and understanding. She knows us, and we know that she knows us. We have the feeling of feeling felt.

Other features in addition to Austen's wide-ranging portrayals of fictional people amplify our sense of empathy. Shared experience makes empathy more likely. If you've felt intense grief for the loss of a loved one, you'll empathize more easily and completely with someone whose grief is of a similar kind. It's also easier to feel empathy for people who are similar to us; the downside of this is how readily humans as a species fail to feel compassion for those who are of different races, cultures, and clans.

Austen's subject matter is very much our own, and so contributes to our sense of a shared framework of feeling and experience. Austen famously claimed to work on "two inches of ivory" with "a fine brush," creating a world that traces the intricacies of human interaction rather than the breadth of human endeavor. She concentrates on interpersonal relationships, an aspect of human life that's universal. All of Austen's heroines embark on a search for intimacy with a trustworthy person who can be both a lover and a friend; the allies and adversaries they encounter along the way include personalities of all kinds, rather than the monsters and warriors typical of the hero's quest.

Such human universals explain why we can relate to literature of many different cultures. Literary critics argue that realism, the extent to which literature can feel true to life, consists of conventions that vary from culture to culture. Nevertheless, some aspects of being human are universal, and we tend to be able to accept the portrayal of such universals as true to life and meaningful, even when they're set in times and places remote from our own. The literary scholar Patrick Hogan has found that love stories are told in cultures throughout the world, and that the same situations and emotions tend to appear within those stories no matter where or when they were written. We might find much about the Latin classic *The Aeneid* alien and even alienating, but we can still identify with Dido's heartbreak when her lover, Aeneas, abandons her. Austen concentrates on this world of ubiquitous feelings and perceptions.

Not only does Austen tell stories of love and friendship of the sort shared by people everywhere, but these take cultural forms that are still easily recognizable to us, our vast advances in technology notwithstanding. We still live in families. We still interact with circles of friends, acquaintances, and colleagues. Marriage and other kinds of intimate partnership are very much a goal for many of us. Austen couldn't completely anticipate our world, nor transcend many of the limitations of her day—she was insightful but not clairvoyant. And so she writes about universal topics with a limited cast of characters: heterosexual, Caucasian, upper- and middle-class families. Some find her off-putting because of this. But many readers are willing to forgive her for being of her age; they recognize her value, as demonstrated by the breadth and diversity of her global readership. I think her attitudes were progressive, given the limitations of her milieu and that her insights have value for all of us, even if they weren't written with all of us in mind. But that's a personal decision.

Austen's style remains as accessible as her stories. She writes in pithy, crystal-clear sentences, creating novels that are paced quickly enough even for our impatient twenty-first-century sensibilities. In Austen, the heart of the matter, which is indeed the matter of the heart, is right there; we don't have to penetrate layers of cultural and stylistic difference to get at it. Because Austen creates a world that has much common ground with our own, there's a strong foundation for empathy.

Austen's stories not only convey empathy through mirroring and identification, but they're about empathy as well—who has it, who lacks it, and how some of her characters deepen their capacity for this important quality. Her novels get us to focus on the experience of empathy (neuroscientists would say they prime us to think about it) by showing its value repeatedly. So we find ourselves reflected in novels that are all about the value of being able to find yourself reflected in other minds and hearts. Yet we're not fascinated by empathy because it's brought to our attention, but rather we pay attention because empathy is essential to our well-being. And this is yet another reason we're drawn to Austen—she understands this about us.

Perhaps it seems strange to characterize Austen's novels as being about empathy. After all, Austen's great subject is love: its different varieties, its frustrations, its nuances, and, above all, its satisfactions. And not just love between couples, but also between friends, parents and children, siblings. Austen certainly understood this most precious of human emotional resources.

But there's no contradiction here. Austen's novels show again and again that the most complete and satisfying relationships rely on perspective taking, understanding, and emotional resonance. Whatever its other features—gratitude, esteem, passion, nurturing—at its core, true love is empathy. Think about all of Austen's happy couples and you'll see that this is the case. Anne of *Persuasion* might be more intuitive and passionate than Elizabeth of *Pride and Prejudice*, but sensitivity and understanding lead to happy endings for both of them.

In placing empathy front and center, Austen knew what she was doing. For Austen is no mere copyist of nature, but a deeply thoughtful novelist who explores the morality as well as the psychology of the social brain, those aspects of the mind-brain that imbue our relationships. This was brought home to me recently when I tried to read the novelist Georgette Heyer, a twentieth-century writer who emulated Austen. Here were all the window dressings of Austen's fiction, the *Masterpiece Theatre* costumes, plots, and themes, but hollowed out, not only of Austen's distinctively brilliant style, but also of her philosophical and psychological depth. With apologies to all the Austen fans who cut their teeth on Heyer, I found her unreadable. In the humble guise of the novel of manners, a genre that focuses on social conduct, Austen's works draw out the moral implications of being human: What do we owe one another ethically, and how do we go about fulfilling this obligation?

The simple answer: We owe one another the kinds of consideration and treatment that help all of us not only to satisfy our basic needs, but to achieve well-being and self-esteem. And this depends on empathy, the key to understanding another person's needs. And so Emma caters to her needy, hypochondriacal, and often ridiculous father in *Emma*. So Edmund becomes young Fanny's friend and advocate in *Mansfield Park*. So Elizabeth in *Pride and Prejudice* tolerates the more absurd members of her family with calm consideration. In that last family, we might note that it's with regard to this fundamental ethical obligation that Mr. Bennet fails so completely. Rather than helping his foolish wife to develop whatever potential she might have, he retreats to sarcasm to console himself for having to endure her company. As a result, she remains as silly as ever, learning only to ignore a husband she can't understand and who doesn't empathize with her.

When Austen's characters demonstrate kindness and tolerance, it's because they're able to imagine and sympathize with life from the point of view others. Emma indulges her father's many absurdities because she can see that his worries are real to him. Edmund imagines what it's like to be young, lonely, and intimidated in a new place, and so he's kind to Fanny. Elizabeth knows that she might not be able to change her mother, but that failing to show her respect would be hurtful and accomplish nothing. Austen's best heroine, Anne Elliot of *Persuasion*, owes her goodness and capability to her capacity for empathy. She can see from others' perspectives, and this guides her feelings and behavior. As Wentworth, the man she loves, eventually realizes, there is "no one so proper, so capable, as Anne."

For Austen, empathy is the core quality of all moral action. Here, Austen agrees with the philosopher David Hume, a near contemporary. In our own day, similar conclusions have been advanced by Simon Baron-Cohen, a neuroscientist who equates evil with a lack of empathy, and Frans de Waal, a philosopher and primatologist who views our capacity for moral action as grounded in empathy, which we find in less developed forms in other primates.

Above and beyond the kindness and understanding that empathy creates, it's valuable because it unlocks the prison house of cosmic loneliness that threatens each of us with a life sentence of solitary confinement. Anglo-European politics, philosophy, and psychology have emphasized our separateness, condemned us without a trial, insisting that we're stuck in a container, the body, looking out through windows, the eyes. We're born alone and we die alone, even if other people are near us for these two defining events in the life cycle of every human.

But the latest work in social intelligence tells us that we're profoundly interconnected in terms of brain, body, and mind. This has been a key insight of the literary imagination all along, that fund of wisdom and observation found in literature. In terms of understanding our connections with one another, no author is greater than Austen. And she shows that such connections depend on empathy, on being able to enter into the thoughts and feelings of others. Through such exchanges, people find meaning and purpose in their lives.

‒‒◇✕◇‒‒

Explaining Austen's appeal in terms of empathy made sense to me, but as with all literary theories, and many scientific ones as well, if truth be told, supporting my hunch was another matter. While I realized I could never definitively prove my claims, I began to wonder if I could nevertheless offer convincing evidence. My take on the intense devotion Austen inspires hinges on the observation that Austen "gets us," that she understands us and captures our attention, because she gets us right, creating fictional people whom real people find extraordinarily true to life.

As I became progressively more interested in the mind and the brain, I began to realize that I could make a case for Austen's accuracy in portraying human nature by drawing on various findings in the mind-brain sciences, fields that include psychology, cognitive science, and neuroscience. I could show that Austen's characters are true to what we know about social intelligence and the social mind-brain to support the claim that Austen's appeal lies in her powers of empathy.

And if these scientific fields could be applied in support of a literary theory, that Austen's empathy is conveyed by her ability to portray people realistically, then literature could also be drafted in the service of science. Austen's accuracy in representing feelings and relationships makes her work ideal for discussing social intelligence, that aspect of being human that most concerned Austen herself: how people relate to one another. Austen's characters provide imaginary case histories that illustrate the workings of the social mind-brain. These two stories, one about social intelligence and the other about Austen's fiction, define one another in yin-and-yang fashion.

As far as I know, all the books that discuss Austen's fiction or her appeal invoke the psychology of her characters in one way or another. My book is no exception. But I go one step further, discussing her characters in depth but with a difference, peering beneath the surface of the mind into the anatomy and neurochemistry of the brain. I like to think about this with a metaphor: Recall those children's books on human anatomy with transparencies overlaid so that each time you turn a page, you go deeper into the human body, beginning with skin and hair until you're staring at the viscera. I view my book as this kind of a page-turner. I look at social intelligence through the psychological analysis of Austen's characters, but then turn the page to find what lies beneath in their physiology.

For those who approach these pages because they're interested in literature, I hope you'll see this favorite author in a new light while learning about a topic that might not be familiar. For those who are interested in the mind-brain sciences, I hope that you'll enjoy reading a book in this field told largely by lively and interesting fictional people. Perhaps you'll read more of Austen's work. I hope that so-called general readers, who are general only in the sense that they generally know more about most things than the rest of us, will find something new to enjoy.

For all my readers, I hope that viewing knowledge about the mind and the brain within the very human context of Austen's characters will yield new insights about your own feelings, relationships, and choices. And die-hard Austen fans will be able to add yet another way in which this favorite author is extraordinary—yet one more honor for our beloved Jane. In addition to the pleasure and wisdom she bequeathed, she gave us some of our most memorable lessons in social intelligence.*

---

*   For the sources for information about empathy, see Chapter Nine, "Empathic Emma."
This chapter returns to the topic of empathy in greater depth.

Jane
on the
BRAIN

ONE

Precious Feelings

"Tell me not that I am too late, that such precious feelings are
gone forever."

—Frederick Wentworth in *Persuasion*

E lizabeth Bennet's feelings have betrayed her. Or so she thinks.
But this is when she is still many months, and many pages, away
from the happy ending of *Pride and Prejudice* that will unite her
with Fitzwilliam Darcy. It's the morning after Darcy's first proposal,
an offer made in highly insulting terms. Darcy confessed that he was
asking Elizabeth to marry him against his "will," his "reason," and
his "character," and that their marriage would mean connecting himself with a family that, with the exception of Elizabeth and her sister
Jane, deserves the contempt that he so clearly and abundantly feels
for them: "He spoke well, but there were feelings besides those of the
heart to be detailed, and he was not more eloquent on the subject of
tenderness than of pride."

Elizabeth was furious, and she rejected Darcy in no uncertain terms as "the last man in the world whom I could ever be prevailed on to marry." Elizabeth has good reasons for disliking Darcy, as she tells him. In addition to the rudeness of his proposal, he made her sister Jane miserable by convincing his friend Bingley that Jane was indifferent to him, and so keeping the couple apart. And Elizabeth believes, as her friend Wickham told her, that Darcy had cheated him out of an inheritance that was rightfully his. And on a very personal note (she keeps this to herself), he insulted her when they first met at the Meryton ball, saying within her hearing that she wasn't "handsome" enough to "tempt" him to dance.

Elizabeth's wounding retort to her would-be lover: "You are mistaken, Mr. Darcy, if you suppose that the mode of your declaration affected me in any other way, than as it spared me the concern which I might have felt in refusing you, had you behaved in a more gentleman-like manner." This is the ultimate insult for an aristocrat like Darcy, who prides himself on being a gentleman.

Darcy was too furious and shocked to reply to Elizabeth in the moment, but he sent a letter the following day, answering Elizabeth's charges, and certainly exonerating himself on the subject of his poor treatment of Wickham. Far from having deprived Wickham of a rightful bequest, Darcy gave him a generous amount of money to pursue his studies—Wickham had claimed to want to be a lawyer. When the money ran out, spent in idleness and dissipation (it's doubtful Wickham ever opened a law book), Darcy refused further aid. Wickham soon after attempted to elope with Darcy's younger sister, attracted both by her inheritance of thirty thousand pounds and the prospect of wounding Darcy where it would hurt the most.

Elizabeth is mortified. How could she have been so wrong? She blames her feelings: "Had I been in love, I could not have been more wretchedly blind. . . . Pleased with the preference of one [Wickham], and offended by the neglect of the other [Darcy], on the very beginning of our acquaintance, I have courted prepossession and ignorance, and driven reason away, where either were concerned." But Elizabeth is harder on herself and her feelings than she ought to be because her dislike of Darcy is actually justified. Although he's behaved himself relatively well since their first disastrous meeting, his proposal of marriage is truly obnoxious. However insufferable Elizabeth's family might be, Darcy's condescension and bluntness make him as rude and insensitive as they are, without the excuse of stupidity. Elizabeth is right to reject Darcy's proposal—he doesn't behave as a gentleman should behave toward the woman he loves.

Imagine for a moment if Elizabeth hadn't had the feelings that caused her to reject Darcy, or if she'd suppressed or ignored her resentment. Imagine if she'd accepted his first proposal. Imagine what it would be like to be married to a man who thought that his marrying you was a huge favor for which you ought to be forever grateful, a favor that canceled out any faults in him you might perceive, and which exacted total submission on your part in return. This wouldn't have been good for Elizabeth. And it wouldn't have been good for Darcy. Without the ballast of Elizabeth's corrective influence—without her unexpected and feisty rejection—he might have turned out to be a more intelligent if equally loathsome version of his snobbish aunt, Lady Catherine de Bourgh. Instead, by the end of the novel, Darcy has rethought his attitudes and begun to act accordingly. He's a better man.

Elizabeth's feelings enabled her to judge a situation correctly, even if she was wrong on some of its details, and to choose the course of action that would be in her best interests. Feelings gave her vital information about how to act at a crucial moment—reject Darcy. This isn't to say that Austen claims that feelings are a foolproof guide, goodness knows! When they mislead us, they can do so spectacularly. Elizabeth's sister Lydia demonstrates the dangers of being thoughtlessly guided by feelings when she elopes with Wickham (of course, Darcy saves the day and this brings him together with Elizabeth, but these benefits don't cancel out the inherently disastrous nature of Lydia's behavior). Like all potentially volatile substances, feelings must be handled with care, assessed and regulated. You should think long and hard before indulging strong impulses. Even so, in Austen's world, as in real life, feelings are valuable for what they tell us, both about ourselves and about others.

———◇◇◇———

WHAT WE TALK ABOUT WHEN WE TALK ABOUT FEELINGS

Although definitions of emotion vary, most psychologists agree with Austen that they're a means of appraisal, of assessing whether something or someone is good or bad, as we see with Elizabeth. They convey valuable information that influences our responses to our inner as well as outer environments—to thoughts and memories as well as to people and events. And they instigate action as well as thought—we often behave in ways that express our feelings. Like Austen, mind-brain scientists don't claim that emotions are a foolproof guide. But nothing in the human brain is foolproof. Feelings must have helped our ancestors survive more often than not because the capacity for emotion has been retained throughout the evolution of mammals. We're simply among the latest heirs.

I especially like neuroscientist Edmund Rolls's definition of emotion because it clearly indicates that emotions are active responses to situations and environments: "Emotions are states elicited by rewards and punishers. . . . [A] reward is something for which an animal (including of course a human) will work. A punisher is something that an animal will work to escape or avoid (or that will decrease the probability of actions on which it is contingent)."* Rolls characterizes emotion as a dynamic force that enables us to achieve both tangible and intangible benefits.

Food and sex are the among the most basic material rewards that animals, including human animals, work to obtain. But Rolls's definition additionally accounts for many of the complicated forms of feeling that have the quality of drives, such as ambition. Ambition isn't a simple response like fear, but it nevertheless shares its evaluative and goal-directed characteristics. Indeed, all kinds of emotions ideally help us to work for rewards and avoid punishers. In the first proposal scene, Darcy is clearly a "punisher," although he later becomes a very satisfying "reward."

Understanding how emotions function neurologically provides a firm foundation for understanding how they work psychologically, in personal reactions and in our social exchanges with one another. In order to shed light on emotional processing, neuroscientist Joseph LeDoux has studied the neural pathways—the routes taken by electrical signals that travel along our nerves (called neurons)—of what might well be the most basic of emotions, fear. Fear is very likely a universal emotion, and with good reason: It helps animals, including human animals, to survive.

LeDoux studied rats rather than humans because he could use research tools that are considered unethical for our species, such as implanting electrodes in the brain and breeding for specific traits. And despite the greater complexity of human brains, it's sound scientific practice to use the brains of other mammals to learn about humans because we share much of their basic neural circuitry. As the human brain evolved, it incorporated and built on the anatomy from which it emerged. Even the human cortex, the crinkly, outermost layer of

---

*   Edmund T. Rolls, *Emotion Explained* (New York: Oxford University Press, 2005), 2.

the brain that enables our higher functions, evolved from the simpler cortex that reptiles possess.

LeDoux proposes that in the mammalian brain, a fear response takes two pathways, which he calls the "low road" and the "high road." Both lead to the amygdala, an almond-shaped, emotion-processing area deep within the middle of the brain (inside the wrapping of the cortex). The amygdala turns on the fear response as well as other types of excitatory reactions. It's what gets our adrenaline pumping, and it was surely very active for Elizabeth as she listened to Darcy's proposal. (By the way, LeDoux's work on the function of the amygdala has found creative as well as scientific expression; he plays with a rock band called The Amygdaloids. Given the quality of classic rock to appeal viscerally and directly to our feelings, the band is appropriately named.)

LeDoux illustrates the circuitry of fear with an example that has become classic in the literature of neuroscience. Let's say you're hiking along a trail and you encounter something long and thin that might be a snake—you're not sure. In order to see whether or not this is really a snake, nerve signals must reach the visual cortex, which is the brain's highest visual processing region, the part necessary for sight. But there are visual areas below the cortex in the brainstem, the brain's lowest processing area. Most visual signals pass through these brainstem areas and continue on to eventually be processed by the visual cortex. But some of these signals take another path, traveling directly from the brainstem to the amygdala.

This has two results. You see without knowing you see; such subconscious, subcortical sensory perception is known as "neuroception," and when it involves vision, it's also called "blindsight." The image formed in subcortical (neuroceptive) areas is not a clear, detailed image, since visual impulses haven't completed their journey to the visual cortex where sensory information is assembled in its final form. Nor are you consciously aware of what you're seeing, or even *that* you're seeing. (Of interest to the social brain, Beatrice de Gelder and her colleagues found that blindsight can detect emotional expression on a person's face, although not a person's identity [that is, blindsight excludes facial recognition], nor can it detect gender.)

Nevertheless, the amygdala learns that there's something long and thin that might be a snake, and it initiates a fear response. And so before your conscious mind even registers what you see or even knows you have something to be afraid of, your body begins to prepare for fight or flight, for defending yourself against an enemy or running away to safety. Heart rate increases and stress hormones course through the bloodstream, along with other bodily changes. Your eyes will probably widen, an expression of fear. This is the low road, from sight receptors to the amygdala.

Most visual signals travel the high road, which refers to cortical pathways, strings of connected neurons that lead from the eyes to the visual cortex, where an accurate and fully conscious perception of what is being viewed is assembled; this occurs only milliseconds after the low-road information has reached the amygdala. You now know exactly whether there's a stick or a rattlesnake in your path. With information coming from the high road, a signal can be sent to the amygdala that tells it to either continue generating the fear that will help you survive, or to halt its red alert because you're safe.

Through the moment when you experience your fear, your reaction matches those of other mammals, including LeDoux's rats. Conscious areas of the brain, mostly cortical areas, read the activity that's going on subconsciously and subcortically and translate it into experience. At this point, whether you're a man or a mouse, your emotional response has been transformed into a feeling. You feel your fear. But if you're human, you'll also become aware of your fear in a self-reflective way, and, if all is safe, aware of your relief. Moreover, you can still feel fear without having to act on it, or else act on it immediately, as you assess the situation accordingly. This might also be true for other great apes, and perhaps some other mammals such as elephants and dolphins. Because you can name or think abstractly about what you're feeling—mind-brain scientists refer to such recognition as symbolic thinking—it can be put into words or images, which symbolize actual experience.

Although high-road information completes its path only milliseconds after the low-road information has reached the amygdala, in the wild, where we evolved, such small quantities of time can determine whether we live or die. If you had to wait until your conscious mind registered a given situation, such as a poisonous snake in your path, it might be too late to marshal the bodily resources needed for coping successfully. Because information has traveled the low road, by the time your higher brain areas realize what's going on and decide on a plan, the body is ready with adrenaline already activated to make your muscles do the extra work needed for running away or fighting. In fact, you might begin to run before you fully register the situation, before you know whether there's a poisonous snake, a harmless snake, or a fallen branch in your path.

Perhaps you've had the experience of feeling your startle reflex kick in even as you realize that there's nothing to be afraid of. This experience demonstrates the workings of the two roads. This has certainly happened to me—I have a rather sensitive startle reflex, the mark of a nervous person. Once I was sitting in a chair reading when my cat Jemima came up behind me. I jumped, the physiological, emotional response appropriate to fear and surprise, at the very same time that I was saying to myself, "It's only Jemima." I don't know what danger signal was sent to my amygdala, perhaps a very ancient biologically ingrained response to the possibility of a predator creeping up on me through the grass. It was the oddest experience, to feel my body generating a physical fear response even as my mind was noting the absence of danger. My low-road response had already been initiated and was ongoing when the high-road response completed its course.

The usefulness of the dual pathway is most obvious with an emotion like fear, and it's possible that other emotions, at least negative ones, follow a similar pattern because it was established by certain primal responses that helped us to survive. In any case, emotions are subconscious reactions that consist largely of physiological responses, whether we (eventually) consciously realize this or not; bodily reaction is the calling card of emotional response, and it precedes our conscious knowledge of our own feelings.

JANE AUSTEN, EMOTION SCIENTIST: EMOTIONS AND FEELINGS

I've been speaking of emotion and feeling as synonymous, without distinguishing a difference, as we tend to do in everyday speech. But mind-brain scientists make an important distinction, even if they don't always agree on terminology.* Emotions refer to subcortical and subconscious neural signals that subsequently travel on to higher brain areas. Feelings refer to our recognition of emotions; they're what we experience when emotions reach those higher cortical areas. As mammals, first we respond; then we feel, translating a mind-body response into a conscious perception. A few species among us have self-awareness—we understand that we feel.

We're used to encountering descriptions of *feelings* in novels; feelings tend to be the stock in trade of the genre. We find it entirely natural for a narrator to enter the minds of characters in order to follow their reactions to events. But Austen, with her extraordinary, one might say clinical, powers of observation captures *emotion* accurately as well, the initial subcortical and bodily response to experience, which is much more unusual. We see this when Darcy unexpectedly encounters Elizabeth and her relatives, the Gardiners, touring Pemberley, his family estate.

Tourism of great estates had begun in the eighteenth century, and a pleasure trip such as the Gardiners and Elizabeth are taking would have included such stops. They had been assured that the family was absent. Elizabeth's last encounter with Darcy had taken place when she rejected his proposal of marriage and he'd sent the explanatory letter that shamed Elizabeth by revealing that she'd been a poor judge of character. She would certainly not have agreed to go to Pemberley if she thought there was a chance of meeting Darcy, but this is exactly what happens:

> As they walked across the lawn towards the river, Elizabeth turned back to look again; her uncle and aunt stopped also, and while the former was conjecturing as to the date of the building, the owner of it himself suddenly came forward from the road, which led behind it to the stables.
>
> They were within twenty yards of each other, and so abrupt was his appearance, that it was impossible to avoid his sight.

---

*   For a description of this difference between emotion and feeling, see, for instance, Antonio Damasio, *Looking for Spinoza: Joy, Sorrow, and the Feeling Brain* (New York: Harcourt, 2003), 27–52.

Their eyes instantly met, and the cheeks of each were over-spread with the deepest blush. He absolutely started, and for a moment seemed immoveable from surprise; but shortly recovering himself, advanced towards the party, and spoke to Elizabeth, if not in terms of perfect composure, at least of perfect civility.

She had instinctively turned away; but stopping on his approach, received his compliments with an embarrassment impossible to be overcome.

The emotional nature of this encounter is conveyed by the presence of telltale bodily signs. Darcy "starts" (as I did with my cat), a reaction that often accompanies surprise, an emotion that has affinities with fear. Darcy displays another distinctive fear-surprise response: He freezes. Both Elizabeth and Darcy are embarrassed, as we see from the "deepest blush" that suffuses their faces. And Elizabeth instinctively turns away, the hallmark gesture of shame, seen even in infants when they experience a rudimentary form of this emotion.

These responses are instrumental in informing Elizabeth and Darcy of how they feel about meeting—terribly embarrassed—and this knowledge guides their actions; feelings as well as emotions help us to work for rewards and avoid punishers. Embarrassment lets them know that they're confronting a delicate situation and that they must behave appropriately. The reward they work toward is a reduction of embarrassment, as well as the chance to repair past misconceptions and misbehavior. The punisher they avoid is continued discomfort and awkwardness. Darcy steps forward graciously and Elizabeth responds in kind, with her best manners. We see emotion and feeling doing their job, telling minds and bodies how to behave appropriately, to lessen if not dodge punishers, and hopefully, to reap rewards.

Emotions and feelings convey important information not only to the people experiencing them but to others as well. This is true for all animals, including humans. Of course, for us, language is a vital component of communication, one of the biosocial advantages that have made our species dominant. But we rely on nonlinguistic communication, called social signaling, to a greater extent than many of us realize. Social signals include gestures; facial expressions; posture; and vocal inflections such as tone, volume, and emphasis, known as vocal prosody (as opposed to linguistic content). Many of these signals, such as blushes and tears, are involuntary products of the physiological nature of emotion. Although such signals often occur when we're by ourselves, they're known as *social* signals because of their vital role in social situations. They might be absent, or more likely muted, when you're alone.

Social signals are a powerful means of communication, as important as speech. Watch a movie in an unfamiliar language with the subtitles off; you'll be surprised at how much you're able to understand. Needless to say, people can disguise their social signaling; our cognitive talents have made us masters of deceit. But their more positive purpose is to reveal rather than deceive, and we share this feature with other mammals.

Elizabeth and Darcy's encounter at Pemberley illustrates the display as well as the appraisal function of emotion. The blush that Darcy and Elizabeth both so wish to avoid sends an important message: They know that they share similar responses and that no one has the upper hand. Of course, Austen might have told her readers what Elizabeth and Darcy were feeling at Pemberley without any physical description at all by eavesdropping on their thoughts, a convention Austen and most other third-person narrators frequently use. But fictional people obviously can't do the same, any more than real people can. They use social signals and speech to assess those around them. Austen shows the value of a nonverbal exchange between Elizabeth and Darcy at a crucial moment in their relationship.

Such signals might have been even more vital in Austen's very polite society than in our own less inhibited culture; information that couldn't be spoken was often expressed through these tacit channels. And Austen is a master of showing the importance of nonverbal signs. She understands that what people miss seeing, or fail to communicate, can be as important as the signals that are successfully conveyed. If Elizabeth had read Darcy's social signals more accurately during her brief stay at Bingley's house (where she and Jane were forced to remain for a few days because Jane caught a fever), she would have known that he was attracted to her and been more prepared to deal with his confession of love. Darcy can't take his eyes off Elizabeth, a pointed clue as to his feelings.

Another even more crucial instance: Elizabeth's sister Jane is deeply in love with Darcy's friend Bingley, but the mismatch between her congenial, low-key manner and the intensity of her love prompts others, including Darcy, to mistake her feelings. Elizabeth believes that such reticence is one of her sister's strengths, and that her calm manner protects her privacy. But Elizabeth's friend Charlotte warns that Jane needs to be more obvious about her feelings or she'll risk losing Bingley: "If a woman conceals her affection [from the man she loves] . . . it will then be but poor consolation to believe the world equally in the dark."

This is indeed what happens; Darcy feels justified in separating Bingley and Jane because he hasn't observed strong feelings on Jane's part. And Bingley, although in love with Jane, agrees to relinquish his hope of marrying her because he also fails to see cues that reveal the strength of her feelings. Absent or misleading social signals can be just as harmful as saying the wrong thing.

JANE AUSTEN, EMOTION SCIENTIST: MOOD AND PERSONALITY

As readers of Austen well know, her novels consist largely of following trajectories of feeling as new experiences confront her heroines and other characters. But she's also acutely aware of the role of more sustained kinds of what's called *affect*, the general term in mind-brain science for responses that involve appraisal and evaluation. Temperament, more often called personality these days, refers to characteristic ways of responding emotionally. Bingley's willingness to relinquish Jane stems from temperament as well as uncertainty about her feelings. He's modest and gentle, whereas Darcy is confident and, in certain situations, assertive to a fault. And so Bingley often bows to the judgment of his forceful friend.

Psychologists Robert McCrae and Paul Costa define personality as consisting of five categories and their opposites: openness to experience; conscientiousness-undirectedness; extraversion; agreeableness-antagonism; and neuroticism, which means a tendency to experience negative emotions easily and to feel nervous and anxious. These can be used to further characterize Darcy. He's certainly conscientious, which makes him a bit too serious, and he's also introverted, which makes him appear disagreeable at times; indeed, his shyness is as responsible as his snobbery for his haughty demeanor. Others misread his cues, and so his introverted behavior is taken for rudeness, making him seem even more intolerant—and intolerable—than he really is. He's somewhat closed to new experiences, although we can't blame all of his self-containment on an aversion to novelty; he certainly sees enough very quickly at the Meryton ball, where eligible bachelors appear to be the door prize, to allow him to make an informed decision to avoid making friends in this company. No doubt, he's highstrung, which means he doesn't take things lightly or in stride. Some personality traits appear to be innate, and shyness is one of these, although a person's environment can have a huge influence in altering natural tendencies. With a different kind of upbringing, Darcy might have been less anxious around others, despite a tendency toward introversion.

We can easily see the difference in temperament between Darcy and Bingley in their respective attitudes toward the Meryton ball. There's a lot there that's off-putting, but also much that's positive, such as Elizabeth herself, as Darcy later comes to realize. Yet temperament influences each man's experience:

> Bingley had never met with pleasanter people or prettier girls in his life; everybody had been most kind and attentive to him; there had been no formality, no stiffness; he had soon felt acquainted with all in the room; and as to Miss Bennet, he could not conceive an angel more beautiful. Darcy, on the contrary, had seen a collection of people in whom there was little beauty and no fashion, for none of whom he had felt the smallest interest, and from none received either attention or pleasure. Miss Bennet [Jane] he acknowledged to be pretty, but she smiled too much.

Bingley and Darcy attend very different balls at Meryton, although they're both present in the same place at the same time. Temperament makes the ball an enjoyable event for Bingley and a zone of endurance for Darcy. Temperament also helps to make the world each of these men inhabits, as it does with all of us. Bingley is pleasant, and so he brings out the best in people. Darcy's haughty behavior invokes the negativity he feels in people's responses to him.

Mood refers to an emotional state that's longer lasting than emotion or feeling, but is not as enduring as characteristics of personality. Darcy refers to mood when he tells Bingley why he won't ask Elizabeth to dance at the Meryton ball: "I am in no humour at present to give consequence to young ladies who are slighted by other men." He implies that in a different mood he might have been more polite, and this is true to some extent, for his behavior toward Elizabeth quickly changes as his feelings for her develop. Even so, Darcy's statement reveals as much about his temperament as it does about his mood.

It's a particularly clever choice on Austen's part to have Darcy use the word *humor* ("I am in no humour at present") because in her day, humor could mean either mood or temperament. The word *humor* derives from medieval and Renaissance physiology. It was thought that the body consisted of four chief fluids, called humors, each associated with a different personality trait. While the theory of the humors had been discredited by Austen's time, the use of the word *humor* to mean personality lingered on, a meaning it has lost in our own day. But it had also come to refer primarily to mood, as it still does.

So when Darcy uses "humour" to mean a temporary state of mind, he inadvertently admits that his antisocial stance is more than a temporary mood, and that it's natural for him to be in "no humour" to dance, or to make an effort to extend himself in social situations. Austen's choice of a word with competing definitions tells her readers that Darcy's discomfort with social situations is habitual rather than passing, although he's particularly grumpy at this moment.

Like more fleeting forms of affect, both mood and personality ideally help us to attain rewards and avoid punishers, although given the complexity of the human brain, there's plenty of room for error at all levels. Nevertheless, the basic principle that the role of affect is to steer us toward the best course of action still applies, even when this is difficult to see. People sometimes possess unhelpful characteristics because these were useful at an earlier time in their lives, possibly the best response to a bad set of options. By being deployed regularly, they become ingrained responses. For instance, some children with emotionally distant parents learn to shun intimacy in order to avoid being disappointed. You might easily imagine that Darcy experienced this kind of upbringing.

It is also true that what might appear to be a negative characteristic from one perspective might well have benefits that aren't immediately obvious. Take Darcy's bad humor at Meryton, which appears to lead to behavior with no redeeming features, at least to Elizabeth's way of thinking. Folk wisdom agrees, telling us that we catch more flies with honey than vinegar, and Darcy is certainly all vinegar. But Darcy doesn't want to catch flies, and indeed the inhabitants of Meryton and nearby villages are ready to swarm around him for the honey he has to offer, in the form of a large fortune and marital eligibility. So his bad humor keeps him from having to interact with a crowd of people with whom he has no wish to be better acquainted.

In fact, it's likely that given his position, a bad mood serves Darcy well much of the time. It certainly keeps his admirer Miss Bingley at a distance. And quite honestly, only someone as good-natured as Bingley could have endured the evening at Meryton with such sustained good cheer and a positive outlook. Darcy quickly sees enough at Meryton, including the behavior of Elizabeth's silly mother and even sillier sisters, Lydia, Kitty, and Mary, to put him in a bad humor.

HUMAN BEINGS, HUMAN FEELINGS

It's widely accepted within the mind-brain sciences that we possess basic emotions, that everyone is born with the capacity for certain physiological-psychological responses that are genetically designed to begin working within the first two years of life. While scientists disagree about the number and identity of these emotions, the standard list in Western mind-brain science includes anger, fear, disgust, sadness, happiness, and surprise. According to basic emotion theory, all other emotions develop from these fundamental categories. This is definitely the reigning paradigm. Open just about any textbook on psychology or cognitive science or neuroscience, and this is the account of emotion you'll find.

Facial expression provides support for basic emotion theory. Psychologist Paul Ekman spent a year looking at his face in the mirror in order to identify all the muscles involved in facial expression, and to match them to specific emotions. Applying this knowledge in the field, Ekman found that certain facial expressions consistently correlate with specific emotions across a wide range of cultures. Some emotions do appear to be universal.

Basic emotion theorists maintain that while a given facial expression might carry a range of meanings, this doesn't contradict the essential nature of basic emotions. For instance, a smile can convey qualitatively different categories of happiness: the happiness of being with a loved one, the happiness of relief, the happiness of achieving a goal, the happiness of triumph, and so forth. Jane's smile when she sees Bingley is very different from Elizabeth's smile as she listens to the folly of her neighbors. Be this as it may, all these instances have a common denominator, a happiness factor. No one smiles as an expression of sadness, although you can smile if you're feeling a mixture of happiness and sadness; you're smiling at the "happy" part. Even a nervous smile or laugh expresses your sense that you've done something funny, something other people might laugh at or find "funny peculiar."

While we're one of the few species who possess the muscles needed to smile, we certainly aren't the only creatures with emotions. Psychologist Jaak Panksepp explains that because our emotional systems are the product of evolution, we share the circuitry for basic emotions with other mammals. Panksepp actually categorizes emotions in terms of basic *systems* rather than single emotions; these include seeking, rage, fear, lust, care, panic/grief, and play. But the principle is still the same; we're born genetically endowed to develop basic circuitry for emotional responses, a capacity shared by all mammals. (By the way, Panksepp has been nicknamed the "rat tickler" in scientific circles because he discovered that rats actually laugh when they're tickled. You can watch Panksepp tickle rats at https://www.youtube.com/watch?v=j-admRGFVNM). Precursors of emotion can even be found in much more primitive animals, as you'll see when you meet the giant snail *Aplysia* in a future chapter. Nevertheless, there are emotions that are not basic, that are found in humans and likely some other species, but which are not ubiquitous among mammals.

Embarrassment is one such nonbasic emotion. Unlike fear, which all neurologically intact mammals are capable of experiencing, embarrassment involves knowing or imagining a witness to your actions or feelings. It also appears to know rules about what's acceptable or unacceptable, rules that are conveyed through language or other symbolic forms of communication. Yet despite its origins in a higher level of awareness than many other mammals are capable of, embarrassment is an emotion—a learned emotion, but an emotion nevertheless. Its physiological signature, the blush, indicates the activity of the autonomic nervous system, which controls involuntary bodily responses; this subconscious physiological reaction makes it as much an emotion as fear.[*]

Embarrassment is definitely the emotion shared by Elizabeth and Darcy when they meet at Pemberley because they each recall their last meeting and the turbulent feelings that accompanied the ill-fated proposal. Neither wants to be reminded of this awkward encounter, especially in public. Darcy would rather not be reminded of Elizabeth's rejection, nor her accurate assessment of his ungentlemanly behavior. Elizabeth doesn't want to be reminded of her lack of judgment or her loss of temper. Each was a witness to the other at a particularly unflattering moment, and so they're embarrassed. Such a sophisticated and nonbasic emotion like embarrassment might be limited to animals with highly developed social capabilities; perhaps only humans feel embarrassment. In contrast, when my cat Jemima startled me, another unexpected meeting, I might just as well have been another cat as a human; another animal crept up behind me and I reacted as any

---

[*]   I'm making a distinction between embarrassment and shame. The *Oxford English Dictionary* gives this definition of *embarrassment*: "Intense emotional or social discomfort caused by an awkward situation or by an awareness that one's own or another's words or actions are inappropriate or compromising, or that they reveal inadequacy or foolishness; awkwardness, self-consciousness." Here is the definition of *shame*: "The painful emotion arising from the consciousness of something dishonouring, ridiculous, or indecorous in one's own conduct or circumstances (or in those of others whose honour or disgrace one regards as one's own), or of being in a situation which offends one's sense of modesty or decency." Embarrassment more specifically includes a cultural context and relies on symbolic thought. Your dog might feel shame after being caught rooting through the trash, but she isn't likely to be embarrassed. Or perhaps your dog doesn't feel shame but rather fear because he knows you won't like his behavior. Along with ethologist/psychologist Frans de Waal, I remain agnostic about animal capabilities but inclined to think that we generally underestimate our fellow creatures. Some languages don't distinguish between embarrassment and shame; for instance, in Spanish, the word for both is *vergüenza*.

mammal would, startling with surprise and fear. But if Jemima were to meet another kitty who'd rejected her amorous advances, she wouldn't feel embarrassed. "Pemberley" doesn't happen in the kitty world.

The complexity of the human brain might also explain why some nonbasic emotions might be culturally specific. Emotion scientists cite the Japanese emotion called *amae*, which many claim we lack in our more individualistically oriented Western societies. *Amae* refers to the sense of well-being that comes from feeling that you're completely part of another person or group of people, especially when you're dependent on that person or group. *Amae*, experienced as an emotion, that is, subconsciously, generates a calm or happy feeling linked to the sense of dependency. A person *reflecting on* the feeling of *amae* would realize that he felt good as a result of being close and dependent on someone else.

However, there's controversy about how exactly to define *amae*, and whether it is a culturally distinct emotion. People in Western societies very likely do experience *amae*, although we don't have a name for it; this suggests that emotions that aren't recognized within a given culture might nevertheless be felt. Perhaps in our individualistic society with its worship of autonomy, we'd rather not admit to feelings that undermine self-reliance. In any case, *amae*, like embarrassment, is not a basic emotion.

Psychologist Lisa Feldman Barrett rejects basic emotion theory altogether. She's certainly not the only one to have done this—in the past thirty years, it's been criticized repeatedly in the scholarly literature. But Barrett's work is in the forefront of challenges to basic emotion theory, and has garnered attention and prestige equal to that of the mind-brain scientists whose theories she challenges.

Barrett argues that emotions are "dimensional" rather than basic. This means that they're brain-body activations that tag experience in terms of "value" and "arousal": whether you feel good or bad about something and whether your feelings are strong or weak. Barrett maintains that emotions consist of ongoing neural and physiological changes in this fuzzy, dimensional sense, in response to the stream of people, events, and thoughts that we encounter each moment.

If you're mathematically inclined, you might think of graphing a given emotional response along an x/y axis, with x being equivalent to value and y to arousal. Responses would then involve changes in position within the space of the graph. Emotions would achieve their specific features only after reaching consciousness, on being experienced as feelings. We can view a dimensional theory of emotion in terms of the emotion-feeling distinction; emotions emerge in our bodies and subconscious brains, and our conscious minds subsequently experience and label them.

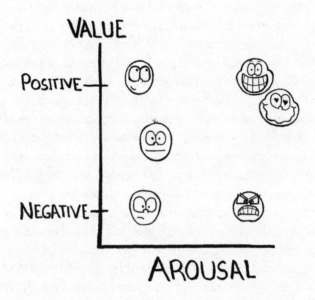

To see how this works, let's look again at Elizabeth's insights after receiving Darcy's post-proposal letter. In retrospect, she understands that "Pleased with the preference of one [Wickham], and offended with the neglect of the other [Darcy], I have courted prepossession and ignorance, and driven reason away where either [of the two men] were concerned." Notice that the word *pleased* refers to feelings that are strong and positive, "offended" to feelings that are strong and negative, but these words fail to capture nuances of response; *pleased* and *offended* are broad descriptive terms. An array of possible emotions can contribute to feeling pleased, including feeling flattered, proud, happy, vindicated; offended can mean hurt, disgusted, disapproving, shocked. These lists are partial, and I'm sure you can think of many other kinds of feelings that fit these umbrella terms.

With similar imprecision, the narrator describes Elizabeth's reactions to the letter itself as "difficult of definition . . . Astonishment, apprehension, and even horror, oppressed her." The narrator appears to grope for words in order to pinpoint a reaction that is, to begin with, much more formless. But again, the description might well embrace nuances of feeling that contribute to Elizabeth's "astonishment, apprehension, and even horror," such as embarrassment and regret.

The general terms in which Elizabeth's feelings are described by both herself and the narrator might be seen as evidence in support of Barrett's view that emotions, our initial affective physiological and subconscious reactions to experience, are fuzzy rather than specific. That is to say, in describing our feelings, at least to begin with, we reach for overall categories because our subconscious emotional reactions are themselves imprecise; we distinguish among nuances when we begin to consciously interpret these responses. Real people's self-reports about emotion tend to be as vague as Elizabeth's; this is part of Barrett's argument against basic-emotion theory.

Barrett challenged the existence of basic emotions after reviewing hundreds of studies on emotion, which led her to conclude that they are not nearly as consistent, uniform, or clear-cut as many scientists believe. Take facial expression, the most frequently cited evidence for the existence of innate, distinct categories of emotion. Barrett found that the evidence is far from clear that facial expressions convey fixed and bound categories of emotion. I must confess that I have a very hard time telling fear from surprise.

Let's return to the example of the smile, which can convey a range of meanings. Where basic-emotion scientists note the common denominator of these meanings, those who favor a dimensional view highlight the differences. They point out that smiles can express meanings so distinct as to signal entirely different modes of feeling. They wouldn't agree that the smile of happiness for being with a loved one has much in common with the smile that comes from listening to the folly of your neighbors. When the same evidence points to two different conclusions, what you think has a lot to do with where you draw the boundary between modes of feeling. I might think these two experiences have enough in common to signal the same emotion, broadly speaking; you might disagree.

Even at the level of bodily response and neural circuitry, the emotions don't appear to be as basic as is widely believed. The amygdala, the structure in rats that LeDoux studied, is definitely involved in fear responses. But it's involved in generating other emotions, such as surprise, even in rats. And it has other important functions, such as tagging an event as important so that we remember it. The same complexity is true for the adrenaline response on the part of LeDoux's rats. Fear definitely triggers the release of adrenaline, but so do other kinds of stress responses such as anger, which calls on many of the same neural areas and shares many of the same hormonal responses as fear. Even positive emotions such as excitement involve adrenaline.

Although Barrett claims that she isn't a pure social constructionist, someone who believes that all our responses, including emotions, are shaped entirely by culture, her theory does argue that influence from the environment is paramount in turning subconscious, dimensional emotions into specific feelings. I think she's right insofar as culture instills values and norms that become second nature to us. But nevertheless, I can't help but feel that she's thrown the baby out with the bathwater. Of course, we need to take the environment and culture into account when considering emotion in humans, and likely in many other mammals as well. But this doesn't mean denying the strong influence of evolutionarily older modes of processing that we share with other mammals.

My objection to a purely dimensional theory of emotion comes somewhat ironically not from the hard neuroscience of emotion, which often aligns itself with the basic-emotion approach, but rather from psychotherapeutic theory, where messiness and indistinctness are often the rule. In Barrett's terms, if a person has a strong negative reaction to someone, specific content will subsequently be attached to that reaction; there's no specific content *before* we recognize or experience the emotion as a feeling. And if emotions have no distinctive characteristics prior to becoming feelings—if they're broad affective responses—then whatever way in which we experience or label our emotions must, by definition, be correct. If what you experience as fear is merely negative and strong at the subconscious level (in other words, if it's dimensional), then repressing that fear wouldn't be possible because it wouldn't exist to be repressed in the first place.

Yet this is certainly not the case with Elizabeth, or with me, or likely with you, either. It's indeed possible to misinterpret your emotions: Elizabeth has a strong negative reaction to Darcy, but she doesn't realize that hurt, humiliation, and fear—the fear of being unattractive and never finding a husband—are as much a part of the mix as dislike and disapproval. If we can misinterpret our emotions, then there must be something there to misinterpret to begin with. Something specific must be happening at the subcortical, subconscious level that differentiates one emotion from another in very specific terms, at least in many cases. And if something specific is happening at the subconscious level of emotional response—that is, if fear and surprise really are different at this level—then a purely dimensional view is incorrect. Even nonbasic emotions would develop entrenched circuits that would generate emotions in the subconscious, and they would be open to misinterpretation by our conscious minds.

I haven't come across this particular objection, but the evidence about basic emotion is sufficiently contradictory that many mind-brain scientists have attempted to reconcile the conflict between these two theories rather than abandon basic-emotion theory altogether. Elaine Fox suggests that we might possess some emotions that are basic, like fear, and others that originate in dimensional terms. This means that they would acquire their specific quality—indeed their identity—only after cognitive input. So the uncomfortable feeling of sensation like embarrassment (a nonbasic emotion) might originate as a strong, negative sense of arousal that gets defined at the level of consciousness, as Barrett maintains.

Jaak Panksepp (of rat-tickling fame) and Douglas Watt argue that affect consists of instinctual primary (basic emotions), secondary (learned), and tertiary (cognitive) levels of responding to and processing information. A focus on these different levels of analysis accounts for opposing perspectives. An emotion such as embarrassment would have a biologically determined component, but then be elaborated by higher-level processes. If you concentrated only on that higher-level input, you'd deny the existence of basic emotions. Along similar lines, psychologists Andrea Scarantino and Paul Griffiths argue that basic emotions, as they are usually defined, are far too inclusive because they follow popular definitions of emotion rather than referring to truly biological and universal responses. These latter kinds of response do indeed exist. For instance, the kind of fear experienced by a sudden loss of support exhibits all the qualities assigned to basic emotions: a distinctive physiological response, a predictable developmental appearance, and an evaluation of the situation that focuses on a motivating factor (snake, young lady).

Jesse Prinz, a mind-brain philosopher, rejects the distinction between basic and nonbasic emotions altogether to claim that the opposition between biology (nature) and cultural construction (nurture) is false. Prinz argues that all emotions, including basic ones that we're biologically designed to develop, contain this mixture of cognitive input and physiological response. If you see a long, thin object in your path, or even a predatory young lady, although your fear might share physiological markers with the fear experienced by rats, for you, knowledge and culture shape your experience of fear in very human ways. Prinz's view dovetails with the others I've mentioned because it suggests that the multiple areas in the human brain contribute input from different levels of processing in emotional responses.

That basic emotions find further processing and elaboration in the human brain makes sense because it follows the general rule of evolution: Creatures adapt and innovate on the structures they inherit, so that these eventually become functionally different from their ancestral forms. Fins became both arms and wings, and while you can see the similarities in all three structures, they are decidedly unlike one another in form and purpose. In this way, humans and some other animals might have developed additional and more nuanced ways of generating and expressing emotions, even basic ones, because these adaptations served us well.

In addition, the density of our interconnections among brain areas means that there are few neural circuits that don't receive input from all over the brain. Different areas of the human brain work together and extend our basic responses in ways that aren't seen in rats, although likely shared with mammals closer to us in terms of evolutionary time and development (or who have developed on a parallel track, such as birds). In short, if rats have basic emotion circuits, then humans do as well, and if culture provides input into those emotions in humans, the same is likely true for chimps and bonobos. Many basic emotion theorists would agree, while still maintaining that universal responses—and dedicated neural circuitry—are involved in some emotions.

We can apply these views of emotion processing as multitiered to Elizabeth's reactions to Darcy. There are many nonbasic aspects of her dislike, which are complicated and depend on cognitive and cultural input. And these feelings continue to develop in complexity and subtlety throughout their relationship. But at the same time, Elizabeth had certainly responded to Darcy's initial insult with at least one basic emotion, fear (that no man would find her handsome enough to marry), and this endured. It was too painful to be admitted to conscious thought, but it exerted a strong influence on all of Elizabeth's responses. If Darcy's remark invoked the basic emotion of fear for Elizabeth, then there is something happening subconsciously that Elizabeth fails to register; she accounts for her negative reaction to Darcy in more palatable ways. Although this fear is itself influenced by cultural input, by the wish and the need for a woman of Elizabeth's class to find a husband, it might have basic core fear circuitry no different from that of a rat.

All these theorists, and many others, acknowledge the complexity of affect in humans. We might possess the circuitry for basic emotion, but in humans, emotions never stay basic for long. And so the seeming indistinctness of emotional responses and expressions, a rationale for the dimensional approach, might be better explained by the complexity rather than the fuzziness of human responses. Although humans do have basic emotions, we can have mixed responses that make it difficult to exactly pinpoint and separate out specific emotions. Elizabeth might use a general word such as *pleased* not because her emotions are vague and dimensional, but rather because there are so many of them involved that it's difficult to parse them. Perceiving Wickham's apparent preference for her, Elizabeth might feel flattered, confident, and hopeful (about her ability to find a husband), all feelings that validate her sense of self-worth and lead to feeling "pleased."

When basic emotion theory is qualified, it is less open to charges of imprecision and nonuniversality leveled by Barrett and other critics. Refining rather than discarding basic emotion makes sense in terms of both evolution and the workings of the mind-brain.

The complex, nuanced quality of human affect doesn't make things easy for humans. We have a lot of sophisticated neural wiring built atop and integrated with some very primitive and basic structures. Much of our mind-brain development, at least half, depends on experience rather than genetics. There's ample opportunity for things to go wrong, much more so than in the case of other mammals, although they too are susceptible to mental afflictions, such as trauma. And, as every pet owner knows, they have distinctive personalities. The "higher up" the animal on any given branch of the evolutionary ladder, the truer this is. Great apes can certainly be characterized using the five-factor personality scale. Even my guinea pigs (Kira and Dax) have distinct characters.

But for simpler animals, life is simpler. What does it feel like to be a cat? If you have food, water, love, and something to do, such as hunt (even if it's plush animals—my cat Thalia does this), play with toys, and explore, and you haven't experienced terrible trauma or aren't predisposed to be anxious, it's probably rather satisfying. But if a cat's life is easier than our own in many ways, it lacks certain joys that are distinctly human and which involve distinctly human situations and responses: For my cats, there are no Pemberleys. No Darcys either. And no Jane Austen.

Whether we experience basic emotions like fear, or more complex emotions like embarrassment, in a normally functioning mind-brain, emotion is involved in every moment of thought, both conscious and subconscious. It took cognitive science the better part of the twentieth century to discover this, although psychotherapy, its scorned poor relation, has known it all along. Nor was mainstream philosophy any more astute about the significance of emotion and other forms of affect to human life and thought. Novelists have been immeasurably more intelligent on the topic. And of course, Jane might well be the smartest of them all.

TWO

Pride and Prejudice and Brains

THROUGH DARCY'S EYES

Let's start with a look, a catching of the eye. Vision is, after all, the sense that most of us rely on for information about the world. So we'll begin with the look exchanged between Darcy and Elizabeth at the Meryton ball, where they first meet.

The ball is a thrilling event for Meryton's excited young ladies and their hopeful mothers since the community has recently acquired two eligible bachelors, Darcy and Bingley. Their presence transforms the ball from a country dance to a matter of life and death—or at least of financial solvency—since in Austen's day, marriage was the only respectable career option for daughters of upper- and middle-class families. Those who lacked family money and failed to marry faced humiliating and potentially harsh options: They would either have to depend on the charity of friends and family, or take a position as a paid companion or governess. (The latter is a prospect dreaded by Jane

Fairfax in *Emma*.) To further complicate things for the Bennet family, they have no male heirs, and so the family estate is destined to go to the closest male relative. The Bennets would have no other residence or source of income upon the death of Mr. Bennet, and so the family needs to marry off all five of its daughters.[*]

As we discussed in the previous chapter, Bingley enjoys himself immensely at the ball, in part because he's falling in love with Elizabeth's sister Jane. But Darcy stiffly endures the event from the sidelines. When Bingley encourages Darcy to dance, he refuses, declaring that there's no one in the room worth dancing with. Bingley gestures toward Jane's sister Elizabeth, who's sitting close enough to overhear their conversation, but Darcy isn't convinced. He looks in her direction and scornfully replies,

> Which [who] do you mean?" and turning round *he looked for a moment at Elizabeth, till catching her eye he withdrew his own* and coldly said, "She is tolerable; but not handsome enough to tempt *me*; and I am in no humour at present to give consequence to young ladies who are slighted by other men. You had better return to your partner and enjoy her smiles, for you are wasting your time with me. [my italics]

Darcy's contemptuous glance begins what well might be the most famous romance in all of English literature. But let's consider it from a more technical point of view, in terms of what actually happens in Darcy's brain when he looks at Elizabeth.

This point of view might not come naturally, or even be all that enticing, to literature buffs. As a society, our education and our interests all too often divide between the arts and the sciences. But I'm convinced that Austen would have appreciated knowing about the brain. Although she wasn't a scientist, she was nevertheless a most astute observer of human nature along what we recognize as scientific principles. She never wrote about things she couldn't witness, such as men's conversations when alone. Equipped with astute powers of

---

[*]   We can assume that some of the land belonging to the estate is rented and that the family also has their own farm, which would provide them with milk, eggs, meat, fruits, and vegetables.

observation, she came to understand people so accurately that we can use her novels to illustrate the science of social intelligence.

Austen would have realized that psychological understanding is deepened and expanded by knowing about the brain as well as the mind. Today, most psychologists no longer think in terms of a mind vs. a brain, but of a mind-brain. And the different disciplines that focus on one or the other of these entities have come to be so intertwined that their boundaries are no longer distinct. Psychologists understand the basics of neuroscience, and neuroscientists explore theories that used to be considered purely psychological. Researchers often identify with more than one of these fields.

This dual focus makes sense because the brain is an important part of the mind. In fact, most mind-brain scientists maintain that the mind and brain are actually the same, and that the difference between the two pertains to an observer's perspective rather than to the mind-brain in and of itself. They believe that they're two sides of a coin, and that the mind arises from the activity of the brain. However, I follow psychiatrist Daniel Siegel's definition of mind, which challenges this conventional view as being too limited.

Siegel argues that viewing the mind as arising *solely* from the activity of the brain fails to do justice to the mind's complexity. While the brain is very likely the physical structure that registers conscious self-awareness, the mind consists of input from other sources as well. Siegel defines mind as the "flow of information and energy" among our brains, our bodies, and one another—that is, our social interactions with other people. In other words, the mind and brain aren't two sides of a coin. The mind arises from brain (neural) activity, to be sure, but the mind also consists of input from the body and from our relationships—from the meeting of minds, you might say.*

This argument makes sense for several reasons. First, while our bodies connect to our brains though neurons that send information (such as commands) from the brain to the body, and which deliver information from the body to the brain, the body can act independently of the

---

* The notion of embodied cognition, that our bodies are central to thinking, has been advocated by other mind-brain scientists, although it doesn't seem to budge the core belief that mind arises from brain. The logic of this conventional view is that even if events in the body affect the mind, such influence is still routed through the brain. Siegel disagrees about granting full primacy to this one organ.

brain to some degree. This is especially true of the enteric system, the digestive system at the core of our bodies, which includes the esophagus, stomach, and intestines (large and small), among other structures.

The enteric system actually resembles the central nervous system (brain and spinal cord), containing neurons that are more brain-like than those anywhere else in body, and that connect with one another to form a system relatively independent of the brain. Every neuro-chemical found in the brain is also found in the digestive system; in fact, most of our serotonin, the neurotransmitter thought to cause depression if there are insufficient quantities available, is found in digestive areas. An anxious girl at the Meryton ball who felt butterflies in her stomach would have demonstrated the enteric system informing the brain about her nervousness rather than the other way around. Psychological reactions in the stomach and digestive system might depend very minimally on brain activity.

The enteric system might be a particularly brain-like bodily area, but many areas of our bodies participate in thinking. Recall that emotions begin as physiological responses that we subsequently register as feelings. Even before Siegel redefined mind, many mind-brain scientists accepted the phenomenon of embodied cognition, the belief that thought and behavior depend on bodily responses to a particular environment as well as neural activity.

That our social interactions belong to the definition of mind also makes sense. Our minds and our brains depend on social contact for both development and well-being. If you confine an infant in a room, providing food alone with no nurture or human contact, you'll irrevocably damage his brain within a very short time. In fact, it's unlikely he'd survive, and if he did, he'd be severely impaired, compromised for life. Social contact continues to be vitally influential throughout our lives, influencing feeling, mood, perception, and cognition. We're designed to pay attention to one another—it's an inherent part of what constitutes our minds, both developmentally and moment by moment.

Psychiatrist Lewis Mehl-Madrona, while not specifically defining mind, supports Siegel's definition with an analogy: "People are neurons in a social brain."[*] By viewing activity within this social brain as a building

---

[*] Lewis Mehl-Madrona, *Healing the Mind Through the Power of Story: The Promise of Narrative Psychiatry* (Rochester, VT: Bear and Company, 2010), 13.

block of individual minds, Siegel takes this insight to the next level. Activity within the social brain and activity within individual mind-brains continually constitute one another in an ongoing feedback loop, a process called "recursivity." (As you'll see in a moment, recursivity is a defining feature of the mind-brain.) There's no mind without other minds; John Donne's famous line "No man is an island" applies to the neurological and psychological findings of our own day. I think Austen would have approved of Siegel's theory, knowing as she does that the real stuff of our lives can be found in our relationships with one another.

Fundamentals about the brain are nevertheless helpful to understanding the mind, even if mind and brain are different entities. You don't need to remember everything in this chapter about the brain, but reading through will give you the basics of how the brain functions. So now, to return to Darcy's contemptuous glance.

For Darcy to see Elizabeth, sensory information from the outside world must reach the conscious parts of his brain. This means that when Darcy "looked for a moment" at Elizabeth, light traveled through the lens of his eye and hit its back surface, the retina. The deepest layer of the retina (nearest the brain) contains millions of photoreceptor cells, some of which are sensitive to light and some to darkness. These cells, and all the others involved in the brain's processing, are called neurons, or nerve cells. (There are other kinds of brain cells, glial cells, involved in maintenance, but neurons appear to be involved in thought, affect, perception, and action.)

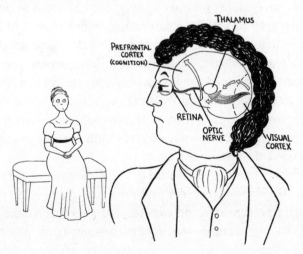

Elizabeth's image caused these photoreceptor neurons to *fire*, the conventional term for referring to the activation of neurons, creating the pattern of her image, much like a photo negative. This in turn activated the retina's output neurons (called ganglions), which sent the image to areas deep inside the brain via the optic nerve, which isn't really a single nerve but a collection of neurons. The impulses carrying Elizabeth's image then traveled upward through many layers of the brain to reach the visual cortex, the brain's highest and most advanced visual processing area.

The journey still wasn't over. The visual cortex as a whole contains a topographic map of the visual field, which means that the neurons in a given area correspond to specific areas in the visual field; each cell is responsible for a small part of the picture, like the pieces of a jigsaw puzzle. Cells of the visual cortex are also specialized to process different aspects of perception, such as form, color, or movement. For instance, the primary visual cortex, known as V1, analyzes patterns and the orientation of forms, such as whether Elizabeth is facing right or left, and whether the lace she's wearing has a regular design. Other specialized cortical areas are needed for recognition of objects and faces, and for the perception of three-dimensional forms. Only when all the different parts of the image contained in various electrical nerve impulses were assembled in jigsaw-puzzle style was Darcy able to see Elizabeth, "not handsome enough to tempt me."

In short, Darcy didn't perceive an image of Elizabeth wholesale, like a boa constrictor eats its prey, but rather, patterns of light and darkness that struck his retina were turned into electrical impulses that, after being registered and assembled by different visual centers in his brain, eventually formed the image of Elizabeth. Yet Darcy remained oblivious to the complicated workings of visual processing. And so it is with most of our perceptions. The workings of many brain areas are involved, yet we experience an end result without being aware of the steps needed to produce it.

Take another example of a brain process: memory. We don't record memories like a video recorder and then play them back; rather, we fashion prior perceptions and experiences anew each time we think of them. The constructed—not recorded—nature of memory leaves plenty of opportunity for error, omission, and variation: You can be sure that if you asked Darcy about the Meryton ball, his account would differ significantly from Bingley's. And when you remember an event, the same areas that were active in registering your initial perceptions work to re-create it. When Darcy later recalls Elizabeth's fine eyes, the visual centers that sprang into action when he first noticed how pretty they are reactivate to form the image in his brain, although in a modified, less intense form. The "mind's eye," an expression that predates the field of neuroscience, is accurate. The mind really does have an eye insofar as the brain has visual processing centers that create mental images. These areas are active whether what we see is real, remembered, or imaginary.

One more crucial point to remember about the mind-brain: There's nothing inside the skull but the brain itself, no little person in a control tower, no vital spirits or other immaterial substances, no ghost in the machine, just a brain gathering information and sending information. Yet the absence of an animating spirit in the conventional sense takes away none of the wonder. Rather than simply glorying in the talents of the human mind-brain, as we've done since time immemorial, we now ask how its abilities can arise from the same everyday processes seen in other mammals, whose mind-brains comprise the same elements as our own: brains, bodies, and social interactions. A group of chimps can't write *Hamlet*, or *Pride and Prejudice*, no matter how much time they're given in front of a computer; you need a human mind for that (and an extraordinary one to boot).* But despite the commonplace materials our minds are made of, even minds like Shakespeare's and Austen's, we can still say with Hamlet, "What a piece of work is man" (and woman!).

---

* This is a reference to a thought experiment known as "the infinite monkey theorem," the origins of which are unclear, but which was popularized in the early twentieth century by Émile Borel, a mathematician, and Sir Arthur Eddington, an astronomer. The premise is that monkeys, given an infinite amount of time in front of typewriters, would eventually type the works of Shakespeare, including *Hamlet*. Virtual monkeys sitting at virtual typewriters have nearly achieved this feat. In my view, using anything but real chimps and real typewriters (or, keeping up with the times, computers) is cheating!

THE DANCE OF NEURONS

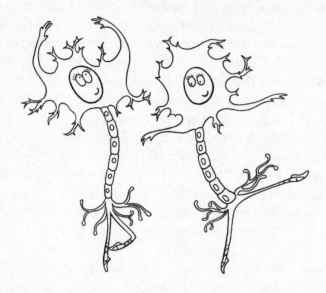

Scientists tend to speak of brain areas as if they were factories where workers accomplish different jobs, but actually, these areas are made of neurons, and neurons alone get the work done. We can't tell the dancer from the dance, neurons from the brain, and it's the endless dance of neural activity that's vital to making us who we are. Similarly, when scientists talk about information being stored in neural circuits, they mean that a particular thought, feeling, or action will happen if a particular configuration of neurons activates.

Neurons are the information processing cells of the brain and nervous system; through electrical impulses, they both give and receive information that travels from one neuron to the next, or from a neuron to an area of the body. You might compare this to the sounds of our voices traveling along telephone wires (or wireless systems), which are transformed into energy that's reconstituted as information at the receiving end. And so knowledge about whether or not Elizabeth is pretty (knowledge involving the entire mind) travels from Elizabeth herself (social interaction, a glance at a ball) to photoreceptor neurons in the eye (body), to cortical neurons that assemble her image (brain). There's an average of 86 billion neurons in the human brain.

Neurons come in many different shapes and sizes, but most of the neurons in vertebrate brains are multipolar. They consist of a cell body, which contains a nucleus; dendrites, which are small extensions that receive electrical impulses through receptors; and an axon, a long, tube-like structure with extensions for sending electrical impulses on to other neurons or body areas. Axons come in all different lengths, and some are long enough to conduct impulses from the brain to the far reaches of the limbs. The multipolar neuron is probably what you think of if you think of neurons at all; its familiarity is shown by its incarnation as a stuffed toy sold by the Giant Microbes company. (They also sell blood cells, bone cells, E. coli, and other cells that nonscientists are likely to recognize from the popular press.)

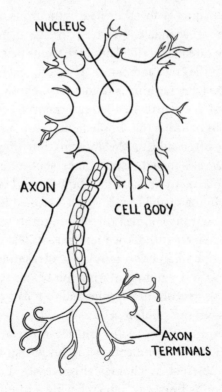

Every one of your thoughts, feelings, and actions involves a cycle of neural activity that begins with a stimulus of some kind, such as exchanging a glance with a young lady at a ball or remembering her fine eyes. This causes electrical current to flow into a neuron via the activity of chemicals called neurotransmitters; these can be likened to other materials that conduct electricity, such as metal or water. For an electrical impulse to travel from neuron to neuron, it must cross a tiny space called a synapse. Small amounts of neurotransmitter are secreted from pouches called vesicles, located in the axons of a sending, or pre-synaptic, neuron and received by receptors in the dendrites or the cell body of a receiving (postsynaptic) neuron. But the transfer of energy from neuron to neuron will take place only if the postsynaptic neuron has receptors for that particular neurotransmitter. Neurotransmitters are like keys, and receptors are like locks; the gates will open only if lock and key fit together.

Most neurons connect to other nearby neurons within a specific area of the brain rather than connecting directly to neurons that have contact with the outside world. There are input neurons that take in information from the environment, as in vision, and neurons that generate information from within, as in memory. These neurons connect to other intermediary neurons, called interneurons, and interneurons connect to output neurons that implement a response.

Interneurons often add to the information they receive before sending it on. Darcy's initial visual intake sent information through many layers of interneurons in various brain areas before reaching the output neurons in the visual cortex that assembled Elizabeth's image. However, some neurons connect directly to target areas, such as the nerve cell that generates the knee-jerk reflex, tested at your yearly physical. But most human brain activity involves interneuron activity for both receiving and sending information before the final output.

The majority of neurons are specialized in terms of functions they enable; as we saw, the photoreceptor cells that sent the electrical impulses that led to Darcy's seeing Elizabeth began their activity in response to light, an environmental stimulus. Other kinds of neurons deal with more abstract psychological processes. But whether we're looking at someone's fine eyes, remembering a humiliating faux pas, worrying about the future, or dancing at a ball, neurons are part of the process, as they calculate input in order to generate responses, moment by moment.

Neural signals can inhibit as well as stimulate the activity of other neurons. In other words, the electrical signal can convey the message "Don't fire" as well as the message "Fire." A receiving neuron's activity, or lack of activity, results from the activity of all the neurotransmitters that are converging on the cell at the same time. That is to say, in each neuron, receiving impulses are literally added together, with inhibitory impulses (Don't fire!) subtracting from the total of excitatory ones (Fire!). This means that neural activity is the result of each neuron's calculation of the excitatory and inhibitory signals it receives; a neuron will fire if the sum of all of its activating impulses is strong enough. Each neuron receives and sends thousands of impulses in any given moment. The math involved in neural activity is one reason many cognitive scientists believe the brain is computational, that it functions like a computer.

You might think that criticism of a physiological, computational view of the brain would come from humanists and literary people. The thought of Darcy and Elizabeth as walking computers, calculating the sum of neural activity, is likely to irritate many Austen enthusiasts. But the critique can be found within science itself, from the undeniable observation that in the brain, the sum of neural activity is greater than its parts. The same is true of the mind, which includes the body and social interaction in addition to brain activity.

Take what neuroscientists call "the hard problem of consciousness," how awareness emerges from the workings of the mind-brain. Even if we were able to trace the activity of every one of the brain's billions of neurons and, incorporating Siegel's views, include the input we receive from our bodies and social information in the environment, we still couldn't say how our awareness of our perceptions (called qualia) and of ourselves emerges from the interaction of these elements. Even the best theoretical explanations can't account for how this happens, which is why figuring out how consciousness emerges is called a "hard" problem. And this is an understatement, because even if you could trace the activity of every neuron in the brain and the body, in addition to calculating every factor in the environment (and of course these tasks are impossible), you still couldn't explain how such activity translates into "how things feel"—the phenomenology of experience. The gap between the workings of the mind-brain and the quality of our experiences might be one that we'll never bridge.

DYNAMIC DARCY

Those who fail to appreciate Austen foolishly (in my view) assume that her novels are dull because her situations tend to be relatively ordinary: Darcy moves into the neighborhood; Anne Elliot's family is forced to rent the family home in order to pay their debts (*Persuasion*); Catherine Morland, who's never traveled, has the opportunity to visit Bath (*Northanger Abbey*). The action is primarily psychological; Austen focuses on feelings and insights that occur as a result of social interactions in a relatively limited milieu. But for humans and other primates, this is the stuff of our most important events. Austen knew that the real drama of our lives most often comes from our everyday encounters with other people.

Such encounters bring challenges in their wake. And people, including fictional people, have various and innovative ways of responding. If this were not the case, every novel would be more or less the same—indeed, we'd have no novels, for what would be the point? We read because we're interested in people and the choices they make as they attempt to navigate their way to happiness.

Psychology explains many of the factors that influence our responses, but for the moment, let's remain at the nuts-and-bolts level of brain function. At this physiological level, we can say that people have a wide range of possible responses to experience because the brain is what is known as a "complex system," also called a "dynamic system," a concept that originated in the field of thermodynamics. (The study of such systems is known as general systems theory.) The mind is also a complex system, but we'll focus on the brain to begin with.

Complex systems are self-organizing systems. As I mentioned earlier, there's no little person, no "mini-me" inside Darcy's skull directing the activities of his brain: And yet despite the absence of this cognitive "author," Darcy and all of us with healthy brains function incredibly well, at least from a mechanical if not always from a social or psychological perspective.

Heating a pot of water provides a nonorganic example of a complex system that anyone who's waited for pasta water to boil will be familiar with. Without heat, the water molecules move in random ways. But when the water is heated, it forms small bubbles, then large bubbles, then agitated coils of water. No one is shaping the water in this way, but it forms noticeable patterns nevertheless. And the sequence repeats every time you boil a pot of water.

Of course, the activity of a complex system is governed by the restraints that are built in to the materials it's made of. Water in a pot is never going to read Austen, even if it's governed by the same principles as the brain. In the case of brains, restraints include basic anatomy and an individual's genetic heritage, the latter estimated to have an equal influence with the environment in the majority of instances.

In complex systems, including both boiling water and the brain, self-organization occurs as the result of feedback loops that affect the functioning of the entire system, a phenomenon called "recursivity." A neuron that sends a signal *out*, either to other neurons or to an area in the body such as a gland or a muscle, is simultaneously taking signals *in* from other neurons, including those that bring information about the environment or the body or other parts of the brain. As signals continue to circulate, some of the impulses received will be responses that have themselves been influenced by the neuron's own output. As noted, this will almost always happen indirectly through relays of interneurons.

Neural networks are so dense and complicated that any one brain area is constantly sending and receiving information to and from a multitude of other areas. So when a complex system confronts a stimulus, as the brain does each and every moment, the changes induced don't ripple through the system one after another like dominos falling; this is linearity. Rather, recursivity, self-organization through feedback loops, means that the stimulus affects the system as a whole. The result is an endless circuit of influence and adjustment, happening at lightning speed.

The mind is also a complex system. To add the mind back in to the equation, we just need to consider bodily and social activity as part of the endless feedback loop that makes us who we are each and every moment. If you could have a freeze-frame photo of all the billions of connections that are being made within and between brains, bodies, and people, you'd have a "screenshot of the self," of the configuration of inputs that forms our identity—all of our perceptions, intentions, thoughts, and feelings (including emotions and bodily sensations), at that particular moment. But of course, within milliseconds, the picture will have changed.

When life confronts us with experiences that can't be absorbed in a routine manner by smooth and continuous reorganization of a complex system, which for the mind translates into taking things in stride and coping well in terms of thought and behavior, we can respond in one of the three ways available to all complex systems: with rigidity, chaos, or adaptive reorganization. Rigidity means failing to change in ways that accommodate or even acknowledge the challenge—rigidly maintaining old patterns. When Elizabeth rejects her foolish cousin Mr. Collins's proposal of marriage, he hunkers down and clings to what he knows. He's so locked in to certain modes of perception that he literally can't absorb what she tells him—that she doesn't want to be his wife.

By contrast, in *Sense and Sensibility*, when Willoughby rejects Marianne in a very cruel and public way by snubbing her at a ball, Marianne has a chaotic reaction, which means that she can't assimilate the information and move on. She's completely overwhelmed, and she ceases to function well or normally. Like Mr. Collins, she clings to cherished beliefs to begin with, thinking that someone must have maligned her to Willoughby, and that's why he's rejecting her. Never mind that such behavior on his part would still be wrong, trauma doesn't stop to examine nuances. Once Marianne realizes that Willoughby alone is responsible for his behavior, she descends into a deep depression. She's lost in the chaos of her pain, which takes her over entirely.

Marianne's state of mind paradoxically involves rigidity as well as chaos, the lack of ability to function normally, in that it follows predictable patterns—sad mood, lack of responsiveness, loss of the capacity for pleasure (anhedonia), loss of appetite. These symptoms indicate a deficit in her powers of emotional regulation, an absence of organization, that leads to the rigidity of depression. Such maladaptive expressions of system overload can be characterized as both chaotic and rigid.

Like Mr. Collins and Marianne, Darcy is also rejected after a proposal (to Elizabeth). But in his case, the rejection initiates a massive
reorganization of thought, perception, emotion, and behavior that
leads to a better system and a better man. Although Darcy is initially
completely taken aback and furious at the rejection, he thinks long
and hard about what's happened, and he changes as a result. Elizabeth
immediately notices how different he is when they later encounter one
another at Pemberley, Darcy's estate. She's surprised by his gracious
and welcoming attitude, especially toward her aunt and uncle, the Gardiners, despite Mr. Gardiner's being "in trade" and so beneath Darcy in
terms of social status. Darcy has shed his defensive, protective armor
and is much more open to experience. He takes in information and
decides on appropriate responses rather than automatically distancing
himself and shutting others out.

After Elizabeth's rejection, Darcy might well have chugged along,
gotten over it, and asked another woman to be his wife à la Mr. Collins—perhaps Miss Bingley's dreams would have come true after all.
Or he might have become deeply depressed and dysfunctional, like
Marianne after Willoughby's rebuff. Instead, he becomes a kinder and
happier person by processing his experience in ways that enable him
to substantially change for the better. Such change indicates flexibility
of mind, and it augurs well for his ability to respond in productive
ways to experience in the future.

In case we're tempted to attribute Darcy's transformation to an
effort to capture Elizabeth's heart, a blip that will have no lasting effects,
Austen makes sure we know that Darcy has processed his experiences—
rethought his attitudes and behavior—and changed as a result. He
tells Elizabeth,

> As a child I was taught what was right, but I was not taught
> to correct my temper. I was given good principles, but left to
> follow them in pride and conceit. . . I was spoilt by my parents,
> who . . . allowed, encouraged, almost taught me to be selfish and
> overbearing, to care for none beyond my own family circle, to
> think meanly of all the rest of the world, to *wish* at least to think
> meanly of their sense and worth compared with my own. Such
> I was, from eight to eight and twenty; and such I might still

have been but for you, dearest, loveliest Elizabeth! What do I
not owe you!

Darcy's mind reorganizes itself to accommodate his experience pro-
ductively. And he can develop with such leaps and bounds precisely
because he—or rather his mind—is a complex system.

When you think about it, one rejection in the context of a lifetime
of experiences shouldn't logically be a life-changing event. And for
Mr. Collins, it isn't. But obviously in Darcy's case, the rejection ripples
through his mind touching on all sorts of issues, perceptions, memories, feelings, desires, and so forth, eventually altering him in dramatic
ways. The change is system-wide and pervasive.

Darcy's transformation points to one of the remarkable qualities of
complex systems, particularly complicated ones like the mind and brain:
Seemingly small events can trigger huge changes. We see this with other
Austen characters as well; they learn, they grow, they become their best
selves, and these changes appear to be disproportionately large compared to the events that instigate them. The recursivity of the mind, its
operation through feedback loops, makes this possible. In Darcy's case,
reorganization is for the better. But recursivity also means that a single
negative or traumatic event can have a seemingly disproportionate negative effect, as with a traumatic experience.

Change can also be gradual and cumulative, another quality of complex systems that's useful to understanding human psychology. Small
changes can occur on an ongoing basis until they form a critical mass,
and then we notice that the system has substantially progressed from
an earlier point. Darcy falls for Elizabeth, hard and fast. But Elizabeth's
love develops slowly, as she gradually realizes Darcy's worth and their
compatibility as a couple, until her thoughts reach a tipping point, a
moment at which she knows that Darcy is the man she wants to marry.

ALL TOGETHER NOW: NEURAL INTEGRATION

Darcy's response to the challenge of rejection is a better one than that
of Mr. Collins or Marianne because it's a more complex one. I mean
this in both a colloquial and a technical sense. Both Mr. Collins and

Marianne respond to crisis in ways that are simple because they're straightforward and predictable, seen in countless other people, real and fictional. Mr. Collins can't adjust his perceptions or expectations because his character is inflexible, while Marianne's despair follows well-known and repetitive patterns that have been seen in countless people who become depressed. This predictability has enabled psychologists to come up with diagnostic criteria for classifying depression as a disorder.

But Darcy's response is more complex because it doesn't follow an expected or familiar pattern. As a result of the shock of rejection, he evolves new ways of responding to people and events, which involve multiple and variable adjustments in thoughts, feelings, values, and behavior. These differ from his habitual reactions, as well as from well-known categorizable, if chaotic, conditions such as depression.

The terminology here is confusing. Of course, both Marianne and Mr. Collins have complex mind-brains in the sense that they have human brains that function through neural feedback loops—recursivity—and so their brains are, by definition, complex. In addition to more localized circuits among brain areas, energy and information are constantly flowing bidirectionally through every brain between bottom and top, left and right (between the hemispheres), and front and back; we wouldn't function at all without such neural activity.

But Darcy's mind-brain exhibits greater and more successful complexity than those of his counterparts. Success in a complex system refers to the extent to which it expands in the best way possible, which involves developing differentiated, specialized modules *and* greater interaction among those areas. When water boils, it begins to function as a whole (interaction) rather than as the collection of separate bubbles we see when at the beginning of the process, and it forms noticeable and various patterns (differentiation) through the eruptions of coils of water. All boiling water will function on par, but some brains will specialize and interconnect (and the latter is particularly important) more successfully than others. Such interconnection is known as neural integration.

Darcy's mind demonstrates complexity as defined in this scientific sense, reconfiguring and creating new neural connections in the body and brain, which means new ways of thinking, feeling, and relating.

The mind-brain's recursivity means that these new modes of being further affect social interaction, brain, body, and behavior—and so the cycle continues. Darcy's responses to experience become more *differentiated* from familiar or default patterns and *integrated* because the brain and body and sociality work together to further his well-being. In terms of the brain alone, a complex response to experience calls on concerted activity from a greater number of densely interconnected brain areas that work together than we see with rigid or chaotic reactions.

Complexity gives Darcy the ability to think creatively and respond in productive and appropriate ways to his experiences. Greater complexity translates into the flexible cognitive and emotional flexibility as well as the successful regulation of emotion. By contrast, both Mr. Collins and Marianne deal with their crises with default modes, rigidity and chaos (depression), one-size-fits-all reactions applied across a wide variety of experiences. Darcy himself emerges from a Collins-like rigidity. You can see this if you compare the automatic, almost rote nature of his responses at the Meryton ball with the quick, varied, and appropriate interactions he has with Elizabeth and the Gardiners when they encounter him at Pemberley.

Greater complexity generally translates into greater stability and flexibility, which means better functioning. As Darcy's mind-brain moves toward greater complexity, it calls upon more working parts, if you will, parts that coordinate their activity in diverse neurological and psychological domains. At the Meryton ball, Darcy is on automatic pilot, responding to experience without really thinking about his words or his actions, guided by feelings that he hasn't really considered. At Pemberley, he behaves with thoughtfulness and consideration; cognitive and emotional brain areas are fully interconnected and working together in concert with bodily responses and social awareness.

The evolution of the human brain offers an illustration of complexity that's easy to grasp because it shows a clear connection between anatomy and function, one that we don't have the tools to trace in terms of the functioning of mind as a whole. Primate brains evolved by developing neural areas that became progressively more specialized and differentiated as different species evolved. The ability to produce speech stems from a part of the human brain known as Broca's area; we find a corresponding area, also responsible for communication in chimpanzees and other great apes. These cousins of ours communicate with one another through vocalizations, social signals, and gestures. With training, chimps in captivity can even be taught to use American Sign Language. (But they can't use language in the way humans can; they can learn vocabulary and convey ideas with words using sign language, but they don't have syntax, the knowledge of grammatical rules for forming sentences). Chimpanzees tend to use communicative gestures with their right hands, which demonstrates left-brain dominance for communication, just as is found in humans. They also communicate meaningfully, just like humans, and indeed their gestures have consistent meanings, like the words in a language. All of this means that chimps have a language-ready brain, which began to evolve in the branch of our common ancestor that gradually became human.

The fact that an area corresponding to Broca's area orchestrates communication in chimps shows that evolution is thrifty, reusing and recycling materials that are already there. In the course of evolution, brains didn't as a rule develop complexity by generating additional brain areas, but by adding neurons to and, even more important, increasing interconnections within and between existing areas. The superior and specialized functioning of Broca's area in humans, the "complexity" of our capacity for language, results from a greater number of neurons and increased connectivity, denser and more complicated wiring.

Density also applies to developing increased complexity within individual brains. Although neurogenesis, the creation of new neurons, takes place in brains, especially during childhood, complexity tends more often to develop through greater interconnection among existing neurons. Darcy's brain functions better, with greater complexity, because it makes a greater number of neural connections than does Mr. Collins's brain. As its neural wiring becomes denser, Darcy's repertory of available responses correspondingly increases. Darcy's neural circuitry builds more roads within the brain, and so he has more routes available on his journey (more neural circuitry) and more towns that can be visited. This means a greater number of options for response, which confers flexibility as well as resiliency to setbacks and rejections. If one road leads to a dead end, take another.

Very simple behaviors such as the knee-jerk reflex involve only one neural pathway running from sensory input neurons in the knee to motor output neurons in the brain. But much of the brain's processing, which includes taking in information and generating responses, happens through processing that takes place simultaneously in different areas and is then assembled. This is called parallel distributed processing.

The pooling of information from different areas of the brain is known as neural integration, a feature found in all vertebrates, creatures that possess a central nervous system: a brain and a spinal cord. For the brain to coordinate input from many different areas, there needs to be an efficient way of bringing neural signals together. To return to the roads metaphor, if you lived in a small rural town in the south of eighteenth-century England, you couldn't travel a direct route to Gretna Green in Scotland, where eloping couples could be hastily and legally married, because the roads for such a journey didn't exist. So you'd first have to travel to the country's hub, London, and from there find roads leading to Scotland. That's why when Mr. Bennet searches for Lydia and Wickham (they've eloped), he travels to London where he knows they'll first have to stop. In the same way, neural signals from different areas of the brain, which have been processed in parallel, need to travel to hubs, known as association areas, where information is assembled and sent along for further processing. But association is almost never the sole function of these areas—far from it. In the process of putting information together, they add their input.

Neural integration is good for the brain, and so for the whole person—the more of it there is, the better. As Siegel explains, the more interconnected the brain is, the more that various circuits work together, the greater the flow of energy and information will be throughout, and the better it will function. The reverse is true as well: Both pathological conditions and less than optimal responses to ordinary experience are often characterized by insufficient neural integration. Think of a quadrille, a popular eighteenth-century dance for four couples. If even only one dancer misses a cue, he'll compromise the dance for everyone. Similarly, if there's a brain area or circuit that isn't working in concert with other parts of the system in the way it should be, this can compromise the functioning of the whole.

You're likely familiar with a very well-known instance of the failure of neural integration: post-traumatic stress disorder. For the unfortunate sufferers of this condition, traumatic memories erupt in flashbacks and dreams because the original traumatic experience can't be processed or "taken in" by various parts of the brain, particularly higher cortical areas. Traumatic experience is registered in emotional and bodily memory, subcortical systems that have no sense of time. And so the sufferer experiences disturbing, intrusive symptoms such as panic attacks and flashbacks that make the experience seem part of the present rather than the past. Neural integration is one route to healing; if cognitive areas can process traumatic experience, for instance, by putting feelings into words that are part of a narrative with a beginning, middle, and end, symptoms are often ameliorated. The experience then becomes part of the past rather than the present.

Marianne's depression similarly involves the shutdown of cognitive areas; negative emotions take over her mind at the expense of all other functions. Other less extreme failures of neural integration happen routinely, as in the psychological process of denial, a defense mechanism that means failing to notice something because it is threatening or disturbing. Mr. Collins must compromise perception and logic to turn Elizabeth's "no" into "yes," even if young ladies did often refuse proposals they eventually meant to accept, as he believes Elizabeth is doing. The affect accompanying her refusal, conveyed by social signals such as facial expression and body language as well as speech, should have convinced him that she was sincere.

Neural integration and parallel distributed processing (which together generate the simultaneous processing and subsequent pooling of information) refer to mind as well as brain. Darcy's glance at Elizabeth, which is itself processed in parallel and assembled in the brain, is only one component of his behavior at that moment. At the same time, he's conscious of his resentment for having to attend the ball and evaluating Elizabeth's looks. Had he simply looked at Elizabeth and seen a young lady sitting there, he wouldn't have made a nasty comment. But vision is integrated with information from other mind-brain areas, such as the emotional areas that tell Darcy he'd rather be elsewhere, from body areas necessary for perception and emotion, and from the social context of viewing a young lady at a ball while knowing that he's the door prize.

Of course, not everyone who responds with complexity to experience, who has an optimal flow of energy and information throughout the mind-brain, is going to dramatically improve their character or marry the partner of their dreams. Jumps between levels of analysis should be handled with care. But in general, complexity of thought in both the colloquial and technical senses leads to more flexibility and more numerous ways of responding, characteristics that are crucial elements of social intelligence.

HEBB'S RULE

Pride and Prejudice has been characterized as a novel of manners, a marriage plot novel, a romantic (and Romantic-era) novel, a didactic novel, a work of great literature, and probably in other ways as well. I'll add one more to the list: *Pride and Prejudice* can be characterized as a Hebbian novel, named for one of the founding fathers of neuroscience, Donald Hebb (1904–1985).

Dynamic systems move toward complexity through change, growth, and development. But they are characterized by continuity as well as flux. A foundational principle of neuroscience, known as Hebb's rule, accounts for the continuity of patterns of thought, feeling, and behavior that characterize the mind-brain. Donald Hebb's important discovery is widely known in the form of a catchy saying: "Neurons that fire together wire together." This means that once a group of neurons has activated at the same time, they're more likely to activate together in the future. Habitual patterns of neural activation are called attractor states.

Continuously recurring neural patterns generate the enduring traits that make up personality. Extraversion, introversion, optimism, pessimism, to name a few features, exist because certain neural patterns tend to repeat. Recurring neural patterns also enable learning; knowledge, like memory, depends on the activation of neural patterns that have previously fired. You repeat certain neural patterns every time you recall a basic fact such as London is the capital city of England. This principle applies in far more complex forms of learning, as well as for habitual ways of perceiving, feeling, and behaving. In short, attractor states generate much of our minds, who we are and what we know. They enable constancy and stability in the mind-brain; they enable us to have a consistent sense of our own identity even though our mind-brains are in a continuous state of flux.

Attractor states are of course responsible for the stubbornness of prejudice. The word *prejudice* as we use it today usually refers to an opinion formed without information. In Austen's day an alternative definition, according to the *Oxford English Dictionary*, was "a premature or hasty judgment." This aptly describes Elizabeth's behavior. She forms a devastating and persistent opinion of Darcy on their first meeting at the Meryton ball, and this is reinforced every time she meets him or thinks about him. Neural pathways that would allow her to correct her first impression can't compete with entrenched responses. Hebb's rule trounces incoming information.

However, this is only part of the story. Although at the neurological level, Hebb's rule explains the persistence of misguided thoughts and feelings—Elizabeth has an attractor state for seeing Darcy as negatively as possible—this explanation is insufficient on its own to account for Elizabeth's prejudice. Whether as a reader of Austen or an observer of human nature (and if you're reading this, you're bound to fit at least one of these categories), you've surely noticed that some misconceptions can be easily corrected while others are ingrained. Certainly, Elizabeth's mind-brain predisposed her to think poorly of Darcy after their first meeting. But she soon had access to additional information that should have contradicted her view of him as past redemption. She herself eventually realizes that she shouldn't have trusted Wickham's story. Elizabeth's misconceptions become entrenched from the start.

This is because they serve a purpose. When Elizabeth complains to her friend Charlotte about Darcy's excessive pride, Charlotte points out that given his money, rank, and personal attractiveness, Darcy "has a *right* to be proud." With her characteristic quickness and wit, Elizabeth rejoins, "That is very true, . . . and I could easily forgive *his* pride, if he had not mortified *mine*." The word *mortified* is telling; it comes from the Latin meaning "to kill," which points to the damaging nature of Darcy's remark. Mortification doesn't kill, but it's very painful, a form of humiliation much more wounding than simple embarrassment. Darcy's words didn't kill Elizabeth, but they nevertheless annihilated her symbolically, pegging her as worthless.

And so Elizabeth misses vital information that would contradict her first impression because she's invested in thinking of Darcy as a bad man. Her "prejudice" is a form of self-protection. If she can believe that he's bad, then she can believe that his judgment is faulty, especially his judgment of *her*. Elizabeth's prejudice is also a form of revenge; if Darcy thinks ill of her, she'll return the favor. But as Elizabeth realizes, it's unusual for her to misconstrue persons and situations so wrongly; in the usual course of events, she "prides" herself on her "discernment."

We can't yet explain how such filtering mechanisms work, exactly how perceptions are distorted. But we know, as in Elizabeth's case, that feelings are responsible. Emotions drive not only the social brain, but the thinking brain as well. Fortunately, emotions drive change and growth as well as distortion and prejudice, as we see in the story that follows that first unfortunate glance at the Meryton ball.

We Janeites accept that we thrill to the romance of seeing a deserving heroine enjoy her Cinderella-esque ending. And many of us additionally congratulate Elizabeth for winning her happy ending on the basis of character and intellect rather than feminine looks or wiles—her eyes owe much of their beauty to her liveliness of mind. But there's an equally thrilling, if more muted story being told about the power of love and, broadly speaking, all positive relationships, to transform us in extraordinary, unexpected ways.

FINDING YOUR WAY AROUND THE BRAIN (AN INTERLUDE)

Understanding neurons, complex systems, and Hebb's rule provides crucial information about how the brain functions. A basic knowledge of brain anatomy can be additionally helpful to understanding the neural processes that contribute to making us who we are. However, those readers who'd rather not pursue this topic can move on to the next chapter; brain areas will be explained as we encounter them.

The brain divides roughly into three areas, which developed chrono-
logically in the course of evolution. They go from lower to higher, and
inner to outer; in general, the higher and more exterior these areas, the
more advanced the functions they oversee. We can imagine the spatial
relationship of these areas to one another by visualizing a cauliflower.
(Actually, the brain looks most like a walnut, a food that's good for
talking about the hemispheres [see below]. But a walnut fails to portray
the brain's levels correctly!)

The first part of the brain to develop in evolutionary time (phylo-
genetically) was the brainstem (the stalk of the cauliflower), which is
responsible for a variety of survival behaviors, such as breathing, sleep,
arousal, and the regulation of heartbeat. The brainstem also participates
in bringing information about the world to other parts of the brain and
conveying commands from these higher levels to the body; it's an information superhighway, continuous with the spinal cord, whose neurons
reach throughout our bodies. Brainstem activity is involuntary and
subconscious. Reptile brains are mainly brainstem, with very primitive
versions of other structures. So if you think your pet snake loves you,
you're projecting your own feelings onto a creature who's cold-blooded in
emotional as well as physiological terms. Unlike mammals, reptiles lack
the neural machinery needed to form emotional bonds. (However, I have
a friend who swears that bearded dragons relate and cuddle in mammalian ways. Perhaps mammalian hubris is as bad as anthropocentrism!)

Next, moving upward, are the subcortical areas, the core of the cauliflower, which includes the structures that make up the limbic system;
these areas are key to the processing of emotion. They include the hypothalamus, which activates the release of important neurochemicals and
hormones, such as the hormone adrenaline. This chemical messenger is
involved in producing excitatory responses of both positive and negative kinds—joy as well as fear. The hippocampus forms new episodic
memories, memories of people and events. And the amygdala, one of
our two "star players" (see below) is central in the activation and recognition of fear as well as other excitatory responses. The amygdala tells
the hypothalamus to send the message to release adrenaline. It's also
one of the brain structures that tags events as important to remember.

The development of limbic brain areas in mammals—this area
used to be known as the mammalian brain—means that mammals

share many of the same basic emotions as humans, as the study of animal behavior and neuroscience have suggested. This accounts for the sociality of mammals, as seen especially in their nurturing of off-spring and their bonding with one another and with humans. Unlike your pet snake, your dog really does love you (and don't believe those naysayer skeptical scientists who continually underestimate animal capabilities). Perhaps this exonerates some of Austen's sporting types such as Charles Musgrove in *Persuasion*, who'd rather spend time with his dogs than with his self-centered and tedious wife. The experience might indeed be more emotionally gratifying. The limbic areas are certainly not the only brain areas dedicated to the processing of emotions, but they're important subcortical ones.

Finally, the cerebral cortex, made up of the flowers of the cauliflower, is the most advanced and recently developed of brain areas (it too has raised and recessed areas, even though it isn't as good a brain look-alike as the walnut). It's the outermost layer of the brain, and it wraps around subcortical areas like a blanket. It's often called the neocortex in humans because it is so new (neo) and advanced compared to the cortex in other vertebrates. The cortex exists in reptiles as a single-cell layer toward the back of the brain. In most mammals, it's a thin layer of tissue surrounding the limbic structures. But in humans and other primates, it's huge in relation to other brain areas.

The cortex expanded in "advanced" mammals by folding in on itself to form grooves (sulci) and raised areas (gyri), thereby providing more surface area and a greater number of cells, resulting in more brainpower. This gives the wrinkly, convoluted appearance most of us picture when we think of the brain. If you compare a hamster brain to a dog brain, you'll see that the rodent has fewer of these convolutions. The more developed the cerebral cortex, the greater the number of sulci and gyri, and the greater the number of capabilities, including social capabilities, an animal possesses. Think of the difference between a pet hamster and the family dog. One has a more developed cerebral cortex, the other, only a very basic one.

Social capability refers not only to depth of feeling, although this is often the case, but to the multifaceted ways that we interact with one another. For despite the common substrate of sociality and emotion we share with other mammals, human cognition adds options for response not found in other species. Perhaps relationships among some of these other animals have dimensions of which humans are unaware, and which surpass ours in complexity and sophistication—who's to say? Although our anthropocentric species has underestimated the mind-brains of other species for most of our time on earth (and many continue to do so), I think that even those who appreciate how smart (cognitively and emotionally) many other species of animals are—and I consider myself in this company—would still grant that the complexities of feeling found in *Pride and Prejudice* are likely not found in other species, not even in chimpanzees and bonobos, who share almost ninety-nine percent of DNA with humans. We can be relatively certain that no chimpanzee will ever type out *Pride and Prejudice* not only because chimps lack the language and intelligence to do so, but just as important, because as far as we can tell, they lack the range and complexity of human feeling demonstrated by Austen's characters and understood by her readers.

It used to be thought that the human brain could be neatly divided into these three distinct areas, a theory proposed by Paul MacLean. According to the theory of the triune brain, the brainstem forms the reptilian brain, the limbic areas form the mammalian brain, and the cortex forms the neo-mammalian brain. The brainstem is responsible for physiology; the mid-subcortical areas generate emotion; and the cortex orchestrates cognition, simple in most nonhuman animals and complicated in humans. MacLean's triune brain makes sense in evolutionary terms since these areas did develop in this order. But his model is flawed in viewing these areas as functionally separate.

As subsequent research on the brain has demonstrated, neither emotions nor other kinds of thoughts and perceptions are processed in a discrete area of the brain. There's no one emotional brain, as MacLean claimed, although we use the term as shorthand for all the systems that go into producing emotion. In the course of evolution, brain areas were not only added but integrated functionally in complex ways with structures that existed already. For instance, mammalian emotions involve input from the reptilian, physiological brain. There can't be a separate emotion system, or any other kind of separate system, because all three "brains" are interconnected through neural circuitry that is astoundingly intricate, even in the lowliest mammals. I stress that the triune brain is an outmoded theory because it's likely that every one of our responses, even simple ones, relies on parallel distributed processing, which means information flowing across the brain in all directions at any given moment. But triune brain theory nevertheless provides a useful way of thinking about the large divisions within brain anatomy.

The brain divides into halves as well as levels. There's a right and a left hemisphere, familiarly known as the "left brain" and the "right brain." These are for the most part symmetrical, with structures present in one half also present in the other. However, areas in each hemisphere differ to some extent in terms of function; this is known as laterality, and it's seen throughout the animal kingdom although most pronounced in humans. In most humans, the capacity for language is located primarily in the cortex of the left hemisphere (you've already "met" Broca's area), while awareness of the body and what it's doing (called body maps) generally takes place in the cortex of the right hemisphere. A skilled writer and a graceful dancer—Jane was both—would need to have excellent capacities in both hemispheres. The "divide and conquer" structure of the brain's anatomy enables different sides to specialize and so do a better job of their given tasks.

Asymmetry applies to subcortical areas as well; for instance, there's a left- and a right-hemisphere amygdala. One of the functions of the amygdala is to decide what's worth remembering, kind of like flagging a page of the novel you're reading. One study concluded that, following the basic differences between the right and left hemispheres, the left amygdala might be more involved in helping us to remember emotional information that involves language whereas the right amygdala might help us to remember emotional information involving images. However, hemispheric distinctions are sometimes subtle or not entirely understood, and for this reason I'll follow the lead of many books about the brain and refer to brain areas without differentiating between right and left hemispheres unless the distinction is relevant.

The cortex further subdivides into lobes, duplicated in each hemisphere; these are called the frontal, parietal, temporal, and occipital lobes. These lobes are carved out of the brain turned sideways. The frontal lobe, the foremost lobe of the brain, contains the motor cortex, which is responsible for initiating voluntary movement. The parietal lobe, on the top and middle of the brain, contains the somatosensory cortex, which governs the sense of touch. The temporal lobe, behind the ear, oversees hearing and language. The most forward area of the frontal lobe is appropriately named the prefrontal cortex. This is the "CEO" of the brain, responsible for executive functions such as planning and implementing behavior, problem solving, and logic. The visual cortex has its own lobe, the occipital lobe, which is located in the back of the brain. This is where Elizabeth's image is assembled, in Darcy's "mind's eye."

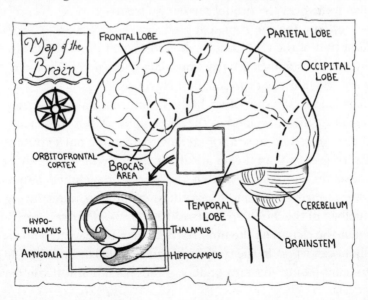

TWO STAR PLAYERS:
THE AMYGDALA AND THE ORBITOFRONTAL CORTEX (OFC)

This rough sketch of the brain doesn't begin to capture its complexity, neither the extraordinary intricacy of its connections nor the abundance of areas that contribute to its functioning. But you don't need to have a comprehensive knowledge of neuroanatomy to understand social intelligence, not even when that understanding incorporates a certain amount of neuroscience. In telling about some of the more physiological aspects of social intelligence, I've decided to let science take its cue from literature once again, using a version of the literary figure known as synecdoche.

Synecdoche is a rhetorical term like *metaphor* and *simile*. It most often means speaking of a part to refer to the whole, as in the phrase "hired hands" to mean workers. It's the workers who are hired, not their hands, but hands stand in for the entire person. A synecdoche can also use the whole to represent a part, as in the phrase "the world isn't treating you well." Only a small portion of the world isn't treating you well, and the rest is completely oblivious to your existence. In true synecdochal fashion, two brain areas will be referenced to discuss the bulk of information about the neurology of social intelligence: the amygdala and the orbitofrontal cortex, hereafter the OFC. (The OFC is also known as the orbital medial prefrontal cortex. According to some sources, the ventromedial prefrontal cortex [VMPFC] includes at least part of the OFC, but the boundaries of the VMPFC have not been firmly established.) The amygdala and the OFC are our "star players" when it comes to social intelligence.

This isn't to say that other brain structures don't play a vital role in social intelligence, or that they'll be ignored, but these two areas will be featured because they are key to enabling our extraordinary sociality, greater than that of any other species. We say "hired hands" because the context in which the phrase developed concerned work done with the hands: carpentry, farming, manufacturing (the etymology of this last also refers to hands). We don't say "hired feet" because the feet aren't the important parts of the person who accomplishes such work. In the social brain, the amygdala and the OFC are significant hands, master builders of the social brain. If you become familiar with the OFC and the amygdala, you'll not only know about two key areas, but you'll also understand how regions of the brain connect and interact in a more general sense.

The OFC is a vital hub, where neural signals from far-flung areas are assembled. Although it's technically part of the prefrontal cortex, the brain's most advanced area, it's located on the underbelly of the cortex, roughly behind your eyes. It sits at the juncture of limbic areas, which are crucially involved in the processing of emotion, and cortical areas, which enable cognition, including logic and reason. Among its many functions, it's responsible for reading social signals, nonverbal expressions of emotion, intent, attitude, and so forth.

The brain is sometimes surprisingly literal in the sense that *where* something is located defines *what* it does (although, as you know, localized function acts in concert with information coming from many other brain areas). The location of the OFC has much to do with its function, for it coordinates information from cognitive and emotional areas. So crucial is the OFC's role in emotional processing that although it's technically considered part of the neocortex, it is more accurately defined as a cortico-limbic structure in terms of function as well as location. In addition, because it's centrally located, more or less at the center of our brains, neural signals moving in every direction cross its path so that it receives information from every other system in the brain. It's a key brain area for neural integration—the London of the brain.

What this means is that the OFC puts information from the external environment, some of which we're conscious of, together with information from our internal environments, again some of which we recognize, such as conscious thoughts, but also endocrine, neurotransmitter, and hormone levels, which we know nothing about. Just as important as the information the OFC takes in is the information it sends out. The OFC has output connections to the amygdala and the hypothalamus, in charge of vital hormones, and to other brain areas where neurotransmitters are produced and released. It therefore orchestrates most of the important chemicals that control thought and behavior, the chemicals neurons need in order to know whether or not to be active. In short, the OFC is central in gathering information, interpreting perceptions, and generating responses.

The OFC is also connected to the brain's reward system, also known as the seeking system. In the mind-brain sciences, reward refers to all the positive outcomes of actions and behavior, from applause after a presentation, to falling in love, to eating a chocolate bar. And speaking of chocolate, one study using fMRI (imaging of the brain in action) found that when people who habitually crave chocolate were presented with images of their favorite treat, their OFCs were more active than those of non-cravers. A related function, the OFC predicts and calculates the magnitude of reward and punishment, such as winning or losing money at gambling. People with damage to the OFC are poor gamblers.

Like all our brain and body parts, the OFC has a range of possible capability. The better the OFC functions, which depends primarily on the more connections it makes, the greater will be the flow of information throughout the brain. A high-functioning OFC leads to complexity. It gives us options and helps us make good choices. It does all this subconsciously, although its input contributes to conscious decision making. We can assume that Darcy's OFC was higher functioning than that of Mr. Collins. Of course, we can say this about their brains as a whole, for Mr. Collins seems to be a very dim light indeed.

The amygdala is the gatekeeper for initiating stress reactions and other excitatory responses. It's especially vital in the processing of fear and anxiety. It's on the lookout for threats, so we can be prepared to confront them, and it activates when we encounter potentially dangerous situations or people, releasing chemical signals that get the body ready for action. It's particularly receptive to visual information, which includes facial expression, so vital a sign for humans. I'm sure Darcy's amygdala was highly active at the Meryton ball. But the amygdala is involved in positive responses as well, helping to generate the neurochemicals we need for excitement, which isn't all that different from fear in terms of pure arousal. This explains why people can find fear and excitement difficult to separate, feeling a certain thrill, or "frisson," as the French so elegantly say, in danger—think of riding a roller coaster.

As noted, the amygdala lets us know what's worth paying attention to, and this again includes positive as well as negative experience. It tags people and events as important, and therefore worth remembering. Elizabeth remembers Darcy's insult because of the amygdala, but this little structure also helps Jane to remember Bingley's charming smiles. Like the OFC, the amygdala connects to areas such as the hypothalamus that control and produce vital neurochemicals. You can see an overlap in function with our two star players—the amygdala also interprets social signals, the OFC also notes what's worth remembering, and both areas initiate neurochemical and physiological responses. But this isn't unusual. Brain areas often duplicate one another in terms of function, varying somewhat in their activity to complement one another. Whatever our brains do, they usually require the coordination of many areas that contribute to or duplicate the same function.

The amygdala is under the jurisdiction of the OFC and must listen to its commands, which is reasonable since the OFC is receiving information from cortical-cognitive areas of the brain as well as subcortical-emotion areas. The amygdala, however, sends the OFC important information about the environment more quickly than cortical areas are capable of doing. Both structures, and indeed all brain areas, have input and output connections that involve them in continuous feedback loops that adjust our perceptions and responses millisecond by millisecond.

The OFC and amygdala pretty much run the social brain because working together, they initiate and regulate emotional responses. And emotions largely determine the nature of our relationships and interactions with others. You can be good at math without emotional input, but you need emotions to be good at relationships. This is ancient wisdom, common-sense "folk psychology." But emotions are at the heart of other kinds of intelligence as well as social intelligence, which isn't as obvious. Emotions are the prime movers of our mind-brains, as we see in the following chapter.

THREE

The Sense of Sensibility

At first glance, *Sense and Sensibility* appears to set up a clear-cut opposition between reason and feeling through the two sisters who personify these traits: Elinor is sense (reason) and Marianne is sensibility (feeling). But we soon begin to see that this split doesn't do justice to Austen's novel: Her heroines are far too complex to personify qualities in this simplistic fashion. Elinor might appear to think more rationally than Marianne, and Marianne to feel more deeply than Elinor—at least in the opening chapters—but *Sense and Sensibility* ultimately shows that feeling and judgment are inseparable.

Austen sets up an apparent opposition only to undermine it (or deconstruct it, as literary critics like to say). To begin with, she knew she could depend on readers in her day to recognize the shakiness of the dichotomy between thought and feeling from the very title of the novel, an advantage we've lost. Austen's readers would have known that the words *sense* and *sensibility* have additional meanings that don't fall into neat and opposite categories. According to the *Oxford English Dictionary*, both words mean perception in a simple sense, the capacity to take in what's around you. Let's say you're at a ball. You can sense, or be sensible of, the conversations of your neighbors.

But this isn't the only way in which the meanings morph into one another. Sense is also defined as emotional consciousness, "a glad or sorrowful, grateful or resentful recognition of another person's conduct, an event, a fact or a condition of things." For instance, Elinor has the *sense* [feeling] that Lucy, her rival for Edward's love, dislikes her as soon as they meet, even though she doesn't yet know about Lucy's secret engagement with Edward. So *sense*, like *sensibility*, can refer to feeling. And the adjective for both words is *sensible*, which means *both* "capable of . . . emotion (feeling)" *and* "endowed with good sense; intelligent, reasonable, judicious." Being sensible can therefore mean possessing either reason or feeling. Sensibility is even, depending on how it is used, listed as a synonym for sense! Here's a sentence no self-respecting author should write, but it illustrates my point: Although Elinor is *sensible* of Lucy's dislike, and *sensible* enough to be disturbed by it, she's sufficiently *sensible* to behave as if they're the best of friends.

Although Austen's readers might have been more likely to catch on to this ambiguity of meaning than we are today, we don't need to rely on a dictionary to see that neither sister embodies pure reason or pure feeling. Elinor appears to be the poster girl for good judgment, but it's a mistake to think she's guided by reason alone, or that she lacks passion. To begin with, if she appears to lack feeling (especially in Marianne's view), it's only because she does not outwardly express what she feels, not because she's apathetic; she has superior powers of emotional regulation, or "self-control," as they called it in Austen's day. And although the excitable Marianne interprets such outward calm as indicating a lack of feeling, this is certainly not the case.

We see this in Elinor's relationship with Edward, the man she loves. Elinor had first begun to see Edward regularly at her great-uncle's estate, Norland, before Elinor's family was forced to move. Norland had been destined to be inherited by Elinor's father from an elderly and childless uncle. Elinor's family had lived with this relative, providing care and companionship in his declining years. But Elinor's father died before his uncle, who then unexpectedly left the estate to John, Elinor's stepbrother from her father's previous marriage. This stepbrother is married to Edward's sister, Fanny. Elinor and her mother and sisters must therefore move from Norland, which they do after a few months of looking for a new home. In the interim, at Norland, Elinor and Edward get to know one another.

In those months while the family was still at Norwood, Edward was a frequent visitor and appeared to be warmly attached to Elinor, although he didn't propose. But when he later visits the family at their new home in Devonshire, his manner is strangely altered. Edward is often moody and distant, although occasionally he's more like his old self. His treatment of Elinor reflects profound ambivalence: "the reservedness of his manner towards her contradicted one moment what a more animated look had intimated the preceding one."

But despite his "coldness and reserve," which leave Elinor "vexed and half angry," she resolves "to regulate her behavior to him by the past rather than the present," and she avoids "every appearance of resentment or displeasure." When Edward leaves, Elinor parts calmly from him, deliberately suppressing the display of the very real anguish she feels. Nevertheless, at the very moment that Elinor is heroically struggling to contain her emotions, Marianne "blushed to acknowledge" her sister's lack of distress, interpreting self-control as lack of feeling.

In addition to attributing Elinor's even temper to an unrefined callousness, Marianne also thinks that Elinor disguises the emotions she *does* feel out of obedience to society's "commonplace and mistaken notions" governing behavior. In Marianne's view, this is another instance of the triumph of reason over feeling, of allowing cold judgment and assessment of a situation to prevail over the spontaneous expression of emotion.

It would have been right in line with ideas of propriety for Elinor to refrain from showing her feelings of distress at parting from Edward. After all, there's been no engagement between them, and so conveying stronger emotions than she would have done at the parting of any other relative would have been inappropriate. A woman wasn't supposed to show her feelings for a man before he had actually proposed. But the struggle that Elinor clearly undergoes to contain her feelings is *not* motivated by knowledge of proper conduct, even though her behavior is socially appropriate. Paradoxically, it is feeling—her concern for Edgar—rather than judgment that drives Elinor to mask her suffering.

By the end of the visit, Elinor realizes that Edward is "melancholy." Had she been distant or cross, or behaved in any way that expressed disappointment or disapproval, she would have added to his pain. Some readers might think that a cold shoulder would have served Edward right for behaving badly—leading Elinor on and pushing her away—even if he did so inadvertently. But Elinor wouldn't agree with them.

Indeed, Elinor consistently exerts self-control to protect others, sometimes at her own expense. Feeling rather than decorum again motivates her restrained affect with her family. Edward's "desponding turn of mind" affects Elinor deeply, and it requires "some trouble and time to subdue," but this is exactly what she does. She contains her distress because she doesn't want her mother and sisters to be upset on her behalf.

Just as Elinor's sense can't be separated from her sensibility, the reverse is true for Marianne: A cognitive, intellectual motive contributes to her habit of responding with quick and strong feeling. This isn't to deny that the sisters are temperamentally distinct, Elinor calm and self-possessed, Marianne skittish and reactive. But Marianne's exquisite sensitivity is also a matter of principle.

In Austen's day, many well-known rules regulated conduct, especially for young ladies; I've mentioned one such rule already, that a young lady wasn't supposed to express her love unless the man she fancied had proposed. Additionally, unmarried women and men weren't supposed to go out together unchaperoned, exchange personal gifts, or write personal letters to one another. Such rules were often published in books that sold very well, a genre known as the "conduct book," which offered a range of advice from dictating behavior in specific social interactions to making life-changing decisions. You can think of these guides as the self-help books of Austen's day.

Marianne finds such entrenched notions of decorum ridiculous, contrary to the goodwill and authenticity of feeling that should ground our close relationships. As the narrator tells us, "[T]o aim at the restraint of sentiments which were not in themselves illaudable, appeared to her not merely an unnecessary effort, but a disgraceful subjection of reason to commonplace and mistaken notions." And so, in Marianne's view, it's unreasonable to behave in ways that her society mistakenly deems reasonable. She thinks it wrong not to express laudable feelings, such as an innocent first love, to their fullest—to "drink life to the lees" as the poet Alfred Tennyson would later write; he wasn't yet born when this novel was written, but he certainly inherited much of the romantic sensibility expressed by Marianne. Perhaps you've known a teenager or two who similarly rebels because she thinks the benighted older generation has invented rules that are stupid, superfluous, and hypocritical. This particular cultural pattern appears to die hard!

Marianne lives by her credo, as we see in experiences that parallel those of her sister. Marianne first meets Willoughby when out on a walk with her sisters. She twists her ankle and he comes to the rescue, carrying her home and, in the process, "sweeping her off her feet" as we say, both literally and figuratively. This begins a whirlwind romance in which neither Marianne nor Willoughby restrains their feelings.

Marianne blatantly disregards the conventions that Elinor respects and observes. She lets Willoughby know how she feels, although he hasn't proposed or expressed serious intentions. She goes on outings alone with him, gives him a lock of her hair, and enters into a personal correspondence with him, all forbidden behaviors. This last convinces Elinor that Marianne and Willoughby must have entered into a secret engagement, although she's wrong about this. Marianne writes to Willoughby although there's been no formal engagement, assuming that their love doesn't need official sanctions, that such guarantees of devotion are beside the point when love is genuine.

Unlike Elinor, Marianne fails to realize that following the rules of conduct and avoiding impulsivity—all the attributes of good sense—can protect against some very unpleasant if not downright dangerous experiences. Society's rules might have restricted freedom in ways that we, as well as Marianne, find silly and unacceptable, but they also protected people, especially women. Women who spent time alone with men, as did Marianne, would be vulnerable to seduction or rape, an event that would banish them from polite society forever. Since Willoughby has already seduced and abandoned one young one woman (Marianne doesn't know this), Marianne might have been lucky to get away with just a broken heart and her reputation intact.

Marianne also fails to think of how her behavior might affect others. When Willoughby takes a sudden leave of the family (paralleling the end of Edward's visit), Marianne's method of coping contrasts glaringly with Elinor's. She gives way to "violent sorrow . . . feeding and encouraging it as a duty." Far from trying to spare her family pain on her account, she lets everyone know she's miserable:

> They saw nothing of Marianne till dinner time, when she entered the room and took her place at the table without saying a word. Her eyes were red and swollen; and it seemed as if her tears were even then restrained with difficulty. She avoided the looks of them all, could neither eat nor speak, and after some time, on her mother's silently pressing her hand with tender compassion, her small degree of fortitude was quite overcome, she burst into tears and left the room.

Despite her constant, "in your face" expression of feelings, Marianne's behavior contains a strong element of decision: "She was without any power, because she was without any desire of command over herself." Austen gets right at the truth here. Marianne succumbs to her feelings so entirely because she doesn't want to control them, believing such control is misguided and hypocritical. Although her feelings are genuine, her extreme sensibility is to some degree a matter of principle, of judgment rather than feeling.

Both sisters possess sense and sensibility; these can't be separated etymologically or psychologically. Austen understood that feelings are influenced by beliefs, and, even more important, no matter how much sense a person appears to possess, it's never free from the influence of sensibility. Nor should it be, because both virtue and sound judgment depend on feeling.

SLAVES OF OUR PASSIONS

Austen's ideas about feelings likely owed much to the philosopher David Hume (1711–1776), a near contemporary—he died the year after she was born. His works were in her father's library, and Austen was a prodigious reader. She wrote a parody of Hume's *History of England* when she was fifteen, so we know that she was familiar with at least some of his writings. Although we don't have proof that she read Hume's *Treatise of Human Nature* (published 1739–40), its fundamental ideas about feeling permeate her novels.

To begin with, Hume believed that emotion, not reason, is the source of virtue; we treat others well because we can take their perspective and feel what they feel—in short, virtue depends on empathy. *Sense and Sensibility* (as well as Austen's other novels) might well have been written to illustrate this insight. All of Elinor's behavior involves such perspective taking, an understanding of how her actions will impact others emotionally. Conversely, for all her emphasis on feeling, Marianne fails to take the feelings of others into consideration. This lapse is what she most regrets, what she realizes has been her most serious moral defect, when she gains new insight after a serious illness. She tells Elinor, "I saw in my own behavior [since meeting Willoughby] nothing but a series of imprudence towards myself, *and want of kindness to others*." [my italics]

Hume wasn't the first philosopher in the Western world to associate feeling with virtue, although he gives the point unprecedented emphasis. His truly revolutionary innovation was to suggest that emotions, or "the passions" as they were called, are inseparable from reason, and that thoughts that appear to be the product of pure reason rely on emotional input. He captured both points in a catchy statement: "Reason is and ought only to be the slave of the passions." Reason *ought to be* the slave of the passions because virtue, and all our best impulses, are born of feeling rather than calculation. And reason *is* the slave of the passions because our supposedly reasonable choices are guided by emotion. Pure reason doesn't exist, at least not in a social or moral context.

By arguing that the passions are an inevitable part of all thought, including reason, Hume marked himself as a renegade, although like many renegades, he's been proved right. By the time Hume entered the discussion, Western philosophy had had a long tradition of seeing reason and feeling as separate and opposed. A famous classic example is Plato's allegory of the charioteer in his dialogue *Phaedrus* (c. 370 B.C.E.). Plato represents the human mind as a chariot. The driver, or charioteer, represents reason, and his chariot is pulled by two horses. One horse symbolizes moral feelings, the feelings that lead us to perform just and benevolent actions. Here Plato and Hume agree that positive actions have their source in feeling. The other horse symbolizes what Freud called the id, the primitive emotions and desires, including those of the flesh, that lead us astray and that need to be managed for a society to function. The charioteer controls both horses, ensuring that the chariot goes only in directions that he approves.

Plato is right in believing that emotion needs to be regulated, guided in the right direction if we're to live together in ordered societies. But he's wrong in thinking that reason, the charioteer, can do the trick. Every one of our supposedly reasonable thoughts or actions or decisions that takes place in a social context—and so most of our cognitive activity—has an emotional component. This means that the thought processes we use in most of our reasoning don't stem from pure reason, and that feeling is woven into the very fabric of our calculations, as we see in the case of Elinor's good sense.

In fact, the only kind of reason that can be exercised without emotional input involves asocial, neutral instances of thought, such as solving quadratic equations, something that isn't inherently tied in with dealing with other people. But this isn't the type of thinking that preoccupies Plato or most other philosophers. They're concerned with the exercise of reason in our dealings with one another, in the wisdom that enables us to behave in ways that benefit societies as well as individuals. If the charioteer can't prevent the wayward horse from running amok, he is likely to hurt or kill all the innocent people in his path, as well as himself.

The mind-brain sciences have confirmed Hume's (and Austen's) insight: "Reason is and ought to be the slave of the passions." Neuroscientist Elizabeth Phelps observes that the more we learn about emotional processing, the more widespread we find its influence to be. Even those instances you might think of as "pure reason," such as our hypothetical math problem, might well turn out to have an emotional component. Perhaps solving an equation will get you a good grade on a test and put you in the running for a scholarship. In that case, no longer is your math problem emotionally or socially neutral. Plato's charioteer is driving toward a dead end.

Neuroscientist Antonio Damasio and his research team confirmed the extraordinary scope of emotion, demonstrating that thought processes that we tend to attribute to reason are firmly grounded in feeling; they depend on input from emotion-processing areas of the brain. Among their groundbreaking discoveries, they found that good judgment often relies on a healthy dose of fear. Remember that emotions help us to avoid punishers, that this is a crucial part of their function, and so it's not surprising that judgment should rely on fear—or surprising only because Anglo-European culture has idolized reason for so long.

The connection between fear and judgment was seen in a research subject, dubbed S.M. This woman has a rare condition, Urbach-Wiethe disease, which destroys the amygdala, the part of the brain that generates fear and other related feelings such as anxiety and apprehension. By the time Damasio encountered S.M., her amygdala was totally nonfunctional.*

Damasio found that although S.M. was competent cognitively and was able to process emotions other than fear in a normal manner, she had an obvious fear deficit. She couldn't recognize fearful faces, nor could she draw them, although she could easily recognize and draw faces with other emotions. This meant that her capacity to read social signals was also impaired. S.M. could be trained to recognize fear by being instructed on what to look for in a person's face, especially around the eyes. But this involved a cognitive override of her automatic emotional responses: S.M. didn't feel fear involuntarily and unconsciously in the usual way. Subsequent experiments throughout the years have confirmed that others with similar amygdala damage also have a fear deficit.

S.M.'s personal life had shown the danger of living fearlessly. She made friends and got involved romantically rather easily, but she'd been repeatedly betrayed by people she trusted. She simply lacked

---

* The lead writer on the paper that first reported this research was Damasio's student, Ralph Adolphs; this means that Adolphs directed the research. Daniel Tranel was the second author listed. Both are currently professors and major researchers in the mind-brain sciences. Damasio subsequently reported and popularized the findings of this team in *Descartes' Error*, and he has continued to work throughout his career with S.M. and others whose emotional processing areas have been damaged.

the feelings that would alert her to warning signs, or tell her to be careful—to avoid punishers. S.M. had been threatened with deadly weapons in more than one mugging (she couldn't detect situations that might be dangerous) and was nearly killed by a domestic partner, yet she remained fearless throughout these traumatic events. Memories of encounters that had turned out badly also failed to engender fear, so she lacked the possibility of learning from past experiences. Since one function of the amygdala is to tag experiences with emotional value, this deficit might have been the result of the loss of two of its functions.

The old saying, "Fools rush in where angels fear to tread" might have been written to describe S.M. Although no one's fool in many respects, her decisions were often reckless because they put her at grave risk. This proverb, which asserts the link between fear and wisdom, also shows that popular culture had bucked the tide of pure reason long before the advent of neuroscience, along with exceptions in the world of letters, such as Hume and Austen.

We see how fear enters into good judgment in Elinor's handling of her friendship with Lucy Steele, who's secretly engaged to Edward. Several years before Edward and Elinor met, he had been a student of Lucy's uncle, Mr. Pratt, with whom he boarded. Lucy was then a frequent visitor at her uncle's house. After an acquaintance of several years, they entered into a secret engagement, an action that Edward has lived to regret, especially since meeting Elinor.

Lucy realizes that Edward wants to break the engagement (he's too honorable to do so), and also guesses his attraction to Elinor. So when Lucy and Elinor cross paths in London because they have acquaintances in common, Lucy strategically shares her secret with Elinor. She claims to want to confide in Elinor because she trusts and respects her new friend. But she really wants to warn her away from Edward and to torment her for so obviously being the woman he'd rather marry.

Hearing Lucy's news about the secret engagement, Elinor is dumbfounded: "[H]er astonishment at what she heard was at first too great for words." For despite her "composure of voice," she experiences "emotion and distress beyond any thing she had ever felt before. She was mortified, shocked, confounded." Although there's nothing she can do about the engagement, she quickly apprehends another danger that *can* be averted: letting Lucy know how deeply she's affected.

Elinor's payoff for her self-control is that she deprives Lucy of her triumph, and so averts the negative feelings she would have experienced in seeing Lucy gloat. Elinor dodges that punisher! She finds great comfort in "convincing Lucy that her heart was unwounded." Elinor can't lessen the loss and disappointment she feels, but she can—and does—protect herself from having salt rubbed in her wounds.

Elinor's good judgment, Marianne's poor judgment, and S.M.'s deficits fall under the category of social intelligence (or lack thereof). While most of us wouldn't use the word *social* to describe S.M.'s beatings and muggings, they were technically social in that they involved dealings with other people. This is the context in which Damasio studied S.M.'s deficits. Damasio is a very philosophically minded neuroscientist, profoundly influenced by the seventeenth-century philosopher Spinoza (another renegade proved right in many respects), so it's not surprising that he had a humanistic focus in studying S.M.'s condition. Indeed, novelists and philosophers, including Austen, Hume, and pretty much anyone else writing about the human condition, tend to consider judgment and ethics in the context of relationships, whether this concerns a relationship between two people, the workings of an agency or institution, the social structure within a society at large, or a personal connection with God.

This focus makes sense because sociality is the most important factor in brain function and development, at an individual and an evolutionary level. In fact, many scientists believe that our extreme sociality led not only to social intelligence, but to all the other intelligences we take pride in as a species. It would make sense that emotions, the very foundation of relationships, are most important in the context of social situations, in our interactions with one another at all levels.

In this respect, there's been an interesting development that sheds additional light on the social brain as well as on Damasio's work. It appears that the brain might indeed distinguish between social situations and other contexts, such as that neutral quadratic equation (which is rarely entirely neutral in the end). In an experiment in which S.M. and others with her condition were deprived of oxygen, they all reported feeling not only fear but panic. This suggests that the brain makes an important distinction between threats coming from the external environment, and purely internal events, such as being unable to breathe. Many threats from the external environment come from our interactions with others; certainly, this was true for S.M. Amygdala damage might be necessary to the experience of fear only when the threat comes from outside ourselves, a qualification that applies to our interactions with others much of the time.

WEIGHING PROS AND CONS, OR THE "WO/MAN OF REASON" IS REALLY "THE WO/MAN OF FEELING"

Willoughby has to decide. He must choose between staying faithful to Marianne, whom he genuinely loves, or marrying the heiress Miss Grey for her fortune. Although Austen doesn't follow Willoughby in the throes of his decision making, he later tells of his struggle in his genuine, heartfelt confession and apology for abandoning Marianne, pledged to Elinor toward the end of the novel. As Marianne lies dangerously ill, Willoughby comes to see Elinor. He asks her to tell Marianne that he really loved her—and still does—and that he made a cruel and terrible mistake that he'll regret until the end of his days.

And it gets worse. His behavior has added insult to injury; his heartless mode of ending the relationship exacerbated the effects of his decision. After Willoughby had abruptly left Devonshire, he stopped writing to Marianne, although she remained a faithful correspondent. When they both ended up in London for a prolonged stay, Willoughby continued to keep his distance. Finally, he snubbed her very publicly at a ball they both attended, greeting her coldly as a casual acquaintance, and not the woman he passionately adores.

In response to Marianne's desperate notes asking him to account for his behavior, Willoughby writes a devastating letter denying that they'd ever had a close relationship or felt anything special for one another. After this, Marianne descends into a deep depression that almost costs her life. We know that stress can negatively affect the immune system; Marianne adds to this with a total neglect of her own health and safety, a common behavioral trait of those suffering from depression.

Marianne's depression leads to the fever that nearly kills her, contracted at the home of a friend on the way back to Devonshire. It's while she hovers between life and death that Willoughby comes to see Elinor. He explains the motives for his behavior. His aunt, who had planned to leave him her money, discovered that he had seduced and abandoned a young woman and disinherited him as a result. Willoughby was left with only one option for an income (or, at least, one option for someone who isn't willing to work for a living): He had to marry for money. And so he engaged himself to Miss Grey and her fortune. It is she who insisted on his cold treatment of Marianne, and who dictated the cruel letter that sent her plummeting into despair.

Many people in Austen's day would have characterized Willoughby's conflict, between marrying for love and marrying for money, as a matter of feeling vs. reason. It was a common dilemma at the time, more for women than men because marriage was the only respectable source of income for women of the middle and upper classes. For men and women, marrying for money or status was seen as practical, leading to solid, predictable benefits, while marrying for love, without a comfortable income, was frowned upon as a choice that could get you into a bad scrape. We can all dream of "love in a cottage," but a large house would be much more comfortable. It's as true today as it was in Austen's time that not having sufficient income can stress a relationship. Many would say, even today, that Willoughby made a reasonable choice.

But Austen makes sure we don't see things that way, in terms of a stark opposition between reason and feeling—not here or in any of her novels. In her view, the marriage choice, as well as every other decision we make, relies on our feelings, and not our powers of reason. "Reason is and ought to be the slave of the passions."

Feelings enable us to make decisions by prioritizing what's important to us. Willoughby's decision hinges on figuring out what matters most, and in the end, his concern for his own comfort wins out over his love for Marianne. He doesn't make a reasoned choice; rather, one desire conquers another. He tells Elinor,

> My affection for Marianne, my thorough conviction of her attachment to me—it was all insufficient to outweigh that dread of poverty, or get the better of those false ideas of the necessity of riches, which I was naturally inclined to feel,

and expensive society had increased. I had reason to believe myself secure of my present wife, if I chose to address her, and I persuaded myself to think that nothing else in common prudence remained for me to do.

Although Willoughby thoroughly regrets his decision—he regretted it even in the course of deciding—he ultimately prioritizes money over love. His statement gets at the truth of how we make decisions. We might consider our choices as conflicts between reason and feeling, but they're really conflicts between one kind of feeling and another. Willoughby knows that his reasonable choice, his action done "in common prudence," stemmed from feelings, from his fear of being poor and his desire for the good life.

It is no accident that the word *rationalize*, which usually means to find reasons to justify one's thoughts or behavior, comes from the Latin word *ratio*, which means reason. Rationalization, in this etymological sense, follows the usual order of things in our brains: First we decide, based on feeling, and then we explain why our decisions make sense. As Austen's narrator says in *Persuasion*, "How quick come the reasons for approving what we like!" (Incidentally, *rationalize* is another word like *sense* and *sensibility*, which has competing and opposite meanings. According to the *Oxford English Dictionary*, rationalize can mean "To explain or justify [one's behaviour or attitude] to oneself or others with plausible but specious reasons, usually unwittingly," but it can also mean "To think rationally." Our very language captures the entanglement of feeling and reason.)

We can look to Damasio's work once again for neurological confirmation of this view of our behavior. By studying another research subject who, like S.M., suffered from brain damage, Damasio was able to chart many of the brain areas involved in making decisions. Not surprisingly, these were emotion-processing areas. Another check to pure reason.

This patient, whom Damasio calls Elliot, was a corporate executive who was referred to him for an evaluation after having been denied disability benefits. Elliot had suffered from a tumor in the lining of his brain that had been removed, along with cortical tissue that had been damaged by its growth. After recovering from the operation, he appeared to be cured, and he returned to work.

But all was not well. Elliot couldn't get tasks done or manage his time. If he had to sort through documents in order to choose the ones that were needed for a given business transaction, he would get endlessly distracted by irrelevant details, or turn to another task. He was fired from his job and then from several subsequent jobs. He engaged in different business ventures until he'd lost all his money. His wife divorced him. A second marriage also ended in divorce. This man was obviously not fully functional.

Yet a battery of tests confirmed that Elliot was cognitively intact. He even placed above average on intelligence tests and other measures of reasoning ability. How could this be the case when he had cognitive deficits so extreme that he couldn't hold a job? Although Elliot's ability to think had seemingly been unaffected by his medical condition, what did emerge from testing, and from Elliot's own perceptions, is that his ability to feel had been greatly diminished. For instance, he could view videos of all kinds of distressing events apathetically, lacking not only empathy, but even horror or disgust or fear or any of the other feelings we tend to have on witnessing danger or disaster. He knew that he'd been able to respond emotionally before the surgery. This lack of feeling was the key to Elliot's cognitive deficits. He had lost access to the feelings that enable us to prioritize tasks.

You might think that Elliot could have decided rationally which of his business accounts deserved attention without input from his emotions. He could have calculated which accounts promised to pay the most, or were due earliest. And had this decision been completely devoid of social content, a pure math problem with no strings attached, he might not have fared so poorly. But he couldn't do this because the very impetus to apply logical reasoning comes from the emotion centers that had been damaged in Elliot's brain.

Lacking in all of Elliot's choices was a sense of urgency, that mixture of fear and desire that keeps most of us focused on what we have to do or on what's in our best interests. Working on an account that was due earliest might have been the logical choice, even to Elliot, but without a sense of urgency, this deduction would lack the punch of true motivation needed to keep him on track.

It's not surprising that Elliot was easily distracted. Sitting here at the moment and writing this book, I have access to hundreds of websites.

Were I to google "research on the emotions," I could spend all day going from site to site, article to article. But my sense of urgency—definitely fear and desire in my case—keeps me focused on my writing. I want people to read my book, which means I have to write it first. I'm afraid that if I fail to concentrate, I won't finish.

Elliot's amygdala was intact, so unlike S.M., lack of fear didn't account for his deficits. Rather, a different area, the orbitofrontal cortex (OFC) was involved in Elliot's damaged capacities. Damasio concluded that Elliot's inability to decide or prioritize and his deadened capacity for feeling had resulted from the removal of ventromedial prefrontal cortical areas, which included the OFC.

The OFC forms part of the underbelly of the cortex, the crinkly outermost area of the brain, which contains our most advanced processing areas and which wraps around other structures in the interior of the brain. Since the OFC is on the inside of this outer wrapping, it also borders on some of the brain's interior areas, in particular the limbic system, which is largely responsible for generating emotion (the amygdala is part of this system). The OFC is therefore perched between cortical areas responsible for thought, and limbic structures involved in emotion. One of its functions is to coordinate information-logic areas with emotional input; the OFC would allow Elliot to realize the importance of factual information, such as "that account is due soon."

Just as important, the OFC enables us to interpret emotional information, which includes the ability to read social signals and to form expectations about the behavior of others. It enables us to predict the rewards and punishers that follow from our behavior. And it regulates emotion (as you'll shortly see in more detail), which helps us to control impulses. A deficit in any one of these areas would have impaired Elliot's ability to choose wisely.

Without these abilities, Elliot was oblivious to how his actions impacted his clients as well as to the effect his behavior would have on those who evaluated his performance—not to mention his wives. He could neither perceive nor predict the disapproval evoked by his erratic, irrational behavior. And so he lost job after job and marriage after marriage. Along with his inability to feel the urgency of current tasks, he was also unable to ignore the distraction of new ones, and so he frequently gave in to the impulse to change his focus. In short, without the capacity to process and pool information normatively, Elliot was forced to make decisions with minimal emotional guidance. Pure reason equated to poor judgment.

THE BRAKING POINT

There are a few instances in which reason and emotion are pitted against one another, mainly in states of emergency. When we're angry or upset or fearful, or in the grip of any very strong emotion, most of us find it difficult to think clearly. How often we come up with the perfect comeback long after the argument is over!

The reverse is also true: If, when upset, you can get yourself to stop and think, you'll probably calm down to some degree. We can see this inverse relationship between reason and feeling in Elinor's reaction when Lucy tells her about her engagement to Edward: "Her astonishment at what she heard was at first too great for words." Emotion runs high, and so cognition shuts down. It's only as she focuses on what she has to do to maintain the conversation in a way that protects herself that Elinor is able to answer, "forcing herself to speak, and to speak cautiously."

Along with reason, the other capacity that shuts down with strong negative emotion is social engagement, the set of various feelings, thoughts, and behaviors that enables us to interact with one another in positive ways. This is, in a sense, self-evident: If you're furious with someone, or in the grip of any strong negative emotion, you're not going to be particularly receptive to what they have to say, or to be socially adept. You're certainly not going to be in the mood to socialize or chitchat when you're in a rage. Elinor must force herself to answer Lucy. But she momentarily loses her ability to speak, among the most social of our capabilities, and certainly necessary if she is to deprive Lucy of her triumph.

Another and more extended instance of social withdrawal can be seen in depression, as in Marianne's situation. Devastated by Willoughby's rejection, she becomes incapable of honoring the most basic niceties of social life. This would have meant more, and been more noticeable, in Austen's day than our own because women had defined social duties that they were expected to fulfill. If someone called and left a calling card, as was the custom, you were obliged to return the visit, unless you wanted to deliberately "cut" someone.

When Marianne emerges from her depression, she regrets her social ineptitude: "Whenever I looked towards the past [the time she was depressed], I saw some duty neglected, or some failing indulged. Everybody seemed injured by me. The kindness, the unceasing kindness of Mrs. Jennings, I had repaid with ungrateful contempt. To the Middletons, the Palmers, the Steeles, to every common acquaintance even, I had been insolent and unjust." Even so, the people around Marianne who care about her recognize that she's in deep distress and respond with compassion rather than blame.

Like all our thoughts and behaviors, the complementary push-me/pull-you relationship between ordinary states of mind and states of emergency operates at a neurobiological as well as a psychological level. These changes are mediated by the autonomic nervous system (ANS). This is the system that controls automatic bodily functions such as respiration, sleep, and digestion, and the physiological responses that generate emotion. It is actually an ur-system, composed of many different interactive systems throughout the brain and body. When we're safe and in business-as-usual mode, our systems are dominated by the branch of the ANS called the parasympathetic nervous system (PNS), again, a system with many subsystems. The PNS enables ongoing processes like digestion and growth, as well as clear thinking and social engagement.

But when the environment poses danger, be it a snake in your path, a nasty rival, or an unexpected rejection, the sympathetic division (SNS) of the ANS takes over. Like the PNS, this subsystem coordinates activities throughout our brains and bodies. It's actually responsible for all our excitatory physiological responses, both positive and negative. Two of its most important subsystems associated with stress are the fight-or-flight response, which generates an immediate response to danger, and the hypothalamic-pituitary-adrenal axis, better known as the HPA axis response, which activates some time afterward (although this can be just minutes later) and which is necessary for a sustained response to stress. The primary chemical associated with fight or flight (and other excitatory responses) is adrenaline (Adrenaline is called epinephrine in the U.S., but the British term *adrenaline* is nevertheless the more widely known term. When have you heard someone speak of a rush of epinephrine?) Other chemicals known as glucocorticoids, particularly cortisol, are released with an HPA axis response, although adrenaline also continues to enter the system. Prolonged exposure to cortisol isn't good for us.*

The more social the animal, the more possible it is for stress responses to activate in response to social as well as physical dangers. Elinor was about as physically safe as a person can be in Lady Middleton's drawing room, where Lucy told her about the secret engagement. But this encounter put her into crisis mode nevertheless. This move toward extending the scope of crisis responses in animals, including humans, was likely related to the increasing importance of social ties to survival.

How we switch from one system to the other—the dance of emotion and its regulation—plays out at the nuts-and-bolts level of brain function in especially interesting ways. Stephen Porges and his colleagues have formulated a convincing and widely accepted theory, which is beginning to impact therapeutic practice. This is "the polyvagal perspective" (also known as the "polyvagal theory"). It is called a perspective rather than a system because it's really a *way of viewing* how the ANS works and what it does.

It can be confusing to read about the polyvagal perspective because it does have many system-like qualities, such as divisions and parts. For instance, the fight-or-flight response and the HPA axis are functions of the SNS, but they are also the second of our significant ways of responding to experience (adverse experience, of course), from a

---

*   These two responses to stress involve two pathways. In the fight-or-flight response, the hypothalamus sends a chemical message to the adrenal glands (to the medulla, an area inside of each gland). The adrenal glands are located on the top of each kidney. These glands then release adrenaline, the primary hormone involved in fight or flight. Adrenaline helps to initiate sympathetic arousal. This pathway is called the "sympathomedullary pathway" or SAM. In the HPA-axis response, the hypothalamus sends a chemical message to the pituitary gland, located directly below it; the pituitary gland then releases a hormone called ACTH (adrenocorticotropic hormone), which travels to the adrenal glands (to the cortex, or outside area, of each gland this time). The adrenal glands then release the hormone (steroid) cortisol, a glucocorticoid, which helps the body maintain blood sugar levels needed for dealing with prolonged stress. Glucocorticoids are helpful to begin with, but when they circulate for too long in the bloodstream, they become harmful. The hypothalamus (the "H" of the acronym HPA) is a small area directly above the brainstem. It's called the hypothalamus because it's located beneath the thalamus, a much larger brain area. The hypothalamus might be a relatively small structure with a derivative name, but make no mistake: It's one of the brain's most important areas, involved in the regulation of bodily functions.

polyvagal perspective. When you look at the ANS* from the polyvagal perspective, you see the areas and functions that constitute its master switch; this is primarily the vagal brake, which we'll look at in a moment. The vagal brake is the mechanism that regulates the extent to which the PNS and SNS each activate. The polyvagal perspective therefore highlights those areas and functions that rule the ANS, determining the input from its subsystems, and thus also determining how our bodies and brains respond to the environment at each and every moment. The polyvagal perspective considers those responses within the context of whether the environment is threatening or safe.

The polyvagal perspective divides into three areas of focus. The first is the ventral vagus, so-called because its neurons run closer to the ventral side of the brain, the side where our stomachs are located. (*Ventrus* is Latin for "stomach.") This is also called the "smart vagus." The second area of focus is the SNS, its fight-or-flight and HPA axis responses. The third is the dorsal vagus, whose circuits run closer to the back of the brain. (*Dorsum* is Latin for "back.")

The vagus nerve originates in the brainstem, the brain's most primitive and lowest part, continuous with the spine; the ventral vagus is one of its branches. In one direction, the ventral vagus connects to the heart's pacemaker, a muscle called the sinoatrial node; it actually extends into the body to do this. A crucial function of the ventral vagus is to vary heart rate in order to enable us to match our reactions to what the environment requires.

As you know, heart rate is an indicator of excitement—I'm sure Elizabeth's heart races when she unexpectedly sees Darcy at Pemberley. Heart rate is also the primary catalyst for changes within ANS. Increases and decreases in heart rate are registered by other brain and body areas that then respond accordingly. Among its most important functions, increased heart rate activates the SNS, and if the heart rate is sufficiently accelerated we go into fight-or-flight, "red alert" mode, and if a threat is sustained, HPA axis mode. If excitement is not required, heart rate slows down, and other excitatory bodily processes also cease, such as the release of adrenaline. Porges calls the part of the vagus nerve that extends to the sinoatrial

---

* Recall that ANS stands for autonomic nervous system, which contains the sympathetic nervous sytem (SNS) and the parasympathetic nervous system (PNS).

node "the vagal brake," an automotive metaphor, because it increases and decreases heart rate, just as the brake on a car regulates speed.

Under ordinary circumstances, the vagal brake keeps our heart rate low so that the PNS, business-as-usual system dominates. When we experience strong emotions, the vagal brake is lifted, and the increase in heart rate signals to the brain and body to increase the activity of the sympathetic nervous system. This is true whether the emotions we experience are positive or negative, although the polyvagal perspective looks at responses to threats and dangers. Incidentally, the command to lift or lower the vagal brake comes primarily from the OFC, that major hub of emotional processing. If you see a snake-like object or a mean girl in your path, the amygdala sends a signal to the OFC, which relays the information to the smart vagus.

The automotive metaphor of a vagal brake makes sense if you think about driving downhill rather than on a level surface. You need to press the brake to keep cruising at an acceptable speed. Without the restraint of the vagal brake, we would quickly go downhill biologically. The heart would beat much more quickly, initiating sympathetic stress responses. And we all know how unhealthy it is to live in a constant state of stress. Actually, without any vagal restraint, the heart would beat too quickly to sustain life. People who are poor at regulating their emotions are said to have poor vagal tone; efficient self-regulators have good vagal tone. Elinor has better vagal tone than Marianne.

The smart vagus controls heart rate in one direction, which induces shifts between sympathetic and parasympathetic systems. In the other direction, it connects to important parts of the social engagement system, which is the set of brain areas involved in emotions, thoughts, and behaviors that activate when we engage socially with others. This part of the vagus is known as the tenth cranial, or head nerve; actually, all cranial nerves are clusters of nerves, just as the optic nerve is not a single nerve but a cluster. In particular, the smart vagus (tenth cranial nerve) controls muscles of the head and face, most crucially around the eyes, which are so important for signaling emotion. It also connects to the stapedius muscle in the ear, which opens passageways to increase our capacity for hearing, vital to conversation. Really angry people might not be able to listen to reason not only because logical thought is impeded during fight-or-flight mode, but also because they literally aren't hearing well.

In addition to inducing both states of emergency, stress, and calm, the smart vagus induces all the states of mind and body that we experience between these extremes. States of rage or terror—full sympathetic dominance—rarely last for long before we return to a less extreme mode of response. Elinor was dumbfounded at Lucy's confession, but the peak of her upset quickly subsided. Emotions impeded her ability to speak for only a moment before parasympathetic regulation began to function again, at least to some extent, and she was able to think clearly enough to answer Lucy.

So while the mutually exclusive relationship between sympathetic and parasympathetic activity applies to extreme emotional states, most of us don't live on the edge in this way. By linking heart rate in one direction with facial expression in the other, the smart vagus connects emotional states, which depend on bodily responses, with facial expression. In other words, in addition to controlling heart rate, which then influences other systems throughout the brain and body, the smart vagus controls our facial expressions, which let people know that we're angry or embarrassed or happy or preoccupied, or any of the other myriad states that our supremely mobile facial muscles are able to convey. Recall that psychologist Paul Ekman studied his face in the mirror for a year to chart the connection between emotional response and facial expression.

Bodies tell faces how to act, but influence can go in the other direction; adopting a given facial expression induces its accompanying emotions to some extent. The vagal perspective describes a complex system (like all systems in the mind-brain, including the mind-brain as a whole), which means that intervention at any point can affect the whole. However, this influence is subtle and obviously limited, or we'd only have to "put on a happy face" to banish distressing emotions. Obviously, this doesn't work well enough to have banished the painful feelings all of us experience at one time or another.

It makes sense that our systems evolved to include a continuum of excitability rather than all-or-nothing alternatives. If an animal is in danger or some other kind of demanding situation is occurring, resources are needed to deal with the emergency at hand, and so cognition shuts down or shifts to automatic pilot. But being able to think clearly is obviously an advantage in all kinds of situations, which is why the ability to down-regulate intense emotions quickly is just as important as the ability to go on red alert.

The careful balancing act between the SNS and PNS applies to positive as well as negative emotions. Although destructive emotions tend to take over with greater force than positive emotions, the latter can reach the fever pitch we associate with fear, anger, and other negative emotions. We can be stymied as the result of rapture as well as rage. When Elinor bursts into tears of joy at finding Lucy has married Edward's brother, she's incapable of doing anything but cry. This isn't a respectable or decorous response—it's worthy of Marianne in her pre-depression days—especially since Edward is the one who conveys the news. Elinor's tears of joy and relief confess her love before Edward has made a formal declaration of his own feelings, definitely a transgression in Austen's day. Even those with strong vagal tone can be overwhelmed.

Along similar lines, I was in the grocery store recently, where I overheard someone say, "I was so ecstatic I couldn't think straight!" Whether or not he was exaggerating, he expressed a common way of feeling that was recognizable to all his listeners. Elinor's reaction is not uncommon. Positive as well as negative feelings can interfere with clear thinking. (By the way, because I was thinking about emotion and reason, that sentence in the grocery store leaped out at me from among all the other conversations that were happening at the same time. Neuroscientists call this priming. If you're thinking of a subject, the neurons that form ideas related to this subject are prepared to fire should you encounter it in the environment; they're "on the lookout" for what you've been thinking about. Have you ever noticed how once you learn a new word, you start encountering it everywhere? It's also possible that I imagined what I heard, that someone said something different but I heard a sentence in line with my own thinking. The power of the human brain to find what it seeks shouldn't be underestimated.)

This comment overheard about the cognitive effects of "ecstasy" brings to mind an old joke popular with biologists: The sympathetic system dominates during the four f's, the basic drives that all animals share: feeding, fighting, fleeing, and, euphemistically, mating. (We'll talk about a fifth "f" in a future chapter.) But actually, most people in caring, intimate relationships would probably say that they remain emotionally engaged during most of what goes on during that fourth "f." Such involvement signals parasympathetic input, although the actual moment of orgasm might involve sympathetic-system takeover. Indeed, all approach behaviors, all the positive emotions that come into play when we seek rewards, need the excitement that comes with sympathetic input because energy and motivation depend on this. But at the same time, most positive emotions are also characterized by a sufficient degree of calm for us to be able to think clearly about what we're experiencing, and to maintain excitement at physiologically healthy levels.

In short, in most instances of both positive and negative emotion, you never release your foot fully from the brake so that you're dangerously careening downhill, nor do you come to a full stop. Such a mixture also characterizes the variety of conflicting feelings that humans are so prone to feel, especially in complicated or delicate social situations. When Edward arrives at the Dashwood cottage to tell of Lucy's marriage and ask Elinor to be his wife, he feels embarrassment and confusion as well as hope, as his stammering and blushing clearly show. When he actually tells Elinor that Lucy has married his brother, information that sends her from the room running and sobbing, Edward is certainly overjoyed to convey the news of his lucky escape and his availability. But he's also embarrassed for his past behavior and anxious as to whether Elinor will be willing to marry him. He's so overwhelmed by his medley of conflicting feelings that he simply leaves: "he quitted the room, and walked out towards the village."

According to the polyvagal perspective, the ventral, smart vagus is the first part of the ANS. The fight-or-flight and HPA axis functions of the SNS make up the second part. The third division, the dorsal vagus, involves the PNS, the calming division of the ANS. This too involves a response to crisis, freezing, the third "f" in our emergency response system of "fight, flight, or freeze." Freezing is an older, more primitive response that kicks in when we're so overwhelmed that fight or flight feels inadequate or useless to protect us, or so we sense, since this decision doesn't involve conscious thought.

Freezing involves an evolutionarily older neural pathway that uses a different branch of the vagal nerve (and so originating in the brainstem), the dorsal vagus, whose circuits are routed closer to the back of the brain. This pathway initiates a different response to danger, the third "f." Freezing refers not only to immobilization, the "deer in the headlights" phenomenon, but also to fainting and other forms of response associated with slow rather than accelerated heart rate, and shutting down rather than revving up.

The dorsal vagal response developed because if an animal freezes, it's less likely to be noticed by a predator, perhaps mistaken for an inanimate object or a dead animal. An example with regard to the human social brain can be seen in Marianne's reaction to Willoughby, when they finally meet at the ball in London where he snubs her:

> Marianne, now looking dreadfully white, and unable to stand, sunk into her chair, and Elinor, expecting every moment to see her faint, tried to screen her from the observation of others, while reviving her with lavender water.

Marianne is indeed like a deer frozen in the headlights, immobilized by Willoughby's behavior. Of course, Marianne doesn't freeze because she's pursued by a predator, although Willoughby has had a predatory relationship with the woman he seduced and abandoned. But the loss of his love feels so shocking and dangerous to her general sense of well-being that a fight-or-flight emergency response doesn't feel adequate to the subconscious parts of her brain/body that make these decisions.

In terms of the automotive metaphor, when the vagal brake is lifted, the car begins to travel so quickly that it crashes, turning off the HPA response. Freeze mode follows.

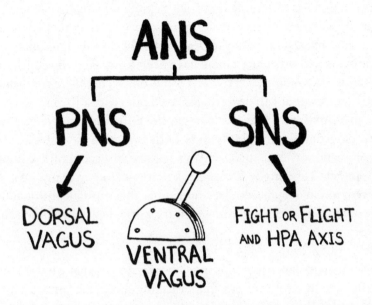

A brief recap. The autonomic nervous system consists of two divisions: the parasympathetic nervous system (PNS), which dominates when we're on an even keel, and the sympathetic nervous system (SNS), which dominates when we're in excitatory mental and bodily states. The vagal perspective highlights those parts of the ANS that determine the degree of input from each of its divisions. The ventral or smart vagus controls the switch between systems by controlling heart rate. It regulates activation of the PNS, including normal bodily functions and the capacity for social engagement, and the SNS, which contributes to normal states of excitement as well as high-stress modes. Most of the time, we experience states of mind that involve input from both systems. The second focus of the vagal perspective references sympathetic stress responses, fight or flight for immediate dangers, and HPA axis activation for ongoing threats. The third part of the vagal perspective, the dorsal vagus, refers to freeze mode; you might think of this as parasympathetic dominance gone haywire so that it *shuts* us down rather than *calms* us down. From the polyvagal perspective, aspects of the vagal functioning succeed one another. When excitement is too much for business as usual, including interacting with others in a regulated fashion, which is orchestrated by the ventral vagus, the vagal brake is lifted and stress modes predominate, fight or flight to begin with and HPA axis activation subsequently. If fight or flight isn't up to handling an emergency to begin with, the dorsal vagus takes over.

Humans and other mammals have been formed by the conflicting pressures of evolution to arrive at a compromise: highly reactive emergency systems that can nevertheless be dampened sufficiently so that we can think. But while this confers flexibility, it has its downside; many of us develop the ability to be both anxious and strategic. Some people spend way too much time in stress mode with cognitive powers fully intact. This might indeed be a prerequisite for many jobs. But before we blame evolution, let's remember that our Paleolithic brains were not meant for a twenty-first century world, or even an nineteenth-century world.

Hume, Austen's favorite philosopher, believed that what we think of as reason is really a form of passion, or feeling. We've certainly seen this with Willoughby, whose reasonable decision to marry for wealth and status clearly matches his desires. Scratch the surface of reason, and you'll find it's a thin veneer covering affect.

We also see this with Marianne, who snaps out of her depression not as a result of deliberate self-control, or the triumph of reason, but because time and reflection lead her to more positive feelings. As a therapist, I've spoken to many people who lament their depression saying that other people have it worse: "I shouldn't feel this way." You'll have more success fighting an E-ZPass fine than your own feelings.

Although deliberate efforts to self-regulate can succeed, this isn't because reason gets the better of feeling. Reason, or logical thinking, can help us to regulate emotion only by shifting our focus to thoughts that bring calm or positive emotions in their wake to replace turbulent or negative ones. Reason can help us to reframe our thoughts so that different feelings come into play. Reason can also distract us, activating cognitive areas that are dormant when we're upset.

Elinor's effort to deal with her sadness and anxiety about Edward's strange behavior and obvious melancholy during his visit illustrates this point. As soon as he leaves, Elinor attempts to distract herself in order to keep her thoughts from dwelling on Edward: "Elinor sat down to her drawing table as soon as he was out of the house, busily employed herself the whole day, neither sought nor avoided the mention of his name, appeared to interest herself almost as much as ever in the general concerns to the family." But as soon as conversation and activity cease, she's left to her own reveries, "to think of Edward, and of Edward's behaviour, in every possible variety which the different state of her spirits at different times could produce: with tenderness, pity, approbation, censure and doubt." Enough turbulent feelings here for even the most romantic of Austen's readers!

By focusing on activities that engage her attention, Elinor gives herself a break from her troubles. She doesn't tell herself to stop thinking of Edward, or try to argue herself out of her feelings, but directs her attention elsewhere. Paying attention to mundane activities brings the mundane feelings that accompany them into play. By redirecting her attention, she also activates cognitive brain areas that inhibit stress reactions, drawing on the inverse relationship between parasympathetic and sympathetic systems. She shifts attention away from distressing thoughts, and so encourages the restraint of the vagal brake.

Marianne learns to do this as well. As she slowly recovers from her illness, she determines to follow Elinor's example and to ward off her feelings of disappointment and grief, rather than courting and encouraging them as she used to do. She determines to follow a disciplined course of study, music, and exercise. When she encounters the many places and things in Devonshire that remind her of Willoughby, she resists despair by directing her mind elsewhere. One poignant instance occurs as she sits down to play the piano:

> [T]he music on which her eye first rested was an opera, procured for her by Willoughby, containing some of their favourite duets, and bearing on its outward leaf her own name in his hand writing. That would not do. She shook her head, put the music aside, and after running over the keys for a minute complained of feebleness in her fingers, and closed the instrument

again; declaring however with firmness as she did so, that she should in future practise much.

Rather than tumbling into an abyss of pain and memory, Marianne anticipates a future of productive work. She can't fully divert her attention away from her sadness at the moment, but she anticipates a time when she'll be able to do so, and that in itself redirects her focus and her feelings.

Controlling our attention is one way in which we can use reason, or cognitive skills, to think ourselves into a better frame of mind. This is the basis of mindfulness, which has become a popular topic within the general population as well as a significant object of study for mind-brain scientists. Mindfulness means being aware of the current moment, of anchoring one's mind completely in the present rather than allowing it to dart through time and space and memory, as minds tend to do. It means stepping back and watching the world, including the world of your own feelings. Such watching involves emotions such as curiosity and tolerance. If you can step back and watch your own anger, you're no longer completely driven by it. Ditto if you can concentrate on a drawing. Your attention and its concomitant emotions have shifted away, at least to some extent, from the upsetting and the negative.

But this is not reason. It's not arguing with yourself or suppressing your feelings or trying to become Mr. Spock, the famous character from *Star Trek* who embodies "pure reason," whose responses are logical rather than emotional (and even he has trouble being Mr. Spock). Marianne escapes the grip of a destructive sensibility only when she can sense alternative and healthier modes of being and feeling, and only when she commits herself, heart as well as mind, to finding her way along a new and better path.

FOUR

I Never Knew Myself

et's return to Elizabeth the day after Darcy's first proposal. You'll recall that Darcy had asked Elizabeth to be his wife in highly insulting terms. Elizabeth had clearly refused, while also recounting the many deficits in Darcy's behavior and character that have infuriated her. This includes his treatment of Wickham, the charming, handsome soldier who's captured her attention. Darcy sends a letter the following day, explaining his actions and seeking to exonerate his character. He no longer has any hope of marrying Elizabeth, but he will at least correct the very wrong impression she has of him.

On receiving the letter, Elizabeth reads "with an eagerness which hardly left her power of comprehension; from impatience of knowing what the next sentence might bring, [she] was incapable of attending to the sense of the one before her eyes." Her thoughts can "rest on nothing." Her feelings are "scarcely to be defined," but they include "amazement," and a hearty dose of anger; she's "still persuaded that

Darcy could have "no explanation to give, which a just sense of shame would not conceal." She must read and reread the letter, taking in a bit more with each attempt, until she's able to accurately understand and assess Darcy's words. As Elizabeth gradually calms down, she absorbs the letter's contents; as you now know, regaining emotional equilibrium (putting the vagal brake on) and clear thinking go hand in hand.

Slowly, Elizabeth realizes that Darcy's letter makes sense, and that she's been misled by Wickham's false version of events. Far from depriving Wickham of a rightful inheritance, Darcy gave him what he was legally due—and more—which he squandered on wine, women, and gambling. After Darcy finally refused to give him any more money, Wickham planned to gain an income, as well as revenge, by eloping with Darcy's beloved younger sister, heir to a substantial part of the family's huge fortune. Fortunately, Georgiana couldn't go through with this plan—she loved her brother far too much to betray him—and she confessed to Darcy. Wickham is the scoundrel, not Darcy.

Elizabeth realizes that her mistakes in judgment have all stemmed from her first encounter with Darcy, when he insulted her at the Meryton ball by saying she wasn't "handsome" enough to "tempt" him to dance. Although he said this to his friend Bingley, the remark was obviously within her range of hearing. On the other hand, Wickham had been warm and attentive right from the start. She now understands that, "Pleased with the preference of one, and offended by the neglect of the other, on the very beginning of our acquaintance, I have courted prepossession and ignorance, and driven reason away, where either were concerned." Elizabeth realizes that she's been prejudiced.

Elizabeth had no idea that her judgment could be compromised by her feelings and desires, that she, who prided herself on her "discernment," on being the only member of her dysfunctional family with an accurate take on events and people, could distort the world as thoroughly as her foolish mother, her cynical father, and her doggedly optimistic sister Jane. She concludes, "Til this moment, I never knew myself."

As you probably realize, Elizabeth's lapses illustrate the psychotherapeutic concept of denial. Denial involves missing or suppressing information that's available. This can be information about our feelings and motives, as when Elizabeth fails to realize that wounded pride clouds her judgment of Darcy and gratified pride clouds her judgment of Wickham. (I never knew myself!) Denial can also refer to distortions of information outside ourselves, to skewing or ignoring our perceptions of the environment or of other people's thoughts and behavior.

Such information can turn out to have been glaringly obvious. When Wickham bad-mouths Darcy and his family to Elizabeth at a dinner party, without any prompting, he's totally out of line. Rules of decorum, which would have been well-known to an intelligent young woman like Elizabeth, prohibited both sharing the story of his wrongs and casting aspersions on another gentleman, especially to a casual acquaintance; Elizabeth has met Wickham only a handful of times. Elizabeth realizes that she should have seen this as a warning sign about his character.

Denial is definitely something we humans do a lot of, an unfortunate but ineradicable aspect of our psychology. It is what psychotherapists call a "defense mechanism," a method our brains have for protecting us from information that would detract from our well-being. Elizabeth's denial of Darcy's good points protects her self-esteem; to acknowledge that Darcy can make accurate observations means that his opinion of her looks (not handsome enough!) might indeed be true.

Denial, prompted by the fear of abandonment, motivates at least some of Elizabeth's sister Lydia's behavior. Months after Darcy's first proposal, Wickham runs away with Lydia, telling her that they will be married. If they aren't—and Wickham has no intention of keeping his word—Lydia will be exiled from polite society; cohabitation without marriage means that she won't ever again be allowed to associate with other women of her class. She also potentially blights the chances for any of her sisters to marry, for no respectable man would marry into a family where a daughter had so completely compromised herself. Fortunately, Darcy saves the day, paying Wickham to marry Lydia, which makes everything all right again.

Throughout this ordeal, Lydia remains oblivious to the moral enormity of her behavior, and to its likely consequences for herself and others. She believes that Wickham will marry her, and appears to be completely ignorant of the danger she's brought on herself and her

family. Her frivolity and lack of social intelligence (and any other kind
of intelligence!) accounts for this in part. But a young lady couldn't
have grown up in Austen's world without a sense of the horrors of such
a transgression. No matter how stupid, spacey, and self-absorbed Lydia
might be, she must be denying the seriousness of her actions and the
truth about Wickham's character to behave as she has. Like many of
us, she sees what she wants to see—Wickham's charm, the fun of being
with him, the adventure in running away—and she believes what she
wants to believe, that they are really eloping.

Denial involves filtering as well as distorting information. The
brain relies on its filters continuously. We couldn't possibly take in all
the information available to our minds and senses; we simply aren't
capable of processing it. So we have filters that select what we notice.
These are rarely emotionally neutral. At a party, you hear a stream
of conversation tantamount to white noise until you hear someone
say your name. You hear that quickly and clearly enough.* When I'm
really thinking about my writing, I can walk into a room and fail to see
someone in full view. My concentration is elsewhere—my mind-brain
told me it was more important to think about what's going on inside
my head than about what's going on outside it. Elizabeth overhears
Darcy's insult, which predisposes her for noticing bad things about
him rather than good; in terms of the brain, she has an attractor state,
a habitual neural pattern for perceiving negative information about
Darcy and filtering out positive information.

Denial and other defense mechanisms show that we're buffeted
about by forces of which we remain unaware. Psychotherapy has
always known this, and the field of academic psychology is beginning
to catch up.

A TALE OF TWO DISCIPLINES

Even though denial and other defense mechanisms appear to be
intrinsic to the human mind-brain, for much of the twentieth century

---

*   This is known as *the cocktail party effect*, a term coined by cognitive scientist Colin
      Cherry in 1953.

they were ignored by the academic discipline of psychology, that is psychology as it was researched and taught at colleges and universities. This was also true of other affectively driven mechanisms of the mind, including emotion itself.

While the reasons for ignoring such a huge dimension of human experience deserve to be studied, I'll leave that complex task to the historians of science and only venture one of the simplest explanations: that psychologists lacked much of the science and technology needed to objectively investigate such mechanisms. Studying subliminal thought became more feasible with the advent of computers that could flash words or images on a screen too quickly to be registered by the conscious mind; experiments of this kind (one is described below) made studying subconscious motivations and perceptions feasible. And when researchers became able to study neurons and neurotransmitters using brain imaging and biochemistry, they began to understand the biological underpinnings of thought and behavior. Until roughly the 1980s, mind-brain science just wasn't there yet.

By contrast, a phenomenon like conditioning was accessible to study with available nontechnological methods. The classic model for this is Russian psychologist Ivan Pavlov's famous experiment with dogs. You pair a natural stimulus such as food that makes a dog salivate (called the "unconditioned stimulus") with a nonnatural stimulus such as a bell (called the "conditioned stimulus"), and after a few trials, dogs will begin to salivate at the sound of the bell. This is so much easier than trying to find out why people love, or hate, or miss vital information. In addition, a rigid emphasis on detachment and objectivity, the zeitgeist or spirit of the times, meant that observation of others and introspection of oneself were not considered reliable methods of inquiry. Today, we know that subjective perceptions can yield important information.

Such limitations led academic psychologists to ignore the study of emotions, drives, and desires, focusing instead on conscious cognitive mechanisms like attention and perception, and observable phenomena like conditioning. By the mid–twentieth century, academic psychology was dominated by behaviorism, a theory that maintained that all thought and behavior results from conditioning. Behaviorism ignored both the existence and complexity of inner mental life. B. F. Skinner, a prominent behavioral psychologist, went so far as to define love as "another name for positive reinforcement."[*]

For strict behaviorists, human nature was no more complex than salivating at the sound of a bell. The unconscious, that dynamic force that dictated so much of thought, personality, feelings, and behavior, was virtually ignored. Academic psychology uncannily illustrated the mechanism of denial by ignoring the subconscious and affective aspects of human experience.

Desires, feelings, defense mechanisms, compulsion, trauma—all the messy stuff we humans are made of—became the provenance of another discipline, psychoanalysis. Famously ideveloped by Sigmund Freud, psychoanalysis soon gave rise to many variations on, and alternatives to, Freudian theory and technique, and it continues to evolve. To include these alternatives and developments, I'll use the term *psychotherapy* rather than the older *psychoanalysis*. And to avoid confusion with the Freudian unconscious, I'll use the term *subconscious* to refer to affect, cognition, and knowledge that the conscious mind doesn't access.

By the mid–twentieth century, psychotherapy became an alternative discipline with its own educational institutions, schools of thought, and publications. It was gospel to therapists, including psychiatrists and clinical psychologists, but professors of psychology and academic researchers rejected its tenets pretty much unilaterally. Psychology had split into two branches.

Of course, Skinner, the champion of theories of conditioning, and all the others of his ilk were wrong. Toward the end of the twentieth century, better techniques for studying the mind-brain began to render the disciplinary ghettoization that split psychology and psychotherapy impossible to maintain. It became clear that most brain activity, about ninety percent in fact, takes place outside of conscious awareness, just as Freud, that bugaboo of the behaviorists, had claimed. Cognitive scientists call this vast area of mental space the "cognitive unconscious."[**]

---

[*]   Actually, a character in Skinner's utopian (or dystopian, depending on your views!) novel *Walden Two* says this, but it's often attributed to Skinner himself. B. F. Skinner, *Walden Two* (New York: Macmillan, 1968), 282.

[**] The term *cognitive unconscious* was originated by J. F. Kihlstrom in a 1987 essay titled "The Cognitive Unconscious," published in *Science* 237, no 4821 (1987): 1445–1452.

Blindsight, discussed in Chapter Two, provides a fascinating instance of this domain. As its name suggests, blindsight is the phenomenon of seeing while not knowing that you're seeing. For us to see and know that we're seeing, visual information must be processed in the visual cortex, as when Darcy glanced at Elizabeth at the Meryton ball. But, as you know, such processing percolates up through lower areas of the brain. These are evolutionarily older pathways that resemble the visual systems of more primitive animals, which makes sense because evolution works by building on what's there already. It's likely that less-evolved and complicated animals see with stringent limitations. A reptile might see the fly that's near enough for him to eat but be oblivious to a landscape with flies buzzing in the distance. And a reptile can't say to himself, "I'm seeing."

Blindsight was first observed on the battlefields of World War I when it was noticed that soldiers who had been blinded were nevertheless successfully dodging bullets. But it wasn't until the 1980s that Larry Weiskrantz tested the phenomenon in the psych lab and coined the term *blindsight*. He showed that a person with a damaged visual cortex whose subcortical vision areas remained intact could locate the source of a light far more often than random chance would dictate. It was possible to see without seeing. One of Weiskrantz's subjects, D.B., had partial cortical blindness; his visual cortex was damaged in places, but his subcortical areas, the areas responsible for blindsight, remained intact. When D.B. was asked to identify the location of a light using only subcortical areas, he accurately located targets although he was unaware of seeing them.

Even though blindsight was known in the years that behaviorism predominated at universities, academic psychologists didn't view this as proof of a motivated, or psychotherapeutic, subconscious. Indeed, blindsight and many other mechanisms of the cognitive unconscious are neutral, merely reflexive, and not influenced by feelings and desires. Blindsight is an earlier neurological stage of normal sight; it's not stuck in the subconscious because it poses a danger to the psyche. However, it might well convey information that's not emotionally neutral, such as "You need to dodge that bullet." Ironically, we can see without seeing in other ways as well; indeed, repression or filtering is the uncanny opposite of blindsight. Elizabeth's blindness to Darcy's adoring looks means that she doesn't see something that her visual cortex actually *can* see. There's much wisdom in the saying, "There are none so blind as those who will not see," a proverb that Austen likely knew.*

Even though much subconscious processing is emotionally neutral, most brain scientists today accept that subconscious emotions and drives determine mental life to a great extent, that they're the undetected motivators of thought and behavior. Academic psychologists, including neuroscientists, now study aspects of the mind-brain that psychiatrists and psychotherapists have long known to be important. In turn, many practicing therapists are incorporating knowledge of the brain and its mechanisms in their practice. More and more therapists are familiar with the basic principles of neuroscience. These practitioners combine knowledge of the brain with psychotherapeutic theory, mapping these disciplines on to one another.

I stress that in discussing psychotherapy as a serious approach to understanding the social brain, I'm being selective. Psychotherapeutic theory, beginning with Freud, has generated many outlandish insights that have on the whole been rejected by most mind-brain scientists and therapists. For instance, very few people today, even ardent practitioners of old-style psychoanalysis (complete with couch, silent therapist, and several sessions a week) support Freud's claims about penis envy, or his theory that memories of childhood sexual abuse are almost always the expression of unconscious fantasies (would that this were true).** But despite some of its zanier and more destructive assertions, two central claims of psychotherapy have stood the tests of

---

*   This saying has its roots in the Bible, specifically Jer. 5:21 (King James version): "Hear now this, O foolish people, and without understanding; which have eyes, and see not; which have ears, and hear not." The proverb has been traced back in English to 1546 (John Heywood), and resembles the biblical verse quoted above. In 1738, it was used by Jonathan Swift in his *Polite Conversation*, a work that Austen might have read.

**   Psychologist Judith Herman suggests that in order to safeguard his career, Freud revised his theory to suggest that most reports of sexual abuse by young women were fantasy. To have suggested that the abuse of girls was rampant within the upper and middle classes of civilized Vienna would have been controversial and likely destroyed his practice. "A Forgotten History," in *Trauma and Recovery: The Aftermath of Violence* (New York: Basic Books, 2015) 7–32.

time and research, and these are germane to Austen's novels. The first is that, as denial shows, we're continually motivated by subconscious emotional forces, the topic of this chapter. Second, people are capable of tremendous growth and change, which will be considered in the following chapter.

These might seem like obvious points to many readers, especially devotees of the novel, but they've been continually challenged. There are still people today who deny the existence of a motivated, subjective subconscious. But their ranks are thinning as we learn more and more about how the brain filters perceptions and we discover the areas that are active in such filtering.

Of course, some information is permanently unavailable to our conscious minds. Although Elizabeth might have figured out that Wickham was not on the level before reading Darcy's letter, she could never have remembered what happened to her in her first year of life, before her brain was capable of making memories of events (called episodic memories). But in terms of considering how subconscious emotions influence our thoughts and actions, this distinction isn't vital. What matters is that subconscious information continuously influences our perceptions, feelings, attitudes, attention, and behavior.

We don't yet know how denial and other subconscious processes work neurologically. And there are very likely multiple processes, systems, and neural routes that accomplish the masking of knowledge from conscious perception. But even if we can't fully explain defense mechanisms neurologically, there are several candidates for the subconscious, for brain areas and systems that process and store emotionally charged information of which we're unaware. Either such information is being repressed (and how this happens remains largely a mystery) or it is neurologically unavailable to our conscious minds. It can influence us in either case.

Three systems can be viewed as candidates for the subconscious: subcortical emotional processing, emotions that we're unaware of (in other words, emotions as opposed to feelings); the right hemisphere of the brain, known familiarly as the right brain; and implicit memory systems. There is frequently a significant degree of overlap among these systems.

CANDIDATES FOR THE SUBCONSCIOUS: EMOTIONAL PROCESSING

Let's begin with basic emotion processing. Emotions are subcortical brain-body reactions that become feelings when they reach higher cortical areas of the brain and are consciously experienced. LeDoux's work with fear in rats illustrated this difference; as we've seen, physiological fear reactions began in his lab rats before fear signals reached cortical areas that enabled the animals to feel their fear. We can extrapolate to humans: We have similar subcortical reactions that cortical areas translate not only into feelings of fear, but also into reflective awareness—the knowledge of being afraid. Emotions can be identified with the psychotherapeutic subconscious only if they exert their influence without our awareness. This is what happens much of the time, just as psychotherapeutic theory suggests, and as Austen's novels demonstrate.

This claim is now accepted by most mind-brain scientists, although it was still (incredibly, in my view) necessary to argue the point as recently as the start of the millennium. Thousands of studies in labs throughout the world have consistently shown that emotions subconsciously influence cognitive activities such as perception, attention, and memory. For instance, in a study I'll dub the "beverage study" (published in 2004) because it involved drinking a fruit-flavored beverage, participants were told that the purpose of the experiment was to look at how "biological rhythms influence reaction times, sensation, and mood." This masked the true purpose of the experiment: to see if emotion that wasn't consciously registered could influence attitudes and behavior. The trial was done twice, both times with undergraduates who were offered extra credit for participating.

In the first trial, participants were asked first to complete a questionnaire rating their current level of thirst. After that, they were asked to sort faces flashed on a screen according to gender (male and female were the only choices). These faces appeared to have neutral expressions, but for some of the subjects, faces with angry or happy expressions were subliminally sandwiched between pictures of the neutral faces, flashed so quickly that these images couldn't be processed consciously.

Some participants were subliminally targeted with happy faces, some with angry faces, and some didn't receive any subliminal images at all, just the neutral faces that they knew they were seeing. Following this alleged gender-classification task, participants were asked to rate the strength and pleasantness of their feelings according to a scale: 5 = unpleasant, 1 = pleasant. They were then given a pitcher of the beverage and told to pour as much as they wanted. Unknown to them, the amounts they poured were measured. They were also asked to rate how delicious the drink was: 0 = not delicious, 10 = extremely delicious.

Subliminal suggestion definitely had an effect, but only on those who were thirsty to begin with, a significant feature of the study. Thirsty participants poured and drank more if they'd been exposed to happy faces, and poured and drank less if they'd been exposed to angry faces. But while priming (the quick flashing of faces) influenced the amount thirsty participants drank, it didn't affect their *perceptions* of their mood; they perceived no change in the strength or quality of their feelings. So although negative faces resulted in a more negative attitude toward the drink and happy faces in a more positive attitude, participants were unaware that their emotions had been influenced or that they felt any different than they had before the trial began.

The second experiment was similar except that at the beginning of the trial, participants were given a small amount of the beverage instead of pouring it for themselves. They also rated their mood by filling in a more extensive questionnaire, rating twenty qualities such as proud, alert, nervous, and so forth on a scale. They then completed the sorting task, complete with the subliminal primes as in the first experiment. The members of this second group were asked at the end how much more of the drink they wanted and how much they would pay to buy the drink themselves. Again, results affected only those who were thirsty to begin with. Participants who had been given happy primes wanted more of the drink and were willing to pay more for it, double in fact. And as with the first round of students, the subliminal faces had no effect on conscious perception of mood or affect, despite the opportunity participants were given to be more specific about feelings through the more detailed questionnaire.

I find this study especially fascinating because despite its simplicity, it captures an essential feature of emotion that's at the core of psychotherapeutic theory. Emotions work in the service of basic drives. Emotions that are strong enough to influence thought and behavior don't just happen, they happen in order to accomplish something. Rolls depicts this aspect of emotion as a dynamic and goal-directed process in his definition of emotion as the mind-brain responses that motivate us to achieve rewards and avoid punishers. We don't have strong emotional reactions, even subliminal ones, about things that are value-neutral. People who weren't thirsty were not affected by the subliminal faces because they weren't invested in the task at hand. A fruit drink? If you're not thirsty, you can take it or leave it. The happy or angry faces have no effect. But if you have a need—thirst, in this case—emotions subsequently come into play.

To take this out of the lab and into the novel, Elizabeth is subconsciously influenced by emotion because Darcy's scorn and Wickham's flattery intersect with vital goals. We are social animals who constantly look for validation from others of our kind. It's undeniable that Darcy is an important member of society, a person whom others look up to, even if for the wrong reasons. And it matters whether an important member of the "tribe" likes you. This is especially true with regard to Darcy because he's an eligible bachelor, and even though Elizabeth scorns the predatory and obsessive husband-hunting of her society, the opinions of handsome young (and single) men do matter to her. She "needs" to get married in order to survive in her society. The social programming of nineteenth-century polite society is right in line with the biological programming we share with other mammals. Finding the best possible mate is one of our most fundamental drives.

Like non-thirsty participants in the beverage experiment, Elizabeth is relatively invulnerable to the effects of negative signals when they come from sources that don't matter. She couldn't care less what Mr. Collins, her foolish and persistent suitor, or Lady Catherine de Bourgh, Darcy's snobbish aunt, think of her. Yes, it's true Mr. Collins is an eligible bachelor, but his drawbacks far outweigh his advantages. And while Lady Catherine possesses rank, she lives an isolated life, certainly far from the people Elizabeth routinely meets. They are off the beaten track of significant drives: Elizabeth remains impervious to their opinions.

One intriguing theory of how emotion affects thought and behavior, called the "somatic marker hypothesis," has been suggested by Antonio Damasio, the neuroscientist who provided convincing evidence that damage to emotion areas of the brain compromises cognition.* The somatic marker hypothesis proposes that in making decisions, we "mark" the consequences of our choices affectively through physiological responses, which is really just to say that we react emotionally to each moment of experience through physiological and biochemical reactions throughout the body. The brain has areas that register the condition of the body—as one author puts it, the body has a mind of its own—and these areas pass that knowledge along to other areas that integrate information, including the OFC (orbitofrontal cortex, an emotion-processing area on the underbelly of the cortex, roughly behind our eyes). The OFC is also responsible for flagging important emotional knowledge.

The OFC is also thought to record, or learn, the association between physiological arousal (somatic markers) and the situations, people, and events we encounter. When we encounter these again, or others similar to them, we draw on this knowledge to evaluate the possible responses that will allow us to achieve rewards or avoid punishers. We remember past reactions, often subconsciously, and apply this knowledge to current situations to choose our course of action. For example, it's likely that Elizabeth's stress hormones and body tension increased when she encountered Darcy after the Meryton ball. Such bodily signals, activations of the sympathetic nervous system (SNS), would alert her to his status as someone not kindly disposed toward her, someone she needed to be wary of. Of course post-Pemberley, she would have experienced excitatory reactions of a very different nature.

The somatic marker hypothesis was tested in a famous experiment called the Iowa Gambling Task. Subjects were asked to draw from four decks of cards that had gains or losses of a given amount of money written on one side. Two of the decks had winning cards that paid very little (e.g., you gain five dollars), but the lose-money cards asked you to forfeit even less (you lose one dollar). The other two decks had very high payoffs (hundreds of dollars) but their losses were even larger. To come out ahead financially, participants had to learn to

---

* Damasio introduced this theory to general readers in his book *Descartes' Error* and returns to it in all of his subsequent books. The somatic marker hypothesis, although more than twenty years old, is still respected today.

draw from the low-win/low-lose decks. Patients with ventromedial/ OFC damage failed to do this, while adults who hadn't suffered brain damage soon began to choose from the right decks. But they did this without knowing that they'd figured out the game. Their bodies knew what their brains did not.

In the course of the game, without the participants' knowledge, skin conductance (temperature), an indicator of stress, was measured. Subjects without brain damage showed an increase in skin conductance response in anticipation of a poor choice. So, for instance, while thinking about choosing from the higher-payoff deck, subjects without brain damage had physiological arousal associated with danger, or lack of reward, while this didn't happen when considering the low-payoff decks. Subjects with ventromedial/OFC damage failed to show differences in skin conductivity response. Damasio concluded that skin conductivity was one somatic marker that helped people react appropriately.

Some scientists have objected to the somatic marker hypothesis because people with spinal cord or other damage that interferes with reading bodily signals (such as muscle tension) still have emotional responses. But according to Damasio, the body need not actually respond to a situation because there's an as-if body loop that lets the brain read the appropriate physiological and neurochemical response without taxing the body and its systems to produce this response. You can have a bodily response minus the body. Integration of this signal with other brain areas (the job of the OFC) would still be necessary to convey information.

CANDIDATES FOR THE SUBCONSCIOUS: THE RIGHT BRAIN

When Elizabeth says, "I never knew myself," she implies that she's two people, the one who knows, and the one who's there to be known. Indeed, having a subconscious is a bit like being two people. This is seen most clearly with the second candidate for the subconscious, the right hemisphere of the brain, the so-called right brain.

The brain divides into two hemispheres (sliced down the center of a head, facing front). These largely mirror one another anatomically, with most structures present in both left and right brains; for instance, there's both a left and a right OFC. But brain function isn't entirely symmetrical. Specialization in each hemisphere (called lateral specialization) evolved because it enabled the brain to take on more functions in the same amount of space. For instance, because the left brain processes language, enabling us both to speak and to understand what others are saying, analogous areas in the right brain can be devoted to other tasks. And language renders our powers of communication paramount among the creatures of the earth. Other mammals, especially primates, have lateralization to some degree, but it's most pronounced in humans.

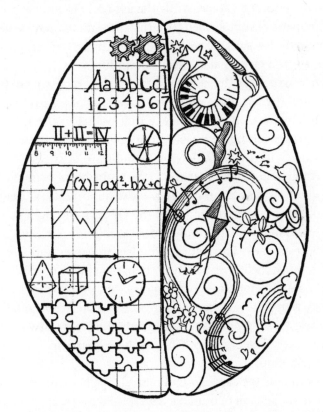

The left and right hemispheres have different jobs, and for that reason they need one another to function well. The left hemisphere is analytical and rational. It processes information sequentially, so it's responsible for our sense of time, our perception of cause and effect, and our ability to understand and formulate a logical argument and the order of events in a narrative. Your left brain makes sense of episodes in a novel: The Meryton ball takes place before Darcy's ill-fated first proposal, and Elizabeth rejects Darcy because she's furious at how he's treated her and her family.

However, if cause and effect is visual, such as a bowling ball knocking down a pin, the right hemisphere tells you this. That's because the right hemisphere processes visuospatial perception. It enables us to navigate through space, to find our way around. In general, the right brain is best at grasping global knowledge, such as seeing patterns at a glance, while the left brain is good at seeing the component parts of complicated patterns; the right brain sees the forest, the left brain the trees. Facial recognition, which involves recognizing the design of a given face, is also a right-brain function.

Evidence associates the right brain with the processing of negative emotions and the left brain with the processing of positive emotions. Along similar lines, there's evidence that points to the left brain as mediating approach behavior (seeking rewards) and the right brain as mediating withdrawal behavior (avoiding punishers). Nevertheless, research also shows that the right brain has a primary role in *all* emotional processing, including, most important, the regulation of emotion; this is largely the job of the OFC on the right side of the brain, which puts the vagal brake on, calming our stressful, negative excitatory responses. The right brain also processes and stores nonverbal reactions, including bodily responses, which are the essence of emotion. Somatic markers rely on right-brain processing. In general, we can say that the right hemisphere is the more "emotional" (more involved in generating and regulating emotion) of the two, although this is a matter of degree; both hemispheres participate in the processing of emotion.

As I mentioned, the capacity for language is a lateralized brain function; ninety-six percent of humans have left-hemisphere specialization for language. But crucial to the social brain, the right brain processes nonverbal cues, social signaling, including facial expression, and these are at least as important as language in conveying emotion. In addition, the right brain perceives significant nonliteral features of language, including tone, and so the emotional quality of a statement, as well as figures of speech such as metaphor, irony, and idiomatic expressions. You couldn't get most jokes without input from the right side of your brain. You certainly couldn't understand the first sentence of *Pride and Prejudice*: "It is a truth universally acknowledged, that a single man in possession of a good fortune must be in want of a wife." The left brain would take this statement literally, and wonder why the narrator was lying. The right brain gets the irony, perhaps even hears the archness in the narrator's voice.

The right hemisphere's lack of language is one reason that it might be identified with subconscious processes. We certainly tend to be aware of left-brain thoughts more often than right-brain thoughts because we usually think in language, labeling and narrating what we encounter; this is one of the earmarks of being human. But even if we don't reflect on right-brain information, we rely on it continually without acknowledging that this is what we're doing. Social signals and the perception of emotion work in this way: We constantly process the affect of the people we interact with without necessarily putting that information into words or being aware of it. And because of its nonverbal nature, right-brain processing often takes the form of hunches or instincts.

Although the right brain harbors a great deal of subconscious information, as we'll see, much of it is accessible to consciousness; we just need to pay attention. Right-brain thinking can be like background music, which, incidentally, is perceived by the right brain. Movies and television shows often have a soundtrack accompanying scenes, but most of us barely notice this, paying attention to plot and dialogue. Nevertheless, the music influences us, amplifying our emotions, as directors well know. But you can "look up" from the story and suddenly hear the music. In the same way, when we consciously decide to pay attention to nonverbal information, we can enlarge our awareness. Therapists are trained to pay attention to nonverbal cues like body language and facial expression, which can often reveal much more, or even be at odds with, what a person is actually saying.

But not all right-brain processing is available to reflective consciousness, and this is where things get really interesting. The right brain can harbor unknown, and sometimes unknowable, emotions, desires, and impulses that the left doesn't want us to realize, but that often influence us nevertheless. In other words, the right brain can be identified with the psychotherapeutic subconscious and the left brain with the filtering mechanisms designed to protect us.

Evidence for identifying the right brain as the repository of subconscious or repressed material comes from studies with so-called split brain patients. In the normally functioning brain, the two hemispheres coordinate and integrate information via a band of connecting tissue called the corpus callosum, which consists of neurons that form a left- and right-brain information superhighway. Each side "reports" to the other, and perceptions, feelings, judgments, behaviors, and so forth emerge from the input of both hemispheres working together. This is one of the most basic ways that we can see how neural integration contributes to the optimal functioning of the brain.

Some people with severe epilepsy have had this connection severed to prevent their seizures, a procedure called a corpus callosotomy. Although surgery might appear to be a drastic solution, for some patients it's the best available option. In most people who undergo a callosotomy, the hemispheres continue to work together, with the left brain dominating and the right brain going along with orders. But in some cases, the right brain can harbor its own agendas that conflict with those of its counterpart. And these can be motivated, purposeful agendas.

This is seen in the bizarre condition known as "alien hand," in which a person's two hands disagree about what they want to do. (The left hemisphere controls the right hand and body and the right hemisphere controls the left; this is because neurons coming from one side of the body cross over in the brainstem before traveling on to higher brain areas.) In one report from the annals of neuroscience, a person's left hand (controlled by the right hemisphere) kept taking goods from supermarket shelves and putting them in the subject's pockets while the right hand (controlled by the left, logical, hemisphere) kept returning them to the shelves or putting them in the cart.

For another subject, getting dressed became an internal civil war. She would select clothing she consciously wanted to wear and then her left hand (dominated by the right hemisphere) would grab something else and refuse to let go. Either she had to wear what the right brain (left hand) had chosen, or she had to call for help to subdue her "alien hand" (the name for this condition!). It's especially interesting that the right hemisphere chose more flashy and flamboyant clothing than the conservative left, in line with typical ideas about repression.

The most amazing story of this ilk concerns a subject, P.S., who had an unusual degree of language in his right hemisphere. His right brain couldn't generate speech, but it could direct P.S. to spell out answers using Scrabble tiles. The neuroscientists Michael Gazzaniga and Joseph LeDoux (of the low and high roads) wanted to ask the right-hemisphere questions, and so they needed to figure out a way to do this without the left answering. This was difficult because the left, when presented with language, would produce an answer, preventing the right hemisphere from communicating. They got around this problem by using pictures to ask questions, presented to the right hemisphere alone.

P.S.'s two hemispheres agreed about many things, but a startling difference emerged when Gazzaniga and LeDoux asked P.S. about his aspirations. First they asked the left brain, and he answered, speaking, "I want to be a draftsman . . . I'm already training for it." But when they asked the right brain (showing him alternative career choices in pictures), his left hand arranged the letter tiles to spell "automobile racer"! As seen in the person with "alien hand," P.S.'s unusually verbal right hemisphere demonstrated that it's possible to have a hidden, censored self that harbors desires and information unknown to our conscious minds.

The split-brain phenomena I've described support psychotherapeutic theories about the existence of subconscious, yet influential, thoughts, feelings, and desires. But this is only part of the story: Defense mechanisms not only suppress information, such as "I want to be an automobile racer," but misinterpret information as well. The division between hemispheres likely enables these distortions. In this case, we don't necessarily suppress our feelings, but the left brain invents reasons for our feeling the way we do, an alternative reality that's more palatable than the truth.

An experiment conducted once again by Gazzaniga and LeDoux demonstrated the left brain's function as an "interpreter" of right-brain information, a nickname coined by Gazzaniga. One large and four small pictures were placed within view of a split-brain patient's left and right fields of vision (so there were ten pictures in all, one large and four small ones for each hemisphere). The left hemisphere saw a large picture of a bird's foot with smaller pictures of a toaster, a chicken, an apple, and a hammer. The right hemisphere saw a snowy winter scene, complete with a large snowman, and smaller pictures of a pickaxe, a shovel, a lawnmower, and a rake. The patient, or rather each of his hemispheres, was asked to match the large scene with one of the four smaller pictures. The left hemisphere correctly picked a chicken to match the bird's foot. The right hemisphere correctly chose the shovel to match the snowy scene.

The left brain could see that the right brain (i.e., left hand) had chosen a shovel, but lacked knowledge of the snowy scene that had motivated this choice. As far as the left brain knew, the right brain was also shown a picture of a bird's foot. When the subject was asked why the left hand (ruled by the right hemisphere) had chosen the shovel, he said that it would be used to clean out the chicken coop! The left brain, capable of speech, was driven to come up with an explanation. Split-brain patients allow us to see the interpreter function in action.

We can extrapolate from this extraordinary condition to conclude that the left brain routinely speaks for the right. And when we put this together with the right brain's tendency to perceive negative information and to harbor hidden wishes, we can see how defense mechanisms would emerge from the mechanisms of the two hemispheres.

Let's split Elizabeth's brain to imagine the contributions of both hemispheres in generating the defense mechanisms that prevent her from knowing herself. Both hemispheres would understand that Elizabeth had negative feelings about Darcy. Elizabeth's right brain would further realize that the insult not only hurt but also frightened her, that the reasons for her dislike have less to do with her aversion to Darcy's snobbery and subsequent discoveries of his misdeeds, but with the magnitude of the wound inflicted by his comment. I mentioned in an earlier chapter that Elizabeth describes Darcy as having "mortified" her pride. The root of this word is *mort*, meaning "death" in Latin, and so her choice of word associates Darcy's remark with a serious wound, even a deathblow. The left brain would protect her from this knowledge, leading her to think that although she resented the insult, the greater reason for her dislike is that Darcy is a bad man.

Why is this insult so powerful? The right brain would say that not only was Elizabeth hurt by Darcy's insult, but that the hurt was deep, not superficial, and that it affected her whole sense of herself and her prospects, and not just her pride. This is because the insult frightened as well as hurt Elizabeth, for it indicated that perhaps other men also found her unappealing, which would make it difficult for her to find a suitable husband. This is something she very much wants to do for her personal happiness, and that she very much needs to do for financial security.

The prospect of being too unattractive to "tempt" a prospective husband, at least one she can bear, also presents Elizabeth with the possibility of a wrenching moral dilemma, one that was common at this time. Elizabeth believes that it's wrong to marry for money, that a young woman should at the very least like and respect the man to whom she commits herself, body and soul. Readers not only attribute this attitude to her as a young woman of integrity, but we also know it from her rejection of Darcy's first proposal, and, even earlier, from her rejection of Mr. Collins and her reaction when Charlotte becomes engaged to him, after Elizabeth herself has turned him down.

Elizabeth knows that Charlotte can't possibly find the prospect of a shared life with this fool appealing. When she talks about it with her sister Jane, Elizabeth suggests that Charlotte lacks not only judgment but scruples as well:

> My dear Jane, Mr. Collins is a conceited, pompous, narrow-minded, silly man; you know he is as well as I do; and you must feel, as well as I do, that the woman who marries him cannot have a proper way of thinking. You shall not defend her, though it is Charlotte Lucas. You shall not, for the sake of one individual, change the meaning of principle and integrity, nor endeavour to persuade yourself or me, that selfishness is prudence, and insensibility of danger, security for happiness.

The moral quality of Elizabeth's language is unmistakable. Charlotte's decision betrays "principle" and "integrity." In clear but decorous language, Elizabeth portrays Charlotte's marriage as a form of prostitution. But that's not the worst of it.

For even though young people of the middle and upper classes routinely married for pragmatic motives, and were even pressured to do so by parents concerned about their welfare or their status, this was totally opposed to the higher morality that allegedly guided every Christian's life—and Austen's England viewed itself as a very Christian society. The marriage ceremony asks that spouses promise to love one another, and if this isn't possible, speaking these words is perjury, forswearing oneself before God. These conflicting ideals, between worldly and spiritual concerns, remained a huge and unresolved contradiction at the heart of attitudes about marriage in Austen's society. But Elizabeth knows where she stands on this matter.[*]

And so Elizabeth characterizes Charlotte's betrayal of principle not only as wrong but perilous; Charlotte's decision reveals "insensibility of danger." This could refer to the vulnerability to adultery that was believed to haunt loveless marriages, a truism of the age; we see examples of this in *Sense and Sensibility* and in *Mansfield Park*. But I

---

[*]   I discuss this conflict at length in my book *Consensual Fictions: Women, Liberalism, and the English Novel*, Toronto: University of Toronto Press, 2005.

don't think Elizabeth worries about Charlotte's falling prey to a Willoughby or a Henry Crawford, the lotharios of those novels who seduce and abandon women. Elizabeth knows that her friend has far too much common sense and far too little romance to stray in this manner.

Elizabeth worries about her friend's soul rather than her reputation, about her lying to God by marrying a man she can't possibly love, and most readers will agree that Mr. Collins is particularly unlovable. On these grounds, Charlotte's marriage is a sin, a word we don't often find in Austen's very secularly focused novels—Austen's not going to preach to us—but which she implies nevertheless. That this sin is a mundane, familiar betrayal of religion and principle renders it no less terrible to Elizabeth.

Elizabeth's left brain must protect her from knowing that Darcy's comment was not only insulting but profoundly frightening. For Elizabeth, admitting that Darcy's statement hurt her would be tantamount to acknowledging that she too might face such a choice. For if what Darcy says is true, and she's unattractive (like Charlotte), she's likely to have difficulty finding a suitable husband. She might end up facing Charlotte's dilemma, although she would never make the same choice. Elizabeth's left brain represses this knowledge. Elizabeth knows she has negative feelings about Darcy; she fails to perceive that she's also hurt and scared.

But the left brain does more than repress: It also interprets. Elizabeth knows she doesn't like Darcy. The danger lies in knowing why. And so she distorts—interprets—both her perceptions and her dislike. She sees Darcy as a conceited, snobby scoundrel whose views are not to be trusted. Whatever he says, including what he says about her, likely stems from evil motives and a twisted, malevolent view of the world. If he finds that she isn't handsome enough to tempt him to dance, this is because he's too snobby to dance with anyone at the Meryton ball. To be fair, she does get that one right!

But even this isn't enough. He could be a snob but still be right about her lack of appeal, and so he must be thoroughly discredited, shown to have faulty judgment across the board. Moreover, the interpreter seeks to avenge as well as to protect. Elizabeth gets back at Darcy by seeing him as utterly despicable. From their first encounter until his revealing letter, she continues to embellish this observation, finding other evidence of his bad character as it comes her way. The interpreter is hard at work.

But why this drive to interpret? Why can't the left brain just suppress information and leave it at that? Why can't Elizabeth decide that she dislikes Darcy because he's a snob without leaping at the chance to believe him a scoundrel as well? She's all too ready to accept all of Wickham's slanders. The answer: We rarely leave well enough alone because our logical left brains demand reasons for everything. We're meaning-making entities, constantly on the search for cause and effect. We see this in children, who can drive us nuts by asking "Why?" about just about everything.

We're driven to interpret because making meaning, viewing the world in terms of cause and effect, is so crucial to survival. Our prehistoric ancestors might have figured out that if you walked through a certain area of the forest, you would likely be attacked by wild animals. They also realized that if you plant seeds in the ground, they'll grow into edible food. If you deliberately plant the seeds of those plants you like best, you'll likely have a steady supply of this plant. We owe the rise of agriculture, the most influential development within human culture, to our ability to understand and manipulate causality. Other animals also learn cause and effect, but they haven't explored its power—for better and worse—to the extent that humans have done.

In many ways, knowing cause and effect is the essence of wisdom. Elizabeth knows that if she were to marry Mr. Collins, she'd be miserable. It's clear to her that not only is he unattractive, but he's also a fool whose company she would find intolerable. However, she also knows that if she were to marry him, she'd be financially secure and that this would benefit her entire family. Since Mr. Collins is the heir to her father's property, neither her mother nor her unmarried sisters would be made to leave if Mr. Bennet were to die before his wife and daughters. If she doesn't marry him, it's possible that she won't get a better offer, or even another offer, and that her family will be evicted from their home. But Elizabeth decides based on her ability to connect actions with consequences. In her mind, marriage to Mr. Collins is by far the greater danger. Charlotte obviously wouldn't have agreed.

Another reason we interpret: As Elizabeth's "prejudice" toward Darcy demonstrates, left brains must often deal with conflicting agendas: to let us know upsetting information that might be helpful (Darcy isn't nice, which is initially true and ultimately helpful to know), while also protecting us from knowledge that might be damaging (I'm not attractive). The solution is to distort information rather than suppressing it entirely. Misinterpretation is a compromise between the hemispheres, and between knowledge and ignorance, with the left saying to the right, in effect, "You can express yourself, but I'll interpret what you say in the way I think best." Perhaps the split-brain subject who couldn't dress herself because of "alien hand" had lost this ability to compromise between the agendas of the hemispheres, and so she faced a conflict between two entirely different styles: flashy, which she enjoyed personally, or conservative, which she knew was appropriate for work. In her previous, presurgery life, she might have resolved the conflict by wearing a conservative suit with a flashy pair of earrings.

CANDIDATE FOR THE SUBCONSCIOUS: IMPLICIT MEMORY SYSTEMS

When most people think of memory, they think of declarative memory, which includes episodic memory and semantic memory. As the name indicates, episodic memories are recollections of the events in our lives. Semantic memory refers to knowledge of facts, meanings, concepts, words, and so forth. Both of these kinds of memories are conscious. By contrast, implicit memories are largely subconscious memories that influence us without our awareness.

As with much of our knowledge about brain function, what we know about implicit memory systems originated by observing subjects with brain damage. This included, above all, psychologist Brenda Milner's groundbreaking work beginning in the 1950s with a brain-damaged patient known for decades as H.M. When he died in 2008, his obituary in the *New York Times* revealed his identity (he was Henry Gustav Molaison, born in 1926) and noted that he was "the most important patient in the history of brain science."

The woman who studied him for decades is equally noteworthy. Milner is credited with being one of the founders of neuropsychology, the study of the effects of brain damage on behavior and the mind, and cognitive neuroscience. She is a pioneer not only for her extraordinary contribution to the mind-brain sciences, but also for her entry into a field that was, and still largely is, dominated by men. In a book that's about the intellectual legacy of one extraordinary woman, I feel it's only right to pay homage to the achievements of another. As I write this chapter, Milner is still alive and professionally active at the age of 98, the Dorothy J. Killam Professor at the Montreal Neurological Institute and Hospital, and a professor in the Department of Neurology and Neurosurgery at McGill University. By the way, her dissertation director was Donald Hebb, the man whose theorem says, "Neurons that fire together wire together."

Milner's patient—let's still call him H.M., the name he had as a living research subject—had severe epilepsy due to a head injury he'd suffered at the age of nine when he was knocked down by someone on a bicycle. His epilepsy was so disabling that his doctors decided to remove the area in which the seizures originated, the medial temporal lobe. This region is part of the limbic area, located in the center of the brain underneath the wrapping of the cortex. The OFC borders this area, which contains many structures involved in the processing of emotions. But the significant area removed in H.M.'s case was the hippocampus, which enables us to make new episodic memories.

The surgery didn't affect H.M.'s cognitive skills. He tested normal for intelligence, use of language, and other abilities. He also possessed "working memory," which isn't properly a memory system, but rather the name given to all the thoughts we have in our conscious minds at any particular moment—what you can hold in awareness in the present. H.M. could retain information such as a visual image or a phone number for a few minutes, but then the information vanished. He could converse normally, holding on to the thread of statements and ideas long enough to understand what was said to him and to respond in a manner that made sense. And he could remember his life before the surgery. But H.M. couldn't remember the people and events he encountered subsequent to his surgery. He was doomed to live in an eternal present.

Yet, although H.M. could no longer remember new events or people, he was capable of making other kinds of long-term memories. For instance, he could learn new motor skills. In one experiment, he was taught to trace the outline of a star while looking at the image in a mirror, a difficult task to master. Each day that H.M. traced the star, his skill improved, which showed that he was learning—learning is indeed a form of memory. Yet each time he traced the star, he had no memory of ever having previously performed this task.

Similar experiments with other patients who had brain damage in the same brain areas yielded the same results. This capability pointed to the existence of procedural memory, the knowledge of how to do things—how to proceed—and it demonstrated that this kind of memory didn't depend on the hippocampus to encode new knowledge. Moreover, procedural memory can operate while bypassing consciousness. If you happen to find yourself at a ball dancing a quadrille, you'll nevertheless be able to carry on an important conversation with your partner as long as you're familiar with the dance. Procedural memory will keep your feet moving correctly while working memory focuses on more important things, such as showing your partner that you're a witty conversationalist. And you might even know the dance well without remembering having learned it. Driving a car depends on procedural memory.

Although procedural memory often refers to motor tasks such as driving or dancing, this system also encodes crucial social-emotional information, including how to feel and behave with others in different contexts. It often involves another memory system, emotional memory. Like procedural memory, the memory of our affective reactions doesn't need the hippocampus to be encoded; it most likely depends on the activity of the amygdala.

Neuroscientists Antonio Damasio and Daniel Tranel devised an experiment with another patient who, like H.M., couldn't make new episodic memories, to uncover the existence of an emotional memory system (let's call him I.N.). They introduced I.N. to three different people, each with a different affective style. Good Guy was kind and friendly. Neutral Guy was neither pleasant nor unpleasant. Bad Guy was rude and abrasive.

Five minutes after this trio left the room, I.N. could no longer remember them. But he encountered them repeatedly after that. When researchers subsequently instructed I.N. to ask one of these men for gum or cigarettes, he chose Good Guy more often than the others—more often than could be expected if left to chance. I.N. retained an emotional memory of people whom he couldn't remember meeting.

We can think of Elizabeth's experience in terms of implicit memory systems. Elizabeth is bothered far more by Darcy's remark than she realizes. The aspects of her reaction such as her hurt and fear, unavailable to explicit forms of memory, are stored in emotional memory. Like I.N. avoiding Bad Guy, she develops a bias against Darcy fueled by the emotions of this hidden memory system. She interprets all of Darcy's future behavior in the worst possible light and misses the very pointed flattery and fascination that follow his initial misjudgment.

Elizabeth learns to know herself better after the flash of insight she has on reading Darcy's letter. We know enough today about the mind-brain and its many facets to understand that this is no mean accomplishment; knowing yourself isn't easy. The "self" is made up moment by moment, strung together by our consciousness and self-awareness to create the sense of having an "I." But we're not the same from moment to moment, and even the unified being we feel ourselves to be contains layer upon layer of perception and identity, some of which is knowable, but much of which is hidden. Generally speaking, the more we know about ourselves, and the more we can unveil and integrate different aspects of our mind-brains, the better off we are. Psychotherapy aims to help people to achieve such understanding, to know themselves so that they can be fully present to see and deal with challenges and opportunities, joys and sorrows. That there are extraordinary benefits to such wisdom, to seeing yourself and others without pride or prejudice, might well be the moral of Austen's most famous novel.

FIVE

Changing Your Mind

usten was well aware that subconscious emotions and desires can influence us without our knowledge long before Freud revolutionized mental health with this observation. Austen also understood psychotherapy's other major insight: Given the right circumstances, people can change profoundly, that our ways of being in the world aren't written in stone—or its equivalent in our day and age, the genetic code. The warp and weft of Austen's novels consists in portraying people who change for the better, psychologically and morally, although of course psychological and moral changes can go for the worse in real life and in Austen's novels (think of the fallen Eliza in *Sense and Sensibility*, or even of Mr. Bennet, whose cynicism appears to ensue from his unhappiness in marriage).*

In her novels, Austen shows, and as many theories in current psychotherapy maintain, that insight is key to personal transformation.

---

* Austen actually refers to just such a change as is implied in Mr. Bennet with Mr. Palmer, a minor character in *Sense and Sensibility*.

For instance, in *Pride and Prejudice* (let's stay with that novel a bit longer), insight plays a huge role in the profound changes experienced by both Darcy and Elizabeth. Elizabeth comes to understand that her judgment is *not* always objective, and that she isn't above being influenced by her feelings. She realizes that she was ignorant of this all-too-human susceptibility, and that she therefore failed to interrogate her judgment or her motives. She'll be wiser in the future.

Even greater changes happen for Darcy. When we meet Darcy at Pemberley several months after Elizabeth's harsh rejection, we see that he has a different way of looking at himself and his place in the world. He's welcoming rather than haughty, and he enjoys the company of Elizabeth's aunt and uncle even though they're in trade, well below him in status. He has obviously spent some time questioning the validity both of his automatic judgments and his customary behavior. He's a different man.

But as psychotherapy—and Austen—also tell us, insight isn't sufficient to bring about these kinds of changes. Knowledge alone rarely changes mind, brain, heart, or behavior. Darcy makes this clear in his account of his psychological and moral awakening. He tells Elizabeth that as a child, he'd been taught to know what good behavior meant (insight), but that the *emotional* lessons he learned contradicted such knowledge: "I have been a selfish being all my life, *in practice, though not in principle*. As a child I was taught what was right, but I was not taught to correct my temper. I was given good principles, but left to follow them in pride and conceit." [my italics] Knowledge without the punch of emotion lacks conviction or power; emotional lessons win out over cognitive ones every time.

More specifically, the emotions that spur us to change are embedded in our connections with other people. According to Dr. Judith Herman, a pioneer in the study of trauma, healing "can take place only in the context of relationships."* Sociality provides the occasion for growth and change in nonpathological contexts as well. Darcy's knowledge of right and wrong remained abstract until his relationship with Elizabeth sparked a psychological and moral transformation: He continues, to Elizabeth, "You showed me how insufficient were all my preten-

---

* Judith Herman, M.D., *Trauma and Recovery: The Aftermath of Violence—From Domestic Abuse to Political Terror* (New York: Basic Books, 2015), 133.

sions to please a woman worthy of being pleased." Because he loves Elizabeth, Darcy is motivated to examine his behavior in the past, including both his proposal, which was condescending and insulting, and his habitual approach to most other people, also condescending and insulting. That is to say, disappointed love gives him the desire to examine his behavior in light of his principles, and so to realize the discrepancy between the two. More important, Darcy acquires the will to change, not necessarily to marry Elizabeth—he thinks that's a lost cause—but rather because he realizes that changing his ways might allow him to please "a woman worthy of being pleased."

Similarly, on reading Darcy's letter, Elizabeth understands that she's been mistaken about Darcy and Wickham. This causes her to question her habitual rush to judgment. Elizabeth becomes less susceptible to prejudice because doing so matters.

Insight and relationship are the two main factors that help people to change, and this is seen in Austen's novels, in real life, and in therapy. Nevertheless, just as the existence of the subconscious was accepted by academic psychology only when empirical evidence grounded in the study of the brain became available, so the claim that psychotherapy works by inducing substantial changes in cognition, feeling, and behavior required some "hard" scientific proof, preferably brain based, if psychotherapy were to be allowed to join the respectable world of evidence-based knowledge. Eric Kandel, winner of the Nobel Prize in Physiology and Medicine in 1990, provided such proof. His extraordinary research showed that learning and experience really do change the brain. The first part of the chapter tells of his findings. With this basic knowledge as a foundation, we can jump from the microscopic world of neurons to the mind-brain to view such changes in a therapeutic mode, as Marianne of *Sense and Sensibility* heals from her debilitating bout of depression.

OF SNAILS AND PEOPLE

The goal of psychotherapy is to effect positive changes for people, to help them, at the very least, to heal from mental affliction, and at best, to find a path to well-being and contentment. And it has worked.

People have been helped by therapy for over a century, although it was only in the last quarter of the twentieth century that psychologists began to collect empirical evidence to measure such improvement. One popular research tool is the Likert scale, which asks people to assess their feelings using a spectrum of possible responses: For instance, "On a scale of one to ten, how depressed do you feel?" Assessments can be made at several times during a course of therapy to see if treatment is making a difference. Or people can be asked to rate the treatment itself. You're probably familiar with Likert scales from visits to the doctor; they're widely used to assess pain.

It was only possible to use measures such as the Likert scale when the intellectual climate of the age had shifted and the field of academic psychology began to take people's reports of their own experience seriously. A type of research called "exploratory" or "qualitative" research, which relies on what people have to say about their experience, on narratives rather than numbers, complements the information gleaned from quantitative evidence, such as the Likert scale and other statistical methods for evaluating various practices. Of course, people have been reporting the benefits of psychotherapy from the get-go, but the difference is that what they have to say is now being taken seriously by researchers.

Even so, such evidence, whether it's quantitative or qualitative, refers to the mind, not the brain. This focus has always been suspect in certain quarters of hard-core neuroscience. People, no matter how astute they are about their mental state, will never provide the impartial proof we see when we chart the activity of the brain. In addition, although we can measure levels of stress through charting blood pressure, the level of stress hormones and triglycerides in the blood, skin temperature (conductance), and other biological indicators, evidence coming from the body rather than the brain doesn't provide irrefutable, direct evidence of the brain per se.

Eric Kandel dedicated his career to the quest for such evidence, to providing neurological proof for the tenets of psychotherapy. As a young man, Kandel had planned to become a psychoanalyst. But he began to wonder where in the brain the id, the ego, and the superego— the three divisions of the psyche established by Freud—were located. One of his mentors, Harry Grundfest, told him that the answer to this question was well beyond the grasp of current biology and that in order to understand these psychological categories in terms of anatomy, we had first to understand how nerve cells work. To understand the mind, we have to understand the brain, one neuron at a time.

Kandel thought this was well worth doing and decided to pursue a career in medical research. Freud's trajectory had been just the opposite. Beginning as a neurologist, Freud realized that he couldn't account for, nor influence, the mind by confining himself to the study of the brain. And so he invented a science of the mind, psychoanalysis. Freud, Kandel, and Grundfest were all ahead of their respective times in realizing that we need to know about both mind and brain because an adequate understanding of either depends on seeing how they relate to one another. Today this is beyond question, a fundamental principle of the mind-brain sciences.

Although inspired by Freud, Kandel didn't direct his research to finding Freud's three divisions of the mind. Rather, he addressed the essential principle of all psychotherapy, that therapy is a form of learning that changes a person's habitual ways of responding—emotionally, cognitively, and behaviorally. Kandel reasoned that the first step in proving that learning changes the brain would involve demonstrating that the brain is transformed physiologically as a result of experience.

Kandel couldn't attempt his proof using the human brain, nor the brains of other mammals, reptiles, or vertebrates, for in these animals the neurons are too numerous and small, and the connections among them too complex, to be able to trace the impact of experience on a single neuron or group of neurons. He worked with the giant snail, *Aplysia*, which has about 20,000 neurons, some of them visible to the naked eye. Compare this to the roughly eighty-four billion microscopic neurons in the human brain.

You wouldn't think that Austen or her characters or you, for that matter, would have any reason to be interested in a giant snail, unless, of course, you decided to read *Sense and Sensibility and Sea Monsters,* one of the many novels belonging to Austen's afterlife. This one is part of a series that considers the challenges posed by various kinds of monsters, rather than the more pedestrian and difficult challenges we encounter in our dealings with other people. But actually, the *Aplysia* can tell us more about ourselves than we might care to admit.

Kandel was able to use the *Aplysia* to discover principles of neuron function in all animals with nervous systems, including humans, because evolution is remarkably conservative and builds on what's already there. The most primitive part of our brains, the brainstem, looks very much like a reptile's brain. This means that neurons work in essentially similar ways in every animal that possesses them. It also means that we share much of our genetic material with "lower" animals, even monstrous snails. Later, influenced by LeDoux's work, Kandel also conducted research on learning and memory with mice. But his dramatic early discoveries focused on the *Aplysia.*

By the time Kandel began this research, some important basic facts were known about neurons: The neuron is the building block of all nervous systems, however advanced or primitive. Neurons send signals to one another through chemical transmission that is converted to an electrical charge within the sending cell (this is the "firing" or "action potential" of the neuron). Firing in turn causes the cell to release chemicals that cross the synapse, the small space between neurons, to an adjacent neuron (or muscle or gland) in the circuit. The receiving cell (or body part) responds according to the content of the chemical message it receives from the sending cell. Neurotransmitters can be excitatory, instructing another neuron to fire (or a part of the body to react), or inhibitory, sending a message to inhibit reaction. But this foundational knowledge didn't begin to explain some of the higher functions of the brain, such as learning and memory, at the cellular level, in biological, physiological terms.

Kandel began his studies of this difficult topic by focusing on the gill withdrawal reflex of the *Aplysia.* When the skin of the *Aplysia* is touched, it naturally withdraws its gill to protect this crucial part of its body. To begin with, Kandel tracked the actual neuronal circuit between sensory and motor neurons that caused this reflex. While the mechanics of neuronal circuits had been theorized (as described above) no one had previously mapped an actual circuit, matching it to the behavior it enables. This was an extraordinary achievement since the neural mechanics of a specific behavior were now known.

Kandel could now build on this knowledge to explore the mechanisms involved in learning. He had to work with very simple kinds of learning, since the *Aplysia* is a very simple kind of creature. No insights about self-deception or denial for the *Aplysia*! But just as this animal's body appears to be vastly different from ours yet possesses the fundamental building blocks of human cognition, so human learning has its analogues with the learning this creature is capable of. An *Aplysia* can't be taught to consciously recognize its prejudices and amend its behavior, but it possesses the basic mechanism underlying all learning, the ability to form habitual ways of responding and, just as important, to change such habits as a result of experience. Kandel worked with three kinds of simple learning—habituation, sensitization, and conditioning—to observe what cellular changes took place as the animal mastered its tasks.

All animals habituate to nonthreatening stimuli that remain constant, which means that they get used to things and stop responding, or respond much less strongly. That's why you might notice a certain smell upon entering a place, but soon cease to be aware of it. Your nose doesn't physically stop smelling it, but your brain no longer responds or interprets those cues to the same degree. Or, you might become startled on hearing a particular loud sound for the first time, but if you hear it repeatedly (such as when there's construction going on outside your office), you soon take it in stride as background noise, perhaps even failing to register it. When the *Aplysia*'s skin was touched repeatedly, its gill reflex became weaker; that is to say, the snail withdrew its gill to a lesser extent and more stimulation was needed to elicit a response.

Elizabeth similarly became habituated to her mother's incessant chatter, which was also an irritant. You can see how habituation would have biological and psychological advantages in creatures that have a central nervous system (brain and spinal cord); habituation spares Elizabeth the continuous pain and embarrassment that her mother's silliness would have evoked had she really listened to every word. When we speak colloquially about getting upset when people "press our buttons," we're often testifying to our inability to become habituated to annoying or provoking behavior.

Kandel next worked with sensitization, the opposite of habituation. This was done by applying a shock to the animal's tail or head, which made the gill reflex stronger, occurring more readily and with less stimulation. Watch how after a scare you remain "jumpy" for a while. When Darcy insulted Elizabeth at the ball, he made her more sensitive to perceiving his negative qualities. Just as the *Aplysia* withdrew its gill reflex more readily to protect itself, so Elizabeth was "sensitized" to picking up on information that would confirm her negative opinion of Darcy. Like the gill-withdrawal reflex, this too was a protective gesture; by attributing Darcy's negative perception of her to his own bad character, she didn't have to admit that his remark had hurt, or that he might have been right in thinking she was "not handsome enough." Of course, as it turned out, there were other explanations than the alternatives "Darcy is a terrible person" or "I'm not attractive," but most reflexive automatic behavior is almost as thoughtless as a gill-withdrawal reflex.

On a related note, I love how the word *sensitize*, from the same root as *sense* and *sensibility*, bridges physical, cognitive, and emotional experience, the latter two pertaining to Elizabeth and not *Aplysias*. Again, usage points to essential features of the human mind-brain, in this case indicating the commonality between the simple defense mechanisms of our evolutionary forbears, many of whom likely resembled the *Aplysia*, and our own responses. Darcy's comment at the ball was also a *shock*, another word that bridges mental and physical divides.

The third kind of lesson for the *Aplysia* involved classical conditioning, the most famous instance being that of Pavlov's dogs.* This is the pattern of classical conditioning: An unconditioned stimulus (such as food) is paired with a conditioned stimulus (such as a bell) so that the subject, be it dog, snail, or human, learns to produce the

---

* Classical conditioning was discovered by Russian psychologist Ivan Pavlov in the 1890s.

unconditioned stimulus response when the conditioned stimulus alone occurs. Kandel was able to condition the *Aplysia* to withdraw its gill when its siphon (connected to the gill) was lightly touched by repeatedly following such a touch with a shock. Eventually, the *Aplysia* had a strong withdrawal response, akin to the negative impact of a shock, when its siphon was touched.

We might say that Darcy was conditioned to be distant and disdainful by one too many experiences of balls like the one at Meryton. Annoying people who make Darcy feel like the door prize in the marriage contest (the unconditioned stimulus) are paired with a type of event (a ball), so that even before a ball starts, Darcy's in a bad mood. However, I would qualify this with my characterization of this behavior as conditioning, as well as my examples of habituation and sensitization in humans, by noting that conscious and subconscious thought of a much higher order than simple association also goes into producing Darcy's bad mood and Elizabeth's sensitivity, or lack thereof. The "conditioning" for both these characters depends on complicated input, both cognitive and emotional, conscious and subconscious, that takes place in many areas throughout the brain.

By observing neurons during these lessons with the *Aplysia*, Kandel saw that at the cellular level, learning involves changes in synaptic strength, how readily a neuron will send an electrical impulse across a specific synapse, the small space separating one neuron from another. Electrical signals must cross this space for a neuron to activate, and so for us to respond. Synaptic strength in turn depends on the amount of neurotransmitter that's required to elicit a response in the receiving cell, the one to which the electrical impulse is being sent. Sensitization means that less neurotransmitter is required to elicit a response from the receiving cell than was formerly required. In this case we say that the synaptic connection has strengthened. Conditioning also involves sensitization, but with the intermediary of the conditioned stimulus (bell, light touch, Meryton ball).

Conversely, with habituation, more neurotransmitter is needed to evoke a response, and so the synaptic connection has weakened. Moreover, the duration of these effects, how long the *Aplysia* holds on to its learning, depends on the length of time of its "training." Kandel found that the longer the training, that is, the greater the number of times the experiment was conducted, the longer the *Aplysia*'s behavior continued. Here was support for Hebb's theorem: Neurons that fire together wire together.

This information was crucial. Kandel's experiments proved that learning takes place initially not by altering the number or kinds of neurons in the nervous system, but by altering the strength of their synaptic connections. Of course in animals with complex centralized nervous systems, a given response will also depend on the sum of signals that both stimulate and inhibit that response, as well as the strength of each individual signal.

The idea that learning depends on synaptic strength was already endorsed by many scientists, but it was by no means accepted by all. Here now was definitive proof that learning, and hence memory, are altered as a result of alterations in the strength of synaptic connections. No new circuitry was required. This contributed support for the idea of neuroplasticity; even in brains that were fully mature, substantial change was possible. Elizabeth and Darcy experience significant changes of mind-brain as adults.

Up to this point, Kandel's research concerned short-term learning and memory. Short-term memories last seconds, minutes, or hours, but long-term memories last days, years, or a lifetime. The changes wrought by psychotherapy, as well as most other kinds of learning, are forms of long-term memory. And so, momentous as his discoveries were, Kandel extended his research to the more complicated issue of how long-term memories are made at the cellular level.

It was known already from observation that for short-term memories to turn into long-term memories, something needed to happen that took some time. If, say, Darcy had a fall from a horse and suffered a concussion, he might forget the events immediately preceding the accident, such as leaving his house and starting his ride. The rather common type of memory loss suggests that a blow to the head can interfere with the consolidation of information, the process of turning short-term memories into long-term memories.

An important clue about what might be happening in cases like this was suggested by Louis Flexner, who discovered that drugs that disrupt the synthesis of new proteins in the brain also disrupt the acquisition of long-term memories. This suggested that protein synthesis was needed for long-term memory. Protein synthesis is also how genes work. They produce proteins that act as chemical messengers, telling the body what to do.

Still working with the *Aplysia*, Kandel confirmed Flexner's results while also making another amazing discovery: Learning can actually cause the growth of new synapses. His previous experiments had shown that in the case of sensitization or habituation of relatively short duration, synaptic strength changes for synapses that already exist. Kandel also confirmed that dormant synapses can begin to activate. In this subsequent phase of experimentation he discovered that long-term sensitization can actually cause a neuron to grow new terminals, new pouches that secrete neurochemicals, and so increase synaptic transmission by increasing not only the percentage of active synapses but the actual number of synapses. Today, we also know that mature adult human brains can even grow new neurons. This was deemed impossible until a short time ago.

Kandel's work demonstrated that learning does change the brain. The difference in synaptic strength that occurs in short-term learning and memory is often the first step of a series of changes that ultimately alter the landscape of brain areas. Short-term memory involves functional changes in the brain's activity, but long-term memory involves anatomical changes to the brain. And what's surprising—and this applies to simple animals such as the *Aplysia* as well as to complex animals like humans—these changes take place using the same chemicals and signaling systems that the body uses to make other kinds of changes. All our biological processes, including the physiological substrate of our thoughts and memories, use the same basic elements.

Subsequent research has confirmed Kandel's findings. For example, two studies conducted in the 1990s, in the wake of Kandel's research, used brain imaging to show that new growth occurred alongside learning in higher animals as well as in simple animals such as the *Aplysia*. Michael Merzenich trained monkeys to get food pellets by touching a rotating disk with their three middle fingers. After several months, the cortical area in charge of these fingers had expanded. Thomas Ebert and colleagues in Germany compared images of violinists' and cellists' brains with images of the brains of people who didn't play an instrument. He found that the area of the somatosensory cortex in charge of the fingers of the left hand—the active hand for these musicians—was up to five times larger than this area in nonmusicians. Areas in charge of the right hand were similar in all groups. There is even evidence that antidepressants encourage neurogenesis in adults in various areas. Among the most important of these is the hippocampus (responsible for memories), which we've long known loses cells and volume as a result of chronic depression.

Kandel published some of his findings about changes in synaptic strength in an article entitled "Psychotherapy and the Single Synapse: The Impact of Psychiatric Thought on Neurobiologic Research." His title indicated that he had begun the important work of providing physical, empirical evidence for psychotherapeutic theory, and just as important, that he had never lost faith in the value of psychotherapy. To find the ego, id, and superego, or whatever other names we give to our mechanisms of thought and feeling, Kandel knew you have to start with neurons, as his mentor had advised. And so he studied the *Aplysia* in order to begin to validate the insights of psychotherapy. The *Aplysia* is like a small detail of a very large painting, one tiny part of the picture of the kinds of activity we find throughout the human mind-brain, but which nevertheless yields important information about the whole. Kandel traveled a path opposite to Freud's, from psychology to neurology, while never losing sight of the need for a synthesis of the two.

Without this awareness, he might have positioned his work differently; the discovery that learning changes the physical properties of the brain is huge, certainly worthy of a Nobel Prize, but it doesn't have to be linked to psychotherapy. But Kandel deliberately referenced psychotherapy, signposting the direction that he thought the mind-brain sciences ought to take. He publicly championed the value of "the talking cure" during an era when its views were discarded by universities and other official research institutions. He courageously bridged the disciplinary divide between the hard sciences and psychotherapy, remaining a champion of the latter throughout his career. For such vision, steadfastness, and courage, Kandel is as remarkable as his discoveries.

In his very readable autobiography, Kandel observes that psychoanalysis has contributed to our understanding of the mind, leading to ideas that are almost universally accepted today. These include the existence of different types of subconscious processes, as well as the complexities of psychological phenomena such as motivation; denial; and transference, the influence of past experiences and relationships on current functioning. It's not surprising that this visionary scientist, who never lost sight of the human aspect of his research, also recognized the value of literature, and spoke of its inspirational power in his own life:

> Until the end of the nineteenth century, the only approaches to the mysteries of the human mind were introspective philosophical inquiries . . . or the insights of great novelists, such as Jane Austen, Charles Dickens, Fyodor Dostoevsky, and Leo Tolstoy. Those are the readings that inspired my first years at Harvard.[*]

Jane is there with the best of them.

MARIANNE IN THERAPY

Changes in the behavior of snails result from physical events and are registered as neurological (anatomical) changes. Changes in patterns of response for humans also involve neurology. If a person's mind (and so their behavior) is going to change, the brain has to change as well, there's no doubt about this. But for humans, a lot of other factors are involved, and we tend to lose sight of this. The human brain is still worshipped as the core of the self. Ninety-five percent of mind-brain scientists will tell you that the brain is equivalent to the mind, and that the mind arises from the activity of the brain, while ignoring the significance of Siegel's emphasis on social connection as a crucial part of mind.

Nevertheless, people tend to change through relationships, one of the key insights of psychotherapy. No one shows this better than Austen. Her characters change their behavior, they change their

---

[*]   Eric. R. Kandel, *In Search of Memory: The Emergence of a New Science of Mind* (New York: W. W. Norton & Company, 2006), 40.

feelings, they change their minds, and they change their lives, but always in the course of engaging with people who matter to them. Austen's novels are all about the transformative power of social connection.

In a broad sense, such changes can be defined as therapeutic. Psychotherapy has always been about changing the way a person perceives and reacts to events and people. It's about changing the core of one's emotional and cognitive habits, and as a result, learning to create a different reality than the one that motivated a person to seek therapy in the first place. Many of Austen's main characters experience such therapeutic change, becoming better or more satisfied people in one way or another. We see this with Elizabeth and Darcy, who become less judgmental, and in so doing, find happiness.

But *Sense and Sensibility* stands out as the most "therapeutic" of Austen's novels, portraying personal development in the context of psychological healing. When Marianne's suitor Willoughby abandons her, she becomes clinically depressed; we can actually diagnose her using *DSM-5*, the diagnostic bible of the mental health profession in the U.S. She eventually recovers through her connection with her sister, Elinor, a relationship with many therapeutic aspects.

Of course, Elinor is Marianne's sister, not her therapist—there *were* no therapists in Austen's day. There weren't even *alienists* yet, the nineteenth-century term for this newly minted occupation. But the relationship between the sisters takes on the characteristics of what's called a "therapeutic alliance," a positive relationship between therapist and client with the express goal of helping the client to heal and achieve a sense of well-being.

A strong therapeutic alliance has been proved to be the crucial element in successful therapies, even those that differ significantly from one another in terms of technique and theory.[*] Psychotherapy was founded on the knowledge that others are instrumental in shaping our minds, and that our most significant transformations in mental states and behavior happen through connections with other people. This is true throughout our lifetimes; from the very beginning, our

---

[*] The importance of the therapeutic relationship is widely accepted. On this point, see Paul L. Wachtel, *Therapeutic Communication: Knowing What to Say When* (New York: The Guilford Press, 2011), 104–105.

mind-brains are linked to those of the people who care for us, dependent on them for their very development. Psychotherapy works by means of our drive to connect with others in order to achieve its fundamental goal: Psychotherapy has always been about changing the way a person perceives and reacts to events and people. It's about changing the core of one's emotional and cognitive habits, and as a result, learning to create a different reality than the one that motivated a person to seek therapy in the first place, to help people lead happier lives.

Elinor begins to relate to Marianne in therapeutic mode the moment Willoughby's treachery becomes too obvious to ignore. After spending most of the previous two months with Marianne, and appearing to be entirely devoted to her, Willoughby suddenly takes his leave from the Dashwood family, saying that he won't be able to return. Marianne writes to him, but he doesn't answer her letters. (They shouldn't be corresponding since they're not engaged, but Marianne disregards this rule.) When Willoughby arrives in London, where Marianne has also traveled and eagerly awaits him, he visits when he knows she's sure to be out, leaving his calling card; he wouldn't have done even this much were it not for the dictates of decorum. Marianne spends day after day on tenterhooks, waiting for Willoughby to seek her out, wondering why he hasn't done so.

When Marianne finally sees Willoughby at a ball, he openly snubs her, which adds humiliation to her sorrow. Marianne is so overwhelmed that Elinor must restrain her from making a spectacle of herself by very publicly demanding an explanation for what is so clear to Elinor and everyone else: Willoughby has jilted her. In the following days, Marianne writes repeatedly to Willoughby, desperate to understand his strange behavior. He eventually responds with what might be the cruelest letter in the nineteenth-century novel, a letter that coldly suggests that their relationship had been no more than a casual and distant friendship. This is the final blow. At this point, Marianne begins her downward spiral into depression.

Marianne becomes withdrawn and dysfunctional, virtually oblivious to her surroundings. When she regains sufficient calm to be able to leave her room, she goes through the motions of living on automatic pilot, truly engaging with very little around her. The only reality she fully experiences is the stubborn presence of emotional pain.

Depression can begin in this way as a chaotic response to an over-whelming event, or it can be purely organic, a feature of a person's mind-brain rather than a reaction to a particular experience. Most depressions involve a combination of organic and environmental-psychological factors. While Marianne's crisis is clearly a response to the dramatic end to her relationship with Willoughby, she might have had a tendency to depression because she's not naturally a good self-regulator. She's much more thin-skinned and reactive than Elinor, a characteristic she's deliberately cultivated rather than sought to curb.

Indeed, what Austen blames Marianne for is her refusal to make an effort—it is *not* for being depressed or inherently thin-skinned. We know today that depression can be so totally incapacitating that it renders a person incapable of doing anything to help himself, but this wasn't known in Austen's day. And so Austen interprets Marianne's lack of effort as a moral failing rather than a psychological affliction. However, readers in our own time can view Austen's judgment as one of those strange but not unusual moments when an author's intention doesn't necessarily prevail in her writing. However judgmental Austen might have been about Marianne, and however much she wanted to punish her character and teach her readers the value of behaving well and staying motivated, she portrays the course of Marianne's depres-sion with a clinical accuracy that garners our sympathy.

I suspect that this might have been true for Austen's first readers as well as for us, despite their lack of knowledge about psychology. In a highly appreciative review of Austen's work, the novelist Sir Walter Scott takes Austen to task for her negative opinion of Marianne's romance, viewing this heroine as far less culpable than Austen likely intended: "Who is it, that in his youth has felt a virtuous attachment, however romantic or however unfortunate, but can trace back to its influence much that his character may possess of what is honourable, dignified, and disinterested? . . . [They] are neither less wise nor less worthy members of society for having felt, for a time, the influence of a passion which has been well qualified as the 'tenderest, noblest and best.'" In writing her novel, Austen's wisdom about human nature exceeded her conscious morality.

Even if Austen blames Marianne more than we and Scott do, she clearly shows that Marianne is suffering and debilitated and that Elinor provides a healing relationship and environment for her sister. Elinor offers a "safe space," as it's called by therapists. When Marianne is at her lowest, Elinor protects her from well-meant offers of help and from the predatory voyeurs who thrive on gossip about the suffering of others. She provides the peace and quiet, the "holding environment" (another therapeutic term), so necessary for the processing of difficult emotions and experiences.

Elinor's quiet strength and anticipation of Marianne's needs further convey empathy, a crucial aspect of the therapeutic alliance. Empathy includes both cognitive understanding and emotional resonance, being in sync in terms of emotional state. Resonance alone is often comforting because it sends the message that our feelings are recognized; most of us need this kind of validation. Empathy amplifies this point, extending fellowship in cognitive as well as emotional terms, conveying that someone else can take our perspective; this too is tremendously validating. In short, empathy sends the message that our problems are real and that we don't have to face them alone. Even good times are made better when shared with people we care about who "empathize" with our happiness. It's a feature of our humanity to want to know that we're recognized in the minds and hearts of others.

Elinor's empathy informs her care of Marianne throughout the course of the depression. Here's one instance of Elinor's behavior that shows her understanding and affirmation of Marianne's pain. This is shortly after Marianne has received Willoughby's letter, ending their relationship:

> Elinor . . . returned to Marianne, whom she found attempting to rise from the bed, and whom she reached just in time to prevent her from falling on the floor, faint and giddy from a long want of proper rest and food . . . A glass of wine, which Elinor procured for her directly, made her more comfortable, and she was at last able to express some sense of her kindness, by saying, "Poor Elinor! how unhappy I make you!"

The glass of wine, given in the privacy of the sisters' room, speaks of Elinor's concern and understanding. And Marianne's observation that Elinor is unhappy on her behalf shows that she recognizes

134

the significance of this interaction, that it's registered as empathy. Marianne knows that Elinor understands and resonates with her own unhappiness.

The therapeutic safe space provides the time and opportunity for Marianne to go through her ordeal in peace and eventually resolve her crisis. This involves dwelling on her sorrow, at least to begin with. Although Austen might have disapproved of Marianne's stasis, she shows that it's an important part of the process of recovery. Psychologists Paul Andrews and J. Anderson Thomson, Jr. argue that the "persistent rumination," the obsessive focus that accompanies many depressions (certainly Marianne's), has an important purpose; it allows for the "slow, sustained processing" that's essential to solving major problems.

Rumination and depression can continue for a long time. But ideally, a person gradually begins to emerge, and she can begin to process the experiences that sparked the depression. This means being able to put her story into a narrative with a beginning, a middle, and an end. And it means recalling not only events, but also the emotions that accompanied them. If the experience can be placed within a finite narrative that encompasses events and feelings, it becomes possible to move on and heal. This is equally important for healing from trauma, a secondary aspect of Marianne's condition. With severe depression and trauma, upsetting events feel timeless; Marianne experiences the pain of her rejection as if it will be her emotional reality forever. Narratives provide closure.

Telling the story to an empathetic, supportive, and objective person works magic much of the time. In terms of the brain, telling the full story in this context to someone who can help us make sense of events, enables neural integration, what psychiatrist Daniel Siegel calls "the free flow of energy and information throughout the brain." The more "integrated" our brains are, the more that different areas communicate with one another so that the brain functions as a whole, the more options we have for responding in the best way possible. To put this in terms of dynamic systems theory, integration allows us to increase complexity, and so to be able to respond flexibly and thoughtfully to situations. Hence the healing that often accompanies something as seemingly simple as talking to someone, and how valuable it can be to have someone you know is empathetic, who doesn't necessarily give advice but simply listens.

We can think of many maladaptive reactions, responses that are inappropriate or detract from our well-being, as failures of neural integration—the result of parts of the brain not working together either because they're inaccessible to, or in conflict with, one another. A word that describes this segmentation is *dissociation*. Depression, trauma, denial, and many other conditions involve dissociation, and the result is that dysregulated emotional responses take over. Cognitive inputs that might modify such negative reactions are off-line. This state of affairs also characterizes automatic responses such as losing your temper or being excessively anxious, which also exemplify dysregulated emotion.

Much of the work of psychotherapy involves increasing neural integration in the brain through work done with the mind, and in some forms of therapy, the body as well. To overwrite bad patterns, whether they're all-encompassing, as in depression and trauma; somewhat incapacitating, as in denial; or they constitute habitual, automatic ways of responding, such as Marianne's tendency to react before thinking (a characteristic we see well before her encounter with Willoughby at the ball), improvement means the integration of emotion with cognition. Higher cortical cognitive areas can provide crucial information that makes a difference to how we respond, and they're also connected with regulatory areas, especially the OFC, that can send the safety message that will stop negative stress responses.

Neural integration is an aspect of the success of all therapies that improve mental health and well-being. "Telling the story," as we do in most therapies, facilitates neural integration because it demands that emotional and cognitive, right and left, lower and higher areas of the brain work together. Even when parts of the story are inaccessible to consciousness, as with memories from infancy or early childhood, clues as to what must have happened can be found in later events, or even in the nature of the client's responses in the present day, so that the story can be told. By "telling the story," the client ideally reshapes it, so that she eventually tells a narrative of healing and resilience rather than of injury and hopelessness. If you asked Marianne to tell her life's story while she was depressed, her response (if she would deign to talk to you in the first place) would differ greatly from her narrative of events after she's become Mrs. Brandon.

However, the *whole* story must be told in order for narratives to be therapeutic, and this means telling of events and feelings in the past, along with commentary by the present-day self—again including feelings—who looks back at past events. An outline of the facts from a detached, impassive, dissociated narrator will not have the therapeutic value of integrating various parts of our brains and selves. And it means telling the story to someone who can empathize and help to reduce our distress.

I believe that the demands of narrative account for one reason reading novels is so gratifying—they involve our whole minds and brains. This feeling of being completely absorbed and present during an activity is known as "flow," and it pertains to all sorts of activities in addition to reading Austen and other all-consuming novelists. Flow days are glory days for writers! Flow is the essence of mindfulness and meditation.

Marianne eventually tells her story to Elinor in terms that show that she has been processing her experience in ways that have helped to heal, to make her mind whole again. She demonstrates that her thinking self (cognition) has begun to influence her reactive, feeling self. As you know, reason cannot suppress or resolve Marianne's turbulent feelings, but it can give her access to other, more productive feelings. She tells Elinor, "My illness has made me think. It has given me leisure and calmness for serious recollection. Long before I was enough recovered to talk, I was perfectly able to reflect." Although Marianne doesn't tell her story during a fifty-minute hour, Elinor's knowledge of her situation and calm presence provide a therapeutic environment in a less structured manner. As in therapy, Marianne first endures, and then begins to process her experience.

Marianne's story is not the one readers might be inclined to tell about her; like Elizabeth in *Pride and Prejudice*, she's far too hard on herself, accepting total responsibility for a situation that's only partly her fault: "I considered the past; I saw in my behaviour since the beginning of our acquaintance with him [Willoughby] last autumn, nothing but a series of imprudence towards myself, and want of kindness to others." Marianne doesn't consider the involuntary nature of her distress, or the huge part that Willoughby played in events. But what's crucial to her healing is that she tells the story in the right way, recognizing her emotions in the past and present. She's thinking about events rather than moving through them. She no longer inhabits a timeless no-man's-land of emotional pain.

ARE YOU MY MOTHER?

Therapy further provides a venue for practicing healthy relationships through transference, one of psychotherapy's most famous concepts. Transference basically means relating to someone in the present as you did to someone in the past. For instance, a client who distrusted authority figures might initially distrust the therapist. Transference allows a client to "redo" relationships, forming different patterns of response. At the neurological level, new and better habitual neural patterns, attractor states, overwrite older maladaptive ones.

Marianne's transference involves "revising" her relationship with her mother. We don't have a narrative of Marianne's childhood, but Mrs. Dashwood's behavior in the present indicates patterns that likely prevailed in the past. I'm inferring past events from present ones, but this is what often goes on in psychotherapy. It is widely accepted today that transference involves the kind of corrective attachment experience that enables a client to create new patterns of relating, as well as altering negative patterns of thought and feeling.

Children need emotional resonance from parents. Resonance means attuning to emotions, being on the same wavelength, as we say. This is crucial to developing social intelligence, including the capacity for emotional regulation (this is the topic of a future chapter). Parental attunement signals both validation and support, saying that you have a right to your feelings and that you're not alone with them.

But for resonance to be effective, it has to be true attunement, not emotional contagion. When a therapist resonates with a client's feelings, she shows the client that she understands such feelings viscerally, in the gut and not just cognitively. But she must maintain the distinction between understanding a feeling and experiencing it firsthand. Entering fully into another's feelings without critical distance ceases to be resonance and becomes emotional contagion. A therapist who's overwhelmed by a patient's distress fails to maintain boundaries. This doesn't help anyone.

A therapist must also maintain cognitive distance, taking the perspective of the client while maintaining her own point of view. She does this in terms of thoughts as well as feelings, and at this point, resonance becomes empathy, full-blown perspective taking. Failure to do this, assimilating another person's point of view cognitively as well as emotionally, is known as introjection. It's useless, and quite often harmful.

In order to comfort children, parents and caregivers also need to maintain boundaries, to resonate and take the child's perspective rather than introjecting the child's experience and feeling it as their own. Older children need empathy as well as resonance; they need to know that the caregiver *understands* what they're thinking and feeling, as well as attuning to emotions. As we've seen, Elinor takes Marianne's perspective both cognitively and emotionally. She resonates with Marianne's distress without taking it on as her own. Marianne understands this, that her sister intuits the pain she's in without being overwhelmed by it. Elinor similarly understands Marianne's thoughts—her sense of disbelief and betrayal—without feeling personally wronged.

We see the failure to take Marianne's perspective in a well-regulated and helpful way with Mrs. Dashwood, who tends to respond with contagion and introjection rather than empathy. This is especially true in her relationship with Marianne, the daughter who is most like her. (Readers have long noticed that Marianne and Mrs. Dashwood are alike, that they tend to have similar responses to experience.) This means that Mrs. Dashwood enters into Marianne's feelings and viewpoint wholeheartedly, that she doesn't maintain the distance needed for conveying empathy. Notably, this applies to her response to Marianne's relationship with Willoughby.

After Willoughby's hasty and uncomfortable visit to the Dashwoods to say that he's leaving Devonshire (where they live), Mrs. Dashwood retires in private for a while, returning with the signs of her emotion obvious: "Mrs. Dashwood felt too much for speech, and instantly quitted the parlour to give way in solitude to the concern and alarm which this sudden departure occasioned . . . In about half an hour . . .

[she] returned, and . . . her eyes were red." Certainly, Mrs. Dashwood is fond of Willoughby, and it would be appropriate for her to be disconcerted on Marianne's behalf, but her behavior clearly shows that she's almost as overwhelmed as Marianne herself, and thus not in a position to help her distraught daughter.

In contrast, Elinor, who's also fond of Willoughby and worried about her sister, keeps her distance and responds with thought as well as feeling—tempered feeling, appropriate to the situation. Elinor wonders why Willoughby has gone so suddenly, and with no intention of returning, as he's made clear. Elinor detects warning signs, things that don't make sense if Willoughby is sincere and on the level. She doesn't know how to explain Willoughby's strange behavior, but she believes that "suspicion of something unpleasant is the inevitable consequence of such alteration as we have just witnessed in him."

Mrs. Dashwood criticizes Elinor for such thoughts, arguing that Willoughby might have reasons for secrecy about his relationship with Marianne, which she's certain is an engagement. She doesn't suspect Willoughby of betrayal, nor have concerns about his devotion. Mrs. Dashwood dismisses Elinor's doubts and vehemently defends Willoughby against all of Elinor's accurate suspicions:

> Oh! Elinor, how incomprehensible are your feelings! You had rather take evil upon credit than good. You had rather look out for misery for Marianne, and guilt for poor Willoughby, than an apology for the latter. You are resolved to think him blameable, because he took leave of us with less affection than his usual behaviour has shewn. And is no allowance to be made for inadvertence, or for spirits depressed by recent disappointment? Are no probabilities to be accepted, merely because they are not certainties? Is nothing due to the man whom we have all so much reason to love, and no reason in the world to think ill of?

This is Marianne's perspective as well. She might be upset at Willoughby's departure, but she doesn't suspect him of treachery. Even after his villainy is clear to all, she still believes that he's behaving oddly because someone must have maligned her to him. Only the letter makes her see the light. Like Marianne, Mrs. Dashwood defends Willoughby until his behavior is clearly indefensible.

In short, Mrs. Dashwood takes Marianne's viewpoint and experiences all of Marianne's emotions uncritically. She grieves, trusts, and hopes almost as intensely as Marianne. She shares her daughter's thoughts and feelings—catches them, if you will—instead of empathizing with them.

The effect of this is to make things worse rather than to provide comfort. After Willoughby leaves, Mrs. Dashwood enables Marianne's theatrical if genuine devastation, failing to set limits or encourage her to calm down. Not only does Mrs. Dashwood neglect her duty to inspire a more peaceful frame of mind for her daughter, but she actually encourages Marianne's distress by her full and uncritical participation in Marianne's feelings. Emotional contagion has this dysregulatory effect, for when people catch one another's emotions, this often leads to a spiral of intensifying feelings. Conversely, when someone empathizes but remains calm—is emotionally involved rather than emotionally overwhelmed—this induces a natural regulatory effect.

Empathy becomes Elinor's job. She understands her sister's feelings but maintains a critical distance, keeping both her own and Marianne's perspectives in view. She does what Mrs. Dashwood ought to have done, and actually takes on a maternal role. It's not accidental that Mrs. Dashwood is absent during Marianne's crisis in London. This makes it clear that Elinor is functioning as the stand-in for Mrs. Dashwood, psychologically as well as pragmatically. Elinor is older than Marianne by a few years, which also facilitates the transference. And indeed Marianne herself regresses to a child-like state of being during her depression, unable to get her own food, or interact with others, or follow the social rules expected of all but the very young.

The transference magnifies the healing effects of Elinor's empathy. As Elinor cares for Marianne, this patient/daughter/sister begins to experience the regulatory influence so missing from her real parent. By being in the care of a mother figure who calms her down rather than works her up, Marianne acquires the lessons in emotional regulation she missed as a child. Elinor's calming influence helps to teach

Marianne to deal with her destructive emotions; the same is true of the relationship between therapist and client, and it should be the dynamic between caregiver and child. Much of this influence happens subliminally. An increased capacity for regulation is instilled simply by being with someone who remains calm, available, and empathetic in the face of one's own turbulent emotions. Elinor helps Marianne just by being herself.

A similar process occurs in therapy. Brain as well as mind is crucial in this respect. When the client is sad, or stressed, or withdrawn, the therapist resonates with this mood but then offers an alternative to the downward spiral by remaining tranquil and regulated. The client subliminally perceives this regulatory force by picking up on social signals, right brain to right brain, and then begins to respond by regulating her own emotions. Emotional resonance, or mood matching, right brain to right brain, gradually and subliminally teaches emotional regulation by inducing the client to habitually regulate rather than escalate strong negative feelings. This is also how we regulate one another outside the therapeutic relationship, and how caregivers regulate the emotions of babies and children.

This might sound mystical but it's scientifically sound. We read emotional signals with our right brains, and we are, as a species, very susceptible to catching one another's emotions. Just as Marianne "caught" her mother's dysregulated feelings (and vice versa), so Marianne absorbs Elinor's serenity. Such influence forms different habits of response and of relating to others at the level of mind, new attractor patterns in terms of the brain.

In a more overt manner, Elinor helps Marianne by suggesting alternative ways of thinking, feeling, and behaving. Therapists also do this, although not until the therapeutic alliance has been firmly established, and always by offering insights and sometimes suggestions—not orders. Elinor's comments are also indirect; she doesn't comment on Marianne's situation verbally, but her own behavior in a situation that's parallel models an alternative. She too has been abandoned by the man she loves, and although this isn't as obvious as it is in Marianne's case since Elinor keeps the secret of Edward's engagement for several months, Marianne knows at the very least that Elinor's beloved has not been behaving as a faithful suitor should.

When the engagement does become known, Marianne at first attributes Elinor's self-command to a lack of feeling. Elinor quickly corrects her sister, recounting the horrific ordeal of losing Edward, without even the comfort of being able to confide in anyone. She concludes, "If you can think me capable of ever feeling—surely you may suppose that I have suffered now." Marianne is instantly contrite: "How barbarous I have been to you!—you, who have been my only comfort, who have borne with me in all my misery, who have seemed to be only suffering for me! Is this my gratitude? Is this the only return I can make you? Because your merit cries out upon myself, I have been trying to do it away."

But guilt isn't the only effect of this knowledge; when Marianne begins to emerge from her depression, she has Elinor's example in mind. Rather than dwelling on her own misery, she determines to channel her energy differently: "As for Willoughby—to say that I shall soon or that I shall ever forget him, would be idle. His remembrance can be overcome by no change of circumstances or opinions. But it shall be regulated, it shall be checked by religion, by reason, by constant employment." This is Elinor's mode, and Marianne has obviously taken the example to heart. Marianne begins to view herself as more than the sum of a broken relationship.

Elinor also models a technique seen in one of the most popular forms of therapy today: cognitive behavioral therapy (CBT).[*] CBT involves training people to consciously replace negative thoughts with positive ones rather than focusing on the processing of experience, thought, and feeling as happens in more traditional (psychodynamic) talk therapy. Reason alone won't bring changes in habitual responses; you can't talk yourself out of a depression. But you *can* practice positive replacement thoughts, talking back to your own negativity with the goal of inducing different, more positive feelings.

This is the theory behind CBT, which provides training in replacing negative thoughts that bring destructive emotions and behavior in their wake, with positive and corrective statements. Of course,

---

*   Beth Lau analyzes *Sense and Sensibility* in terms of CBT in "Optimism and Pessimism: Approaching *Sense and Sensibility* Through Cognitive Therapy," *Persuasions: The Jane Austen Journal* 33 (2011), 40–52.

reframing, viewing one's situation differently, is an aspect of all successful psychotherapy. But CBT aims to achieve this goal by imposing such well-being through cognitive channels, rather than encouraging its development emotionally, as is the way with most talk therapy. It works "top down" rather than "bottom up."

Elinor teaches CBT by modeling such self-talk, recasting her situation in ways that make the best of a bad deal. She predicts that Edward will marry Lucy, and that she herself will meet another appropriate suitor because "after all that is bewitching in the idea of a single and constant attachment, and all that can be said of one's happiness depending entirely on any particular person, it is not meant—it is not fit—it is not possible that it should be so." We see Eleanor talking herself into this constructive attitude after she tells Marianne about Edward's secret engagement. She's reassuring Marianne, but her statements serve to convince herself as well:

> I would not have you suffer on my account; for I assure you I no longer suffer materially myself. I have many things to support me. I am not conscious of having provoked the disappointment by any imprudence of my own [ouch to Marianne!], I have borne it as much as possible without spreading it farther. I acquit Edward of all essential misconduct. I wish him very happy; and I am so sure of his always doing his duty that though now he may harbour some regret, in the end he must become so. Lucy does not want sense, and that is the foundation on which every thing good may be built.

Like a lot of people who engage in CBT scripts, Elinor says all this in an attempt to believe it. I leave it to Austen's readers to determine how successful she is! (Incidentally, such techniques of self-talk have trickled down to a general public today in much the same way as awareness of psychoanalytic categories did in the last century. (I find it fascinating to watch this kind of positive self-talk in action on Facebook, as people publicly talk themselves into better modes of thought and feeling.)

CBT is one of many new methods in the rapidly evolving world of psychotherapy. Many new therapies differ radically from traditional talk therapy (psychodynamic therapy), which relies heavily on insight in addition to the therapeutic alliance and other mechanisms. CBT claims to be able to bypass the need for insight altogether.

Some of these newer therapies that have proved highly successful involve the body as much as speech, or even primarily the body. Take Eye Movement Desensitization and Reprocessing (EMDR), which uses eye movements or tapping, and is believed to help people heal from trauma by integrating right- and left-brain experiences. Traumatic memories, involving such reactions as panic and fear, are thought to be stored primarily in the circuits of right-brain areas. As noted, processing them so that their power is curbed means integrating them with left-brain activity. It is believed that EMDR takes a shortcut to neural integration by having a client look right and left (or to do the same with tapping), while remembering and speaking about the traumatic event; this appears to help integrate parts of the experience, such as cognitive (left-brain input) and emotional (right-brain input), that had been dissociated.

That such a mechanical process can work transformations within the mind is a potent reminder of the physicality of all our thought processes, and of what it means to have a mind-brain. Recall that Siegel defines the mind as consisting of our brains, bodies, and relationships—our interactions with other minds. The mind is neurological, physiological, and relational. These are the three elements that interact to create the dynamic system that constitutes our minds.

They're also the three elements involved in any effective therapy. While talk therapy might not be as obviously physiological as more body-focused therapies, responses during sessions are registered in the body as well as the brain; this is automatic. All psychotherapies involve changing our bodily and neurological responses (brain and body) by using the therapeutic alliance (relationship).

Another example of a promising therapy that addresses all the aspects of mind is Accelerated Experiential Dynamic Psychotherapy (AEDP). This works largely by putting a person in touch with "core affects," the essence of how they really feel, thereby connecting the cognitive observing self with the feeling reactive self, including bodily reactions, in the context of an empathetic therapeutic relationship. This facilitates health and change, even when it forces a confrontation with negative feelings. Progress occurs in leaps and bounds rather than baby steps.

Psychotherapy shows that changing your mind in substantial ways involves addressing all the mind's different facets. This happens in everyday life as well, often through the magic of our loving connections with others (the relationship aspect of mind). When Elinor finds Marianne in her room, debilitated with grief, she brings her sister a glass of wine, not the treatment of choice for our puritanical, anti-substance era, but often an effective stimulant. She tends to her sister's weakened physical condition (her body), and her depression (brain, the neurological processing of physiological, cognitive, and emotional signals), showing her love through her attention and care (relationship). Elinor comforts Marianne in many other instances as well, never flagging in her careful attention and care.

But even though new techniques such as CBT and EMDR have been successful, and many other newer kinds of therapy that differ from traditional talk therapy appear promising, they nevertheless all rely on the strength of the therapeutic relationship. Bessel van der Kolk, a leading expert in the treatment of trauma, stresses that relationships are crucial to the healing process. He particularly criticizes the use of CBT without an emphasis on the therapeutic alliance by pointing out that cognition alone is inadequate to treating conditions like trauma or depression. Without a strong therapeutic alliance, many people fail to believe a word of their chosen mantras.

The therapeutic relationship can help a depressed or traumatized person to stay connected to at least one other person, providing an escape from the often relentless solitude and misery of these conditions. It might enable a person to endure until her condition improves. Even at her very worst, Marianne still cares deeply for Elinor and can rouse herself to express this care, as we see at a social gathering, when Marianne is at the nadir of her depression. Elinor's sister-in-law Fanny Dashwood compliments Elinor's artwork. Then fearing she's been too kind (Fanny isn't a kind person), she compares it to another young lady's paintings, on which she lavishes much greater praise. Marianne is indignant: ". . . such ill-timed praise of another, at Elinor's expense . . . provoked her immediately to say with warmth, 'This is admiration of a very particular kind!—what is Miss Morton to us?—who knows or cares, for her?—it is Elinor of whom *we* think and speak."

This is the first sign of interest in anyone that Marianne has expressed for many weeks. It suggests that her love for her family, especially for Elinor, will provide her with a way back to health by reminding her that she can care for others besides Willoughby, and that there are better ways of loving than the desperate hunger she feels for him.

Marianne nearly dies from the aftereffects of a relationship, which led her to stop caring about her health and even her life. Her reawakening to the many other important connections in her life, especially her connection to Elinor, rescues her from her depression and reconnects her with the living. She begins to process and integrate feelings that had been overwhelming. She thinks—thinks hard—rather than merely reacting. She gains insight about herself and what's happened, weaving her experiences into a narrative that looks to the past and the future. In the words of Daniel Siegel, she moves from being "the passive victim of trauma to the active author of the ongoing story of . . . her life.* At the nuts-and-bolts level of the brain, this process brings analytical left-brain, cortical processes to bear on right-brain, subcortical emotional processes, creating new neural pathways that allow for greater cognitive and emotional flexibility. Marianne is able to come to this empowering resolution of a bad experience largely because of Elinor's love and protection. Elinor provides the therapeutic environment—the empathy, safety, transference, and constructive thought—that enables Marianne to heal.

---

*   Siegel, *Developing Mind*, 53.

SIX

The Map of Love

TOO CLOSE FOR COMFORT?

J ane Austen writes about incest. Well, almost. She doesn't exactly
write about incest per se, but she certainly flirts with the topic.
Take Emma. She marries a man old enough to be her father. To
be sure, this wasn't all that unusual in the nineteenth century; men
and women of the middle and upper-middle classes often married late
due to financial considerations. Edmund of *Mansfield Park* can't marry
until he has a way to support himself; ditto for Edward of *Sense and
Sensibility*. Although Edward is engaged to Lucy—who fortunately jilts
him—many men postponed courtships as well as marriage until they
were financially stable. At that point, they could look to a marriage
pool that included younger women in addition to their contemporaries.
And given the high mortality rates for childbirth, men often married

more than once, and the second marriage was often to a younger woman. Many bridegrooms were therefore significantly older than their brides.

And why not? It was a buyer's market for financially stable men, and youth was no less attractive in the nineteenth century than it is today. But for a woman living in a small community, as do most of Austen's heroines, the chances of meeting and marrying the man of their dreams, or any eligible partner, were slim; think of how many available bachelors are actually residents of her villages. It was less of a long shot if her family was wealthy enough to spend part of the year in London, where the marriage pool was larger, or if she was willing have low standards for an acceptable partner à la Charlotte Lucas. (Of these heroines, only Emma marries someone from her own village, but even she realizes that Frank Churchill, an outsider, is the obvious choice of a partner for her.)

That's why Austen's heroines get their chance when their community changes; either they leave their small villages or an unexpected visitor arrives. The excitement over Darcy and Bingley at the Meryton ball might have been tactless and obnoxious, but in light of demographics, we can understand it nevertheless. We hear of no other eligible bachelors within the Meryton community throughout *Pride and Prejudice*. Even Mr. Collins's insufferable expectations of success with Elizabeth make a bit more sense in this context.

So marriages between older men who'd had a chance to establish themselves financially and younger women waiting to be asked were not in and of themselves bizarre. People didn't look at such couples and think, as we often do in pop-psychology fashion today, *She must need a father figure in her life* or *He needs to date younger women because he's scared of getting old*. Austen's brushes with incest lie in the psychological quality of the relationships she portrays rather than in the ages of her characters.

This is true of her first major novel, *Northanger Abbey*, in which Henry Tilney behaves like Catherine's older brother rather than a lover (he's twenty-six, and she's eighteen when he proposes); he definitely has the upper hand in their relationship, and he feels himself Catherine's superior in terms of intellect and experience. Catherine acknowledges this superiority and is indeed dazzled by it. The dynamic of guide and guru, brother and sister, father and daughter, explains their attraction. She's starstruck, he's flattered, and that's enough to begin a romance.

In *Sense and Sensibility* incest shadows the relationship between Marianne and Colonel Brandon in various ways. Early on in the novel, the colonel confesses to Elinor that as a young man, he was in love with a young woman named Eliza, one of "[my] nearest relations, an orphan from her infancy, and under the guardianship of my father. Our ages were nearly the same, and from our earliest years, we were playfellows and friends. I cannot remember the time when I did not love Eliza." That these two were not only blood relatives but also raised together from infancy suggests multiple sources for the taint of incest.

But their marriage was not to be; Colonel Brandon's father insisted that Eliza marry his eldest son so that her fortune would go to the heir to the family property. Trapped in this loveless marriage with Colonel Brandon's brother, Eliza succumbed to a seducer and was exiled from polite society as a result. It was a truism in Austen's era that entering a loveless marriage would make a woman more vulnerable to seduction. We find this belief over and over again in novels of the period; we see it again in Austen's *Mansfield Park*. Colonel Brandon learned about the disgrace of his beloved on returning to England—heartbroken, he had fled to avoid reminders of their unhappy separation. He supports her illegitimate child, also named Eliza, who's later seduced by Willoughby.

The "incest" here is not only in Eliza's relationships with the brothers but also in Marianne's subsequent marriage to Colonel Brandon, and not only because he's old enough to be her father. When Colonel Brandon shares this personal history with Elinor, he refers to Eliza as "a lady he had once known . . . resembling, in some measure, your sister Marianne." So Marianne is associated with his pseudo sister Eliza in Colonel Brandon's mind (and so for Austen's readers as well).

Moreover, Colonel Brandon has also acted as a father to Eliza's child, also named Eliza, and that child has recently been seduced by Willoughby, Marianne's beloved. So Marianne is again a stand-in for a close relative, in this case, Colonel Brandon's "daughter," adopted in psychological and financial, if not legal, terms. The incest factor occurs through a series of symbolic replacements: Marianne stands in for both of the Elizas, mother (Brandon's beloved "sister") and daughter (we might think of this as incest twice removed). In psychological terms, Colonel Brandon has a paternal relationship to Marianne, at least from her perspective. Their marriage provides her with the emotional security and consistency she needs. If you think about it too much, you might find yourself in the famous scene in Roman Polanski's great movie *Chinatown*, saying along with Faye Dunaway, "my sister, my daughter." But let's stay in Austen's world.

In *Emma*, when Mr. Knightley asks Emma to dance at a ball, she replies, "Indeed I will. You have shown that you can dance, and you know we are not really so much brother and sister as to make it at all improper." Emma refers to an in-law relationship—their siblings have married one another. In this context, her statement makes little sense since there were no laws or social taboos against two brothers from one family marrying two sisters from another. And dancing together was certainly allowed! The effect of Emma's odd comment is to evoke the idea of incest for the reader. Here as elsewhere, Austen deliberately calls attention to the familial nature, either literal or psychological, of a romance.

But we're more likely to think of Mr. Knightley as a pseudo-father than brother. For not only is he twice Emma's age, but throughout Emma's life, he has consistently provided the guidance and the tough love that was lacking on the part of her own ineffective parent. When Mr. Knightley scolds Emma at Box Hill for insulting poor Miss Bates, he's very much in parental mode, and we see this at other times as well. In retrospect, you might say that he's had a hand in creating the woman he loves, molding Emma's character to make her a suitable wife. A psychotherapist might say that he means to do this subconsciously; we can guess that Mr. Knightley had been attracted to Emma long before he considered doing anything about this.

Yet, despite this *parental* element in Austen's relationships, especially that of Emma and Mr. Knightley, Austen might have been criticizing *paternalistic* views about female education, a popular topic in novels of her day. In particular, in 1762, the French philosopher Jean-Jacques Rousseau published a novel, *Émile*, in which an educator tries to mold a woman into the perfect wife for his protégé, Émile. This young man has been given an ideal education (in Rousseau's terms, anyway), attuned to nature rather than corrupted by civilization. Austen would have had many reasons for disliking this novel, foremost among them Rousseau's sexist ideas about women. I believe she was indirectly addressing Émile in *Emma*—talking back to Rousseau—by saying that if you want to "educate" a woman to be a proper spouse, the only way to accomplish this task that isn't completely absurd is through friendship and advice of the kind Mr. Knightley offers, and even then, his readiness to comment reveals an element of condescension. Mr. Knightley eventually apologizes for his behavior, for his sense of entitlement to criticize and comment on Emma's conduct, revealing a self-consciousness about his privilege that makes him worthy of Emma's love.

In *Mansfield Park*, Austen raises the issue of incest at the very beginning of the novel, when Mrs. Norris (Lady Bertram's sister) proposes to the Bertrams that they take Fanny into their household. Sir Thomas worries that one of his sons might fall in love with this young cousin. As a poor relation from a downwardly mobile branch of the family, Fanny was considered completely unsuitable as a daughter-in-law by the status- and money-conscious Sir Thomas. So keen is he to have his children marry money that even when he realizes that something is lacking in his daughter Maria's feelings for Rushworth, he chooses to look the other way. It's not surprising that he voices fears about the dangers of allowing Fanny to join their family.

Mrs. Norris reassures him: "You are thinking of your sons—but do not you know that of all things upon earth *that* [a marriage between Fanny and one of the sons] is the least likely to happen; brought up, as they would be, always together like brothers and sisters. It is morally impossible" While Mrs. Norris isn't usually a reliable source of information, she's right on this point: Being raised as brother and sister would tend to prevent romantic feelings for many people. (Of course, this isn't always the case, even for actual brothers and sisters.) As you know, Mrs. Norris is wrong, and the cousins do eventually marry.

Biological as well as social closeness is also a factor. Fanny and Edmund are first cousins, and while marriage between such close relatives was legal and socially acceptable in England in the nineteenth century, it borders sufficiently on incest to be controversial if not outlawed in many English-speaking places both today and in the past; it was actually forbidden in England until the sixteenth century. In any case, Fanny and Edmund are very close in terms of bloodlines, regardless of legality.

We're also continually reminded of the fraternal nature of the couple's relationship, at least on Edmund's part, by the way he relates to Fanny throughout the novel. He mentors Fanny, much as an older brother would guide a beloved younger sister. Austen overtly calls attention to the familial aspects of this relationship by equating Edmund with Fanny's brother William: "She loved him better than any body in the world except William; her heart was divided between the two."

Indeed, it well might be that Edmund marries Fanny on the basis of these brotherly feelings, for we never actually see a transformation in his attitude toward her—and this is a novel in which the various lovers' thoughts and feelings are conveyed very clearly by the narrator and by the characters themselves. So when we're told that Edmund learned "to prefer soft light eyes [Fanny's] to sparkling dark ones [Mary's]," we have to assume either that he's decided that the feelings he has for Fanny are a sufficient ground for a successful marriage, or that he's developed romantic feelings for his cousin.

At this point, the novel goes into interactive-fiction mode: Write your own ending. I vote for the first. I believe that Austen's omission of the full story is quite deliberate, for she was certainly capable of showing us how relationships might undergo sea changes—witness Elizabeth and Darcy. The effect of Austen's withholding is to leave us with the image of Edmund as older brother, and the relationship as characterized above all by fraternal feelings—again, at least on his part. But you still have the option of thinking that he falls for Fanny romantically, if that's what you want to do.

CULTURAL PRESSURES AND INNATE SYSTEMS

Four of Austen's six major novels feature pseudo-incestuous lovers, and although *Pride and Prejudice* doesn't flirt with incest, it still features a partner, Elizabeth, who feels deep affection rather than romantic love. But suddenly in *Persuasion*, Austen's last completed novel, she drops the subject of incest altogether and writes the most romantic of all her stories. Why did Austen champion domesticated love (with some relationships almost too close for comfort), and then abandon the topic when she wrote *Persuasion*?

This has everything to do with the kinds of relationships she wants to endorse for her young female readers. Austen's hints of incest act as shorthand to suggest that the kind of steady affection and care we tend to have for family members is a suitable basis for marriage. In *Mansfield Park*, by showing that Fanny is *like* a sister to Edmund in several literal ways (close cousin, raised with Edmund), Austen underscores Edmund's brotherly feelings for her.

Austen wasn't alone in having such an agenda: Many novels as well as the conduct books (advice literature) of her time attempt to counter the idealization of romance found in so much of literature—equivalent to the idealization of romance in chick lit and Hollywood today. Many thought that a belief in romance could be dangerous, leading young women to have unrealistic expectations about love and marriage. This is a point still made everywhere today, from serious books about psychology to women's magazines. It would have been even more necessary to stress this in Austen's day when marriage was an economic necessity for women. But novel readers, on the whole, tend to want passion rather than staid affection to triumph.

Perhaps only a writer as skillful as Austen could have gotten away with this, writing novels so compelling that we don't miss the absence of romance for some characters. In *Pride and Prejudice*, Darcy's rescue of Lydia, which saves the entire Bennet family from degradation, is so dramatic that we barely notice that Elizabeth hasn't actually fallen in love in the way we usually think of this experience. Movie versions of the book certainly ignore this point. Anyway, Darcy has enough romance for both of them, and what gives us our thrill is their finally seeing through their pride (and prejudice) to realize that they are perfect for each other.

By the time she wrote *Persuasion*, Austen was in a different frame of mind, and in this novel, she champions romance and feeling above other motivations for marriage. Yet, even though she'd shifted her emphasis, she didn't betray her principles. Although Austen thought that staid forms of affection were a firm foundation for marriage, and she stresses this in her novels, romantic love, passionate and often overwhelming, still rules many hearts and happy endings throughout her work. Elizabeth might feel deep affection and admiration for Darcy, but he's bonkers for her. Fanny might have fraternal feelings for Edmund, but she also has passionate yearnings, complete with the jealousy and agony that so often accompany romantic love. Marianne might end up with a stable but satisfying marriage to Colonel Brandon, but Elinor marries the man she's hopelessly (literally, for much of the novel) in love with.

Defining different types of love has been a persistent theme in Western literature, beginning at least as early as Plato's *Symposium* (385–370 B.C.E.). These two options, romantic love and attachment love, are found in the works of countless other authors as well as in Austen's novels. Sometimes a choice between kinds of love is shown, as in *Mansfield Park*: Should Edmund marry Fanny (attachment) or Mary (romance)? Or let's go further back, to the Knights of the Round Table: Guinevere loves King Arthur (attachment) but can't resist Lancelot (romance). (And it definitely doesn't end happily for anyone when she gives in to her passions—the moral of many an English novel as well.) Often, literary works dwell exclusively on one or the other of these types of feeling, with romantic love garnering the most attention. As literary critic Patrick Hogan has demonstrated, the archetypical plot of thwarted romantic love, including narratives in which obstacles are overcome is a narrative universal.

The mind-brain sciences shed light on why Austen and so many others keep returning to these particular kinds of feeling, and why they're often portrayed as distinct choices. The representation of feeling across situations, characters, authors, and cultures remains consistent because romantic love and attachment love are ingrained in the physiology of our brains. They correspond, respectively, to bio-psycho-social systems that have the force of drives.

TENDER LOVING CARE: THE ATTACHMENT SYSTEM

Austen would have found an important literary precedent for the kind of companionable, "familial," love she portrays in a famous French novel of the seventeenth century, *Clélie*, by Madeleine de Scudéry. We know that Austen was familiar with *Clélie*, which isn't surprising given her interest in novels and the popularity of this work in England as well as France. She probably read it in the original because most educated women of her class learned French. And she would have had plenty of opportunity to practice her language skills with her older cousin, Eliza de Feuillide, who married into a French aristocratic family. Eliza was a frequent family visitor in the Austen household during Jane's childhood and again later, when she returned to England to flee the turmoil of the French Revolution. (Eliza's husband, however, was guillotined.) But Austen needn't have known French at all since these popular novels were translated into English soon after publication.

There was plenty of adventure in *Clélie*, a ten-volume novel published in installments from 1654 to 1660. But what really caught the devotion of the reading public were its discussions about love, in which characters analyze the traits and challenges of intimate relationships. The most important of these conversations is accompanied by "the map of tenderness" (*"la carte de la tendre"*), a real map of an imaginary land called Tenderness. This was a brilliant marketing ploy, the ancestor of board games like Monopoly, and it was almost as popular, inspiring many imitations and parodies. The map accompanies a famous scene in which the novel's heroine, Plotine, offers instructions on how to gain the love and trust of a good woman by interpreting the symbolism of the map (an early visual teaching aid).

The goal of relationships, as explained by Plotine, isn't necessarily marriage or sexual consummation, but the achievement of a quality called "tenderness," represented by several destinations on the map. For instance, Pretty Verse and Sincerity are en route to a town called Tenderness on the River. But if you take a wrong turn to Negligence, you're on the way to Obliteration, losing your beloved friend or lover. The final destinations are Tenderness-on-Gratitude and Tenderness-on-Esteem. Ring a bell? These are Elizabeth's motives for marrying Darcy. As the narrator tells us: "If gratitude and esteem are good foundations of affection, Elizabeth's change of sentiment will be neither improbable nor faulty." By the time Elizabeth becomes engaged to Darcy, she certainly feels tenderness for him.

Tenderness is a caring response to another person. It isn't necessarily sexual, although it can accompany other sexual aspects of a relationship. Plotine says,

> To define what tenderness means, I think it has to do with a certain sensitivity of the heart, which makes certain people sincere, passionate, and empathetic in their friendships. They feel all the griefs and joys of those they love. It makes them devoted to and supportive of their friends. It is tenderness that makes them prefer to condole with a friend in need rather than go out and have fun. Friends who feel tenderness are also willing to go to great lengths to help one another. They are forgiving of one another's faults. Tender friends trust one another. In effect, it is tenderness alone that gives joy and a particular closeness to friendship without all the chaos that can accompany romantic love, although it resembles such love in many ways.

In short, tenderness refers to a loving, bonded connection with another person. It involves devotion and is grounded in empathy. It can inform a variety of types of relationships, close friendships as well as intimate partnerships. Tenderness applies to the kinds of relationships that form our support systems, our connections with people to whom we turn to in times of need or distress. Plotine might well have been describing the relationship between Edmund and Fanny, which is "tender" right from the start.

Tenderness, or "attachment love" as I'm going to call it, is a mode of feeling that the mind-brain sciences have also recognized and mapped, not onto paper but within the neural circuits of the brain. It's governed by the attachment system, one of three systems that motivate us to form close relationships. The other two systems are the seeking system (responsible for romantic love) and the sexual system. The attachment system orchestrates caring, affectionate, and companionable connections with others. Attachment relationships are also the kinds of relationships that form our support systems, the people whom we turn to in times of need or distress.

All three systems involve all levels of the brain, from our lowest brainstem areas in charge of automatic processes such as breathing, to the prefrontal cortex, which orchestrates our higher executive powers, including judgment and self-awareness. Emotion-processing areas are especially important to these systems. They're also connected to the brain's reward circuits, those areas that activate when we have pleasurable thoughts, sensations, or experiences, and they involve the release of endorphins (a contraction of *endogenous* and *morphine*), the brain's natural opioids, feel-good, pain-killing neurochemicals. Although these systems express themselves in complex ways in humans—indeed, this is the stuff of literature—they're found in other mammals as well.

The primary bonding neurochemical of the attachment system is oxytocin, also known as "the cuddle hormone." It's associated with females more than males because it's the hormone that induces maternal care. As many studies with animals demonstrate, oxytocin ensures that parents, especially mothers, will become attached to their children. For instance, an ewe ordinarily responds only to her own lambs. But if her brain is infused with oxytocin before introducing another ewe's lamb, she'll adopt it. Virgin female rats who are given oxytocin begin to care for rat pups, which doesn't happen ordinarily.

We haven't done experiments of this nature with humans for ethical reasons, but we do know that oxytocin is abundant during pregnancy and nursing. Oxytocin also induces the contractions of labor. That's why when a woman's labor isn't progressing quickly enough, doctors often administer oxytocin. It might well be that the link between oxytocin and labor evolved because oxytocin readies the mother for the nurturing work that lies ahead. But the cuddle hormone is also important to male bonding, especially with offspring.

The effects of oxytocin extend well beyond parental behavior. Oxytocin is the hormone of friendship as well as parenting. It generally fosters positive, nonerotic social connections for both men and women. Animal lovers will be glad—if unsurprised—to learn that when dogs gaze into their owner's eyes, oxytocin levels increase for both parties.

Oxytocin is also important in sexual responses. It's released during sexual arousal and surges during orgasm for both men and women. The association between oxytocin and both nurture and sexuality suggests that systems designed to govern attachment between parents and offspring might have evolved to bring couples together for mating, although the reverse might also be true, that sexual bonding led to bonding with offspring. In either case, bonding for intimate erotic partners and parental nurture are connected to one another in terms of biochemistry and evolution.

Another hormone, vasopressin, also contributes to attachment, especially in pair bonding for males. Oxytocin and vasopressin are made in the hypothalamus, the ovaries, and the testes, which points to their involvement in both sexual and reproductive functions. Both sexes process both neurochemicals, although the concentrations, timing, and key target areas differ in men and women. Oxytocin and vasopressin are chemically almost identical, differing by only two amino acids, but this makes a huge difference.

Vasopressin actually contributes to attachment in ways that might not be all that tender, generating mate guarding and aggression on the part of males toward other males who threaten sexual competition. Interestingly, vasopressin in females also appears to generate aggression, but in the service of protecting offspring rather than mate guarding or other versions of defending one's territory (one's land, status, possessions, etc.). To each their own!

Oxytocin and vasopressin are the chemical motivators not only for attachment but also for monogamy, as mind-brain scientists learned from studying prairie voles. The prairie vole would be just another nondescript rodent had it not achieved fame in neuroscientific circles for proving that oxytocin in females, and vasopressin in males, induces pair bonding. The prairie vole is one of the few monogamous species that exists (about three to five percent of all mammals are monogamous), and research has shown that oxytocin and vasopressin create the difference between happily "married" couples and their promiscuous relatives, the montane voles.

Bear in mind that the cultural definition of monogamy differs from its scientific, technical definition. In the latter sense, monogamy doesn't mean sexual exclusivity, but rather an emotional and social bond that results in living together and caring for offspring. It doesn't preclude copulation on the side when the opportunity presents itself. This definition might be more accurate than the social or religious definitions of monogamy to which we hold ourselves—or perhaps others—but that's another issue.

Prairie voles form pair bonds after mating. They don't fall in love with one another first, nor are they motivated to choose a mate out of affection or friendly feelings such as "gratitude and esteem," or even calculation. But like all mammals, they seek sexual contact, and sex activates the neurochemicals that lead to attachment and pair bonding. Studies of these animals show that when a female prairie vole has copulated with a suitor, she develops a preference for him that's accompanied by a fifty percent rise in the amount of oxytocin found in her brain. But with a hefty infusion of oxytocin into the brain, she'll pair bond even if mating hasn't taken place, which rarely happens in nature. Conversely, giving prairie voles antagonists that block absorption of attachment neurochemicals in crucial brain areas will prevent pair bonding.

Another neurotransmitter involved is dopamine, which is the key neurotransmitter in the circuitry of pleasure. Bonding occurs because of the joint release of dopamine and attachment neurochemicals in crucial brain areas that are part of *both* reward and attachment circuitry. Experiments with blocking either oxytocin/vasopressin or dopamine in prairie voles reveal the interdependence of the two systems for pair bonding.

The same is true for humans. This makes sense: Close bonds with others are pleasurable, whether you're a prairie vole, a dog, or a human.

Partners who bond and stay devoted to one another engage the attachment system, which is at the neurological core of all long-term, bonded relationships in which people care about one another and seek or provide support. For Elizabeth in *Pride and Prejudice*, feelings of attachment suffice to draw her to Darcy. But although Darcy certainly feels tenderness for Elizabeth, his feelings are much more intense. Both lovers want to be together, and they both love one another, but, to use a somewhat dated expression, "They're coming from different places." If we apply this expression quite literally to the brain, their desires are coming from different places, or at least from different areas of the brain. Darcy falls in love, and that involves a different system, with different neural circuits and a different combination of neurochemicals.

DESPERATELY SEEKING: ROMANTIC LOVE

Romantic love is what most of us probably think of as falling in love. It involves focusing on a special other. It's love in the mode of Romeo and Juliet, Lancelot and Guinevere, Bohe and Dihua, Layla and Majnun, Janie and Teacake, Ennis and Jack, Sabrina and Jorie—love so overpowering that it influences crucial life choices, sometimes leading to behaviors that are uncharacteristic of a person, and which are often portrayed as transgressive in literature.* Darcy realizes "the danger of paying Elizabeth too much attention," but he finds himself succumbing to such danger and proposing nevertheless.

---

*   I expect that the stories of Shakespeare's Romeo and Juliet and Lancelot and Guinevere (made available in English in the fifteenth century by Sir Thomas Malory) will be familiar to all readers. Layla and Majnun are lovers in a twelfth-century poem written by Nizami, an Iranian poet; Bohhe and Dihua are lovers in the Chinese novel *The Sea of Regret* written in 1906 by Wu Jianren. Janie and Tea Cake are from *Their Eyes Were Watching God* by Zora Neale Hurston. And Ennis and Jack are the lovers in Annie Proulx's short story "Brokeback Mountain." Sabrina and Jorie are characters in the novel *Maybe Next Time* by Karin Kallmaker. The last two are contemporary texts that feature same-sex lovers. But I would characterize many same-sex friendships in earlier literature as exemplifying romantic love under the guise of intense friendship, or masked in some other way. In previous eras, it was difficult to write openly about same-sex love, at least in many cultures.

Falling in love usually involves obsessing about the loved one; indeed, such thoughts can become intrusive and compelling. In his first proposal, Darcy tactlessly confesses that he can't subdue his fascination with Elizabeth. For romantic lovers, mood and well-being depend on how the relationship is going—exhilaration if things are working out, pain if they founder. People in love also tend to have tremendous energy and direct much of it toward their special relationship. The need for sexual exclusivity and hence sexual possessiveness also enters into these unusually intense feelings. But there's a yearning for emotional union with the other even more than for sexual union. Romantic love usually predominates from twelve to eighteen months after it begins, and indeed, who could tolerate such intensity for longer?

Romantic love is likely governed by the circuits and neurochemicals of what neuroscientist Jack Panksepp calls the "seeking system," an overarching emotional system associated with motivation, and which is part of the reward circuitry of the mammalian brain. We can view this in the context of Edmund Rolls's definition of emotion: "Emotions are states elicited by rewards and punishers . . . [A] reward is something for which an animal will work. A punisher is something that an animal will work to escape or avoid." The seeking system embraces all the feelings associated with working toward rewards, including curiosity and hope, which cause us to engage with the world. We seek many different objects for many different reasons, and so it makes sense to think of seeking as a general arousal system that activates when we engage in behavior that we hope will lead to gratification—to finding—whether our object is food, shelter, sex, friendship, or a sense of accomplishment.

In other mammals, the seeking system initiates exploratory behavior as well as the search for basic physical requirements, as in foraging, and including the search for a mate. Prairie voles don't fall in love before they bond, but they do seek sexual contact. Panksepp eloquently describes the function of seeking throughout the animal kingdom:

> Although the details of human hopes are surely beyond the imagination of other creatures, the evidence now clearly indicates that certain intrinsic aspirations of all mammalian minds, those of mice as well as men, are driven by the same

ancient neurochemistry. These chemistries lead your companion creatures to set out energetically to investigate and explore their worlds, to seek available resources and make sense of the contingencies in their environments. These same systems give us the impulse to become actively engaged with the world and to extract meaning from our various circumstances.[*]

The primary neural pathway of the seeking system is the meso-limbic cortical reward circuit; it's the primary pathway the brain uses to signal the possibility of reward. It isn't necessary to memorize all the areas associated with this circuit, but if you hear the name (it's basic knowledge among mind-brain scientists) you'll know that seeking and reward are involved. As with all of our feelings, this circuit involves all the levels of the brain such as the ventral tegmental area in the brainstem (the lowest brain region) and the amygdala in the middle of the brain; however, for humans, the prefrontal cortex, our most advanced area, is especially important to the calculus of love, to monitoring gains and losses, making plans, plotting the next chapter, hopefully a happy one.

Dopamine is the primary neurotransmitter of the seeking system. When a gambler enters the casino, a rush of dopamine generates his excitement, and ditto for Darcy when in Elizabeth's company. Dopamine generates other qualities associated with romantic love, in addition to highly focused and goal-directed seeking behavior. It's been linked to exhilaration, energy, sleeplessness, and loss of appetite. Dopamine has also long been known to be significant to movement: Parkinson's disease, a disorder of the motor system that produces muscular rigidity, a hallmark tremor, and the loss of voluntary movement, results from the degeneration of dopamine-producing neurons. It makes sense that dopamine would be central to both movement and the seeking system, since impulses need to lead to actions in order to enable animals to reach goals or rewards. Interestingly, an excess of dopamine is thought to be one of the causes of schizophrenia.

---

[*]   Jaak Panksepp, *Affective Neuroscience: The Foundation of Human and Animal Emotions*, Series in Affective Neuroscience (Oxford, England: Oxford University Press, 2004), 145.

Other neurochemicals active on the reward circuit also contribute to the experience of being in love. Like dopamine, norepinephrine (a form of adrenaline also known as noradrenaline) is associated with increased energy, elation, sleeplessness, and loss of appetite, as well as heightened powers of memory for new stimuli, all recognizable attributes of romance. Norepinephrine may also contribute to sexual arousal. Endogenous opioids, endorphins, generate many of love's pleasurable feelings.

The neurochemical serotonin is important to romantic love through its absence. Dopamine and serotonin are mutually inhibiting, so that an excess of dopamine in the system will depress levels of serotonin. And low levels of serotonin have been associated with obsessive-compulsive disorder. That's why selective serotonin reuptake inhibitors such as fluoxetine (Prozac) are often prescribed for this ailment; they increase brain levels of serotonin by preventing cleanup (reuptake) chemicals from removing excess serotonin from cerebral fluid, thereby raising levels of serotonin available for use as a neurotransmitter. But when it comes to romantic love, people don't seek a cure if the relationship is going well. Romantic love, with its natural endorphins, is a powerful and intoxicating opiate.

In line with its role in initiating behaviors associated with desire, the seeking system is activated with the *anticipation* of pleasure even more than its fulfillment. There's been a change in thinking here: This seeking-reward circuit was initially thought be associated with gratification, but research has shown that it fires with anticipation and seeking in general even more than with its fulfillment. For this reason, the pleasure circuit motivates us to alleviate negative situations as well as to quest for happy ones; the absence of evil is a very muted form of pleasure.

But even if the system is associated with desire rather than fulfillment, the condition of wanting and anticipating appears to be extremely pleasurable in and of itself—even if it's accompanied by stress, and even if wanting brings pleasure of a different kind than having. If the mesolimbic cortical circuit is electrically stimulated in animals, they'll vigorously demonstrate exploratory, search behaviors rather than the calm that comes with satisfaction, which we usually think of as reward. For instance, rats will investigate their environment, sniffing excitedly. And if a rat is taught to press a lever that stimulates this circuit, the animal will continue to do so until he collapses from exhaustion.

It's impossible to ask a rat to parse the nuances of feeling, and we humans often have difficulty with that as well. But if you've ever postponed fulfilling a desire in order to enjoy the state of anticipation for a longer time, you've experienced one rewarding aspect of seeking. Less happily, if you've ever stayed in a bad relationship because you just *know* it has potential (Marianne of *Sense and Sensibility* is sure someone has spoken ill of her to Willoughby and all will be well if she can set the record straight), you've had experience with its less benevolent side.

The connection between romantic love and the seeking system is demonstrated by the innovative work of neuroscientist Helen Fisher, who studies the brain in love. Fisher conducted a series of experiments using functional magnetic resonance imaging (fMRI), which can tell which parts of the brain are active at a given moment. (Regular MRI is magnetic resonance imaging that takes a static picture of inner structures.) After selecting people passionately in love, as determined by a questionnaire, Fisher looked at lovers' brains as they gazed at pictures of their beloved. Many areas became active, but two important areas, smack in the middle of the mesolimbic cortical circuit, the reward circuit, were correlated specifically with being in love. This strongly suggests that romantic love is a kind of seeking. (The ventral tegmental area and the caudate "lit up.")

Throughout the period in which romantic love dominates, for most people the first six to eighteen months of a relationship, romantic lovers seek for one reason or another. First there's pursuit of the beloved, before they know that their love is requited. And if it's not, or one of the lovers changes their mind, this difficulty often fails to shut down the system. In fact, this circuit tends to fire more vigorously when we encounter obstacles, in order to step up seeking efforts through pumping more dopamine through the circuit. The circuit usually ceases activity when we lose hope altogether, or run out of the energy to sustain anticipation.

But this can take a long time. Being abandoned by a lover can breed terrible misery, but many among the heartbroken continue to hope until the signs are indubitable, and sometimes beyond that point. Marianne has many indicators of Willoughby's loss of interest, but she pursues him until he snubs her so directly that she must accept the truth. I leave you to draw the analogy with crazed lever-pressing rats. Until it finally relaxes its grip, romantic love is incredibly addictive, which explains the obsessiveness of those in love. It's not all that surprising that the mesolimbic cortical reward circuit also governs addiction to cocaine and other drugs. The circuit can also dominate for a long time before an actual romance begins; Fanny is in love with Edmund for years.

Even when both partners are equally involved and feel relatively secure in one another's love, seeking doesn't stop because the romantic lover seeks total merging with the beloved. This is what John Donne depicts in his poem "The Ecstasy," a description of orgasmic union so perfect that it causes the lovers' two souls to leave their bodies and intermingle in the air above.

> As 'twixt two equal armies,
> Fate Suspends uncertain victory,
> Our souls (which to advance their state,
> Were gone out), hung 'twixt her and me.

Ecstasy comes from the Greek word *extasis*, which means "out of the body," and it's telling that we apply the term to pleasures that make us lose consciousness of ourselves as bounded entities, whether the pleasure is derived from religion, nature, drugs, or another person. But even when lovers feel Donne's sense of union with a beloved, this is obviously a state of feeling that's impossible to maintain for long periods of time, and so it keeps the system activated.

For the fortunate couples whose relationships survive the loss of romantic intensity, the attachment system begins to dominate. But the shift from romance to attachment doesn't have to be absolute. Some people manage to maintain high levels of desire and excitement in their relationships over many years. They might not maintain the obsessive quality of romantic love, but these lucky partners nevertheless retain the ability to rekindle romance while incorporating other qualities into their relationship. The anticipation of sexual and other pleasures likely tweaks seeking neurons. Getting away from it all can also help; marriage counselors often recommend vacations away from home to rejuvenate a flagging marriage in the hope that the dopamine stimulated by new surroundings will generate romantic feelings in the marriage as well. In any case, there's great joy in attachment as well as in romance; endorphins, which generate feelings of pleasure, are important to both systems. But the state of intense and sustained passion yields to other, less hyperaroused feelings in most romantic relationships.

LUST BUT NOT LEAST

There's attachment, there's romance, and then there's pure sex. Well, actually, for humans, pure sex is a myth. Lust is never as pure and simple as we'd like to think. Here, as in other forms of relationship, higher brain areas contribute to choosing objects of desire. Even with simple preferences—short or tall?—the decision is routed through cortical regions to form the endless mind-brain feedback loops that give rise to our thoughts, feelings, and actions.

Blame the human mind-brain for making everything so complicated. For humans, sexual activity involves emotional and cognitive dimensions of experience that go beyond the largely instinctual behavior that drives many other species. While there's a social aspect to sex for other mammals as well, it doesn't run the show so completely as it does for us. In fact, the larger and more intricate the brain, the more likely that a variety of factors will embellish basic drives. The greater complexity of factors in human sexual relationships as compared to those of chimps matches the greater complexity of our brains, and chimps have a far more complicated social life than rats.

To put this another way, the more complex the brain, the more input there is from the mind, and the greater the ratio of the social to the instinctual. For humans, inner environments, consisting of memories, thoughts, and feelings, inevitably spur or inhibit sexual desire, complicating our relationships and our choices. The old usage of the word *conversation*, which could refer to either talk or sexual intercourse, nicely captures the evolved nature of human sexuality: We're still the only primates with fully developed speech and language, and the only primates to make such a huge fuss about sex, for better or worse.

But even without the greater cognitive input from the cortex, the neurochemistry of sex, likely shared with most mammals, is complex, involving multiple systems throughout the brain. In humans, testosterone is the neurochemical of sexual desire for both men and women, and the septum, an area in the brainstem, appears to be a crucial area for sexual arousal; our species shows significant increases in electrical brain activity in the septal area during arousal. The septum appears to be associated with sexual pleasure in other mammals as well, since rats will press a lever to stimulate this area (as with the seeking system). But right from the start, with the identification of this region, boundaries begin to get blurry. The septum is also one of the targets of the mesolimbic-cortical reward pathway along which dopamine and endorphins travel. So, not surprisingly, sex involves reward centers and neurochemicals of the brain. (You probably don't need neuroscience to tell you that sex is pleasurable, but it can tell you why this is so at a basic neurological level.)

The overlap in all three systems with reward systems shows that while we can delineate sufficient differences in behavior, circuitry, and neurochemistry to talk about three different systems, they're actually only semiautonomous—and semi-interdependent—for they frequently connect to one another in vital ways. We can speak of one system as being dominant, but they almost never act alone. In addition, one system can trigger or inhibit the activation of another depending on the ratio of neurochemicals and the circuitry that activates. Alcohol response provides an analogy. A little alcohol can make a person feel lively and confident, but a lot can cause confusion and depression. A similar modus operandi applies to love's neurochemicals.

The sexual system provides a clear example of the complexity of interrelationship among systems of sex and social affiliation. We've seen that oxytocin plays an important role in sexual activity and desire. But attachment neurochemicals can drive down testosterone. For many men, testosterone levels decline with the birth of a child. Conversely, testosterone can interfere with attachment. Men with high testosterone levels appear to have greater difficulty bonding than those with levels within the normal range.

Take another combination. Dopamine and norepinephrine, romance neurochemicals, can trigger the release of testosterone, the hormone of sexual desire. That's why we almost always feel sexual desire when we fall in love. But dopamine and norepinephrine can also stimulate the release of oxytocin, which, as we just saw, can dampen sexual excitement. And although romance can lead to attachment, attachment can dampen feelings of romance because elevated levels of oxytocin and vasopressin can interfere with dopamine and norepinephrine pathways. This explains, neurochemically at least, why lovers can turn into "just friends." But the reverse is also true. You might feel you're entering into a friendship with benefits only to fall in love because testosterone can stimulate the release of norepinephrine and dopamine, romance chemicals. Or, you can find yourself becoming attached to your friend in a way that defies the original terms of the agreement since sex stimulates release of oxytocin.

If you're confused, that's a good thing, because it means you have an accurate sense of the strange complexity and interactive nature of the systems and neurochemicals that govern sexual and social affiliation in mammals, and which orchestrate human love in its various forms. You also have an idea of how incomplete our knowledge of the brain remains. Although we know in principle that the effect that one system has when interacting with another depends on the quantity, location, timing, and interaction of neurochemical release, we're missing details. We have a long way to go before we understand the neurochemistry of love in all its forms.

Nevertheless, the intricate and entangled nature of relationship areas and neurochemicals, including the prefrontal cortex, provides a clue as to why human relationships are so variable and complicated. When we say that love (or sex) is never the same with two people, we might well be speaking the truth of our neurology as well as our feelings.

LOVE'S BLURRED BOUNDARIES

Austen's characters show the blurriness between systems and the kinds of love they involve. Let's take *Mansfield Park* and start with

Henry Crawford. Most of Austen's readers would immediately have recognized that Henry is a libertine, a familiar figure in eighteenth- and nineteenth-century novels. The libertine rejects all notions of attachment. Yet, while seduction is his goal, the seeking system motivates him as strongly as his desire for sex. But it's not the same kind of seeking that predominates in romantic love; the motives and the objectives are different. The libertine doesn't seek union, but rather power and domination, and sex is often pleasurable more for the power it signifies than for its sensual or emotional aspects.

True to type, Henry sets out to make the Bertram sisters fall in love with him as soon as he arrives in the neighborhood of Mansfield Park. While he doesn't actually become involved with either of them sexually until his eventual elopement with Maria, he gets what he wants, control over their minds and hearts. Power, not sex, is the motor of seduction.

Henry then sets his sights on Fanny. But Fanny has the best inoculation against his charms that she can possibly have: She's in love with another man. In the literature of the period it was a truism that being in love with one person made a person immune to the attentions of another. And this is actually correct in terms of the brain's love systems. The obsessive nature of romantic love makes us seek only one person at a time in this special way. It's certainly possible to love two people at once, but this almost always involves different kinds of love. For instance, it is possible to be in love with one person and attached or sexually attracted to another. But again, the drives come from different systems.

Although Henry has a "tainted mind," a cynical, opportunistic, and amoral take on life, he nevertheless finds himself genuinely in love with Fanny to the extent that his shallow character will allow for such feelings. And he begins to be attached as well. At first, he's motivated by the challenge of having control over so pure and moral a woman—what a trophy for the seeking system! But in line with other famous libertines, Henry finds himself "hoist with his own petard," genuinely attached to the woman he meant to entrap. And he would likely have succeeded in winning her had he been steady in his pursuit. For although romantic love often persists for a while after hope is gone, and Fanny is quickly losing hope that Edmund will abandon her rival Mary, even the most tenacious of seekers eventually lets go.

But ironically, it's not the libertine's quest for intellectual and moral power that motivates Henry to run away with the newly married Maria Bertram, but rather, sexual attraction. There would be no glory whatsoever in winning Maria from Rushworth since it's obvious to all that Maria has never loved her husband or even pretended to respect him. Henry's social and economic status surpasses that of the Rushworths, so he wouldn't be motivated by class antagonism, another typical libertine motive. And Henry has already conquered Maria; the libertine customarily abandons his victims when they no longer present a challenge. This is just what he'd done earlier when he failed to propose to Maria as she'd expected, leaving her to endure a lifetime with a dull man whom she despises.

The libertine, however, is also a great indulger of his physical appetites, and he frequently consorts with prostitutes and other loose women who present no challenge whatsoever. Here we can say that the sexual system truly dominates. What's attractive to Henry is Maria's availability, the promise of easy pleasure. Austen makes sure that her readers realize that Henry, despite his handsome face and charming ways, goes as low as you can go, which also means as subcortical as you can go in terms of the mind-brain's systems of love, and as primitive as you can go in terms of the evolution of these systems. Even lizards have a sex drive.

Other characters similarly show the overlap of systems. Edmund exhibits the obsessiveness and idealization typical of the romantic lover. Because Mary plays the harp, he suddenly develops a taste for this instrument and visits Mary every day to hear her practice. He can talk of little else but Mary, and so she becomes the subject of most of his conversations with Fanny, although he's oblivious to how much he's hurting his cousin. Fanny wonders how Edmund can remain so unaware of Mary's moral shortcomings, which are so obvious to her.

It's clear that Edmund downplays the bad and emphasizes the good to justify what he feels. He attributes all of Mary's moral lapses to "resulting principally from situation," especially the bad influence of the people who raised her. Here again we see denial in action, Edmund's left-brain interpreter works hard to justify his right-brain emotions. If he loves Mary, she must be worthy of his love.

Edmund is so head over heels that he compromises his principles a number of times in order to please Mary. Love makes him inconsiderate and thoughtless; indeed, there's little room in the lover's mind-brain for any thoughts other than those of the beloved. Edmund agrees to act in the home theatricals that the young people of the house are producing even though he's well aware that his stern father Sir Thomas would disapprove (Sir Thomas is away on business). Even worse, because Mary likes to go horseback riding, a newly acquired skill, he lends her Fanny's horse without thinking that his cousin's health might suffer if she's deprived of her main source of exercise. When he realizes that Fanny has fared poorly because of this, he's angry with himself although regretful that his pleasure jaunts with Mary must come to an end. He feels guilty and contrite, yet he nevertheless longs to continue his rides with Mary.

Austen cleverly chose riding as a topic, for it symbolically points to the sexual nature of Edmund's feelings for Mary; he feels more than simple worship. The highest forms of idealization are rooted in love's lowest system. Horseback riding has traditionally had sexual implications, as we see from the vocabulary common to horsemanship and sex: *mount, jump, ride, unbridled passion*. It's significant that Edmund and not someone else offers the horse to Mary; one kind of physical offering stands in for another. Although Edmund was also responsible for introducing Fanny to riding, the emphasis and quality of the gift were different. Edmund taught Fanny to ride for her health; he teaches

Mary for her pleasure. And Mary's obvious relish and quick mastery of the sport contrast with Fanny's timid and measured equestrian style. Mary's hearty physicality calls attention to the erotic component of her own as well as Edmund's feelings.

The restraints of the age caused Austen to resort to symbolism. But she was also as direct as she could be, telling us that as Mary leaves the room, "Edmund [looks] after her in an *ecstasy* of admiration of all her many virtues from her obliging manners down to her light and graceful tread. . . . 'How well she walks!'" Edmund watches Mary's body as heterosexual men have eyed attractive women since time immemorial. The connotations of the word ecstasy would not have been lost on Austen, who was extremely well versed in English literature (she would certainly have read "The Ecstasy").

Fanny loves Edmund with as much passion as he feels for Mary. Her feelings for her cousin had initially consisted of strong attachment: Edward provided, and continues to provide, support and solicitude for Fanny: "From her earliest days at Mansfield, he was always true to her interests, and considerate of her feelings . . . giving her advice, consolation, and encouragement." She responds appropriately: "Her sentiments towards him were compounded of all that was respectful, grateful, confiding, and tender."

But at some point Fanny's feelings for Edmund evolve to include romance, which is why she finds his conversations about Mary so painful. When Fanny hears Edmund call herself and Mary "the two dearest objects I have on earth," she feels all the sexual possessiveness of the romantic lover and all the pain of unrequited romantic love. "She had never heard him speak so openly before, and though it told her no more than what she had long perceived, it was a stab." She's sure of Edmund's attachment, but Mary owns his passion. His unavailability keeps her own seeking system activated, and would likely have done so until the moment Edmund married Mary and was truly out of reach. But an equally strong component of attachment binds her to Edmund. She's as totally devoted as a person can be.

Why does it all have to be so complicated? Evolution provides some answers.

LOVE AND EVOLUTION

We can blame our conflicting drives and desires on evolution, at least to some degree. The systems that govern love were formed in response to the challenges our species faced as we evolved, and these systems are different because they're solutions to different problems. The behavior and psychology of intimacy, such as choosing why and when to enter into relationships, whom to pursue, and whether to stay or leave a partnership have been influenced by the same ancient pressures of survival that all animals face. But keep in mind that this applies only to the parameters of the choices, to the reasons the basic systems exist and the forms they take, and not to any one individual's behavior. It would be silly to say that Henry Crawford seduces women to ensure his evolutionary fitness, the survival of many offspring. Our motives are far more complicated. Nevertheless, this kind of argument is often found in literary criticism that takes evolution into account. Drawing simple one-to-one correspondences of this sort between evolutionary forces and individual actions has given evolutionary studies a bad name in some humanistic circles.

In the Paleolithic Age, when our species emerged, survival was quite a challenge, so just getting to reproductive age was an accomplishment. And having and raising a baby was even more daunting back then than it is today (at least than it is for people born into the middle and upper classes in developed countries, whose infant mortality rates are low). The human infant is born the most helpless of all primates and takes longest to reach an age when she or he can self-feed. This means that human infants have always been incredibly expensive in terms of time and resources. So our species needed to hedge its bets with respect to reproductive fitness, survival of the species. Members of a species who manage to reproduce pass their genes on to offspring, and this includes genes that determine the systems that influence behavior. Behaviors that led to reproductive success would likely survive.

One practice that would help fathers to achieve evolutionary fitness is promiscuity. Sex with as many women as possible would put the reproductive odds in a man's favor, making it likely that some of his offspring would live to reproduce. It would also ensure variety in the gene pool, which is always a good thing in the long view, since it offers the chance for more genetic variety and avoids the perils of inbreeding. And since human babies take nine months to gestate, getting several women pregnant at once makes good reproductive sense. (Again, this is why the impulse to promiscuity evolved, although individuals remained unaware of the benefits of their behavior to the species.)

Yet, even though promiscuity might benefit the species and be a pleasurable lifestyle, a man likes to be certain that the females (or female) he has sex with will produce his genetic offspring and not someone else's.* Since human females have concealed ovulation, and are (theoretically) sexually receptive at all times, it would be difficult for a man to be sure of paternity. One way to put the odds in his favor would be to stick around, a motive for proto-marriage. This might be done in the spirit of suspicion, a human counterpart of the mate guarding found in other animals that wish to possess their mates (and, inadvertently, ensure paternity). In addition, by offering help and protection to the mother of his child, he would also be increasing the odds that his child would survive to adulthood, another motive.

But he might have reasons for staying with a particular woman that have more to do with the woman herself than her status as the mother of his children. Biology prompts us to want to live companionably and intimately with others, a behavioral tendency that characterizes our species because it's been key to our survival. A close mate would provide such company. So a man might pair bond because he feels an emotional connection with a particular woman, which at the molecular level accomplishes the same goal as mate guarding and increases the chances of his child's survival.

In short, one of nature's solutions to the fitness problem would be to make men promiscuous, impregnating as many women as possible. But another solution would be to encourage bonding with a single mate. Of course, there's also the option of bonding with a woman and then indulging on the side, a solution that often creates as many problems as it solves for humans. Needless to say, this is an option that has stayed with us throughout the ages. And there's also the option of serial monogamy, which is common in Western societies today. But

---

*   Humans have understood the connection between sex and reproduction for at least the
       past 50,000 years.

life was short and brutish in prehistoric times, leaving little time for long successive relationships.

A woman would face the same conflict with a few variations. Sex with more than one man would raise the odds not only of her being impregnated, but impregnated with the best man's sperm since sperm cells themselves compete for the honor of fertilization. And the same selective pressure to vary the gene pool would be at work for women as well as men, covertly influencing behavioral tendencies. However, a woman needs help and protection to successfully raise a child. And while men were probably not any more dependable in Paleolithic times when we evolved than they are now, which means that many men were Darcys and many were Henrys, having a man around was still a goal worth pursuing. This argues for a neurophysiology that encourages pair bonding.

Even if a woman had been promiscuous, she might decide to commit herself to a man who could offer attractive resources. This need not be the biological father of her child (she might not even know who he is), but a man who believed he was the father, or who was willing to support her and her child in any case. But she might have a spare lover-father (or more!) in the wings, perhaps a man who believed the child was his and was willing to contribute support on the sly, another solution that's endured. The craving for reliable companionship would motivate women as well as men to bond with a single sexual partner.

So it appears that we're buffeted by different and contradictory evolutionary mandates. In terms of reproductive fitness alone, and putting aside moral, psychological, and religious considerations, promiscuity pays for both spouses. But so does pair bonding, which appears to involve sexual exclusivity much of the time. Such contradictions get us into uncomfortable and sometimes painful situations because what works at the level of evolutionary fitness doesn't always work well in individual lives. Our contradictory impulses make it possible for us to love two people at the same time, to stray from monogamy even when we're committed to our partners, and to engage in relationships and sexual behavior that we want and don't want at the same time.

What's a human to do? This isn't the kind of book that proposes to answer that question, but we can at least begin to understand the pressures that gave rise to the complexities of human intimacy.

LOVE AND CULTURE

While Austen was half a century too early to know about evolution and two centuries too early to understand the complex neurological underpinnings of her characters' feelings, she understood that cultural pressures affect individual choices. And she knew that by telling stories, she could give her opinions about the meaning of such choices within a larger societal context. For many literary critics, detecting Austen's views on social and political issues by analyzing her stories has become a primary focus.

Taking literary criticism on Austen in this direction was the brainchild of the twentieth century. Before roughly the 1980s, Austen had been thought of as a brilliant but totally domestic writer, interested in how human nature played out in her small communities but oblivious to larger political and social issues. Marilyn Butler's *Jane Austen and the War of Ideas* and Claudia L. Johnson's *Jane Austen* were groundbreaking books in terms of changing this view; it's now generally accepted that Austen engages with such issues. But she does so subtly, commenting on social and political topics through her portrayals of private lives. For instance, her characterizations of women as intelligent, self-aware, and capable are right in line with her contemporary Mary Wollstonecraft's feminist tract, *A Vindication of the Rights of Woman* (1792). But Wollstonecraft was hated in many circles whereas Austen was almost universally loved. Two clever women, but one winning flies with honey rather than repelling them with vinegar.

Or take marriage. The opposition between marriage for love and the sensible mandate to take material factors into account played into an ongoing class struggle. Those who had believed that love was important tended to have liberal views about class mobility. If marriage was based on love, factors like social class and economic status receded in importance. Marriage for love therefore implied that intermarriage between people of social classes was acceptable, which was a progressive view. But if you were, let's say, an aristocrat who thought it was unacceptable to marry a commoner, then you necessarily believed that love shouldn't be the most important factor in a marriage; status would be more important then love, a conservative stance. Complicating all this was the increasing awareness of married love as a Christian duty; to swear to love someone when you couldn't was therefore a sin. A compromise position was to endorse attachment love since it left a person rational and likely to behave in character and in line with social expectations. Many conservatives could accept this option while thinking outright passionate love matches were to be distrusted.

But Austen's work doesn't divide along such party lines. She understands that every person's story is different, and that this is true at various levels of individual and social context. With novels that continue to amaze each new generation, she portrays the complexity of the bio-psycho-social factors that conspire to create each life. This makes it difficult to pin her down, although we keep trying. Our brains are designed to categorize, to reduce complexity to generalities. And so we ask, is Austen conservative or progressive? A feminist or an anti-feminist? In general, I would say that she's progressive, but that doesn't mean that she always takes the expected progressive position. She's way too smart to toe a party line.

Romantic love, attachment love, and sexuality emerge again and again in her plots. But the value of such feelings changes with situations and characters. Although Austen is polemical to the extent that she wants to endorse attachment love as a perfectly acceptable motive for marriage (perhaps because this gives women more choices), she doesn't insist that this is the only option. She doesn't advocate attachment at the expense of more romantic modes of feeling, not even within the same novel. And not even within what appears to be the most conservative and cautious of her novels, *Mansfield Park*.

Austen's flexible approach applies to many of the issues she portrays, which tended to have coded meanings within her culture. Take cousin marriage, which tended to be favored by conservatives because it protected a family against outsiders (think of all the hemophilia in nineteenth-century Europe from inbreeding among royal families). In *Mansfield Park*, cousin marriage does close the family in on itself, protecting it not from unwanted and "inferior" outsiders, but rather, rendering it a bastion of tradition against the corrupting influences of London and "the world," represented by the Crawfords, of course. Whether you think that is a good or a bad thing is a different matter.

But cousin marriage and attachment love have a very different status in *Pride and Prejudice*. There, the cousin marriages that loom for our protagonists are between Mr. Darcy and Miss de Bourgh, and Elizabeth and Mr. Collins. Here, as in *Mansfield Park*, cousin marriage would consolidate the family, enclosing it in on itself. But this is not a good thing; Darcy needs the vitality and freshness of an outsider like Elizabeth. Anyway, the cousins here are totally unsuitable: Miss de Bourgh is a cipher, Mr. Collins a fool. And so our hero and heroine hold out for something better.

But what that "better" consists of is different for each of them. As noted above, Mr. Darcy marries for romantic love, the kind of obsessional passion that can lead to endings that are aren't so happy, as with Colonel Brandon's two Elizas in *Sense and Sensibility*. We can assume that romance led to the marriages of the Prices (Fanny's parents) in *Mansfield Park* and the Bennets (Elizabeth's parents) in *Pride and Prejudice*, whose households certainly fail to demonstrate wedded bliss. The moral in these instances appears to be "Marry in haste and repent at leisure," whether such leisure consists of a retreat to the library (Mr. Bennet) or the alehouse (Mr. Price), immersion in domestic chores (Mrs. Price), or in gossip and worry (Mrs. Bennet). But romance works for Darcy.

Austen's love plots serve ideological purposes to be sure. And they express the influence of basic systems that guide all mammals. But whether or not readers understand or care about the specific historical and neurobiological aspects of such choices, they find situations they can recognize and identify with. Most readers understand the longing of romantic love, the hurt when it's thwarted, as it is for both Marianne and Elinor. They accept, more or less, Marianne's disappointment, and for the most part, we trust that she's happy in the end.

But Elinor's fate is the more conventional, and for many of us, the more gratifying ending. Neurologically speaking, Elinor's feelings for love draw on all of love's systems. (We'll assume she finds Edward attractive since sexual chemistry is usually a part of romantic love. Of course, Austen wouldn't speak directly of such matters.) Integrating aspects of the mind-brain is always a good thing for us humans. Or put more simply, it's very gratifying when we love with all our hearts, minds, and souls.

This isn't the only way to be happy in love, and Austen knows this. But she also knows that it tends to be the most satisfying ending for her readers. Marianne's choices and her personality preclude such an ending for her. But Elinor, with her exquisite powers of patience and restraint, has the wherewithal to deal with such excesses of feeling. And—this might not sit all that well with readers of today—she deserves a romantic ending; Marianne forfeited this privilege. But that's okay—or at least Austen wants us to find this acceptable. The sisters live "happily ever after," although not in the unrealistic mode of the fairy tale, but in the true-to-life kinds of stories that allow us to find ourselves in Austen, again and again.

SEVEN

Ties that Bond

F anny Price is a very lucky girl. Or so her mean and tactless aunt, Mrs. Norris, keeps telling her. Mrs. Norris thinks Fanny is lucky because she's been adopted by her wealthy relatives, Sir Thomas and Lady Bertram. They whisked her away from her own large, chaotic family, with too many children and too little money, to become a member of the household at Mansfield Park, their country estate. Lady Bertram is Fanny's maternal aunt who married well—that is, married a man who was socially and economically superior to her own family. Fanny's own mother married beneath her in these socioeconomic terms, and against her family's wishes, falling in love with a poor naval officer with very uncertain prospects.

Fanny's adoption, at the age of nine, comes about as a result of Mrs. Norris's scheming. Following her downwardly mobile marriage, Fanny's mother was promptly disowned by her family. But after a hiatus of ten years, Mrs. Norris, the third sister, suggests that they reach out to Mrs. Price and lighten her burden by taking one of her children.

A stingy, petty woman, Mrs. Norris has no intention of contributing financially to Fanny's upbringing. But she has no problem offering charity on behalf of the Bertrams. Mrs. Norris is stingy in spirit as well as purse, never letting Fanny forget that she's a poor relation, inferior in every way to her female cousins Maria and Julia.

In material terms, the move to Mansfield Park promises opportunities that Fanny would never have had with her own family. Yet despite her great fortune, when Fanny arrives at her new home, she doesn't feel very lucky. In fact, she feels terribly sad and lonely. It appears that no one there will be able to understand her or enter into her feelings, a kind of connection that we all crave. That is, until her cousin Edmund finds her crying alone. He asks Fanny what's wrong and discovers that she misses her family, especially her brother William. When Fanny tells Edmund that she's promised to write but has no writing supplies, Edmund quickly procures pen and paper for her. More important, he offers the friendship Fanny needs.

From this moment on, Edmund takes the time to understand Fanny. He quickly realizes her value: She's intelligent and sensitive, and possesses "an affectionate heart and a strong desire of doing right," core moral qualities. Edmund decides that Fanny deserves "positive kindness." And this is exactly what he gives her, consistently and abundantly.

Edmund becomes what's known in the study of human attachment (called "attachment studies") as "a secure base" for Fanny, someone she can go to for emotional support. She can turn to him when she's in trouble or needs *refueling*, the technical term for such support, to deal with the challenges of life. At Mansfield Park this generally means coping with the substandard way in which she's treated by all the other members of the family. Because of Edmund, Fanny is able to feel comfortable in her adoptive home. She's further able to depend on Edmund to supplement her education and fill her hours of leisure by the many books he recommends and the many discussions they have together. Edmund shapes Fanny's mind and heart as she grows from a girl to a young woman.

Edmund is the only one of his family who's truly caring and sensitive, and he habitually pays attention to the feelings of others. So it's not surprising that he nurtures Fanny. However, as Fanny grows up,

Edmund reaps unintended benefits from his kindness. As so often happens with adults who enter into attachment relationships, the support begins to go in both directions. Edmund begins to come to Fanny for refueling, especially as he copes with the heartache of having fallen in love with Mary Crawford.

Mary and her brother, Henry, have come for an extended visit with their relatives, the Grants, who are the Bertrams' neighbors. Similar in age to the young people at Mansfield (Fanny is nineteen at this point), Mary and Henry are soon accepted into the family circle. Their attraction lies in their liveliness, a strong counter to the dependable quiet—some would say dullness—of Mansfield. Children of London and fashionable society, with its worldly values and goals, the Crawfords bring turmoil of one kind or another to everyone at Mansfield Park. They disrupt the household's quiet way of life and tempt its family with enticing alternatives. But ultimately they teach the lesson, "All that glisters is not gold"—a lesson needed by everyone but Fanny, who is wise beyond her years.

Edmund's problem is not the usual one, unrequited love, that makes many a heretofore stoic man seek a confidant. Ironically, that's Fanny's problem, for she has fallen deeply in love with her kind cousin from the very beginning, even as a child. Mary actually reciprocates Edmund's passion. The problem is that she's far too worldly and ambitious to marry a poor clergyman, and the clergy is Edmund's chosen profession. Or so she thinks, and Edmund fears. Or perhaps it's Mary who fears that she'll succumb, and Edmund who hopes this will be the case. Both acknowledge their irreconcilable differences, each yearning for the other to change. The stress of this relationship causes Edmund to look to Fanny for strength and guidance.

We see the tables turned in this way in a moment in which Fanny hopes to get support from Edmund and ends up having to offer it instead. The Mansfield cousins and the Crawfords are involved in putting on a play, a lighthearted and fun endeavor that both Fanny and Edmund (and only they) feel is totally inappropriate given Sir Thomas's absence in the West Indies, where he's looking after business interests. The serious Sir Thomas, a man who loves quiet domestic comfort, would never have approved of home theatricals, and they ought not to be taking advantage of his absence in this way. This is especially true since Sir Thomas potentially faces grave dangers posed by transatlantic travel and residence in Antigua, including tropical fevers and a precarious political situation. This should be a time of sober reflection and prayer for the family, not a period of revelry and release, mice playing while the cat's away. To make matters worse, the chosen play, *Lovers' Vows*, is inappropriate, way too racy for an upright English household. And worse yet again, Maria Bertram plays opposite Henry Crawford, whom she's fallen in love with, despite her engagement to the slow-witted and unappealing Mr. Rushworth.

Fanny faces a dilemma. The other young people, with the exception of Edmund, pressure her to perform a small part in the play. She detests the thought of acting, especially in these questionable circumstances, but she wonders if she's being selfish and cowardly by refusing. Fanny is sitting in her room, hoping that Edmund will stop by and support her decision to refuse, even though she's so self-doubting, so used to complying to the wishes of others, that she wonders if even "Edmund's judgment, . . . his persuasions of Sir Thomas's disapprobation of the whole, [would] be enough to justify her in a determined denial in spite of all the rest." Edmund does stop by, but not to listen to Fanny's troubles—rather, to voice his own.

The young people have threatened to ask an outsider to join them because they have no one to play Anhalt, one of the leads. Edmund comes to Fanny supposedly to tell her that he's decided that taking the part himself will be the lesser of two evils, the other being to ask an outsider to join their theatricals. This would make the performance even more inappropriate, extending it beyond the family circle and going public to a degree. Of course, Edmund indulges in a hearty dose of self-deception here because it would be immensely pleasurable to him to play the part of Anhalt, a clergyman who falls in love with and eventually marries the young girl whose character he reforms, played by Mary; indeed, the script embodies Edmund's dearest hopes and fantasies for their relationship.

Edmund knows in his heart that acting is wrong, and is troubled by his choice, and so he turns to Fanny for comfort and validation of his feelings. These are some of the psychic treasures that the person who functions as a secure base can offer. While Fanny can't fully endorse his decision, she shows enough true sympathy for his plight, and an understanding of his supposedly noble motives, to convey the support that he needs.

From that moment on, we see Edmund turning to Fanny when he's upset or depleted, as she's done with him throughout the years. His need becomes more pressing as difficulties with Mary increase. After one particularly upsetting encounter, Edmund seeks out Fanny because "his mind was fagged"; he's psychologically exhausted, in need of refueling, and it's only with Fanny that he can find the "repose" he needs. He later painfully confides his hopes and fears to her as he gets ready to propose to Mary. Yet Edmund doesn't go through with his plan because he fears he'll be rejected; he realizes, after traveling to London to see her, that he must compete with a rival as insuperable as any flesh-and-blood challenger, the fashionable world. When he returns to Mansfield Park, more uncertain than ever, he again turns to Fanny for comfort. Finally, when circumstances force Edmund to see Mary's deeply flawed character and he realizes he can never marry her, Fanny becomes the companion of his many hours spent in lovelorn moping. That is, until Edmund learns "to prefer soft, light eyes to sparkling dark ones" and marries Fanny.

EMOTIONAL RESONANCE

When Edmund comes to Fanny because he's uneasy about acting in the Mansfield home theatricals, he hears what he wants to hear, interpreting her attempt to put the best spin on things as being much more positive than it really is. His perceptions are accurate in one respect: Fanny does empathize with him, more than he can know, since she herself is also desperately in love and so understands his longing. And without being false in any way (indeed Fanny *can't* be false), she conveys this understanding to Edmund. He would of course like to hear that he's doing the right thing with more enthusiasm than Fanny can muster, but he needs her understanding even more than he needs her permission.

This sense of being understood that Fanny provides is known as emotional resonance, also called affective empathy and [emotional] attunement; it means that another person has recognized your emotions and is on the same wavelength, as we say. It's one of the building blocks of empathy—you can't have empathy without it. But unlike empathy, resonance can operate subconsciously, without our awareness. You can grasp someone's feelings implicitly, without thinking directly or consciously about your perceptions. This also means that you implicitly know that these feelings are someone else's, and not your own.

We detect attunement largely by the same channels we use to express our emotions: through social signals, especially facial expression around the eyes (blind people have other equally effective ways of detecting emotions). This is a subconscious process that links the right brain of the person who sends social signals to the right brain of the person who reads them. Recognition can be implicitly acknowledged as well, usually by mirroring: smiling in response to a smile, looking worried in response to distress. Of course, we can be aware of resonance and social signals consciously as well as implicitly; conscious and subliminal perceptions often happen simultaneously. You can know intuitively that your friend is happy while at the same time consciously observing her smile.

Resonance is one of the most important pathways for human bonding and a prerequisite for well-being. Throughout Austen's novels, lovers, friends, sisters, parents, and all those who have genuine, close emotional connections, attune to one another's feelings and moods. When all the responsiveness goes in one direction, or is lacking altogether, this is a problem. Fanny is able to endure the insensitivity of those around her because she has Edmund. Without him, she would have suffered years of emotional isolation. Social creatures that we are, we crave resonance. And this need is not exclusive to humans; all mammals need emotional connections with others, and they establish such connections by whatever the means available to their species.

Resonance not only tells us that someone has registered our feelings and so we're not alone, but also subtly confirms our sense of self-worth, our inalienable right to be here. When our feelings are recognized, even subliminally, we feel validated. The definition of *validate* is worth citing: "To cause (a person) to feel valued, significant, or worthwhile; to affirm that (a person's feelings, opinions, desires, etc.) have validity, truth, or worth." The absence of feelings of validation, poor self-esteem, is often a factor in common pathological conditions such as depression and self-harm; many afflicted with these painful illnesses lacked resonance during critical or formative periods. So crucial is emotional resonance to feelings of self-worth that suicide-crisis hotline workers are trained to acknowledge their callers' feelings, even when there's nothing they can do to alleviate what's wrong. Such "reflective listening" often makes people feel better. Similarly, Fanny can't fix the situation for Edmund so that his desire doesn't betray his duty, but she can recognize the strength of his feelings and the difficulties involved in his decision.

I noted earlier that *Sense and Sensibility* conveys this validating, existential aspect of resonance especially well through Elinor's therapeutic relationship with Marianne. Ironically, we also see the value of resonance in the context of a failed relationship, Marianne's romance with Willoughby. Attunement appears to distinguish this relationship right from the start. Marianne and Willoughby have the same tastes and opinions, but this matters only because it demonstrates how exquisitely they resonate with one another emotionally. Who's to say if Willoughby really shares all of Marianne's refined, artistic tastes, but love prompts him to enter into all her enthusiasms even if he doesn't come by them on his own. Their attunement lies in their love for one another, and this organizes itself around other shared feelings and experiences.

Or so it seems. In the heartless letter that ends her hopes, Willoughby denies having felt anything but mild friendship for Marianne and virtually accuses her of having imagined their love. The possibility that this might be true, that Willoughby never loved her and that she imagined the resonance they felt with one another, might be even more toxic than Willoughby's abandonment.

Marianne's sustained focus on Willoughby's character and motives distinguishes her story from less nuanced tales of deserted lovers. Long after Marianne knows that Willoughby has jilted her and that her dream of a life with him has come to naught, his feelings and motives continue to matter to her. This is clear in a conversation between the sisters that takes place after Marianne has received Willoughby's heartless letter and has shown their full correspondence to Elinor. Marianne has just corrected Elinor's mistaken belief that they'd been engaged, a plausible assumption on Elinor's part because a young lady was allowed to correspond with a man only if they'd been engaged:

> "I felt myself," she added, "to be as solemnly engaged to him as if the strictest legal covenant had bound us to each other."
>
> "I can believe it," said Elinor; "but unfortunately he did not feel the same."
>
> "He *did* feel the same, Elinor—for weeks and weeks he felt it. I know he did. Whatever may have changed him now (and nothing but the blackest art employed against me can have done it), I was once as dear to him as my own soul could wish. This lock of hair, which now he can so readily give up, was begged of me with the most earnest supplication. Had you seen his look, his manner, had you heard his voice at that moment!"

What's notable here is Marianne's appeal to the truth of social signals, and her urgent insistence that she's read them correctly, that Elinor would have thought the same. She clings to the hope that someone has maligned her not because she thinks that she'll be reunited with Willoughby once the misunderstanding has been cleared up, the plot of many an eighteenth-century novel, but rather because it's unthinkably painful to her that she could have been so wrong about Willoughby's feelings. As she tells Elinor, "I could rather believe every creature of my acquaintance leagued together to ruin me in his opinion, than believe his nature capable of such cruelty. . . Beyond you three [her mother and sisters] is there a creature in the world whom I would not rather suspect of evil than Willoughby, whose heart I know so well."

Reader, if you've ever been in love with someone who returned the feeling, then you know the joyful sense of elation, of liveliness, of "being-thereness," if I may coin a word, that accompanies the experience. This is abruptly truncated for Marianne, long before the first flush of romantic love has run its course. But painful as this is, the more devastating blow is that, in her own mind, this experience calls into question her ability to form authentic and meaningful relationships. We can say, using contemporary psychotherapeutic language, that Marianne would have appeared to herself as someone who had projected her own desires on to Willoughby, and as someone who wasn't safe because she couldn't assess character accurately or judge the authenticity of her relationships correctly, with anyone but her immediate family.

Teasing out the implications of this a bit further, we can say in that case, Marianne would be condemned to a kind of existential loneliness, imprisoned within her own perceptions and alone with her own feelings because she's unable to connect emotionally in the ways that link us to one another. If Marianne doesn't know Willoughby's heart, then what does she know about anyone or anything, including herself? How can she trust herself, or anyone else, ever again? She saw herself reflected in Willoughby's eyes, but maybe nothing was there.

The validation that she found in Willoughby's love is gone, and it has taken with it the very ground of validation itself. The experience is *annihilating*, and the definition is of this word is worth citing. To *annihilate* means "To reduce to nonexistence, blot out of existence," and "To extinguish virtually; to reduce to silence, powerlessness, or humiliation." Marianne has been annihilated by Willoughby's betrayal, humiliated, silenced, and reduced to nonexistence in psychological terms. She's been made to feel like nothing, as someone living a life that didn't really exist, a reality that was a reflection of her own desires. And if you're not really here in terms of mind and heart, if you're not really connected to your world, why be here at all? The logical consequence of such feelings of annihilation is suicide. As psychologist Thomas Joiner observes, suicidal thinking involves feelings of not belonging and of being ineffectual, powerless to make a mark on the world you live in. One reason that validating the feelings of suicide-hotline callers can have a positive effect is that it counters this sense of nothingness by acknowledging the reality of the caller's feelings.

Indeed, Marianne's depression is a subconscious attempt at annihilation, to act out the death sentence of nothingness delivered by Willoughby's actions. Marianne makes this clear to Elinor once she's recovered from the nearly fatal illness brought on by her disregard for her health and many weeks of depression, which, as we know today, weakens the immune system. She tells Elinor, "My illness, I well knew had been entirely brought on by myself, by such negligence of my own health, as I had felt even at the time to be wrong. Had I died, it would have been self destruction."

Ironically, it's by imagining herself dead, de-realized, that Marianne rediscovers the affirmation that had been lost to her in her depression. To Elinor again: "Had I died, in what peculiar misery should I have left you, my nurse, my friend, my sister! You, who had seen all the fretful selfishness of my latter days; who had known all the murmurings of my heart! How should I have lived in *your* remembrance! My mother too! How could you have consoled her!" By picturing the devastating effects of a real rather than a psychological annihilation, Marianne is able to find herself again, present in the minds and hearts of those who love her, and so there to herself as well.

As if in reward for being able to turn away from the annihilating deathblow delivered by Willoughby and to focus on the affirmation she finds in the love of her family, Marianne finds out that her perceptions had been accurate, that she hadn't been wrong about Willoughby. When she lies ill with her life in the balance, Willoughby comes to see Elinor in the dead of night with a message for Marianne. He tells Elinor that he had indeed loved Marianne, that his feelings for her were genuine, and that he disregarded them to marry a woman whose fortune would pay his debts and enable him to gratify his expensive tastes. The cruel letter that nearly killed Marianne had been dictated by the woman who's now his wife. He deeply regrets his behavior and wants Marianne to know that their love was real.

Despite the insights she gained during her illness, this still matters to Marianne. Even when she's well again and has determined to live a "regulated life . . . checked by religion, by reason, by constant employment," she still wishes to "be satisfied on one point . . . If I could be allowed to think that he was not always acting a part, not always deceiving me. . . . If I could but know his heart, everything would become easy." Fortunately, Elinor can assure Marianne that what she saw and felt was real: Willoughby did love her. Marianne can now move on emotionally to make the happy marriage with Colonel Brandon that concludes her story.

THE ATTACHMENT SYSTEM

Both Marianne and Fanny's stories show that resonance is at the center of attachment relationships, those close connections we have with others that offer a secure base and refueling. Edmund's attunement to Fanny enables her to thrive at Mansfield Park. When Marianne loses her ability to benefit from the attunement of those she's close to, when she *detaches* rather than attaches, she suffers intensely. As years of research in the mind-brain sciences have demonstrated, Austen was right about the connection between resonance and attachment.

The study of attachment was cofounded by the great twentieth-century psychologists John Bowlby and Mary Ainsworth. Attachment studies initially focused on babies and children, but we know today that the drive to connect with others in ways that bring support and well-being continues throughout our lives.

Bowlby proposed that the quality of a baby's relationship with her mother influenced the child's emotional and cognitive profile throughout her lifetime, rendering the nature of attachment a strong determinant of personality, behavior, and expectations about future relationships. Bowlby's theories, particularly his insight that children need attachment figures to thrive, have had a significant pragmatic impact; they were endorsed by the World Health Organization, and this led to major changes in the care of hospitalized children in Europe. I'd like to think that Bowlby was inspired by Jane Austen. Perhaps this is true since one of his daughters became an English professor who has written about Austen, analyzing her portrayal of parenting.

According to Bowlby, the foundation of attachment is emotional resonance (attunement, affective empathy), an insight that's generally accepted within the mind-brain sciences. Bowlby and his researchers observed that the most successful kind of attachment relationship, which they called "secure attachment," depended on the degree to which caregivers were available emotionally to reflect and acknowledge a baby's feelings through social signals and caring behavior—that is, emotional resonance. Their findings suggest that from our very first months of life, attunement conveys validation, and it continues to do so throughout the lifespan. To feel safe, secure, and meaningfully connected to their world, people need to feel that others are attuned to their emotions

However, this doesn't mean that a caregiver needs to be on-target a hundred percent of the time. Far from it. By experiencing lack of attunement, ruptures with the caregiver that are later repaired, children learn that although this is not a perfect world, we can recover from challenges and setbacks. They also realize that relationships will have their ups and downs. Attunement at a level of about fifty percent translates into what the great twentieth-century psychoanalyst/pediatrician D. W. Winnicott called "good enough parenting."

Bowlby's collaborator Mary Ainsworth devised a protocol for categorizing attachment, called the Strange Situation, which has been reproduced countless times in psychology labs all over the world. Participants in this experiment, mothers and babies, were visited in their homes by psychologists throughout the babies' first year. Assessments were made of how mothers interacted with their children. Researchers paid particular attention to whether or not mothers were responsive to their infants' needs on a contingent basis, which means responding with attunement. Attuned emotional responses almost always accompany actions that also convey understanding, such as picking a baby up when he cries, or letting her rest when she's tired.

When these babies were about twelve months old, the mother-child dyads were invited to Ainsworth's lab to complete the experiment. A mother and baby entered a room full of attractive toys. For twenty minutes the baby alternately stayed with the mother, with the mother and a lab worker (the Stranger), with only the Stranger, and alone. Each of the intervals without the mother lasted for a maximum of three minutes. Separations and reunions thus occurred several times in the course of the experiment.

Babies responded in ways that consistently correlated with the ways their mothers had interacted with them at home. Mothers who had resonated with their baby's emotions and needs tended to have babies who were securely attached. These babies explored the room full of toys when they first entered with their mothers. They were distressed at each of the separations, fussing and even crying, especially by the second separation. On each reunion with the mother, however, they greeted her with touching as well as vocalizing, and they were clearly happy to see her. They were a bit more clingy after repeated separations, but nevertheless, and here's what's important, they soon settled down and returned to independent play and exploration of the room with its many attractive toys. These babies were comfortable using the mother as a secure base from which to extend themselves into the surrounding world. They were able to refuel, and thereby recover, after each of the separations.

Reactions that didn't follow this pattern indicated insecure attachment. Behavior indicating insecure attachment also followed predictable patterns, enabling researchers to categorize attachment styles. Mothers who'd been emotionally distant from their babies during the home visits, such as by habitually ignoring a crying baby or failing to show much affection, tended to have children who were avoidantly attached. These babies appeared to be relatively uninterested in their mothers and didn't fuss when she left or returned to the room, neither seeking contact nor displaying anger. They focused on the toys throughout the Strange Situation. During the reunion following the separation in which the child was left alone, which was the most stressful time for all the babies, some of these avoidantly attached children actually turned away from their mother when she returned. Others who were able to show they were upset were willing to be comforted by the Stranger as well as their moms. Through most of the experiment, these babies maintained emotional and physical distance from their mothers, and they appeared to be calm even though physiological measures of heart rate and skin conductance (temperature) indicated their distress. They displayed a denial mechanism at work, hiding their feelings from their mothers, and quite likely from themselves. As in most denial mechanisms the logic was: "If I don't care or notice, I can't be hurt."

Anxious attachments, also called "ambivalent" or "resistant" attachments, were formed by mother-baby dyads in which the mother had been inconsistently available and responsive. These mothers tended to inflict their own moods on their babies rather than responding to the child's cues. A baby who wants to go to sleep doesn't want to be hugged and played with no matter how positive such behavior is on its own terms. Sometimes such a parent will be preoccupied or self-involved, perhaps distractedly ignoring a crying child, while at other times right on target, reading the baby's signals accurately and responding appropriately. Children of these mothers therefore didn't know what to expect, which made them anxious.

When rewards are intermittent, people and animals tend to develop the kind of insecurity that characterizes the anxiously attached. Feed a dog every day at the same time and place, and he'll be there without fail, happily waiting for you. Stop doing this, and he'll be distressed to begin with, but will eventually give up and go about his business during the expected feeding hour. But feed him intermittently at this time and place, and he'll be there every day, nervously waiting to see what happens, perhaps whining and begging, asking for what he craves in the ways his doggy mind knows best. So it is with children and adults who attach anxiously. They're nervous and clingy in close relationships because they've learned not to expect the reward of having their emotional needs met with any consistency or dependability.

The anxiously attached babies were often distressed even before the mother left the room. They tended to be fixated on their mother's presence and availability; they sought frequent contact, both social and tactile. They were on the whole less willing to play with the toys in the room because they were preoccupied with the activities of their mothers. These babies also showed caution and distrust of the Stranger, right from the start. At reunions with their mothers, they couldn't be comforted, and some responded with anger or passivity as well as distress—hence the "ambivalent" component of this category. They didn't return to exploration and play, as securely attached children did.

Mary Main, another formative researcher of attachment, added a fourth category, "disorganized/disoriented" attachment. Parents who showed or inspired fear, or conveyed even more extremely contradictory responses than the preoccupied caregivers of anxious/ ambivalent babies, had children who were disorganized/disoriented in their attachment. These infants responded in ways that are called disorganized or disoriented because they didn't add up to a coherent whole, just as the parent's behavior was also incoherent—sometimes loving, sometimes frightening. The babies faced an irresolvable paradox: that the parent, their source of safety, was also a source of fear. Upon reunion, these babies displayed bizarre behavior such as freezing with a catatonic expression, hands in the air, only to collapse in a fetal position the next moment. They might cry and cling to the mother while also leaning away from her and avoiding her gaze. While this category is not considered technically pathological or abusive, it adversely affects development and renders a child vulnerable to pathologies later in life.

Two additional categories, classified as pathologies, are reactive attachment disorder and social engagement disorder, in which, respectively, the child fails to develop attachment relationships altogether, or readily attaches to all adults, with no preference. These conditions are usually seen in children who've been raised in institutions where they were neglected or had no opportunity to form relationships with specific caregivers.

Attachment is so vitally important because in addition to getting us support when we need it, the attachment system grows the social brain, those skills and areas of our brains that are most important to the processing of emotions and interacting with others. All babies with normally functioning brains (called neurotypicals in autism studies) are born ready to engage emotionally and attach to their caregivers. But attachment style depends on what happens after birth. Attachment doesn't exist outside of a collaboration between nature and nurture, genetics and the environment, because even though attachment is an innate system, it depends on experience for development. In other words, there's no "what this person would have become without environmental influence" because there's no becoming without such influence.

Bowlby explained that interactions with the primary attachment figure train babies to develop "internal working models" of the world of emotions and relationships. These are general expectations abstracted from countless exchanges with caregivers. To use the language of cognitive science, internal working models are schemas or prototypes of what relationships look and feel like, general concepts or images derived from multiple specific examples. For instance, we all know that Darcy looks exactly like Colin Firth (LOL!) because he played Darcy in both the hugely popular 1995 BBC miniseries of *Pride and Prejudice*, which propelled him to stardom, and in the 2001 movie *Bridget Jones's Diary,* a film based on a modern remake of the novel. But how did Sue Birtwistle, the producer who wanted Firth for the miniseries and had to convince him to take the job (lucky for him), decide that Firth was Mr. Darcy? To begin with, she wanted a man who was stereotypically handsome, whose looks screamed out "heartthrob," and many a viewer would agree that she chose wisely.

Firth matched Birtwistle's internal schema for "handsome man." Although she wasn't necessarily aware of the existence of this schema, it was there. This means that she had extracted traits from many different faces to come up with an ideal that Colin Firth matched, or closely matched. In a similar fashion, my schema for "house" looks much like the kind of house a kindergartner might draw: a door, a window, and a slanted A-frame roof. This isn't because I'm incapable of more adult ways of thinking about houses—on the contrary, I'm fascinated by distinctive architectural features and have an advanced case of house envy—but rather because I've abstracted a simple model based on what most houses have in common: doors, windows, roofs.

Incidentally, what most of us think of as handsome or beautiful is by definition a schema. We cull the most regular and symmetrical features from the thousands of faces we see and from this generalized composite form a schema for attractiveness. Nevertheless, attractiveness is largely culturally determined even if regular features tend to be favored. Scholars have concluded that Mr. Darcy didn't look like Colin Firth because nineteenth-century standards of attractiveness were different from our own.

In the same way that we form generalized schemas about houses and good looks, a baby culls the common features of his interactions with his mother or other close caregivers and develops a schema of what relationships look and feel like. A securely attached baby develops an internal working model of close relationships as warm and supportive because most of his encounters with his mother or other close caregivers have been characterized by such qualities. For securely attached children, malattuned or inadequate responses are quickly repaired most of the time. Sadly, an avoidantly attached baby learns that intimacy is likely to be painful and disappointing—better to keep your distance. An anxious-ambivalent child learns that people are not dependable.

To put this in neurological as well as psychological terms, repeated instances of attunement on the part of caregivers create the right neurochemical environment for babies to develop the neurological structures that correspond to secure attachment. The experiences that generate insecurity also create stress, and stress is toxic for developing neurons and developing brains. If the child's environment is sufficiently stressful, actual brain damage or diminished development might result. This topic will be considered in more detail, especially with regard to the capacity for emotional regulation, in future chapters.

In addition, our understanding of what relationships feel like is stored in emotional and bodily memory, while our knowledge of how to behave in relationships and what to expect of them is stored in procedural (how-to) memory, candidates for the subconscious discussed in Chapter Four. The neurological content of this knowledge consists of neural patterns, the particular neurons and network configurations that are key in forming our thoughts and behaviors. Hebb's theorem explains that this knowledge becomes neurologically ingrained because "Neurons that fire together wire together." Once a neuron has fired, it's more likely to fire again, and when two neurons fire simultaneously the linkage of activation has a better than random chance of recurring. The child's knowledge about relationships is stored in this dispositional form, in the likeliness that the neurons that represent this knowledge will activate.

Habitual neural patterns translate into knowledge, feelings, and actions in relationships. They also translate into expectations; the world you've come to know is the one you often create. People who avoid forming close relationships with others tend to produce conditions that confirm their sense that such relationships aren't possible. Darcy keeps his distance, and so he lives in a world in which distance from others is the norm.Conversely, when we're able to form relationships that contradict our expectations, that's when change, and often healing, are possible. This is also true of Darcy, who begins to change in essential ways as a result of his relationship with Elizabeth.

ADULT ATTACHMENT STYLES AND AUSTEN'S FICTIONAL PEOPLE

It's widely accepted that intimate relationships tend to be attachment relationships for adults. The same is often true of close friendships. As with babies and their caregivers, these are people with whom we not only feel a strong bond, but to whom we turn in times of stress for refueling, as we see with Fanny and Edmund.

Like babies, adults also have attachment styles, and these categories correspond to those of infant attachment. Mary Main, who devised the category of disorganized-disoriented attachment, also formulated adult attachment categories, thereby extending Bowlby's discoveries. Adult categories of attachment (the corresponding infant categories are in parentheses) are secure (secure attachment), dismissing or dismissive (avoidant), preoccupied (anxious-ambivalent), and unresolved-disorganized (disorganized-disoriented). I won't consider this last category because it leads to extremely impaired functioning in relationships. None of Austen's heroines or their partners illustrates such extreme dysfunction, although other characters demonstrate pathologies (to be discussed later).

Main and her research team devised a tool for assessing adult attachment style, the adult attachment interview (AAI), which is still used today. The AAI is a series of questions that invites people to talk about their pasts, particularly their childhoods. While the Strange Situation assesses behavior, from which psychologists infer the babies' states of mind, the AAI enables researchers to directly assess mental content, to capture attitudes toward attachment. By the ways people answer these interview questions, through the content of their answers and their narrative style, especially the degree of coherence and collaboration (with the interviewer) in their responses, attachment categories are deduced.

Collaboration exemplifies attunement in the sense that it involves participating mindfully in a conversation, with attention to what the interviewer is asking and to speaking so that she can follow your narrative. Those who received attunement tend to be able to offer it as well, and participating with attention in a conversation demands attunement. For attachment researchers, how people speak as well as what they say—form as well as content—reveals more than the subjects answering the questions realize. It also demonstrates that attachment styles motivate not only feelings and behavior, but also the very ways we think about relationships, our cognitive and verbal habits.

As you'd expect, securely attached adults tend to have coherent accounts of the past. They discuss relationships (including those with parents and caregivers) realistically, and they're able to acknowledge both good and bad experiences. They answer the interviewer's questions without digressing or interrupting their train of thought, which demonstrates collaboration. They say enough to give a sense of the past without speaking at inappropriate length about their experiences, which might reveal an obsessive focus on attachment issues.

Those with preoccupied attachment attachment tell narratives that are contradictory and disjointed; the past often intrudes into accounts of the present because they are "preoccupied" with the care they received when younger. They stray from the focus of the question and miss conversational cues, and so their answers lack collaboration. They were not attuned to, and so they don't attune. For instance, one respondent answered a request to tell about his earliest memories saying, "We were a close-knit family. We used to play all the time, have fun, walk around. There were never any times when things became too loud, or sometimes they would." This respondent then recounted a time that his uncle took the family to Disneyland, adding, "Last week my parents took my brother's kids there and they didn't even call us. Why they do this I don't know." This adult hadn't gotten over the injuries of inconsistent attunement and was still preoccupied with his parents' love and attention; this insecurity about relationships, past and present, characterizes preoccupied adults.

Dismissing adults tend to recount the past in very generalized and positive narratives that lack detail. They ignore the invitations extended by the interviewer to elaborate on relationships, and so their discourse lacks a collaborative quality. Their narratives are so threadbare because avoidant-dismissive people do their best to avoid emotions, a strategy that helped them to downplay the pain of the neglect and lack of attunement they experienced.

While the AAI is a remarkable research tool, the most significant indicator of attachment style is not measured in the lab, but seen in our relationships. Let's call upon Elinor and Marianne (*Sense and Sensibility*) and Darcy (*Pride and Prejudice*), who illustrate the most common attachment styles—secure, preoccupied, and dismissive—with textbook accuracy.

The two sisters again provide a telling contrast, with Elinor demonstrating a secure, and Marianne a preoccupied (anxious-ambivalent for the babies) attachment style with their romantic partners. At the start of the novel, nothing indicates Marianne's insecurity; the Dashwoods are a loving family, and Marianne feels safe and comfortable. But a preoccupied attachment pattern would be likely to emerge in new situations, and perhaps especially in romantic ones, where even very secure people can feel unsettled and distracted. This is exactly what happens.

Marianne demonstrates a preoccupied attachment style when she becomes involved with Willoughby. She enters into this relationship impetuously and with abandon, attaching strongly. She focuses on Willoughby obsessively, lacking the energy or desire to think of anyone else. Although people in love do tend to be obsessive, they aren't always as anxious as Marianne.

Even when Marianne believes that Willoughby loves her and will be faithful, she's nevertheless extremely edgy when they're apart. She's miserable when he leaves Devonshire, more engrossed with him than ever. When the Dashwood sisters subsequently arrive in London, where Marianne knows she'll be seeing Willoughby, she writes to him immediately and nervously awaits an answer. She can't help obsessing about this relationship to the exclusion of everything and everyone else in her life, like those poor babies in the Strange Situation who couldn't take their eyes off their mothers long enough to play with a room full of enticing toys. And London was indeed enticing—as Samuel Johnson said, "The man who is tired of London is tired of life." At this time, Elinor notices "a flutter" in Marianne's "high spirits"; she remains happy and expectant, but nevertheless "agitated." When Willoughby finally leaves a calling card to show that he'd attempted a visit, Marianne becomes even more nervous, even though no one yet doubts his devotion. "From this moment her mind was never quiet."

As evidence of Willoughby's deliberate neglect begins to accrue, Marianne tightens her grip, writing increasingly desperate notes to him. This is the pattern of preoccupied attachment; when the attachment figure is unavailable, a person clings and pursues all the harder. Marianne writes to Willoughby even after it's likely that he's snubbed her by not attending a small dance given by mutual friends, and even though he hasn't answered any of her previous letters. On that fateful evening when they finally encounter one another at a ball, where ignoring Marianne is no longer an option, Willoughby greets her formally and coldly, as if he barely knows her, a devastating blow. This only makes her cling all the harder; she writes three additional desperate notes in succession, not waiting for answers to her first two before writing again. People with preoccupied attachment styles (anxiously attached) can't let things rest, and by acting rather than waiting, they often make things worse for themselves. Marianne's frantic letters are finally answered by the "impudently cruel letter" that nearly kills her.

Elinor, who has a secure attachment style, responds very differently when faced with similar circumstances. Edward appears to be falling in love with Elinor as they get to know one another in Sussex, where her family is living at the start of the novel. Yet when Edward subsequently visits the Dashwoods at their new home in Devonshire, Elinor notices an odd ambivalence: ". . . the reservedness of his manner toward her contradicted one moment what a more animated look had intimated the preceding one." Rather than pursuing him, clinging, and seeking signs of his affection, as a person with a preoccupied attachment style would do, Elinor keeps her head and her distance. When Edward leaves, she tries her best to distract herself from dwelling on him, keeping as busy and useful as possible.

Throughout a trial similar to the one Marianne experiences, involving love, separation, doubt, and despair, Elinor never loses her sense of herself as a social being who has the obligation to maintain her relationships with others and to behave appropriately within her community. This isn't easy, but she does it. When Elinor learns that the reason Edward has been behaving so strangely is that he's engaged to another woman, knowledge that appears to end all possibility of a future together, she does her best to temper her grief and move on. She's just as attached to Edward as Marianne is to Willoughby, but there's a less desperate quality to her love.

Darcy, dismissively attached, errs on the other side of Elinor's golden mean. He's emotionally distant from others, in denial about his emotional need for people who can provide a secure base and refueling. To be sure, practical considerations explain his behavior to some degree; he must maintain his distance or he'd have to interact with all the annoying daughters and mothers who hope to capture him in the marriage hunt. But his standoffishness goes beyond this pragmatic, protective mechanism. Bingley welcomes other people into his life, although he too is a wealthy, eligible bachelor. And Darcy keeps his distance even with Bingley, his closest friend. Although we can't know what Darcy says to Bingley in private (Austen never wrote scenes with men alone because she refused to write about something that she couldn't witness), given Bingley's behavior, we have no reason to think that Darcy has confided his love for Elizabeth. He keeps himself to himself.

For the dismissively attached, the desire for closeness signals danger, and so Darcy struggles to resist his attraction to Elizabeth, to maintain his distance. This might be true right from the start. Although it's possible that Darcy fell in love with Elizabeth *after* the

Meryton ball, we can view his rude comment and his refusal to dance at this event as an attempt to ensure that his initial interest in Elizabeth won't lead him to get close to her. In other words, Darcy's insult might well be a defense mechanism. For even though they haven't been introduced, it's likely that Darcy is attracted to Elizabeth at first sight (after all, the novel was originally entitled *First Impressions*).

Although Darcy has only exchanged a glance with Elizabeth, his feelings of attraction aren't necessarily superficial, since social signals are capable of conveying large amounts of information. Perhaps something of Elizabeth's amusement, her ironic detachment from the social scene, conveys itself in her posture and facial expression. Certainly, her liveliness would be legible in her features. Her bright eyes, so alluring to Darcy, would convey her shrewd intelligence, even at rest. And it makes sense that if Darcy felt himself attracted to Elizabeth, he would defend against his desire with a nasty comment. Indeed, his insult protests too much; he could easily have declined dancing without launching such a pointed and audible attack. Fortunately, his love for Elizabeth eventually triumphs, and he overcomes his pattern of avoidant attachment.

Showing another tendency of dismissing adults, Darcy defends against his own needs and weaknesses by projecting them onto others and being concerned with their well-being to the exclusion of his own. We see this in his attitude toward Bingley. Darcy is worried that his friend's love might involve him in an alliance with a most undesirable family, and so he acts to protect his friend. It's likely that he projects his own fears onto his friend, for Bingley's situation is uncannily similar to his own. Darcy acknowledges his own needs only when his love is so insistent that it breaks through all his attempts to conquer it, as he so tactlessly tells Elizabeth when he proposes the first time.

AUSTEN'S FICTIONAL PEOPLE AND THE CHILDHOODS WE NEVER SEE

In her research on adult attachment, Main discovered that the primary attachment style people have as adults predicts with remarkable accuracy the style they develop with their own children. This means that attachment styles are transmitted intergenerationally. (Unfortunately, the same is true of abuse.) It would make sense that the attachment style developed early in life would have a strong effect on the way we relate to our own children. Similar contexts evoke similar responses (a variation of Hebb's theorem), and so the old patterns of parent and child interaction would tend to reassert themselves. Even more simply, attitudes, feelings, and behavior about relationships, as well as strategies for dealing with people, emerge in the context of interacting with our children, as they do with others to whom we are close.

Although Austen doesn't usually chronicle the childhoods of her characters (Catherine Morland in *Northanger Abbey* is an exception), we can use historical context as well as evidence from Austen's novels to infer the conditions that influenced the development of our three representatives of attachment styles, Elinor, Marianne, and Darcy. It's a fair bet that their parents' attachment styles were transmitted to their children. Take Darcy and avoidant attachment. An avoidantly attached person isn't in touch with emotions much of the time, his own and those of other people. Such a parent or caregiver would tend to be insufficiently attuned to the emotions of a baby, and so produce a child who is also avoidantly attached.

There's evidence that Darcy's parents maintained their distance. Darcy speaks well of his father, but he never even mentions his mother. She might not have been a very loving or even a very nice person. Mrs. Reynolds, the housekeeper at Pemberley, also speaks well of Darcy's father, while keeping silent about his mother. Only Lady Catherine de Bourgh, Darcy's snobby, insufferable aunt whose opinion is not to be trusted, speaks of Darcy's mother (her own sister) with affection.

Moreover, Darcy's praise of his father as "excellent," "revered," and "all that was benevolent and amiable" conveys admiration rather than closeness. These are character assessments rather than expressions of feeling, or comments on the quality of their relationship. No doubt, nineteenth-century language was more formal than our own, but compare this to Wickham's effusions, admittedly insincere, but which are nevertheless far warmer than Darcy's restrained assessment: Mr. Darcy (senior) was "one of the best men that ever breathed, and the truest friend I ever had." Wickham not only praises his godfather's character but also conveys a sense of the closeness of their bond.

Darcy's parents probably determined his attachment style to a large extent, but other factors likely influenced him as well. It's not even certain that he actually had much contact with his parents, especially during the crucial formative years of infancy and toddlerhood. Children of upper- and upper-middle-class families were often sent out to be raised by others for the first few years of life, as was Austen herself. In any case, in an aristocratic household, it's doubtful that the mother (and certainly not the father) would have been the primary caregiver. So maybe Darcy had emotionally remote nurses, governesses, and tutors. His own natural tendency to shyness would have been a factor to some extent, certainly making him more prone to distance himself from others. But environment likely played a large role in forming his character.

As to the Dashwoods, we might ask why two sisters, close in age, develop such different attachment styles. To begin with, the sisters are different temperamentally, so innate characteristics might have contributed to this discrepancy. A sensitive person might be more prone to develop insecurities. Even so, the way they are raised would have had a significant influence. Children can grow up in the same household yet inhabit very different environments in social and emotional terms. Marianne, because she's innately more sensitive and reactive than her sister, would likely have elicited different responses from Mrs. Dashwood than Elinor. Mrs. Dashwood might have cared for a calm baby in a calm manner, while feeling completely overwhelmed by a fussy baby, unable to cope in a helpful way.

When a child is screaming and upset, it takes a lot of stability to respond rather than react, to remain attuned without becoming distressed. If a caregiver habitually gets upset in response to her baby's distress rather than comforting the child—responding with emotional contagion rather then emotional resonance—this creates insecurity. It sends the message that the world is a place in which you can't depend on close people to provide comfort or relief, and so you have to try all the harder to make your go-to person pay attention to your needs. Perhaps Mrs. Dashwood's responses were erratic, sometimes on target, sometimes leading her to ignore her baby or, more likely, to become upset herself, which does no one any good. The child becomes clingy rather than self-sufficient, desperate in the hope that the comfort she craves will be forthcoming, because sometimes it is. And it makes her anxious, worried about whether or not relief will be available or unavailable. Think of those dogs being fed intermittently.

Given what we see of Mrs. Dashwood, who's a lot like Marianne, she doesn't appear to possess the stability to deal with a difficult child without becoming engulfed in the distress herself. We've seen that Mrs. Dashwood fails to maintain a critical distance from Marianne during her crisis with Willoughby, tending to absorb or catch Marianne's feelings rather than resonate with them. This behavior might go way back, even to Marianne's infancy, because once patterns of relationship are established, they tend to endure unless work is done to change them.

Because of the family's socioeconomic level, the girls might not have been raised by Mrs. Dashwood at all in the early years. Perhaps they had very different kinds of caregivers. Or perhaps Elinor was sent out of the house and Marianne was raised at home. Or maybe Mrs. Dashwood was able to cope with one child, but not two. In any case, Elinor might well have had more dependable caregiving than Marianne, as their attachment styles suggest.

Additionally, Marianne might have learned to be more insecure with men than women because she's found that they're undependable. Her great-uncle willed his property to Marianne's father, Henry Dashwood, with the stipulation that it descend after his death to Marianne's half brother, John (her father's son by an earlier marriage), who's already well off. He neglects Marianne and her mother and sisters, Henry Dashwood's second family, who really need the money.

This was unexpected, and Austen is rather savage about this betrayal. Henry Dashwood and his wife and daughters had been devoted to this elderly relative, but John Dashwood's child "had so far gained on the affections of his uncle, by such attractions as are by no means unusual in children of two or three years old; an imperfect articulation, an earnest desire of having his own way, many cunning tricks, and a great deal of noise, as to outweigh all the value of the attention which, for years, he had received from his niece and her daughters." And although John Dashwood promises to honor his father's deathbed wish by providing for his stepmother and her daughters, he reneges on this responsibility. Marianne might be naturally more liable to insecurity than Elinor because of her attachment history early in life, and so when she encounters unreliability, it activates powerful insecurities that then become associated with these subsequent circumstances. Marianne learns to expect that men will behave badly, and while she never consciously thinks this will apply to Willoughby, her insecurity likely runs deep.

HEALING OLD WOUNDS WITH NEW STITCHES*

Research on attachment shows that the attachment style you develop in childhood tends to correlate with the attachment style you have as an adult. In particular, romantic relationships tend to be attachment relationships, at least those that last beyond the period of infatuation. It makes sense that the ways we learn to relate early in life, and the expectations we have about relationships, influence us throughout our lives. But even though early experiences with the primary caregiver, often the mother, are highly influential, the correlation between the attachment style you have as a baby and the one that dominates your later relationships isn't absolute. Change and development are possible. The insecurely attached can overcome their difficulties in relating, even if this takes work, and perhaps a bit of luck, as with Darcy.

We also need to take into account the array of influences we experience, even in the first years of life. Anthropologist Sarah Blaffer Hrdy points out that babies have significant attachments with other people even when the mother is the primary caregiver. These other relationships also develop our brains and our personalities. The profusion of relationships most of us have throughout our lives, even in infancy, means that we're capable of developing a variety of attachment styles that can emerge at different times and in different contexts.

Hrdy's claims are supported by variations in results of the Strange Situation experiment. When the experiment is conducted with different people, such as the father rather than the mother, it often

---

*   This wonderful phrase about the possibility of repair is the title of a book of poems by Meggie Royer. *Healing Old Wounds With New Stitches* (Portland, OR: Where Are You Press, 2013).

produces different results. Indeed, Bowlby was misguided in focusing on maternal relationships to the exclusion of these other connections. This was understandable in mid-twentieth-century England and elsewhere in the Western world, including the United States. These were cultures in which a single woman was almost completely responsible for the care of a child, which took place to a large extent in isolation, a form of social organization rarely seen elsewhere. With most primates, it not only *takes* a village to raise a child (a troupe if you're a chimpanzee or a bonobo), but there *is* a village or community available to do this work.

Even when attachment styles are consistent, change is possible because our mind-brains are malleable, or plastic, as neuroscientists say. Experiences and their effects are not written in stone but in neurons and bodies, and as we've seen, experience changes the mind-brain. Provided we haven't suffered intensely traumatic infancies, we have many opportunities, especially through relationships later in life, to correct or compensate for what might not have been so good in our early years. A strong, secure attachment with a mentor, a partner, a friend, a therapist—with any close, caring, attachment figure—can transform our mind-brains, improving social intelligence, the quality of our relationships, and our general sense of well-being. Habits of perception and behavior—internal working models—can be changed by such experiences later in life.

Main acknowledged this optimistic possibility by adding another category to adult attachment: earned secure attachment. This describes people who've had significantly flawed caregiving and who developed insecure attachment styles as children, yet who can be classified as securely attached adults, or who at least have many of the attributes of secure attachment. Perhaps Elinor earned her secure attachment status. I, for one, think that Darcy's transformation will extend to his attachment style, and he'll be a warm, openly emotional parent as well as a loving husband. He'll have a more fulfilling personal life than anyone would have predicted, including Darcy himself, before he met Elizabeth.

Austen was well aware that a certain degree of pure contingency, just plain chance, often decides whether or not we marry happily. In

Persuasion the narrator tells us that although Anne and Wentworth are genuinely in love, "[h]alf the sum of attraction on either side might have been enough [to invoke such feelings], for he had nothing to do, and she had hardly any body to love." Had Bingley not rented a country mansion in the neighborhood of Longbourn, Darcy would never have seen Elizabeth. Perhaps Darcy and Elizabeth, with their intelligent, "seeking" minds and high standards, are also a bit bored and lonely. In *Mansfield Park*, Edmund marries Fanny because Mary has proved to be unsuitable and Fanny is available. Austen conveys the contingent quality of this last match in the offhand, almost comical way in which she describes Edmund's change of heart as learning to prefer "soft light eyes to sparkling dark ones."

But of course chance turns to luck only if a deep connection can be forged, or in Edmund's case, if it's already there. There's nothing accidental about Edmund's deep regard for Fanny, "founded on the most endearing claims of innocence and helplessness, and completed by every recommendation of [Fanny's] growing worth." And to be honest, Edmund might have had enough of romantic love and its edginess to last him a lifetime. He's ready to marry for less glamorous reasons. Austen's worthy and long-suffering heroine, Fanny, gets to have it all, marrying the man of her most romantic dreams, who's also her best friend.

EIGHT

Growing Regulation

As you recall, in *Mansfield Park* Edmund finds his young cousin Fanny alone and weeping on her first night in her new home. She's distressed because she doesn't feel safe. Of course, the weeping Fanny isn't in physical danger; she's not hungry or under attack or lost. On the contrary, in the sheltered world of Mansfield Park, she's just about as physically safe as anyone can be.

Yet Fanny is in emotional danger. Sent to live with her aunt and uncle whom she's never met, she's been whisked away from her own family, everyone she knows and loves. These are her attachment figures, the people who provide a secure base in emotional terms. At Mansfield Park, she feels that she has no one to turn to for refueling, for the understanding and support that enable us to go out into the world and deal with the challenges that assail each life. The adoption feels more like an abandonment than an opportunity, and all young mammals fear abandonment. Edmund comes to the rescue, offering such support, and letting Fanny know that he'll be there for her. He connects Fanny with caring others, both by bringing pen and paper so that she can write to her beloved brother, William, and offering friendship on his own behalf.

This episode shows one purpose of the attachment system, to ensure that we have supportive others in our lives, people who can provide emotional as well as physical safety. The extent to which we receive attunement and comfort as babies determines our attachment styles, at least to begin with. When Fanny realizes she'll still have one such person to turn to, someone who can make her feel safe, she calms down and feels better. Here we see the other purpose of the attachment system: the regulation of emotion, particularly negative emotion.

Experience tells us that these two functions, emotional support and emotional regulation, belong together because, as we see with Fanny, when we get support from others in times of distress, we tend to feel better. Edmund's proposal of help and friendship swiftly quiets Fanny's loneliness and anxiety. This occurs at a neurochemical as well as a psychological level; the hormone oxytocin (the cuddle hormone), which activates when we bond with others, reduces stress. However, we don't rely exclusively on others to manage our emotions; much of the time we do this for ourselves. Emotional regulation often means *self*-regulation, which refers to our capacity to avoid, control, and recover from negative or unproductive emotions.

All of Austen's heroines, with the exception of Marianne of *Sense and Sensibility*, are good self-regulators. Even though they're different from one another, *very* different with respect to some traits, they share the ability to remain on a fairly even keel and to express emotion in ways that are appropriate to a given situation. They experience negative emotions sparingly and judiciously, only when really called for. And when they *do* respond with fear or anger or other negative feelings, they can usually regain their equilibrium quickly; they aren't rattled for long. Even when emotions can't be dampened, good regulators can usually control the display of emotion, the extent to which they let others know they're upset. Just as important, they don't overregulate, deny, or detach from their feelings. Regulation is not repression.

We see all of these qualities in Fanny. She makes the best of her separation from her loved ones, carving out a rewarding life for herself at Mansfield Park. She calmly endures her inferior position as the poor relation, taking the many slights from her aunts and cousins in stride. And although she's heartbroken when Edmund falls head over heels in love with Mary Crawford, Fanny keeps her feelings to herself; this includes her true feelings about Mary, whom she dislikes not because she's a rival, but because she's immoral and dangerous. In short, Fanny has many reasons to feel depressed, unloved, and angry during her years at Mansfield Park, but she's able to focus on the positive parts of her life there, above all, her friendship with Edmund.

Yet resilience is not the same as spinelessness. Although Fanny tends to be deferential and eager to please, she nevertheless remains firm, calm, and confident when such qualities are needed, as when Sir Thomas pressures her to marry Henry Crawford. Even though she's always felt intimidated by Sir Thomas, when standing her ground is crucially important, she keeps her anxiety in check. Still, many readers have felt frustrated with Fanny for her quiet acceptance of her poor treatment so much of the time. Many think she's overregulated, or to put this less charitably, that she plays the martyr. But what purpose would protest have served? In the end, Fanny's way turns out to be the better choice. She gets all that she wants while also proving her worth to those who underestimated her.

The capacity for self-regulation is linked to attachment style. As we see with Fanny, securely attached people tend to be good self-regulators. In our own day, we might find it surprising that Fanny has a secure attachment style when her parents were so willing to let their daughter be raised by relatives. How could people who could so easily let go have made their child feel secure? But the Prices were actually giving Fanny the opportunity for a far better life than would have been her lot had she stayed with them in their crowded, chaotic household with "too many children and not enough money." Love and even strong attachment can be factors in letting someone go. Fanny's very sadness testifies to her having felt loved and supported by her parents and siblings, especially her brother, William.

People with a preoccupied attachment style tend to be poor self-regulators; the very term *anxious attachment*, which refers to babies and children, indicates a compromised ability for regulating emotions. As Marianne of *Sense and Sensibility* demonstrates, people with a preoccupied attachment style experience emotions easily and intensely, specifically in the context of relationships. The morning after Willoughby leaves Barton, his first parting from Marianne and well before he begins to behave badly, Marianne is "awake the whole night." The agitation she feels waiting for Willoughby to contact her when she arrives in London similarly reveals poor powers of self-regulation. And when Marianne realizes that Willoughby has abandoned her, her lack of control is painfully obvious. At this point, Marianne completely loses the ability as well as the desire to tone down the despair she feels, or to temper the self-destructive and antisocial behavior to which it leads.

While Austen highlights Marianne's determination to be flamboyantly passionate, and portrays her failure to regulate her emotions as the effect of a romantic creed—her belief that reserve and self-control are equivalent to hypocrisy—this is only part of the picture. However much Marianne's romantic notions contribute to the disaster with Willoughby, Austen makes it clear that Marianne has a hard time managing her feelings. She lacks her sister Elinor's self-possession, and she's inherently more thin-skinned and reactive. As her agitation in good as well as bad circumstances demonstrates. Marianne has a small window of tolerance for excitement of all kinds. At the end of the novel, reassuring her readers that Marianne really does love Colonel Brandon—and I fear many have doubted this—Austen writes, "Marianne could never love by halves; and her whole heart became in time, as much devoted to her husband, as it had once been to Willoughby." Even in this description of appropriate emotional expression, there's a quality of excess, of not being able to put the (vagal) brake on.

Emotional dysregulation can mean being overregulated as well as underregulated. This can involve both inhibition, not being able to express emotions, and repression, hiding them from oneself. For the dismissively attached, overregulation is often a response to strong feeling. The avoidantly attached babies of the Strange Situation study were too young to be able to tell researchers whether or not they felt numb or emotionally neutral in the company of their mothers. But the Adult Attachment Interview, which indicates attachment style, suggests that dismissively attached adults distance themselves from their feelings, overregulating as well as suppressing. And not being in touch with emotions can compromise a person's ability to form positive social connections. We see this with Darcy, who has a dismissive attachment style, and who's also overregulated. People dislike him. They take his lack of expressiveness for standoffishness and think he's proud in the worst sense of the word; they think he's a snob. Well, yes, he is a snob, and this accounts for his behavior to some degree, but he's also shy and ill at ease with people.

The marriage proposal scene in *Pride and Prejudice* shows how different attachment styles lead to different ways of dealing with negative emotion. In response to Darcy's highly insulting proposal, in which he confesses that he's condescending to marry Elizabeth in spite of her dreadful family, Elizabeth loses her temper. I think that most readers will agree that this is an appropriate response. Elizabeth, who has a secure attachment style, is a good self-regulator most of the time.

Darcy, on the other hand, becomes less expressive than ever in response to Elizabeth's anger. He doesn't repress his feelings, but he doesn't voice them either. This impulse comes from habit as much as from strategy; emotional expression feels dangerous, and inhibition is often Darcy's first line of defense. He leaves Elizabeth in Mr. Collins's drawing room, preferring to tell his feelings in writing, at a safe distance from the fallout of strong reactions, both his own and Elizabeth's.

This is yet another turn to regulation. Writing brings cognitive, prefrontal, regulatory processes to bear on emotions, which is why keeping a journal is therapeutic for many people. Writing integrates right-brain emotions with left-brain thoughts. Responding in writing to Elizabeth is actually not a bad idea in this instance because it enables Darcy to begin to make sense of his experiences and emotions, a process that continues well beyond the aftermath of his rejection. But good or bad, right or wrong, Darcy's behavior indicates his tendency to rely on thoughts rather than feelings. I wonder what would have happened if Darcy had defended himself in the moment, if he and Elizabeth had continued to thrash out their different perceptions. This would have made for a very different *Pride and Prejudice*. I leave this question to be answered by the many who rewrite, sequelize, and prequelize Austen's novels.

HOW TO BUILD A TEMPERATE TEMPERAMENT

Attachment and regulation styles correlate because they both emerge from the same set of experiences. Just as our relationships with caregivers lead to different attachment styles, these relationships also instill differing capacities for managing our emotions. In addition, because emotions are always physiological as well as psychological responses to experience, these two domains are linked for humans and for all mammals throughout their lifespan.

We see this clearly with newborns, who use their mothers' bodies to maintain homeostasis, the body's stabilization of vital processes such as heart rate, respiration, and temperature. This happens through bodily contact, being held or touched by another warm body. The behaviors that manage an infant's physiology are therefore nurturing behaviors; holding a baby conveys love as well as warmth. Babies who receive little or no nurturing die or fail to thrive (as you know, extreme sympathetic stress activity can interfere with normal growth). For human and other mammal infants, love is not a luxury but a life raft. Throughout our lives, we continue to benefit from touch, because it releases oxytocin, which quiets stress.

Additional, more properly psychological elements begin to be crucial as newborns wake up to their worlds. The first step in offering comfort to babies, even comfort that appears to be primarily physical such as changing a diaper, usually involves resonating with the baby's emotional state. This is the very same behavior that fosters attachment. Mirroring is involved; the caregiver's expression usually briefly mimics that of the child. Imagine yourself picking up a crying baby and feel what your face is doing: I think you'll see what I mean. Mirroring allows the caregiver to convey his understanding of the child's distress. The same understanding applies to positive emotions.

But then think of your behavior after this mirroring. I'll bet you're calm and relaxed, conveying words and facial expressions of comfort. This is the next step: The caregiver's expression will convey his own regulated, unstressed condition, which has a calming effect, a benevolent form of emotional contagion. The baby actually attunes to the caregiver's calm mood, using his right brain to connect to the affect conveyed by the caregiver's right brain. Such communication is possible even for infants because the right brain, responsible for expressing and reading emotional information conveyed by social signaling, begins to develop earlier than the left, in the first year of life.

Nearly all the information being shared between caregiver and child is emotional information in the early months of life. This isn't conscious information *about* affect (*I know that my mother is happy or sad*). In fact, recognition of this reflective kind is impossible for infants since they lack the language to reflect on feelings and the sense that people have minds whose contents can differ from their own. Babies might begin to understand words at about six months, but they'll probably not have the sophisticated cognitive skills to reflect on feelings until well after they've learned to speak. And the ability to fully understand that their thoughts and perceptions can differ markedly from those of others is not completely developed until age four or five. What *is* conveyed to the infant, then, is not information about another person's affect, but *the affect itself*. Again, we might think of regulation for babies as a form of emotional contagion. Comfort, attunement, regulation: They're a package deal, the inseparable triumvirate that forms attachment and emotional regulation.

This means, of course, that conveying affect as well as regulation—or dysregulation—can go both ways. The goal is for a parent's calm state of mind to comfort a distressed baby. But even the best of caregivers would admit that sometimes the influence goes the other way, and the caregiver catches the baby's distress. In this case, the caregiver experiences contagion rather than offering resonance. Resonance (empathic attunement) means keeping track of the distinction between self and other, of knowing that the distress is the baby's and being able to maintain a regulated self-state in the face of it. With good enough caregiving, this happens most of the time.

Adults certainly dysregulate as well as regulate one another, responding with contagion rather than resonance. When Elizabeth angrily rejects Darcy's proposal, he similarly responds with anger, although his anger leads to an icy-cold withdrawal rather than the heated protest we see with Elizabeth. Both reactions feed into one another, leading to a spiral of negativity, and they're both content to be done with one another. Fortunately, Elizabeth visits Pemberley.

By moderating the child's negative emotions countless times, the caregiver teaches the child to regulate her own emotions. For instance, an infant might be terrified when alone. But after crying out and being comforted time and again, she eventually learns that being alone isn't necessarily dangerous and that if she calls for help, it will usually be available. Just as important, she learns that this is a world in which her needs will be met, and so she doesn't have to deny them to avoid being disappointed, or proclaim them loudly and constantly to attract attention. These lessons often lead to a realistic sense of self-empowerment and good self-esteem. A child learns that she's worth the attention she craves.

Through repeated experiences with caregivers who regulate emotion, a baby learns to do this for herself. In technical terms, the child develops procedural schemas for self-regulation. A procedural schema is a set of internalized, automatic instructions. Like knowledge- or image-based schemas, which include everything from the way you picture a generic house to your ingrained expectations about relationships, procedural schemas extract a general idea from many specifics: In this case, what is learned and eventually becomes automatic is a plan of action.

Take horseback riding, which requires a specific set of physical actions. When Fanny was learning to ride, she had to think of these instructions in her first few lessons, but they soon became second nature. Young ladies at a ball know they must wait to be asked before they can dance. No one has to rehearse this rule to herself on entering a ballroom. Remaining calm, or quieting upsetting emotions, also involves a set of steps that we gradually learn, internalize, and use automatically. We can also think of procedural schemas as attractor states, patterns of neural activation that are likely to occur because they've repeatedly fired in the past.

It might well be that a baby who lies there contentedly sucking her thumb might be alleviating distress by picturing the mother's face, or recalling the feeling of being held or fed. Although this very young person can't make episodic memories yet (memories of events), she can retain images, and she can form bodily and emotional memories. Emotional memory is a right-brain process, mediated by areas that are developing in the first year of life; it's believed that this is true for bodily memory as well. (The structures responsible for episodic memories, the memories we can remember, begin functioning at about age three.)

Learning to self-soothe means learning to be comfortable with yourself, to have an internal sense of security that often helps you to be strong and independent (although this doesn't mean being isolated—far from it!). Secure-autonomous older adults and children have this internalized sense of security, which might be subconsciously or even consciously related to thinking of the presence and availability of attachment figures. Securely attached people can be separated from others without feeling unduly isolated or panicky.

THE AMERICAN BOWLBY

Neuroscientist-psychiatrist Allan Schore explains the development of self regulation at the nuts-and-bolts level of neurology. Nicknamed "the American Bowlby" for his extraordinary contributions to our knowledge of human development, Schore has woven the separate strands of attachment studies, neuroscience, and psychotherapy into a narrative that accounts for emotional regulation from cradle to grave. But Schore parts company from Bowlby by asserting that the primary purpose of the attachment system is to foster the capacity for emotional regulation—both self-regulation and co-regulation—and that making social connections is a collateral advantage. In any case, the system can be properly called an attachment-regulatory system.

Schore explains that while a child is learning procedural schemas for managing her emotions, her experiences are actually growing her brain in ways that enable this capacity, as well as shaping her attachment style and other features of personality. What happens at the psychological level also happens at the neurological level because the brain is part of the mind. Experiences continually shape our brains, developing attractor patterns, the likelihood that neurons will fire to form a particular pattern.

Animals, including humans, have critical periods of development—windows of rapid development during which a brain area or body part is particularly sensitive to certain kinds of stimuli and will develop in accordance with the quality of the stimulation it receives. If you learn French before puberty, you'll likely be able to speak it without an accent; afterward, you can become completely fluent, but you probably won't sound like a native. The time before puberty is a critical period for learning a new language. The critical period for developing the attachment regulatory system takes place during the first two years of life.

The ability to regulate emotions depends on the development of the orbitofrontal cortex (OFC). Recall that the OFC is a brain area located at the underbelly of the cortex, the outer wrapping of the brain, and which borders many emotional-processing areas. It's deep in your brain, behind your eyes. The OFC determines the ratio of input between the parasympathetic nervous system (PNS), which maintains routine functions such as digestion as well as social engagement, and which dominates when we're calm, and the sympathetic nervous system (SNS), which orchestrates many negative emotions such as anger, fear, and anxiety; the sympathetic nervous system is responsible for the fight-or-flight response, as well as the hypothalamus-pituitary-adrenal (HPA) axis response, systems that deal with short-term and long-term stress, respectively. Sympathetic activity generates excited positive feelings as well, such as joy.

We can think of the OFC as a thermostat in charge of both heat (sympathetic system) and air conditioning (parasympathetic system). If the heat or air conditioning is defective or breaks, your house will be too cold or too hot. And if the switching mechanism (OFC) isn't effective, the house will also become uncomfortable, responding too slowly to changes in temperature or stuck in one mode. With some luck, if the damage isn't too extensive, you can have your malfunctioning heating-cooling system repaired, or at least get it to work better than it has been. In the same way, the deficiencies in our emotional-regulatory systems can also be repaired much of the time through healthy relationships or therapy. Elizabeth surely readjusts Darcy's set point of avoidance and disengagement.

The caregiving behaviors that create secure attachment, attuned interactions between an infant and primary caregiver, maintain a healthy neurochemical environment for the growth of the OFC and its circuits during its critical period. When a caregiver soothes a distressed child, he also down-regulates the stress response that's a part of negative emotion, such as fear, anger, and frustration. If this doesn't happen, if a child's distress is neglected to an abnormal degree, the developing brain, including, perhaps most significantly, the OFC, is bathed in a kind of toxic soup that can destroy existing neurons and prevent the growth of new neurons, new receptors, and new synaptic connections.

This toxic soup consists of stress hormones and neurochemicals, notably glucocorticoids (such as cortisol), which flood the brain and bloodstream during HPA axis responses. Somewhat paradoxically, they're also present in parasympathetic responses to danger (including social danger), freezing, and parasympathetic stress reactions. Think of the numbing that's a response to trauma, the infant's exhaustion that follows rage at protest at neglect, or Marianne's depressive shutdown in response to Willoughby's treachery. Severe stress can prevent a child from fulfilling his potential for managing emotions in the best way possible, negatively affecting physiological as well as psychological and behavioral development. Active abuse, which creates unmanageable levels of stress, is even more toxic and damaging.

Even for adults who are well past this critical period of brain development, stress responses become harmful when they go on for too long. Prolonged or chronic stress can cause heart disease, high blood pressure, reduced immunity, and a host of other problems. Stress also affects brains. People who've been depressed for a long time, a condition that involves both excitatory and dampening stress reactions, have a smaller hippocampus, the structure (found in both hemispheres) that's responsible for making new episodic memories. Sustained trauma often results in reduced cognitive functioning. In short, if you're stressed out for too long, your ability to think clearly is compromised not only because negative thinking is often unproductive, and stress inhibits cognitive activity, but also because stress neurochemicals damage neurons.

Successful development of the attachment-regulatory system during the first year of life, especially for the sympathetic circuit, further depends not only on down-regulating distress, as discussed above, but also on joyful, playful interactions between baby and caregiver. Emotional regulation includes being able to deal with good as well as bad kinds of excitement. In addition to provoking the release of oxytocin, the "cuddle hormone" that reduces stress, these playful, exciting interactions induce the release of endogenous opioids (endorphins), pleasure neurochemicals that encourage growth of the brain. These actually accompany all instances of bonding, but they increase with play and other pleasurable exchanges. Oxytocin also encourages growth of receptors that mop up stress neurochemicals, especially those nasty glucocorticoids. As episodes of attuned excitement, joy, and pleasure repeat, the infant begins to develop a tolerance for higher and higher levels of arousal.

As with all emotional communication, facial expression is key in conveying pleasure, especially around the eyes. The sound of a caregiver's voice is also vital: The sing-songy tone that we are apt to adopt when talking to babies and pets, known as "mother-ese," also contributes to such pleasure. My cats know exactly when I am talking to them; their little ears perk up and they look at me. If you're a dad or other man in a baby's life, don't worry. An infant can engage in this attuned way with more than one person, and men as well as women can speak mother-ese. And for infants with sensory deficits such as deafness or blindness, other senses with accompanying neural pathways can convey playfulness and attunement, as conveyed by facial expression and tone of voice. Deaf babies babble with their hands. And touch, which releases oxytocin, is crucial. The more people an infant has in his or her young life engaging their different senses and opening up these neural pathways, the better.

As a baby enters the second year of life, attuning to his emotions and needs begins to involve the caregiver's repeatedly soothing states of sorrow and deflation that are bound to occur as the baby discovers just how small and powerless he is. Up until this time, he usually got whatever he wanted, but now he begins to want things that are unattainable, like that pretty vase way up high on the shelf. Disappointments also occur in the course of discipline. By discipline I don't mean harsh treatment, which can lead to serious problems, but simply letting the child know that some behaviors are unacceptable and forbidden. This includes even the mildest of rebukes undertaken for the child's protection, and these become necessary as the toddler becomes more social and mobile. (Discipline is both useless and potentially harmful before the age of one because infants can't understand prohibitions or the purpose of scolding.)

But discipline, even when necessary and well-intentioned, and other checks to the child's will, evoke shame, a stressful response. In the simplest psychological terms, shame means having your wishes or expectations disappointed. It describes the toddler's feeling when she looks for customary approval from the caregiver and she receives a rebuke instead, as when she reaches to touch the hot stove. Although adult shame is often more complicated and nuanced, this kind of disappointment is at the core of this emotion. Shame might well be an inborn response because its physiology and symptoms appear to be cross-cultural; in addition to heightened stress activity, these can include blushing and an averted gaze, as when Elizabeth "instinctively turned away" on unexpectedly meeting Darcy at Pemberley.

A child who experiences a lack of sufficient attunement or of playful, joyous experiences, might learn to shut down emotionally to some extent, and will have a system dominated by the parasympathetic (calm) nervous system. A child kept in constant anxious suspense as to whether she'll receive a sensitive and appropriate response might be on edge much of the time, developing dominant sympathetic tendencies without the ability to tolerate these high levels of excitement her nervous system generates. Those with over-regulated and underregulated attachment-regulatory systems, all insecurely attached people, tend to have a small window of tolerance for excitement. The dismissive find it threatening, and the preoccupied find it overwhelming. How this can happen is best illustrated by turning the clock back once again to visit some of Austen's fictional people in childhood.

PEOPLE WHO NEED PEOPLE (WITHOUT CLINGINESS OR DESPERATION) ARE THE LUCKIEST PEOPLE IN THE WORLD

We can return to the childhoods of our three exemplars of attachment style, Marianne, Elinor, and Darcy, to look at how emotional regulation develops from the attachment system.

Darcy likely developed an avoidant attachment style, with the accompanying tendency to overregulate because he was raised by caregivers who didn't attune to his emotional needs and who were themselves emotionally remote. Cultural ideals and child-rearing practices of the well-to-do in the nineteenth century, as well as the personalities of his parents, might have contributed to his denial and suppression of his feelings. Darcy would likely have been encouraged to have a stiff upper lip—that clichéd but nevertheless accurate description of upper-class ideals of manliness that largely prevailed. He would have been encouraged to keep his emotions in check, even as a very young child.

We can imagine the baby Fitzwilliam (Darcy), crying in his crib, his stern governess remaining impassive because he must be taught to be tough and self-sufficient. Darcy's mother might have visited the nursery or had her child brought to her once or twice a day, but she remained aloof during these visits. Perhaps she planned to start truly interacting with her son once he got past those difficult first few years and began to be a reasonable being, capable of rational thought and conversation. Or maybe she had little interest in interacting with her children at all; everyone's silence on the topic of Darcy's mother suggests she wasn't a very warm or nice person. In any case, given child-rearing practices of the wealthy, we can see why Darcy's sister, Georgiana, was attracted to the scoundrel Wickham; he seemed to promise the warmth and vitality she lacked in her close relationships with her family. Even with her beloved brother, Darcy, there was distance and reserve. We can sense her palpable joy when she meets Elizabeth for the first time—a potential "sister" she can connect with, who is warm and empathetic, unlike the calculating and sarcastic Miss Bingley.

To protect himself emotionally in this environment, baby Darcy soon learned to dampen down his emotions, to detach or dissociate from them. He developed a tendency to avoid closeness because he had learned that close relationships are disappointing. He might not have been able to avoid the hurt deep down, but he could seem neutral to the outside world, and would keep to himself much of the time. Dignity was preserved, another strong value among aristocrats. Had baby Darcy been tested in the Strange Situation, he would have ignored both the presence and absence of his mother.

In addition to leaving Darcy to manage his own distress, neither Darcy's governess nor his mother likely indulged him with the joyful play that stimulates growth of the sympathetic system, and which creates a tolerance for excitement. As a result of Darcy's detachment and his lack of positive excitatory experience, his parasympathetic, dampening-down nervous system would have begun to dominate.

Parasympathetic dominance, however, wouldn't mean that Darcy was free of stress. It would just mean that he had defense mechanisms for distancing himself, not only from others, but from his own feelings. And so Darcy would have developed little tolerance for excitement and therefore would have tended to overregulate in order to control his anxiety. He would have attractor states for withdrawing and shutting down in response to stress and to strong emotions. Alone in his crib (or cot, as the English say), baby Darcy would detach rather than self-soothe. Imagining his mother or his nursemaid's face would not be comforting, but denying his distress would insulate him to a great extent.

In short, Darcy's calmness would develop from a tendency to over-regulate—to dissociate from strong feeling—that is as unhealthy as being at the mercy of turbulent emotions. This is a protective reaction, for by having a dominant parasympathetic system that keeps his excitability in check he avoids situations that are likely to be stressful, such as emotional closeness or intense excitement. Avoidant attachment with its parasympathetic dominance can be very adaptive, but only within limits, for not having close others in one's life is also stressful. People who live alone tend to have diminished life expectancy as compared to those who live with others.

Darcy's dismissive attachment style and extreme reserve were created in the context of relationships with his family, and it's only through other relationships that he can break free of these patterns. This is true in general: Damage to our attachment systems and the social brain can be repaired through positive, close relationships with others, whether they're relatives, partners, friends, or therapists. Darcy is lucky enough to meet Elizabeth and wise enough to realize her value, although the attraction takes a much more visceral, less intellectual form: He simply can't resist her. His love for

Elizabeth and their encounters, especially her rejection of his first proposal, transform Darcy. He begins to break the vicious cycle of withdrawal and reserve that distances him from others and from his own emotions.

When we part from Darcy and Elizabeth at the end of *Pride and Prejudice*, he still has work to do to repair the ruins of the past. Elizabeth realizes that he has little tolerance for being teased in the playful manner she would like to engage with him, but she also realizes that he'll continue to develop important aspects of himself that have been neglected for far too long. Readers are left with confidence that theirs will be a long and happy marriage.

Marianne's preoccupied attachment style was formed by different challenges. We know that Mrs. Dashwood is excitable and prone to catch rather than attune to emotions; it's likely that she too has a preoccupied attachment style. We can imagine the baby Marianne tired and wanting to rest, but Mrs. Dashwood, driven by love and goodwill, scooping the child up in her arms to hug and play. We can imagine Marianne fussy and needing attention while Mrs. Dashwood zones out, absorbed by her own schemes and fantasies. And worst of all, we can imagine Mrs. Dashwood overwhelmed by her fussy infant's emotions, getting upset in response rather than soothing her child much of the time.

Such constant lack of resonance would breed problems for the mind-brain. Marianne would be on the alert, anxious to get the right responses from her mother, and so she would learn to be apprehensive and to expect uncertainty from close relationships. She would develop procedural schemas for responding with anxiety to her own needs. Alone in her crib, baby Marianne wouldn't be able to self-soothe; calling up her mother's image was likely to be upsetting rather than comforting, reminding her that emotional sustenance was unpredictable—sometimes abundant, sometimes scarce.

At the neurological level, the excitatory pathways of her sympathetic nervous system would be engaged far too much of the time, reinforcing her innate edginess. The pathways of this system would continue to grow neurons and synapses, while also ingraining attractor states, habitual neural pathways that correspond to excitability. At the same time, the stress of malattunement, of never knowing whether she's going to get what she needs from her mother, would diminish input from Marianne's calming parasympathetic system. Because the parasympathetic system would be underutilized, this system would be recessive, and she would therefore be more vulnerable to stress, and in general more emotionally reactive, than someone with a secure attachment style. In addition, she would have a low window of tolerance, even for positive events that evoke excitement. (However, when she succumbs to depression, her parasympathetic system contributes through the pathways of the dorsal vagus. But this kind of shutdown isn't an instance of healthy parasympathetic regulation but rather the collapse of her usually active mind.)

Ironically, Marianne and Darcy share an inability to manage excitement, although they respond in different ways to this lack, behaviorally and neurologically. Darcy is withdrawn and overregulated, the result of a dominant parasympathetic system, while Marianne is edgy and overemotional, the effects of a dominant sympathetic system.

Elinor exemplifies the regulated state of a person with a secure attachment style. She might have been born with a stable, placid temperament, but she likely had her emotions attuned to and her needs met after she was born. As I suggested earlier, perhaps she was sent away for the first few years of life, or perhaps her mother was very different with her than with Marianne. It's likely that in those early years, she learned to self-soothe and so to regulate her stress, which helped her to develop procedural schemas and neural-attractor states—the neurological capability—for the regulation of emotion. Elinor feels things deeply. As discussed in previous chapters, she is sensitive to the feelings of others, constantly adjusting her behavior to accommodate their needs. But Elinor can also cope with strong feelings. She illustrates emotional balance, neither overly controlling of her feelings, and so repressed and distant, nor continually and powerfully overwhelmed by them.

We don't have the backstory (again, writers of prequels, get to work!), but Bowlby and Schore would both agree that these sisters are so different not only because of innate temperament, but also because of different experiences in the critical years when attachment styles and the capacity for emotional regulation are initially developed.

TEND AND BEFRIEND, NOT FIGHT OR FLIGHT

When Edmund finds Fanny weeping her first night at Mansfield Park, she hasn't meant to attract attention with her tears. But whether she meant to or not, that's one of their purposes. Crying is a social signal that lets others know we're in trouble so they can come to our aid.

Fanny's tears are part of the workings of what psychologist Shelley E. Taylor has called the tend-and-befriend system (also, the tending instinct). As you might notice, this catchy phrase, complete with rhyme, alludes to the well-known shorthand for our stress responses known as fight or flight. The parallel wording mirrors a parallel process: Both are ways of dealing with danger. But tend and befriend involves not fighting or fleeing, or even freezing, the third term in the familiar trio of responses to stress, but rather reaching out to others who can help, and in turn, helping others in need.

It's likely that tend and befriend originated with the maternal nurturing behavior we find in female mammals. It's an outgrowth of the attachment system, characterized by two of its defining features, social connection and emotional regulation. Although tend and befriend occurs in response to threats, it depends on the same pattern of interaction that we see in attachment relationships: the turn to another for comfort and emotional regulation. We can think of tend and befriend as the attachment-regulatory system writ large, at a community-wide as well as an individual level of interconnection, and in the context of the day-to-day maintenance of well-being.

In the prehistoric times in which our species evolved, when women spent much of their time nursing and caring for children, those who formed friendships and networks of care increased the odds of survival for themselves and their children. It makes much more sense for a woman with babies to respond to danger by calling on friends and protectors to help her get her young and herself out of harm's way than to try to fight or flee an aggressor. A man could stand his ground and do battle, or flee quickly from an enemy or predator, but this isn't so easy to do when you have a couple of children hanging on to your clothing and a baby at the breast (although the behavior of human and nonhuman animals of today suggests that females will certainly stand and fight to protect their young when necessary). Taylor points out that even in our own time, women are more likely than men to respond to danger with tend and befriend rather than fight or flight, although it's difficult to say whether biology or culture plays the larger role in shaping these responses.

Like fight or flight, tend and befriend originates in immediate emotional reactions; fear and anxiety activate both systems. And their catchy names refer both to individual psychological and behavioral reactions, as well as the bodily and neurochemical machinery that accompanies these responses. But in other ways, these systems are opposed and complementary: to the extent that one dominates, the other recedes. Fight or flight depends on the dysregulation of emotion, on excitatory negative emotions. Tend and befriend depends on, and induces, regulated, prosocial emotions (as does the attachment system). This is true in terms of thought, behavior, function, and anatomy, and the opposition goes all the way down the line.

When we're in danger (which includes modern dangers such as anxiety about work and all the modern ills our flesh and brains are heir to), the amygdala tells the OFC to lift the vagal brake, thereby inducing a stress reaction. (This is because the vagal nerve connects to the sinoatrial node of the heart, which is responsible for regulating heart rate.) When the brake is lifted, heart rate speeds up, which tells all the activating, sympathetic areas in our brains and bodies to get to work. Stress neurochemicals flood our brains and bodies, particularly adrenaline and, if the HPA axis activates, cortisol, which results in the inflammation that is so bad for our health if sustained for too long a period. But when tend and befriend begins to work, and we receive help or comfort, the OFC puts the vagal brake on; heart rhythm slows down and we return to a more regulated condition.

As with most instances of the tug of war between sympathetic and parasympathetic systems, mediated by the vagal system, our brains rarely enter an all-or-nothing state. And stress might well continue to exist alongside the feelings induced by tend and befriend. Conversely, befriending is important in battle, even when aggression and fighting predominate. But on the whole, tend and befriend has a regulatory effect. Edmund's kindness rescues Fanny from the toxic sense of abandonment and isolation that she feels on her first evening at Mansfield Park.

For tend and befriend to work its magic, however, Fanny has to be receptive to the help that Edmund offers. And indeed she is. Fanny, who obviously possesses a secure attachment style, whatever other insecurities about her place or abilities she might have, can generate sufficient calm and control to be able to make use of the emotional support that Edmund provides. Her situation is certainly scary enough to have produced a different scenario. Abandonment is one of the most stressful circumstances a young mammal can experience, and Fanny is young enough at nine to feel the separation from her family intensely, as danger without a foreseeable endpoint. Depression in these circumstances wouldn't have been an unusual or even an inappropriate response. But this isn't Fanny's way or her story.

But it *is* Marianne's story in *Sense and Sensibility*. She also experiences an abandonment, a separation—from a lover rather than her family—but in emotional terms, the situation is nevertheless similar to Fanny's. Marianne is with her closest friend and confidante, her beloved sister, who's ready to do everything in her power to comfort her. And unlike Fanny, who only has Edmund, Marianne can avail herself of an entire network of people who care about her. Even if such care can be intrusive and annoying at times, it's meant kindly, as Marianne comes to realize when she emerges from her depression.

In similar circumstances, Fanny would have recovered much earlier with such a network of encouragement. (Of course, Fanny would never have gotten herself into such a predicament in the first place.) But Marianne can't get enough of a grip to take the good things on offer. She spirals into the chaos and depression induced by extreme stress. She must first learn and heal before she can take advantage of the tending and befriending that the people who love her are so willing to give.

Taylor describes a system that relies on social affiliation as a form of protection. But of course, sociality has a positive effect that extends well beyond protection. Psychologist Barbara Fredrickson has written about a similar but more extensive system that she calls "broaden and build." She doesn't view this as necessarily a response to threats, nor as a gendered system. Broaden and build refers more generally to our tendency to make connections and build networks of people who can help us to achieve our goals, or who make our lives better or easier in some way. Positive emotions and social engagement are crucial components of this system. And Fanny's positivity consists not only in her being able to accept help, but to her ability to deepen her relationships with the people she knows while learning how to deal with new players in her life. In this, she is similar to the protagonists in Austen's other novels. *Broaden and build* is indeed an apt term for the blossoming of personal qualities and positive relationships that we see with all of Austen's heroines.

DOES MARIANNE'S STORY *REALLY* HAVE A HAPPY ENDING?

At the end of *Sense and Sensibility*, the narrator tells us that Marianne is happy. But many readers don't believe her. They don't care for the ending of this novel. They grudgingly wish Elinor joy, although they can't quite understand what she sees in Edward. But they're positively upset with Austen over Marianne.

These readers aren't unreasonable. Sure, all but the dreamiest of us understand that it wouldn't have been realistic to have Marianne end up with Willoughby. It's believable that her faithless lover would repent, and that he'd regret the love he abandoned from the safety of his wife's 30,000-pound dowry. But it wasn't in Willoughby's nature to say no to this fortune and to remain true to Marianne. We accept this. But many of us are nevertheless prone to say, "But really, Jane, Colonel Brandon of the flannel waistcoat? A man for whom Marianne has never felt a spark of anything but disdain and pity? Couldn't you have found a more romantic suitor for Marianne? You might easily have created another minor character—perhaps Mr. Palmer has a younger brother."

It is a rather drastic transformation for Marianne to go from adoring Willoughby, who swept her off her feet both literally (she had a broken ankle and couldn't walk, and I'm sure Austen was playing here, making the metaphoric expression literal) and figuratively, to Colonel Brandon. But there was wisdom as well as tough love in Austen's decision.

Austen tells us that Marianne's "whole heart became in time, as much devoted to her husband, as it had once been to Willoughby." But devotion is not romantic passion, and Austen wisely doesn't claim this quality for Marianne's feelings about Colonel Brandon. Austen knows that Marianne might have wanted to spend her life with a dashing, charismatic soulmate—at least when she met Willoughby—but given her preoccupied attachment style, this kind of man couldn't have made her happy. Self-involved as Willoughby is, he could never have shown her the gentle devotion that Marianne needs to feel secure.

Once the first flush of romance was over, Willoughby would have been off doing his own thing much of the time. We see that his hunting absorbs his attention and frequently takes him far from home. A lot of social time spent exclusively with other men accompanies the sporting life, so Marianne would have ended up as a "hunting-season widow." And I doubt very much, given his history as a lothario and his readiness to capitalize on his charisma and good looks—so attractive to women—that Willoughby would have remained faithful. Marianne would have found herself often wondering and worrying about where her husband was, whom he was with, and, even worse, wondering and worrying about his feelings for her. An Emma or an Elizabeth could have kept Willoughby in line, giving as good as they got, but this wouldn't have been an ideal marriage for them either. For Marianne it would have been disastrous.

To the disappointed and incurably romantic among Austen's readers, I offer lyrics from a few centuries later: "You can't always get what you want/But if you try sometimes, you just might find/You get what you need." I was one of those disappointed readers, but in the fullness of time, I've come to understand that people don't always want what's good for them, and that getting what you need rather than what you want often brings happiness in the long run. I've come to appreciate Austen's wisdom in arranging Marianne's fate, "at nineteen, submitting to new attachments, entering on new duties, placed in a new home, a wife, the mistress of a family, and the patroness of a village." Marianne is happy and much better off with the staid and flannel-waistcoated Colonel Brandon than she ever would have been with Willoughby. With Colonel Brandon, she finds just the right mix of sense and sensibility.

NINE

Empathic Emma

Austen's "clever, handsome, and rich" heroine Emma Woodhouse gets herself into a very uncomfortable predicament. She's just dined with her family at the home of her beloved former governess, Mrs. Weston. As people are sorting themselves into groups for the short ride home, she finds herself sharing a carriage with Mr. Elton, the young vicar of Highbury who is on the lookout for a wife. For the past two months, Emma has assumed that Mr. Elton is in love with her friend Harriet, a pretty young girl with neither family nor fortune. But earlier in the day, Emma's brother-in-law, Mr. John Knightley, suggested that Mr. Elton actually likes Emma, not her friend, and he warned her to be careful of encouraging unwanted attentions. Although Emma dismissed this observation as ludicrous, in the course of the evening she has begun to realize that she, rather than Mr. John Knightley, might be mistaken, and that she, rather than Harriet, might be the object of Mr. Elton's devotion. She steels herself to deal with the awkward situation promised by the ride home but is nevertheless unprepared for the shock of what follows once she's alone with her tipsy suitor:

> To restrain him as much as might be, by her own manners, she was immediately preparing to speak, with exquisite calmness and gravity, of the weather and the night; but scarcely had she begun, scarcely had they passed the sweep gate and joined the other carriage, than she found her subject cut up—her hand seized—her attention demanded, and Mr. Elton actually making violent love to her: availing himself of the precious opportunity, declaring sentiments which must be already well known, hoping—fearing—adoring—ready to die if she refused him; but flattering himself that his ardent attachment and unequalled love and unexampled passion could not fail of having some effect, and, in short, very much resolved on being seriously accepted as soon as possible.

Most of us probably recognize this particularly embarrassing type of error, mistaking someone else's romantic feelings in one direction or another. (I still blush to think of my own mistakes of this kind.) This generally happens because of lapses somewhere along the way in what is known informally among philosophers and mind-brain scientists as "mindreading," which means inferring the beliefs, intentions, and feelings of others. Humans mindread in this way continuously and automatically, and many believe that we're the only species to do so. Evidence suggests that other great apes share this ability, although if they do, it's not as finely developed in them as it is in humans.

The ability to mindread confers an advantage that clearly helped us to survive as a species: Knowing someone else's intentions and inner states can be used to predict behavior, which might be friendly, neutral, or threatening. And this helps us to respond in appropriate ways to dangers and benefits of all kinds. When Emma realizes what Mr. Elton is really thinking, she quickly tones down the volume, although too late to prevent his exuberance.

By describing scenes from an objective viewpoint while also allowing us to eavesdrop on Emma's thoughts, Austen enables us to see where Emma is going wrong long before Emma does. The reader, like Mr. John Knightley, realizes that she's headed for trouble. There's the time when Mr. Elton and the two ladies are out for a walk and Emma pretends to have "an alteration to make in the lacing of her half-boot" so that Harriet and Mr. Elton can walk on alone. When she catches up to them, she overhears not the sweet talk of lovers, but Mr. Elton giving Harriet an account of "yesterday's party at his friend Cole's." Emma is perplexed, but she reasons that "This would soon have led to something better, of course." And she explains away the oddity of this allegedly passionate lover's strange choice of topic: "[A]nything interests between those who love; and anything will serve as introduction to what is near the heart. If I could but have kept away longer."

An extended sequence of misunderstandings takes place in the portrait episode. Emma offers to paint Harriet's portrait, and Mr. Elton enthusiastically supports this plan. We might think that Emma makes a reasonable assumption in attributing Mr. Elton's enthusiasm for the portrait to love for Harriet since people often commissioned portraits of their loved ones, just as we have photos today. Mr. Elton, however, focuses on the artist rather than the subject of her work. When Emma exclaims, "It would indeed be such a delight to have her picture!" Mr. Elton answers with a long tribute to Emma's talent rather than Harriet's beauty:

"Let me entreat you," cried Mr. Elton; "it would indeed be a delight; let me entreat you, Miss Woodhouse, to exercise so charming a talent in favour of your friend. I know what your drawings are. How could you suppose me ignorant? Is not this room rich in specimens of your landscapes and flowers! and has not Mrs. Weston some inimitable figure pieces in her drawing-room at Randalls?"

Mr. Elton so clearly gushes about the artist rather than the model that Emma again notices that his behavior doesn't make sense. "Yes, good man! thought Emma, but what has all that to do with taking likenesses? You know nothing of drawing. Don't pretend to be in raptures about mine. Keep your raptures for Harriet's face." This time, she doesn't even try to account for Mr. Elton's strange responses. Such is the power of denial! And when he specially travels to London to have the portrait framed, Emma still believes that Mr. Elton wants to possess the image of his beloved rather than the handiwork of the woman he intends to marry.

Emma is not unusual in misreading other people's thoughts in light of her own concerns and desires. This is a common human failing, known as cognitive solipsism in the mind-brain sciences. Although Austen focuses on its dangers in all her novels, in *Emma* it's the primary moral problem and the thematic core of the novel.

In light of this theme, that our perceptions can easily be distorted because we fail to transcend our own desires and points of view, Emma's portrait of Harriet serves as a symbol as well as a prop. As Emma sketches Harriet, Mrs. Weston points out the inaccuracies in the likeness: "Miss Woodhouse has given her friend the only beauty she wanted [i.e., lacked] . . . the expression of the eye is most correct, but Miss Smith has not those eyebrows and eyelashes. It is the fault of her face that she has them not." Mr. John Knightley observes, "You have made her too tall."

These improvements are meaningful. Emma imagines that Harriet comes from an aristocratic family, and so she gives her physical traits that are stereotypically associated with noble birth, such as delicate features and elevated height. Whether Emma draws Harriet as she actually sees her or deliberately improves her appearance is beside the point: The episode tells the reader that Emma shapes reality to match her preconceptions and desires, as in attributing aristocratic origins to Harriet, just as she creates a flattering, idealized image on her canvas. The episode becomes an allegory of the very human tendency to view reality in light of our own biases.

Emma isn't the only one who makes mistakes of this kind. Austen suggests that we're all vulnerable to such lapses, and she hammers home the theme of egocentricity through the many variations it takes in the lives of her characters. Sometimes such self-centeredness is crude: One comic scene depicts a conversational tug-of-war between Mr. Weston, who wants to discuss his son Frank's visit, and Mrs. Elton, who wants to brag about her family's wealth. But more often, we witness the unconscious influence of biases. Episode after episode stages the inaccuracy of perceptions due to egoism, even on the part of ethical and well-meaning people.

Mr. Woodhouse, whom we meet in the first pages of the novel, sets the stage for what will follow, illustrating egocentricity in an absurd, almost parodic manner. When Emma's former governess Miss Taylor marries an affluent local businessman, a stroke of incredible good fortune for a middle-aged woman in service, Mr. Woodhouse pities rather than rejoices. Because he's sorry to see her go, he assumes that she too must be unhappy about her good fortune. To him, she's "Poor Miss Taylor," and not lucky Mrs. Weston. Everyone else in the novel has similar if less extreme lapses; even the clear-sighted and generous Mr. Knightley is driven by jealousy to think that Frank Churchill is far worse than he really is.

Of course, the main culprit is Emma herself. After her embarrassing enlightenment in the form of Mr. Elton's drunken proposal, Emma vows that she's cured of her matchmaking tendencies. She isn't. More to the point, she isn't cured of her wish to see things her way, and her mindreading errors continue throughout the novel. Just as she'd thought Mr. Elton was in love with Harriet, she thinks that Frank Churchill is in love with her (he isn't) and that he might be persuaded to transfer his affections to Harriet (not a chance). She dismisses Mr. Knightley's suspicion that there might be a covert romance between Frank and Jane Fairfax—in fact, they're secretly engaged.

A mistake that turns out to be much more serious than any of these lapses is Emma's failure of insight with Harriet (the model for the portrait). Emma assumes that she can read the naïve and inexperienced Harriet like a book, and this is true for a while. At the start of their friendship, Harriet is so dazzled by her superior friend that she not only agrees with everything Emma says but waits for Emma to tell her what to think. As a result of Emma's manipulation, Harriet rejects a proposal of marriage from an eligible farmer, Robert Martin, whom she really likes; Emma has a more ambitious match in mind. But as Harriet becomes accustomed to the privileged status Emma imagines for her, she begins to have aspirations well beyond those that Emma has envisioned.

Several months after the debacle with Mr. Elton, Harriet visits Emma to tell her she's gotten over the heartbreak of Mr. Elton's apathy

(Emma had encouraged her to expect a proposal from him); she now understands that he would never have considered marrying her. Although Harriet confesses that someone has replaced Mr. Elton in her affections, a familiar cure for the lovelorn in life as well as novels, she nevertheless declares that she'll never marry. Emma correctly guesses that Harriet's vow of spinsterhood stems from the superior social position of the man she loves, which would make a match unlikely. But she's wrong about who this is.

At this point Emma misinterprets Harriet's thoughts in such a way that all her misreadings—all her mistakes of cognitive solipsism—boomerang back, and she herself must suffer the hurt and shame that she's caused others: Harriet, Robert Martin (the young farmer who loves Harriet), and even Mr. Elton, who was certainly humiliated by Emma's mistakes even if his heart remained intact.

Harriet tells Emma that she loves this man in part because of gratitude for the noble deed he performed in rescuing her. "I have not the presumption to suppose—indeed I am not so mad. But it is a pleasure to me to admire him at a distance, and to think of his infinite superiority to all the rest of the world, with the gratitude, wonder, and veneration which are so proper, in me especially." Emma thinks that Harriet pines for Frank Churchill, but she actually fancies Mr. Knightley, a lifelong friend and neighbor of Emma's family (it's his brother who warned Emma about Mr. Elton).

Just as they think of different men, they're thinking of different rescues. Their misunderstanding reveals the egocentric bias of each. Emma recalls that Frank Churchill rescued Harriet from a band of gypsies who were attempting to rob her. This dramatic deed falls right in line with Emma's romantic notions about Harriet, especially the belief that she's really from a family of rank and fortune and forced by circumstances to live a humble life, like a princess in a fairy tale. And like princesses so afflicted, she's sure to marry a man who restores her to her rightful heritage. Emma has been thinking that Frank Churchill will be that man, and so she assumes that Harriet is thinking along similar lines.

But Harriet refers to the time that Mr. Knightley danced with her at a ball after Mr. Elton had snubbed her. Had he not intervened, she would have been the only young woman not asked to dance, and, after Mr. Elton's pointed and very public refusal, an object of pity. Mr. Knightley rescues her from such humiliation. When Harriet realizes the mistake, she tells Emma,

> [I]t was not the gypsies—it was not Mr. Frank Churchill that I meant. No! (with some elevation) I was thinking of a much more precious circumstance—of Mr. Knightley's coming and asking me to dance, when Mr. Elton would not stand up with me; and when there was no other partner in the room. That was the kind action; that was the noble benevolence and generosity; that was the service which made me begin to feel how superior he was to every other being on earth.

Harriet has Mr. Knightley in mind because no matter how much more dramatic the rescue from gypsies, or how much real mischief they might have done, in Harriet's view, the social snub was the greater threat to her well-being. The attempted robbery was an accident of fortune, but the snub was a blow to self-esteem. Harriet's gratitude and the love that goes with it are inspired by rescue from the harm that, to the social-emotional mind-brain, was the greater danger.

As with her other mistakes, Emma assumes that her ideas are shared by someone else, in this case that Harriet is in love with Frank Churchill. But Harriet's new and grandiose self-image shows that the distortion of reality can go in both directions. If we tend to mistakenly project, to attribute our thoughts and feelings to others, we also introject, appropriating other people's thoughts and feelings as our own. In both instances, an egocentric bias causes us to confuse *meum* and *tuum*, "mine" and "yours," as the classical saying goes. In both cases, projection (*You must have the same thoughts and feelings I have*) and introjection (*Your thoughts and feelings are really mine*), the self asserts its supremacy, intruding where it doesn't belong.

Before meeting Emma, Harriet has a realistic idea of her identity and prospects. She has never met either of her parents and doesn't even know who they are, although she knows she's illegitimate. She's been placed at a boarding school by a benefactor, presumably her father. It is assumed in Highbury that she is at best from a lower-middle-class family—indeed she would have attended a more prestigious institution than Mrs. Goddard's boarding school if she had come from the upper classes. Harriet accepts her status, as we know from her wish to marry Robert Martin, a well-to-do farmer. For a girl with Harriet's background, this is a great match. Harriet certainly wouldn't have rejected Robert Martin without pressure and manipulation on Emma's part.

In a society in which it seems that everyone is scheming to marry either themselves or their relatives to a moneyed or influential family, Harriet is singularly unambitious, modest, and unassuming about her prospects. Her naïveté is one of her winning qualities. Another young lady in Harriet's position would have realized the advantages of being Emma's friend and plotted a brighter future for herself. But plotting your advancement requires the will and ability to strategize, as we see so clearly with Mr. Elton, who's out to marry a woman with money. Harriet, to her credit, lacks what it takes to succeed in this fashion. Nevertheless, constant exposure to the strong-minded Emma eventually has its effect. Harriet never reasons that she should have high hopes for a brilliant marriage, nor acts to bring this about. But she gradually acquires a sense of entitlement from Emma, introjecting Emma's perspective.

Both projection and introjection have been demonstrated in the psych lab. One protocol took place in a room that had a grid on the wall on which various small objects could be placed, such as staplers, pens, plates, the kinds of things we find in offices and kitchens. Participants were instructed to hide a roll of scotch tape inside a bag before the experiment's director entered the room. When he arrived, he instructed participants to place the objects he named, all of which were visible in the room, around on the grid. Even though the participants knew that they'd hidden the roll of scotch tape, and also knew the instructor didn't know about this, when he called out "tape," referring to a videotape, a number of participants retrieved the scotch tape that had been hidden and put it on the grid. That we make mistakes of this nature shows just how difficult it is to keep track of whose mind is whose, how easy it is to project.

Another experiment that showed that people regularly appropriate other's thoughts and feelings was designed to test whether the connotations of words could influence behavior, a well-known form of introjection popularly called suggestion.

Researchers asked subjects to form sentences from short lists of words, each of which could be associated with a stereotype. After this exercise was supposedly finished and the group dismissed, researchers continued to observe the participants; this was actually the real focus of the experiment. The group that was given a list of words connoting old age, such as *Florida* and *gray*, took longer to walk to the elevator than those who were given other lists, just as if old age were slowing them down. In a similar experiment, one group was given a list of words associated with the stereotype of professors, while another group was given words associated with stereotypical ideas about secretaries. These subjects were then asked to play Trivial Pursuit. Guess which group played the better game! Given the permeability of boundaries between mind-brains, we shouldn't be too hard on poor Emma, or on ourselves, for finding it difficult at times to escape our own desires, thoughts, and plans.

Emma sees the absurdity of her ideas when she realizes that Harriet aspires to marry Mr. Knightley. While marriages took place between people of unequal wealth and status—witness Elizabeth and Darcy in *Pride and Prejudice*—the difference in standing between Harriet and Mr. Knightley is simply too great to be condoned. (Such prejudices were of ancient origin and long duration, and even Austen didn't escape them entirely. When in the nineteenth century, Albert Munby, a gentleman, married a servant, Hannah Cullwick, they kept the match a secret because of their respective positions in society.) Of course, most of us today would reject the snobbish reasons that make this match a bad idea in the eyes of Austen's society. But we can nevertheless appreciate a more suitable reason: Harriet just doesn't have what it takes to be a true companion to Mr. Knightley. They aren't a good match in terms of intelligence, wit, or temperament.

With the threat of a marriage between Mr. Knightley and Harriet, however remote, Emma suddenly realizes that "No one must marry Mr. Knightley but herself!" In a flash of insight, she knows that she feels much more than friendship for this lifelong friend. And so she is remorseful, not only for the possibility of losing the man she loves to another woman, but also because the match is likely to be unhappy.

Emma further realizes that Harriet would never have set her sights on Mr. Knightley without her influence. Harriet has indeed internalized Emma's view of her; Emma has created this monster. *Frankenstein* was published four months before Austen died, and given her illness, it's unlikely that she read it. But she would have appreciated the allegory. And so Emma suffers—a punishment richly deserved!

MINDREADING: THEORY OF MIND

Mindreading runs the gamut of awareness from lower levels of automatic and nonconscious apprehension such as emotional resonance and emotional contagion, which we share with other mammals, to fully conscious and self-reflective awareness, which some mind-brain scientists believe to be a uniquely human trait. Mindreading is an impressive feat, for it allows us to perceive much more about others than they tell us. Although it evolved in simpler times and environments, and initially for fairly basic tasks such as determining whether someone is friendly or hostile, the complexity of human culture has pressured us to expand and depend upon our mindreading capability. People must routinely infer one another's thoughts, feelings, beliefs, and intentions to function normally; this is a necessary social skill.

Mind-brain scientists have distinguished between two different kinds of higher-level mindreading: theory of mind (ToM) and empathy. ToM means knowing that other people have minds different from one's own as well as inferring the content of their minds, which includes their thoughts, feelings, intentions, and so forth. Psychologist Peter Fonagy uses an alternative term to describe ToM: *mentalizing.* I like this term—less awkward than ToM—as well as his definition, which elaborates on the essential psychological and social implications of ToM. In addition to understanding that people have minds that contain thoughts and feelings, Fonagy stresses that mentalizing includes the knowledge that what a person thinks and feels usually influences their behavior, and that people can change their minds—what they think, feel, and believe. I'll use ToM, mentalizing, and a third term, *reflective capacity,* interchangeably. ToM can include awareness of feelings in an abstract sense, called cognitive empathy: knowing what another is feeling rather than actually sharing those feelings. The latter is the provenance of empathy.

We use our ToM by interpreting social signals such as facial expression and body language as well as by listening to what people say. As with most capacities, people are able to mentalize to greater and lesser degrees, with the exception of very young children and people who have autism and other atypical conditions; they lack this reflective capacity. But using ToM can be difficult even for cognitively typical adults, as we saw in the tape experiment discussed above.

As you know, Emma's mistakes are largely errors of mentalizing. She gets into her scrape with Mr. Elton because she ignores and misinterprets social cues. Before the carriage ride debacle, Mr. Elton behaves enthusiastically toward Harriet and Emma, and Emma mistakenly believes this is due to Harriet's charm, failing to perceive that she's the true object of his affections. Mr. Elton also misreads Emma's behavioral cues; Emma behaves warmly toward Mr. Elton on Harriet's behalf, and Mr. Elton mistakes her friendliness as a sign of love. Yet, while the errors of each are similar to some degree, they're not equivalent. Even though Mr. Elton turns out to be unworthy of Emma in many respects, we must give him his due: Emma misconstrues some very clear signals while also giving Mr. Elton reason to think that she returns his interest.

Of course, mistaking someone's intentions is not always the result of faulty mindreading. Our devious species is adept at manipulating the signs that others read, and so there's always the possibility of deliberate deception, as in the all-too-familiar tactic of seduction, broadcasting serious interest in order to gain sexual favors. This isn't the case with Mr. Elton for a number reasons, both moral and practical. It wouldn't do for the local vicar to seduce a parishioner. And Mr. Elton longs to share Emma's wealth and status at least as much as he longs to share more intimate aspects of a life together, a goal that a "dangerous liaison" would make impossible. When Austen tells us that Mr. Elton made "violent love" to Emma in the carriage, it doesn't mean what it would mean to us today; it simply indicates that Mr. Elton declared himself rather forcefully. But on another famous literary carriage ride, in the eighteenth-century novel *Clarissa* by Samuel Richardson, a young man behaves as though he has his companion's interests at heart when he's really out to seduce and abandon. Richardson was one of Austen's favorite authors, and I'd bet a lot of money that she had *Clarissa* in mind when writing the carriage scene in *Emma*. With a wink at her readers, who were sure to be familiar with this eighteenth-century bestseller, she deliberately chooses to echo that same scene and use phrases like "violent love."

Let's return once more to the portrait episode, which as you've now realized provides a clear instance of mentalizing in action. Recall that in a burst of enthusiasm for Emma's sketch, Mr. Elton decides to go to London to have the portrait of Harriet framed. All that Mr. Elton says is that he thinks it would be a good idea to have the picture framed and that he plans to do it. From this, Emma infers his state of mind. She concludes that he must love Harriet, because a man wouldn't want a portrait of a woman unless he had special feelings for her; if the woman is not a relative, those feelings must be romantic ones. This is actually one of her most reasonable errors. Emma also infers Mr. Elton's beliefs about the function of the portrait: that it will express his love publicly and give him pleasure by allowing him to dwell on Harriet's image when she's not there. And she assumes that he believes certain things about portraits in general: that they should be framed for display and that framing gives them a special, formal status.

Incidentally, I've engaged in a bit of mentalizing myself, as do all readers, for *Emma* doesn't spell out all of these conclusions. In fact, authors routinely depend on us to make these kinds of inferences. Much of the humor of Emma's misadventures with Mr. Elton comes from our ability to infer states of mind from Austen's descriptions of speech and behavior. This gives readers the opportunity to congratulate themselves on their social intelligence, on seeing much more than the flawed heroine.

MY MIND TO YOUR MIND: EMPATHY

Empathy is the other higher-level mindreading ability, the most complete form of mindreading available to humans, and perhaps to other mammals high on the evolutionary ladder. Barring psychic phenomena, which haven't been accepted by the majority of the scientific community, mindreading is as close as we get to a Vulcan mind-meld, to completely inhabiting another person's mind. It's the quality I'm suggesting Austen possessed in abundance, and which has attracted her deservedly huge following.

Empathy studies are a bit of a mess, not least because a standard definition of empathy doesn't exist. To cite two crucial differences, some mind-brain scientists include an appropriate emotional response such as caring or sympathy as part of empathy, while others define it as seeing and feeling from someone else's perspective without including the feelings or actions that follow. I'm going to define empathy as consisting of four elements: taking the perspective of another person cognitively, and so understanding their thoughts and feelings; actually feeling what they feel; regulating your own emotions so that you don't become overwhelmed by the other person's feelings; and paying attention because we don't empathize without focusing on our perceptions.* Empathy is the highest level of mindreading we can attain, incorporating lower-level means of apprehending other minds.

I'd like to go up through the levels, to trace the processes involved in empathy, as well as the pitfalls of contagion that it avoids. You'll recognize these categories, because I've mentioned them all in one context or another, but it's worth listing them to have a full understanding of empathy.

- Perception of action refers to understanding that another animal is actually there and moving. You don't need to understand its motives and intentions, just that it's a being different from you. This likely requires a central nervous system. Reptiles and fish distinguish themselves from

---

* My definition relies on these two sources in particular: Jean Decety and Philip L. Jackson, "The Functional Architecture of Human Empathy," *Behavioral and Cognitive Neuroscience Reviews* 3, no. 2 (2004), 73 and Nancy Eisenberg and Natalie D. Eggum, "Empathic Responding: Sympathy and Personal Distress," in *The Social Neuroscience of Empathy*, ed. Jean Decety and William Ickes (Cambridge, Mass.: MIT Press, 2009). Decety and Jackson note, "There are many other definitions of empathy, almost as many as there are researchers in the field." Be that as it may, in my view, a definition that takes cognitive and affective elements into account without asserting that these necessarily lead to sympathy or action provides the most elegant and useful way to think about empathy.

other living animals. The giant snail *Aplysia* does not, as far as we can tell.

- Emotional contagion means catching someone else's emotional state. If you see someone frightened, you become frightened. Panic appears to be particularly contagious. In *Pride and Prejudice*, the mania for soldiers seen in Elizabeth's sisters Lydia and Kitty, as well as, I'm sure, all of the silly young ladies in the neighborhood, likely owes much to emotional contagion.

- Emotional resonance (also known as attunement and affective empathy) means feeling someone else's emotions, being on the same wavelength, while attributing the emotion to someone else rather than feeling it as your own. This happens implicitly; we don't say to ourselves, "Oh, I feel sad, but wait a minute, the sadness belongs to my friend and not me." Resonance isn't subconscious in the way of some mind-brain mechanisms, but it occurs beneath the threshold of attention and awareness. This isn't unusual for emotions; we often experience emotions without consciously acknowledging their presence, or even being aware of them. Emotional resonance is at the core of attachment and the attachment system. It's likely that many mammals are capable of emotional resonance because it doesn't require self-aware, third-order consciousness. It involves a degree of emotional regulation (this is also subliminal) in order to keep it from becoming contagion.

- Introjection is contagion at a cognitive as well as an emotional level, as seen in Harriet's absorption of Emma's ideas.

- Theory of mind (ToM), also known as mentalizing and a reflective capacity, as has been discussed above. A quick recap: It means understanding that people have separate minds and being able to take the perspective of another person, understanding what they are thinking and feeling at the moment.

- And finally, there's empathy. Empathy comprises perception of action; affective empathy (emotional resonance), feeling their feelings; and theory of mind/mentalizing, which includes cognitive empathy (inferring what someone is feeling) and cognitive perspective taking (inferring what another person is thinking). It means fully inhabiting the point of view of another person, putting yourself in their place. Attention and emotional regulation are crucial for empathy. In order to empathize, you need to pay attention and be relatively calm (have the vagal brake on).

Let's take Mr. Knightley's empathy with Harriet, which motivates him to ask her to dance when she's been insulted by Mr. Elton. To begin with, he sees her facial expression and body language (actions) that convey her sadness (they're social signals). He understands that she's upset by attuning to her feelings, implicitly apprehending that these feelings belong to Harriet even though he experiences them to some degree himself (emotional resonance), while also subconsciously regulating his emotions. Mr. Knightley then mentalizes to understand Harriet's thoughts and feelings (the latter is cognitive empathy), consciously taking her perspective, a knowing entry into her point of view that requires his paying attention. All this means that he feels her sadness and humiliation intuitively—in the gut—as well as understanding it cognitively. But he doesn't become agitated as a result. And although care, sympathy, or some other appropriate emotional response isn't technically considered part of the definition of empathy, these sorts of responses often follow. Sometimes we act on our empathy as well. And so Mr. Knightley asks Harriet to dance.

Emma possesses both a strong ToM and empathy. We certainly see this in her relationship with her fussy father. Attuned to his point of view, she anticipates his wishes and knows how to reassure him. She's exquisitely sensitive to his feelings and is troubled when he's upset. She's also a consummate hostess, which involves plenty of mindreading tasks such as figuring out what people want and what will make them comfortable, introducing topics of conversation that will be interesting, making sure compatible guests have an opportunity to talk, and managing disagreements between those who don't get along.

But with all her capability, Emma commits a heinous empathic error at the picnic on Box Hill, insulting Miss Bates in a cruel and humiliating fashion. This gathering has been anticipated with pleasure by Emma and her friends, but things don't go well. To begin with, everyone is out of sorts. Whether the bad mood originates with Emma or with one of the other of these grumpy revelers, it's contagious, and no one does well. Emma and Frank make things worse by ostentatiously flirting, which makes others uncomfortable, although Emma doesn't realize how much this hurts Jane Fairfax, who's secretly engaged to Frank. (Frank, on the other hand, has no excuse.)

Frank and Emma propose a game in which everyone is required to say "one thing very clever, be it prose or verse, original or repeated—or two things moderately clever—or three things very dull indeed." Miss Bates readily agrees to the terms, and this gives Emma an opening for her insult:

> "Oh! very well," exclaimed Miss Bates, "then I need not be uneasy. Three things very dull indeed. That will just do for me, you know. I shall be sure to say three dull things as soon as ever I open my mouth, shan't I?—(looking round with the most good-humoured dependence on everybody's assent)—Do not you all think I shall?"

Emma could not resist.

> "Ah! ma'am, but there may be a difficulty. Pardon me—but you will be limited as to number—only three at once."

Miss Bates feels this deeply.

Mr. Knightley later scolds Emma for her behavior, a task that no one else is willing or courageous enough to undertake. But he doesn't reprimand Emma for the rudeness of her remark, which, in this decorous society, certainly deserves criticism. Nor does he upbraid her on abstract moral grounds saying, for instance, that it's not right to insult people in public, especially one's elders. He focuses instead, in a very personal way, on how Emma's witticism has made Miss Bates feel. He paints such an accurate description of Miss Bates's circumstances and state of mind that he invites Emma to become Miss Bates for a moment:

> How could you be so unfeeling to Miss Bates? How could you be so insolent in your wit to a woman of her character, age, and situation?—Emma, I had not thought it possible. . . . Were she a woman of fortune, I would leave every harmless absurdity to take its chance, I would not quarrel with you for any liber-ties of manner. Were she your equal in situation—but, Emma, consider how far this is from being the case. She is poor; she has sunk from the comforts she was born to; and, if she live to old age, must probably sink more. Her situation should secure your compassion. It was badly done, indeed! You, whom she had known from an infant, whom she had seen grown up from a period when her notice was an honour, to have you now, in thoughtless spirits, and the pride of the moment, laugh at her, humble her—and before her niece, too—and before others, many of whom (certainly some) would be entirely guided by your treatment of her. This is not pleasant to you, Emma—and it is very far from pleasant to me; but I must, I will—I will tell you truths while I can, satisfied with proving myself your friend by very faithful counsel and trusting that you will some time or other do me greater justice than you can do now.

Emma, deeply remorseful, attempts to repair the damage of this and many other lapses in feeling. She visits Miss Bates, paying full and respectful attention to her conversations, however dull they might be. And she realizes that she has slighted Jane Fairfax because of jealousy of her accomplishments. Envy of Jane's accomplishments has kept her from empathizing with Jane's plight, a bleak financial future that will force her to work as a governess, one of the few jobs available to genteel women.

We might notice how important attention is in this instance. Atten-tion is an executive function over which we have some control—that is, if we have free will in anything, another question debated within the mind-brain sciences. Emma knows that Miss Bates is a woman on the brink of old age who depends on the kindness and charity of her neighbors to alleviate her poverty and her loneliness. But she knows this intellectually, in a theory-of-mind sort of way. But when Mr. Knightley scolds Emma for her cruelty at Box Hill, she starts to pay attention to what these constraining circumstances must feel like to the people who suffer them. She experiences the world from their perspective. Mr. Knightley rouses Emma's powers of empathy by making her pay attention.

Emma's lack of attention at Box Hill is unfortunate, since it leads to hurtful behavior that she later regrets. Yet, even so, zoning out isn't always a bad thing. Filtering information is crucial to our ability to function. A generation after Austen, another great novelist, George Eliot, commented on the value of filtering information, especially concerning the distress of others. She writes in *Middlemarch*, "If we had a keen vision and feeling of all ordinary human life, it would be like hearing the grass grow and the squirrel's heart beat, and we should die of that roar which lies on the other side of silence. As it is, the quickest of us walk about well wadded with stupidity [i.e., a lack of sensitivity or perception]." We need the silence. We can't take in all the world's pain and suffering because this would be entirely too much for us; we would destroy ourselves and be useless to help others. The challenge is knowing how to be compassionate while still maintaining boundaries that ensure your own well-being. As we all know from air travel, put your own oxygen mask on first.

Emma is well aware of this. While she's sensitive to the nuances of empathy, aware of its role in motivating compassion and "good works," she regulates her emotions so that she offers helpful responses rather than pointless guilt. (She's aware of boundaries, as therapists say.) She devotes time and energy to relieving the distresses of the poor of Highbury because she understands their plight both emotionally and cognitively. But with clarity of insight that reveals a well-regulated psyche, she comments, "If we feel for the wretched, enough to do all we can for them, the rest is empty sympathy, only distressing to ourselves."

But when Emma makes an effort to be mindful, when she's awake to situations that call for empathy, she's capable of genuinely moral and appropriate responses. Her very capability accounts for Mr. Knightley's anger—he knows that her callous behavior betrays her better self. Indeed, Emma is one of a minority of characters in Austen's novels, certainly in her own novel, with sufficient social intelligence and active goodwill to be able to live a genuinely self-aware and ethical life. This is one reason that Emma and Mr. Knightley are well matched, despite the differences in their ages and temperaments.

EMPATHY: IT'S NOT JUST FOR WOMEN ANYMORE

It's generally believed that social intelligence began for us humans with the nurturing of the young common to all mammals. Because human babies do much of their developing after they're born, they need extensive care, far more than is required by other great ape babies. The entire troupe of early humans, including men, was needed to protect mothers and help them raise their young.

The prosocial emotions involved in helping and care turned out to be advantageous in many other ways as well—for example in hunting—and so the tendency to work together was preserved within the genome. Our extraordinary cognitive intelligence as well as our sociality was likely jump-started by maternal care. Our need to cooperate in order to survive (we're really a weak and puny species compared to, say, chimps) likely instigated the expansion of the human brain, leading to our cognitive intelligence and flexibility, as well as our ever-increasing social intelligence. Not only has our intelligence in both domains enabled us to dominate every other species on earth, but it's also allowed us to shape our environments (in good and bad ways), to transcend our biology (we're not limited by our puny strength), and even to alter it, as we make ever more dizzying forays into genetics.

What this means is that the cradle of civilization was actually the cradle, and that prodigious cooperation and caring distinguishes our species as a whole, men as well as women. There's no doubt about this, despite the widespread belief that women are more emotional than men, that their friendships are more nurturing, and that they lack the awareness of hierarchy and a subtle jockeying for power that's seen among men (spend ten minutes at a girls' table at your local middle school cafeteria if you want to challenge this last claim). And the kicker: Women are more empathetic than men; this is the essential difference between male and female responses to experience.

Well, perhaps. But it's also widely known and accepted that men are capable of care, compassion, and other nurturative, positive emotions, and that these emotions lead to prosocial behavior. Plenty of men have close friends, love their partners and their children, and care about the welfare of others, extending their "circle of care" beyond their own kin.

This is true of our close cousins, the chimpanzees, even though they possess less developed social capabilities, such as speech. Dominant males spend a lot of time arbitrating disputes among other members of the troupe, getting them to "kiss and make up." Even after an alpha chimp has won a dispute, he frequently works to reestablish a friendly relationship with the defeated. In fact, excellent social skills are necessary for assuming the alpha position, and chimps and other mammals who lack such skills sink to the bottom of the hierarchy, or are even ousted or shunned by others. Nevertheless, discussions of the social capabilities of humans nearly always end up by pointing out that women and men show profound differences in the ways they bond with others, and that women are better at care, nurture, altruism, and empathy than men.

It's important to keep in mind that in order to enter this discussion to begin with, you need to accept that clear-cut categories such as male and female exist. However, this might be true mainly with respect to anatomy, and even here there are exceptions. Human gender identity is so fluid and open, so "queer" even among the "straightest" of us, such a mixture of male and female qualities, that the gendering of personality traits feels like diving into quicksand. But okay, let's stay with male and female with the understanding that we're talking about a spectrum of sexualities, gender identities, and traits. We can say that a certain linkage of male vs. female sexual identity and anatomy has been statistically associated with the appearance of certain characteristics, and from this starting point, determine first whether or not these assessments are accurate, and, if so, whether biology is responsible for the differences we find.

It's certainly true that differences between male and female mind-brains exist. I think it's the height of anthropocentric arrogance to suggest that humans are the only species to escape biological deter-minism altogether. I believe in basic emotions and innate program-ming for attachment. Even so, given that our mind-brains do so much of their developing after birth, it isn't nature vs. nurture that we ought to think about, but as science writer Matt Ridley aptly puts it, "nature as nurture." The study of animals supports this approach; in general, the larger the brain of an animal in proportion to its body, the less the depen-dence on instinct. Chimps make choices about how they'll behave that simply aren't options for mice.

We come into the world with tendencies, but what we become depends as much on experience as it does on innate characteristics. Take a child born with a sunny disposition—an "easy baby"—and subject him to neglect or abuse, and you'll turn him into a deeply disturbed person who struggles with depression and the effects of trauma, including compromised physical health. Or take a child born "highly sensitive," thin-skinned and vulnerable to depression, and give him optimally nurturing caregivers, and watch how he blossoms into a secure, resilient, caring person. No one is born with a specific attachment style, only tendencies. Much of the same logic applies to differences between males and females.

All known cultures begin to treat their males and females differ-ently, in subtle but determinative ways that influence mind-brain development, right from the start. The different treatment we accord female and male babies begins shaping personality at birth, and even earlier if parents know the sex of the fetus. For this reason, drawing the line between culture and nature in determining why women are more empathetic than men, and all the other myriad differences people discover in their explorations of "Mars" and "Venus," becomes nearly impossible.

If this debate were confined to the realm of theory, it wouldn't matter nearly as much as it does. But because so many of us expect male and female children to be different, we treat them in ways that produce those differences. Boy babies often receive less comforting because we expect boys to be tough. And so we produce men who tend toward dismissing attachment styles, who find closeness and emotion difficult or threatening. Schoolchildren receive subtle signals about what subjects are gender appropriate, so many girls dislike math and science. And these differences have material consequences. There's certainly gender discrimination in the workplace. Indeed, discrimination on the basis of gender remains stubbornly present across personal and professional life, and across other intersectional identities such as race and class.

This is nothing new. Pointing out the differences between men and women is as old as the hills on which early humans foraged. And in general, women lose this culture war, with men elevated as the first and superior sex. The argument that such differences are determined by culture rather than nature is also older than you might think. In Austen's day, Mary Wollstonecraft in *A Vindication of the Rights of Woman* (1792) argued that the traits that men point to as proving women's inferiority arise from cultural training rather than innate differences. Girls are deprived of adequate education and encouraged to be vain and silly. Lydia and Kitty in *Pride and Prejudice* definitely come to mind. Every educated, reasonable woman is an argument against sexual difference. And if women are more nurturing than men, that's because nurture is what they're trained to do. Boys learn Greek and Latin; girls are given baby dolls to take care of when still babies themselves. Wollstonecraft argues that with a different upbringing, many differences between men and women, especially those that indicate women's inferiority, would not emerge.

Austen very likely read *A Vindication*. And if she didn't know it first-hand, she was familiar with the popular novel *Hermsprong* (published in 1796 by Robert Bage), which expressed many of its ideas. (Austen was a voracious reader of novels.) Hume was also an influence. His belief that virtue stems from feeling rather than reason, and that this is true for men as well as women, posed a huge challenge to existing ideas about gender. Reason had traditionally been viewed as the provenance of men, distinctly absent or inferior in women. And men were seen as more moral than women precisely because they had superior powers of reason. How could men still be better than women if feeling rather than reason was the source of virtue? Hume might not have meant to undermine sexual difference, but he nevertheless challenged well-entrenched ideas about men and women.

Here's an example of what Wollstonecraft and Austen were up against, the tradition that uses sexual difference to assert male superiority, thereby justifying male privilege: Men are essentially different and better than women. Samuel Johnson, whom Austen greatly admired, had the following response when told that women as well as men preached among the Quakers: "Sir, a woman's preaching is like a dog's walking on his hind legs. It is not done well; but you are surprised to find it done at all." This was typical. Johnson associates women with dogs, and so with animals other than humans and with nature, while suggesting that it's fitting and normal that men preach—that they expound on virtue—because they have superior reasoning capability, a quality that enables them to write good sermons and ultimately places them higher on the scale of creation than women. Men are associated with reason, intellect, and morality, while women belong with nature, instinct, and feeling. Women are from Venus, men are from Mars. As the French say, *Plus ça change, plus la même chose* ("The more things change, the more they remain the same").

Throughout her novels, Austen portrays women who challenge gender stereotypes and enjoy parity in their relationships with their beloveds, a move that was right in line with radical feminist arguments of her day. Austen's heroines are thinking, educated, cultured women, and the men they end up marrying respect them for these qualities. Austen's successful marriages are loving partnerships. Women might not be the equals of men in social or political terms, but the realm of private life provided a space where equity could be achieved within personal relationships. Of course, no one in Austen's day was talking about the degree of empathy in male and female mind-brains because no one was talking about mind-brains in any respect. But the equivalent of that focus, the "women are more nurturing and caring" dictum, was certainly in full force and glory. So, who's the most empathic person in *Emma*?

Mr. Knightley, of course! He's the one always taking other people's perspectives, understanding what they're thinking and feeling, showing consideration and compassion. He even empathizes with Emma for having had to put up with him: "I have blamed you, and lectured you, and you have borne it as no other woman in England would have borne it."

Austen not only undermines truisms about sexual difference through her romances and characterizations, she also suggests that such differences stem largely from culture rather than nature, another radical move on her part. As is often the case, the point is made seemingly in passing, but in Austen's work, every sentence counts. When Mr. John Knightley (Mr. Knightley's brother) and his wife, Isabella (Emma's sister), come with their family for a visit, the two men greet one another in muted, masculine fashion, as the narrator points out: "'How d'ye do, George?' and 'John, how are you?' succeeded in the true English style, burying under a calmness that seemed all but indifference the real attachment which would have led either of them, if requisite, to do everything for the good of the other."

These brothers care deeply about one another and would certainly act on that care, but they're men, and English men at that. Someone merely observing the scene, without benefit of the narrator's comment or knowledge of these two brothers, might have explained this tepid greeting with the widely held belief that men have less feeling and empathy than women. But the narrator makes a point of saying that these brothers have strong feelings and care deeply about one another, that they're ready to respond to one another's distress with empathy, compassion, and altruism. Austen subtly suggests that upbringing— with regard to both gender *and* nationality—has much to do with sexual difference.

If this point slipped by you, or even if you think it's a stretch, that's part of Austen's plan. By writing about private relationships that, at first glance—and only at first glance—reveal a narrow focus, Austen protected herself and her family. As progressive as many of her ideas might have been (and I'm of the party that sees her as progressive), she couldn't have openly challenged the existing social order of her day. She was the daughter of a vicar who lived with her family her entire short life. She wasn't about to make waves in any obvious fashion because she needed to be totally respectable. She also wanted to appeal to a wide readership, which depended on her novels being deemed appropriate for women, the primary readership for this genre. She wasn't about to throw down the gauntlet in the fight for women's rights.

And so she slips her radical points about gender in there in ways that most people don't notice. Who can object to her saying that the Knightley brothers are devoted to one another but keep their feelings muted because it's the English way? You have to stop and think to see the implicit challenge to ideas about gender and nationality. Emma is a strong, confident woman who generally gets her own way, wrong as it is. Well, you can explain that by her having been spoiled rather than by reference to the generally unacknowledged fact that strong women exist who aren't monsters of waywardness or (gasp! heaven forbid!) feminists like Wollstonecraft. And if all her heroines are rational and well-read, that's okay because no one with moderate views was going to object to women applying themselves to rational pursuits—so long as such pursuits didn't interfere with their feminine duties.

I believe that Austen also chose to makes her points about people, societies, and human nature through stories about individuals, rather than direct commentary, narrative rather than polemic, because she understood that human mind-brains attune to narrative. We're much more likely to remember and absorb when a message comes in the form of a story. Still, you might object that one or two people do not a statistic make, and you can't extrapolate from stories about individuals to draw conclusions about people in general. But that isn't necessarily true; you can't say anything about anything without generalizing. Even large protocols with control groups and the full regalia of scientific approval still make generalizations.

In addition, there's a powerful and long-standing tradition in English literature of commenting on the macrocosm, the public arena, through the microcosm. Mr. Knightley's excellent and compassionate character pervades his role as landowner and leader in the community as well as his personal life. For Austen, having a public persona way different from a private one is nothing more than hypocrisy, and you can assess someone's character and ethics by looking at his behavior in specific, private instances.

For years and years, Austen's writing was just too brilliant to deny her membership in the pantheon of great English authors, but she was definitely there as lovely, talented Aunt Jane, a chick-lit genius of sorts, rather than the biting, incisive Jane Austen our own era recognizes. This had much to do with her nephew's brief biography, more like a hagiography, which characterized Austen as an "angel in the house" who focused on the domestic and social concerns that were the proper sphere of women. But this chick-lit designation also had to do with Austen's choice of subject matter, her two inches of ivory—small communities where the primary action consists of social interaction rather than politics or history.

This shows that working within the microcosm, especially if you focus on personal relationships, has its dangers. You can be so discreet that people don't know what you're doing. In addition, as the culture changed, people were more likely to miss the subtle implications of her stories. Readers today don't necessarily recognize that portraying a reasonable, well-educated woman challenges entrenched notions about women's inferiority. (Perhaps we should, but that's a different matter!)

Scholarship of the second half of the twentieth century discovered the falsity of this chick-lit view of Austen, revealing the coded ways she wrote about all kinds of issues pertinent to the public issues of her day.* But Austen is so clever and subtle that it's easy to miss the philosophical and psychological depths of her work as well as its references to "the war of ideas" ongoing in her own day. Try to get most high school males to read *Pride and Prejudice*, and you'll see exactly what prejudice consists of, both on and off the page. Most young men are deaf to the crucial issues embedded in her style and stories, and can't get past the idea that Austen's world is a woman's world, completely alien to anything they might deem important. If you want to see how this works, even with older, highly educated men familiar with the era in which Austen wrote, read William Deresiewicz's book, *A Jane Austen Education*. Deresiewicz dismissed Austen as beneath the notice of a true intellectual until required to read her novels for a course in graduate school. He saw the light, and his book does homage to Austen's wisdom with all the zeal of the converted (well-deserved in this case), and the accuracy of an astute reader.

Early on in *Emma*, when Mr. Elton still hopes to marry our heroine, he characterizes her in a word game as a "lovely woman" who "reigns alone." Although this is romantic nonsense on Mr. Elton's part, it nevertheless captures a social truth: Emma does indeed reign over Highbury society, and she reigns alone in the sense that no other

---

*   The phrase "war of ideas" is a reference to Marilyn Butler's book, *Jane Austen and the War of Ideas* (Oxford: Oxford University Press, 1988), which was largely responsible for focusing literary criticism on Austen's political and social awareness. I will include examples of other works in this tradition in the sources for this chapter.

woman can challenge the leadership she enjoys, due to her personality and her circumstances.

But from the perspective of Austen's values, it's neither Emma's beauty, brains, nor wealth that renders her fit to "reign," and hence to be a guardian of the welfare of others. Nor do any of these qualities make her the perfect consort for Mr. Knightley, who cares for his "subjects" with the heartfelt paternalism that his courtly name suggests. It is Emma's capacity to care for others that renders her a worthy leader, and we see this caring even when it's distorted by her fantasies; in the end, she really does want the best for her friend Harriet.

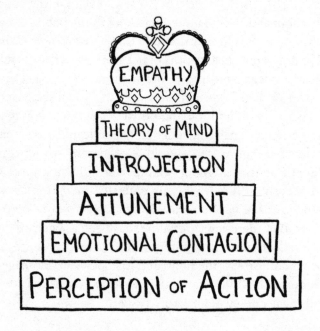

Although Emma is certainly wealthy enough to adorn herself with expensive trinkets, the crown jewel that this queen of Highbury wears is empathy, a capacity of mind rather than a precious gem. It is a crown because it sits atop all the other systems involved in mindreading, incorporating aspects of different levels (cortical, subcortical) and domains (cognitive, emotional), including ToM. It is a jewel because of its value in connecting us to one another. Empathy is indeed the crown jewel of social intelligence.

TEN

Mentalizing and Reality

TO SEE OURSELVES AS OTHERS SEE US

Since I first read *Emma*, long before I became interested in the mind-brain, I was intrigued by the doubling of Emma's enlightenments: When Emma begins to make an effort to understand other people accurately, she begins to know her own mind. Her clarity about others and her clarity about herself appear to be connected.

Emma's newly acquired powers of discernment begin after the Box Hill picnic. As a result of Mr. Knightley's scolding, Emma begins to pay attention to what people are thinking and feeling. She understands that her joke at Miss Bates's expense was hurtful. She also realizes that Jane Fairfax faces extremely difficult circumstances and that her own jealousy of Jane's accomplishments has kept her from extending an offer of friendship that might have been a comfort. Emma doesn't yet know that Jane and Frank are engaged, and that her flirting with Frank at Box Hill was therefore hurtful, but she does begin to empathize with Jane's distress at her unfortunate situation: To have been raised as a lady and look forward to a future as a governess is indeed extremely difficult.

Emma's insights into her own thoughts and feelings are equally astute. When Harriet reveals that she's in love with Mr. Knightley and wants to marry him, Emma suddenly realizes that "no one must marry Mr. Knightley but herself." Readers have long known that Emma loves Mr. Knightley through some mentalization of our own, but this is intimate self-knowledge that Emma has failed to grasp.

We might attribute Emma's sudden insight about her feelings to the shock of Harriet's confession, which jolts her into self-awareness. This is right, but it's only part of the truth, and it raises another question, Why now? Emma has had other moments when jealousy might have prompted awareness. When Mrs. Weston had earlier suggested that Jane and Mr. Knightley might marry, Emma dismissed this possibility out of hand. She argued that Mr. Knightley would never wish to deprive his nephews of the inheritance of his property, Donwell Abbey, which would happen if he were to have children of his own. Emma has a passing moment of anxiety, barely acknowledged, at Mrs. Weston's suggestion, but after watching Jane and Mr. Knightley closely for a few minutes (which cues readers to her true feelings—she cares enough to investigate), she sees that they're behaving as friends rather than lovers.

Nevertheless, a match between Mr. Knightley and Jane is a much more likely scenario than his marrying Harriet. He and Jane are peers with respect to education, intelligence, interests, and social standing; in all of these, Harriet is markedly inferior to the object of her affections. And friendships do develop into romances; this is what ultimately happens for Emma and Mr. Knightley. In terms of probabilities, Emma should be much more worried about Jane than Harriet.

But this isn't the case. Rather, Emma gets scared and realizes her own mind only when Harriet confesses her love, and not when Mrs. Weston suggests a much more realistic pairing. It's all in the timing: It's no accident that this conversation takes place after Box Hill, when Emma's mentalizing powers have been activated, when she's actually paying attention to reading other minds rather than projecting her fantasies onto them.

A closer look at mentalizing explains why Emma's understanding of others is linked to understanding herself. A reflective capacity involves awareness about minds in a general sense: the knowledge that people have minds; that the contents of those minds, including perceptions, thoughts, feelings, and reasoning, can differ from person to person; that what we think and feel influences how we perceive and behave; and that the contents of minds can change. Since mentalizing is a general capability, it isn't limited by specific context. Having the ability to reflect on other people's minds goes hand in hand with being able to reflect on your own mind as well. That is, unless there are strong sub-liminal reasons for hiding knowledge from yourself, as when Emma fails to realize that she's in love with Mr. Knightley.

When you think about what you're thinking or feeling, you actu-ally see yourself from outside yourself, from a third-person perspec-tive. As neuroscientist Simon Baron-Cohen explains, "self-awareness means imagining yourself from another's point of view." This wisdom was captured by Austen's contemporary, Robert Burns, long before the mind-brain sciences affirmed its truth: "O wad some Power the giftie gie us/To see oursels as ithers see us!" Mr. Knightley raises Emma's self-awareness by showing her how others see her, how her behavior appears in his eyes (really bad) as well as from Miss Bates's point of view (really hurtful).

LEARNING TO MENTALIZE

Another way to think of Emma's newfound astuteness: When Emma begins to read minds accurately, she has a better grasp of reality, mainly social reality, which is largely where it's at for humans. A person who can mentalize perceives reality not only in terms of the physical universe but also in light of mental states. This means that Emma understands herself, other people, and people in relationship to one another much more fully and correctly than before Box Hill. She can deal authentically with others.

The title of this chapter, "Mentalizing and Reality," points to this relationship between accurate perception and a reflective capacity. It's also a reference to the work of the great twentieth-century psychologist and pediatrician D. W. Winnicott, whose *Playing and Reality* explained that play, a child's participation in imaginary scenarios, is crucial to developing one important aspect of social reality, an authentic sense of self—the ability to know your own mind and heart. For Winnicott, one of the preconditions of successful child's play (in this psychological sense) is "good enough" parenting, the types of behaviors that develop secure attachment. He also observed, decades before Bowlby, that resonance with a child's emotions helps to create secure and emotionally healthy children. The psychiatrist Peter Fonagy and his research team have built on these observations to formulate a convincing account of attachment and social development that considers both resonance and play.

The originators of attachment theory, Bowlby, Ainsworth, and Main, viewed attachment as an innate psychobiological tool for enabling people to form close relationships that foster safety and well-being. Attachment experiences develop all of the habitual ways people relate to others, called attachment styles. Ideally, children become securely attached, with all the accompanying benefits of such security. Continuing the work of these psychologists, neuroscientist Alan Schore stressed the function of the attachment system as a tool for developing emotional regulation in terms of both brain and mind. While Fonagy agrees with the empirical findings of these other theorists of attachment, he has a somewhat different emphasis. Fonagy views the development of a reflective capacity (also called theory of mind [ToM] and mentalizing)* as the primary goal of the attachment system rather than a consequence. Relationship styles and emotional regulation are collateral effects, benefits that stem from mentalizing, both its exercise on the part of parents and its development in children.**

---

*   Some people make a distinction in defining terms; others don't. I think they refer to the same basic process, the cognitive understanding of mental states, even if one wants to make small distinctions.

**   Everyone who works in attachment considers all three elements, attachment style, emotional regulation, and mirroring as important. But different theorists stress different aspects. Fonagy began to stress mentalization as the most significant factors in the attachment system, crucial to mental health as well as emotional regulation and positive relationships, as his research progressed.

Fonagy agrees that a child's attachment styles and capacity for regulation are determined by the quality and frequency of caregivers' ability to resonate with the child's emotions. But he regards not only resonance but also mentalizing as crucial to developing a healthy psyche. Fonagy argues that mentalizing on the part of parents, expressed in ordinary interactions and episodes of play, is central to a child's ability to develop an accurate understanding of reality; this includes an accurate knowledge about one's desires, capabilities, and shortcomings, as well to be able to understand the behavior of others and to be able to relate authentically in mutually supportive relationships.

Let's revisit the behaviors that develop attachment and emotional regulation in light of Fonagy's theory that teaching mentalization is the primary task of the attachment system. Recall that the parent comforts a baby by attending to physical needs and providing emotional support through emotional resonance (aka attunement). Attunement is conveyed largely by mirroring behaviors, especially the caregiver's matching of the baby's facial expression. This is the fundamental way by which caregivers tell a child that they understand her emotions and needs. Such understanding weaves the very fabric of security. It also develops ToM.

Through the parent's mirroring, a baby learns to associate inner feelings with particular mental states. For very young infants, feelings of all kinds are differentiated solely in terms of good or bad, a morass of comfort or discomfort, even though they are distinct neurologically. But when infants begin to see that certain internal mind-body states routinely evoke certain expressions on the parent's part (i.e., mirroring), which are conveyed through social signals (the parent's facial expression, body language, tone of voice), they begin to be able to differentiate feelings such as sadness, fear, loneliness, and so forth, to know that these are separate and distinctive ways of feeling.

However, such mirroring must be "marked" to distinguish the caregiver's reflection of an emotion from contagion. A marked facial expression is different from the spontaneous expression of emotion; it's usually exaggerated. (Try imagining your facial expression when you comfort a baby, or some other cute, dependent creature; a cat will do.) As the child develops speech, conversation contributes to the development of mentalization. Sensitive caregivers tend to talk about feelings with children, thereby giving them countless opportunities to name and think about their own and other people's states of mind.

Repeated acts of attuning to, mirroring, and naming the child's mental states begin to build a ToM right from the start. Through seeing herself reflected in her caregivers' minds as a being who thinks, feels, believes, and desires, the child gradually acquires the ability to mentalize. She learns that what she thinks and feels influences how she behaves, that her thoughts and feelings can differ from those of other people, and that they can be recognized and shared. She learns how to keep minds in mind.

A reflective capacity gradually comes on line, as we say today. Mentalization builds on our basic ability to distinguish self from other, a capability we're born with. Younger children and, very likely, some nonhuman animals (especially great apes) might lack a fully developed ToM, but are aware of other minds nevertheless. For instance, eighteen-month-old babies can begin to take the perspective of others in a rudimentary way. One experiment showed this through the toddler's sharing. When the researcher indicated his aversion to a certain food such as fish crackers, and his relish of another food such as broccoli, the toddler offered him broccoli. Children of fourteen months aren't capable of such perspective taking, which isn't only a precursor of mentalization, but of empathy and sympathy as well; the child understands another person's state of mind and responds appropriately. All aspects of the attachment system develop gradually, in this fashion. Mentalization, like attachment styles and emotional regulation, are fostered by the cumulative effects of caregiving, which interact with the unfolding capacities of the mind and brain.

Children don't generally have a fully developed theory of mind until about age four when they can pass the false-belief test, the generally accepted milestone indicating mature reflective capacity. Here's one version of the test: Two children see someone put a candy bar in a drawer. One child is asked to leave the room. The candy is then moved to a cabinet. When child two returns, child one is asked where she will look for the candy. To pass the test, child one must realize that child two will look in the drawer. This means that child one understands that in child two's mind, that's where the candy is. She understands that a mental state can differ from reality. Children who haven't reached this developmental point say that child two will look in the cabinet. The false-belief test represents a very advanced level of ToM that might depend on well-developed language skills. Nevertheless, it's precisely this advanced capability, involving language, that's important in Fonagy's work.

The overlap of these three functions—attachment style, emotional regulation, and mentalization—is seen in the intergenerational transmission of attachment styles. Main had proposed that a person's state of mind with respect to attachment, the attachment style revealed in the Adult Attachment Interview, accurately predicted the attachment style that would characterize their yet-unborn children at twelve months. Main was right: Her studies revealed that Strange Situation classifications matched Adult Attachment Interview classifications 68 to 75 percent of the time. However, there were some parents who didn't have secure attachment styles as children but who managed to achieve sufficient security as adults to avoid replicating an insecure attachment style in their children. As a result, Main added a category that she named "earned secure attachment."

Fonagy's research refined this observation. He and his research team devised a questionnaire for measuring mentalizing capacity: the reflective functioning scale. In a longitudinal study (one that follows subjects over a given period of time) of 100 expectant couples, they found that parents—mothers *and* fathers—with a strong reflective capacity were three to four times more likely to have children who demonstrated a secure attachment style at twelve months. They also found that if a parent was able to mentalize, this could compensate for a problematic past that, in the usual course of events, would lead to an insecure attachment style being passed along to their children. Using the reflective functioning scale, they studied mothers who had experienced severe deprivation as children, such as growing up with a mentally ill parent, prolonged separation from parents, and other potentially damaging experiences. All the mothers with strong reflective functioning had securely attached children. But only one out of seventeen with poor reflective capacity managed to have a securely attached child. Earned secure attachment appears to depend on having developed the ability to mentalize.

There's no separating out the different facets of the attachment system. Whether we see the primary goal of the system as being the ability to form close, secure relationships that provide safety and refueling, the ability to regulate emotions, or a reflective capacity, it hardly matters because these functions are so completely inter-twined. To begin with, the behaviors that develop one capacity also develop the others. But they're functionally as well as develop-mentally linked. The ability to form close relationships depends on being able to regulate emotions, which means that you're able to be comfortable with closeness and enjoy it without anxiety, while also being able to resonate and empathize without catching someone else's distress. In turn, the capacity for emotional regulation corresponds to attachment style; the dismissively attached overregulate, the pre-occupied underregulate. Those with secure attachment styles also have a strong ToM, while those with insecure attachment styles tend to be poor mentalizers. We can go round and round, switching the priority of terms—attachment style, emotional regulation, mental-ization—but the truth is that they all go together.

All three capacities are aspects of social intelligence. Let's consider this in light of one of Emma's boring visits to Miss Bates. Secure in her relationships, Emma knows that no matter how she behaves, Mr. Knightley will still be devoted to her. This enables some pretty awful behavior, as at Box Hill, but during most of her encounters with Miss Bates, Emma's strong powers of emotional regulation kick in, and she masks the boredom and frustration she inevitably feels. Having a strong ToM gives her a compelling motive for self-control by enabling her to take Miss Bates's circumstances into account most of the time, and to treat her with the same degree of tolerance she habitually grants her father. When Emma fails to mentalize, she also fails to self-regulate, and she acts on her boredom, expressing the irritation she feels in response to Miss Bates's pointless, compulsive chatter.

REALITY CHECK

Our mind-brains create our realities. Whatever might be "out there," we only have access to it through our perceiving selves. This doesn't

mean that reality is relative, up for grabs, because people do have perceptions in common, and we trust that these refer to a material world
that really exists. But it does mean that reality is subjective, that we
perceive through the filter of our thinking, feeling selves. In *Pride and
Prejudice*, when Darcy and Bingley attend the Meryton ball, they both
realize that they're at a public dance, that other people are in the room
with them, that Jane Bennett is pretty, and (using ToM) that people
are eager to meet them. But the reality of the ball is nevertheless different for each: Bingley sees a room full of friendly people; Darcy sees
a room full of predatory mothers and daughters. Bingley has fun and
Darcy is miserable.

By claiming that we possess experiences in common and can agree
about "what happened," I'm bypassing a huge topic, the status of reality
(the "if a tree falls in the forest . . ." problem), to take for granted that
we share perceptions of the world, that people with normally functioning mind-brains usually agree about the bare essentials of a given
situation. Nevertheless, because reality is subjective (but not relative),
some people have a more accurate take on events than others. And the
extent to which we get it right or wrong varies tremendously. This is
especially true of social reality, of our interactions with one another.
Emma is all about this issue.

A good ToM enables us to get it right much of the time. It enables
us to live in a nuanced world in which we understand the complexity
of individual motives and social interactions, a faculty that helps us
in countless ways. We see an instance of what's at stake in *Pride and
Prejudice*, when Elizabeth's failure to mentalize almost destroys her
friendship with her best friend, Charlotte Lucas. But Elizabeth uses
her reflective capacity in time to keep this from happening.

Let's return to Elizabeth's reaction to her good friend Charlotte's
marriage. As you'll recall, when Elizabeth learns that Charlotte has
accepted her dull cousin Mr. Collins's proposal, she's shocked and
outraged to begin with, viewing this as almost a form of prostitution—certainly, she thinks her friend has traded body and soul for
a home of her own. She doesn't stop to consider the motive that led
Charlotte to her decision, her desire to avoid the bleak future that
awaited poor spinsters in Austen's society. Perhaps even if Elizabeth
had taken Charlotte's perspective, she wouldn't have exonerated her

friend completely—after all, Austen backed out of a similar marriage of convenience because she just couldn't go through with it. But for this very reason, the episode attests to Austen's own capacity for empathy if not Elizabeth's—although Austen couldn't behave as Charlotte did, she writes about this character with sympathy and zero judgment. She also understands the almost instinctive repulsion that Elizabeth feels for Charlotte's marriage.

But Elizabeth comes around, condoning if not agreeing with her friend's choice. When she visits Charlotte in her new home and real-izes that she's happy with the life she's chosen, Elizabeth accepts that people have different feelings and attitudes. Just because Charlotte's view of marriage differs from her own doesn't mean that Charlotte is corrupt. Elizabeth's reality changes from *Charlotte is a bad person for making this marriage* to *Charlotte has her reasons, and they're valid even if they aren't my reasons.* One scholar has even suggested that Char-lotte's decision to marry Mr. Collins influences Elizabeth to accept Darcy. After all, she marries out of "gratitude and esteem," not passion, and also after realizing that "to be Mistress of Pemberley might be something!" I don't agree, but the point is worth considering.

Most of us likely have lapses of ToM that lead to faulty judgments. Certainly, all of Emma's misunderstandings are errors of this type, since her take on reality is generally solid; for instance, she under-stands the dynamic of her own family perfectly. But for some people, ToM can be so compromised that they have a slim grasp of reality altogether, at least social reality. If you can't mindread, you inevitably have a low social IQ. Autistic people have this disability; their deficits in social interaction are obvious. But disabilities, like abilities, lie along a spectrum, and some people who are neurotypical nevertheless have great difficulty understanding and recognizing states of mind.

Fonagy characterizes the condition of being unable to mentalize much of the time as the mode of psychic equivalence. For people dominated by this mode of perception, the external reality and the internal world and of thoughts and feelings are equated, which means that they're often unable to distinguish between beliefs and facts. They're prone to think that if they're treated badly, or someone thinks ill of them, they must actually be bad. Or the reverse, that if they think someone is evil, this must be true. They often fail to perceive psychological boundaries between self and other, and so don't realize that mental states don't necessarily reflect or express the truth. This of course means a slim grasp of the reality concerning the effects of one's own behavior and of the dynamics of social relationships. This describes Miss Bates pretty accurately.

Although readers who've written about *Emma*, including literary scholars, are fully aware of Emma's empathic lapse at Box Hill, her failure take Miss Bates's perspective, no one (to my knowledge) has remarked that ironically Miss Bates is guilty of the same error. The usual content of Miss Bates's compulsive conversation (I'm willing to bet that readers as well as characters tune her out), shows that she fails to realize how she comes across to many of her listeners, at best irrelevant, or how they feel in her presence, tolerant and compassionate, like Mr. Knightley, or bored and impatient, like Emma. Miss Bates's lack of mentalizing may well be a defense mechanism whose purpose is to block an empathic response. If her stream of thoughtless chatter prevents her from knowing how tedious she is, it also blots out the sadness of her situation, as reflected in the compassion it evokes; indeed, few of us are comfortable with being the object of pity. Her nonstop compulsive talking would additionally prevent her from seeing herself as pathetic, not least by keeping her from really thinking about much of anything. She doesn't take the third-person perspective that would enable her to see herself as others see her, and so she doesn't acknowledge the seriousness of her plight.

But after Emma's insult at Box Hill, she has a moment of revelation. To know how Emma sees her is to know something important about herself, that her incessant and empty chatter isn't interesting or socially appropriate. This is hurtful knowledge, but also important knowledge, an insight that might lead her to adopt a more dignified way of being in straightened circumstances that would gain the respect as well as the compassion of her neighbors. Think of Mrs. Smith in *Persuasion*, Anne's resilient friend who's fallen on hard times.

But unfortunately, this moment fails to lead to true mentalizing for Miss Bates. To begin with, Emma gives her opinion, and although many might agree with her, this isn't so of everyone. Mr. Woodhouse doesn't find Miss Bates dull. But Miss Bates simply accepts Emma's belief (*You are dull*) as fact. If she'd been able to see Emma's insult as one person's perception rather than as gospel truth, she would have been less vulnerable. Perhaps she would have been motivated to change her conversational style, taking Emma's comment as rude but constructive criticism. And she would have been able to put the offensive remark of a spoiled young lady into context.

That context would have included a sense of how totally inappropriate Emma has been. Given Miss Bates's low socioeconomic status in Highbury society, it's doubtful that she would have given the obvious retort that Emma deserves, even if she'd been able to think of it—that rude statements are as inappropriate as dull ones. But she might have ignored what Emma said, or responded with, "Since my contributions wouldn't be appropriate, I'd rather not play the game." She could have answered Emma's comment in a way that would have led to Emma's discredit and not to her own feelings of humiliation; Emma would have been the one to blush, not Miss Bates. Instead, she simply folds under the weight of Emma's statement, equating opinion with truth. This is the mode of psychic equivalence.

We see a benign and I suspect unusual form of this condition in Mr. Woodhouse, Emma's hypochondriacal father. Mr. Woodhouse is well-intentioned and cares very much for other people, especially those he loves. But he lives in psychic equivalence mode much of the time, demonstrating very poor powers of mentalization. We might be tempted to say that he displays empathy without ToM, except that empathy by definition includes accurate mentalizing. Mr. Woodhouse certainly feels sympathy, all the compassion and caring we associate with empathy, but without the cognitive perspective taking that empathy involves.

I've already mentioned that Mr. Woodhouse pities Mrs. Weston for her fortunate marriage because her departure from his household has been unfortunate for *him*; for that reason she'll always be "poor Miss Taylor" in his eyes. This is but one among many examples of Mr. Woodhouse's cognitive limitations. Here's another: Because he can't tolerate rich food and lives on gruel, which he greatly enjoys, he assumes that others also suffer from sensitive digestive systems and possess equally questionable culinary tastes. He offers his guests abstemious servings of food, such as a small egg and wine diluted with water. Fortunately, his socially aware daughter, who indeed possesses a reflective capacity—vital for hosting the frequent card parties her father so enjoys—saves his guests from such a fate. One such gathering demonstrates her habitual way of dealing with him: "Emma allowed her father to talk—but supplied her visitors in a much more satisfactory style, and on the present evening had particular pleasure in sending them away happy."

Most people tolerate Mr. Woodhouse's foibles because they care about him and they know he means well. But his son-in-law, Mr. John Knightley, isn't as charitable as his older brother, Emma's own Mr. Knightley. He nearly loses his temper when Mr. Woodhouse insists that his family's seaside vacation, recommended by their doctor as healthy for all, must have been harmful. Mr. Woodhouse keeps insisting on this point of view and urging his son-in-law to have his family seen by his own trusted doctor. Fortunately, before things get too heated, Emma manages to steer the conversation in a different direction.

Miss Bates and Mr. Woodhouse both show deficits in their ability to converse, symptomatic of a weak reflective capacity. Miss Bates might talk more than Mr. Woodhouse, but both engage in social exchanges by laying bare the contents of their minds without taking their listeners into account in any meaningful way. (We might say their conversation lacks collaboration.) Miss Bates tends to direct her focus outward, offering a running commentary on events because she lacks a sense of an interior self, while Mr. Woodhouse projects his own values and feelings pretty much nonstop. The style is different but the lack of true engagement is similar. Most of us edit our minds before speaking without even being aware that we're doing so, at least much of the time. But without a mentalizing capacity, and with a weak sense of the boundaries between inside and outside, Miss Bates and Mr. Woodhouse fail to take that third-person perspective that makes us mindful of what we say. And so they have no idea of how they come across to others.

I think I know what this is like. As a writer, I frequently talk to myself, verbalizing the thoughts and observations that come to mind. Writing is a lonely business, and the urge to talk to someone, even oneself, can be overpowering. This has become a habit, so sometimes I find myself uttering this stream of conversation aloud to members of my family. When someone says, "What did you say?" I'll suddenly realize that no one is really interested in where my purse is, or when I fed the cats, or what I plan to wear that day. I catch myself and stop talking. Miss Bates and Mr. Woodhouse never catch themselves.

It's a fine touch of Austen's that Miss Bates and Mr. Woodhouse get along so well together. When you lack the capacity for perceiving or appreciating the nuances of social interaction, it well might be that affect is what matters the most in conversation, and these two have abundant good nature. Perhaps Miss Bates's stream of irrelevant patter distracts Mr. Woodhouse from his own worried thoughts at a level that he can tolerate. And it hardly matters to Miss Bates what others say—she barely hears them anyway—as long as she has the comfort of their company.

CHILD'S PLAY

Newborns begin life in psychic equivalence mode. They gradually develop skills such as self-soothing, which might involve picturing the caregiver's face, and object constancy, knowing that if people and things disappear from view (as in a game of peek-a-boo), they aren't gone forever. The ability to have ideas that are distinct from immediate perceptions is the beginning of ToM.

Fonagy, building on the work of Winnicott, viewed play as another crucial step in the gradual development of a ToM. Fonagy named the phase of play between the onset of play behavior and the development of a full theory of mind "pretend mode." When children begin to play games involving make-believe, perhaps as early as two for some, they begin to understand that the mind can create a set of circumstances and expectations different from those of the real world. A three-year-old playing Batman knows that it's possible to be Batman in a game and a kid in the rest of life. Reading stories to children also establishes a space of thought and action apart from everyday life.

Adults know that when we pretend, and this includes adult modes of play such as reading and writing fiction, we draw on elements known to us in the real world to create an alternative imaginative world. We know that this mental space doesn't really exist. Indeed, much of the pleasure of reading comes from forgetting that fact temporarily, by engaging in a "willing suspension of disbelief," as Austen's contemporary, the poet and critic Samuel Taylor Coleridge puts it. But however lost in books we might become, deep down we know that Elizabeth, Darcy, Emma, and all the others we've come to know and love, or know and dislike, are fictional people. Our disbelief is suspended, but willingly, and we understand the difference between fiction and reality.

But the young child who's beginning to play and understand stories lacks the ability to make this distinction. He understands that the imaginative world is different from the real world, but to him, they're both real in the moment. In pretend mode, the world of make-believe is "decoupled" from reality, but it's genuine on its own terms. Pretend mode provides good practice for ToM because it involves being able to clearly establish a space where what you think is separate from what's out there.

Pretend mode is also crucial to developing the ability to mentalize because imaginative spaces provide occasions for thinking and talking about feelings, and therefore the opportunity to deliberately focus on the contents of our own and other minds. For instance, you might ask a child why Batman is angry with the Joker (he wants to rob a bank!). Books certainly deal with characters and their feelings, and this is often true even of very basic board books, written for babies. (My favorite is *Duck and Goose, How Are You Feeling?* definitely a book for therapists' kids!). And we often ask children about their *own* feelings about games and books. All this is practice for mentalization.

Fonagy recounts examples that demonstrate pretend mode in children. One father bought his three-year-old son, who loved playing Batman, an elaborate costume. When he looked in the mirror, he was terrified of his own image. He refused to wear the costume and returned to using his blanket as a cape. An alternative universe was acceptable so long as its elements weren't too realistic; he wasn't afraid of his own image in a cape made of a blanket because it wasn't threatening. But when he actually began to resemble Batman, this other reality became too scary. He was scared of his image, as he would have been scared if Batman had really appeared.

Another child, age four, was frightened by a story his mother read to him. When told that the story wasn't real the child replied, "But it's real to me." A wise child, that one! The ability to fully mentalize, just around the corner developmentally for these children, means that you understand that the pretend world is different from, but also related to, the real world. You know that the world of play draws on elements of reality, but that what you pretend actually is pretend, not an alternative universe. You understand that play involves taking elements of the real world and transforming them—and so a doll becomes a baby. You build a bridge between playing and reality by learning that pretend is a state of mind, and that states of mind can alter actual circumstances. This is the core of mentalizing. (Of course, even adults don't always escape pretend mode. We believe in the reality of fictional worlds as we read, and sometimes it's almost as difficult for us to make the distinction between make-believe and reality as it is for these children. If you've ever been scared by a thriller, you know how these children feel!)

When I read Fonagy's work, I knew immediately that I'd witnessed the stage of pretend mode in my daughters. When Jocelyn was two, she had a passion for elephants. She had an elephant pillow, elephant stuffed animals, and several books about elephants. We also watched nature shows on elephants. I decided to take her to the zoo to see real elephants. We approached the elephant exhibit, my heart pounding with excitement at the prospect of this meeting. But it turned out that this was much more thrilling for me than for anyone else on that trip.

A crowd of elephants stood together gawking back at us as we gawked at them. I pointed them out to Jocelyn, "Look there are the elephants." She didn't react. She didn't even recognize them as elephants. Elephants were those cute fuzzy animals who lived in her bedroom, or the images that we saw in books and nature programs. These huge pachyderms standing before us weren't elephants in her view. She ignored them and me. She was very likely confused. I'd like to think that she objected to their being housed in a zoo, but I'm fast-forwarding. Today, Jocelyn is an activist who stands up for treating people and nonhuman animals with the basic, allegedly human decency that we all too often forget.

With similar naïve delight, I looked forward to reading versions of the classics written for children to my daughters. We began with a starter version of *Pride and Prejudice*, which I'm happy to say, both

JANE ON THE BRAIN

girls enjoyed. But when we got to *Frankenstein*, three-year-old Maggie was terrified. I wasn't even allowed to bring the book into her room; the mere sight of it panicked her. And so it was consigned to storage. She has since read Mary Shelley's wonderful original, which suited this (now) young woman's interest in psychology and philosophy.

Pretend mode is a step on the way to developing the ability to mentalize. By roughly the age of five, children who follow a normal developmental path have this capability and they understand that play is play, and that beliefs can differ from reality. But adults who have a weak theory of mind have been unable, for one reason or another, to successfully use the lessons of pretend mode. They often fail to understand that what you think or believe, or what someone else thinks or believes, might not be accurate. Of course, they don't live in the same kind of alternative reality that kids in pretend mode inhabit. In the rather unlikely event that Miss Bates puts on a costume to attend a masquerade, she isn't going to get scared of her reflection in the mirror.

Winnicott maintained that play is the precursor of creativity. By definition, creativity involves the ability to play with reality, to imagine alternatives, including alternative ways of thinking and feeling. Creativity is a form of mental flexibility. To put this in terms of dynamic systems theory, creativity involves complexity rather than rigidity. It's not surprising that people whose development has been compromised, who haven't been able to use pretend mode to develop a fully functional ToM, also tend to demonstrate rigidity and a lack of imagination. Miss Bates and Mr. Woodhouse are prisoners of their limited points of view.

By contrast, Emma, with all her faults and insensitivities, is the most creative of Austen's heroines. Sure, she makes mistakes in reading minds, but we all do that; that's one of the key insights of this novel. But Emma also imagines possibilities about herself and others, fully aware that she's "playing with reality." She weaves a story of guilt and passion between Jane Fairfax and her adoptive father, but she realizes it's speculation. She thinks of the match between Mr. Weston and her governess long before it happens (and so mistakenly takes credit for making this match). After Frank Churchill rescues Harriet from the gypsies, she begins to think of a marriage for these two, but she doesn't assume that they're in love.

A marriage between Harriet and Frank—what a happy ending this would have been, so much like a story in one of the novels Austen read voraciously, especially if Harriet turned out to be an aristocrat in lowly circumstances! So unlike the plot of *Emma*, with its marriages that stem from ordinary events and acquaintances, but which Austen brilliantly renders just as romantic as any of the dramatic stories popular in her time. And *Emma* is instructive as well, telling readers that in order to live an ethical and compassionate life, in order to be fair to others at the very least, and empathetic at best, we need to get over ourselves and pay attention.

But *Emma* is nevertheless about the pleasures as well as the dangers of the imagination, of the joy of playing with reality, and the resources imagination affords a person. Early on in the novel, soon after Mrs. Weston leaves Emma and her father to take up her life as a married woman, Emma misses her companion sorely: "[S]he was now in great danger of suffering from intellectual solitude. She dearly loved her father, but he was no companion for her. He could not meet her in conversation, rational or playful." Surely Emma's imagination, as destructive as it can be at times, also gives her the resources that make life interesting for herself in very limited circumstances. Emma's rich imagination makes her into what literary critics call "a figure for the author," a kind of literary double for Austen herself. For what does Austen do if not spin stories from the ordinary materials of daily life, working her magic to turn flax into gold?

The ending of *Emma* reminds me of another great book, although one in a totally different genre, *The Wonderful Wizard of Oz*. At the end of this classic, Dorothy finds that the fantastic life she sought in Oz exists right at home. Much the same happens for Emma. The romance of her life has been there from the start, her Prince Charming lives in her backyard. She learns this because she "has eyes to see," as the saying goes. Playing with reality also means being able to view it flexibly, and for Emma this means seeing the everyday as no less wonderful than the stories we spin. But as with Dorothy, it takes imagination and insight to understand this point. You need to be able to "imagine" yourself from outside yourself, and to have sufficient powers of insight to know your own mind. Mentalizing enables us to have such insight, for ourselves and others.

THEORIES AND MIRRORS

We understand in a basic, literal sense that people are individual entities. There are areas in the brain that enable us to distinguish self from other, and which give us a sense of agency, that we, and not someone else, is acting. All normally functioning brains can make distinctions of this kind. Whatever Miss Bates's deficits in mentalizing, she understands that Emma speaks the insult, and that she hears it. She knows who is who.

Being able to mentalize and empathize, to recognize states of mind as such and assign them correctly, is a much more complicated process, one that's vulnerable to the many mind-brain glitches and deficits that block accurate perception. Mindreading is, however, a relatively recent innovation among the earth's creatures; it might be unique to humans (although evidence suggests that some other species share this ability, particularly our closest relatives, the great apes, as well as dolphins and elephants). Given how new and complicated the processes involved in mindreading, it's not surprising that it poses challenges.

Evolution conferred this gift, but it's also largely to blame for its defects. Evolution is like a mechanic in an antique auto shop who has to keep updating an old car. He can't junk the whole thing and start from scratch but must work on improving the specimen he has while using available materials. Perhaps at a certain point he'll have replaced so many parts that the car is quite a different vehicle (as when dinosaurs became birds), but the changes are cumulative and never happen all at once. And when something—a car or a brain—is built on top of an older structure using only what comes to hand, there are likely to be many flaws. This is especially true if it's built quickly, and indeed, the human brain was constructed at an incredible pace in terms of evolutionary time.

We understand the thoughts, feelings, and intentions of others with reference to ourselves—our own thoughts, feelings, and intentions. Given our evolutionary heritage, this self-referencing makes sense. To begin with—quite literally at the beginning of animal life on earth— creatures had only themselves. For millennia and millennia, animals, and by this I mean even single-celled animals, survived by putting their own needs above all else. They didn't think about this, because they didn't think at all; they lacked even the fundamental sense of being here, called core consciousness, for which you need a central nervous system, a brain. You also need a central nervous system to experience emotions, the foundation of social intelligence.

For a creature without core consciousness, like the *Aplysia*, the giant snail that neuroscientist Eric Kandel worked with, things in the environment are either edible, neutral, or threatening. The ancestor of emotion, what we might call "proto-emotion," consists literally of approach and withdrawal behavior, the basis for our own far more complicated emotional system. But for the *Aplysia*, this behavior is starkly literal: The creature either approaches, stands still, or withdraws. The *Aplysia* reacts, but it doesn't relate.

Reptiles are far more advanced; they possess a central nervous system, including a rudimentary cortex, the seat of reason and cognition in humans. Yet, although they might be consciously aware of others of their kind (we really can't say), they certainly don't form meaningful connections with one another, or with anyone else. Reptiles mate, but this is instinct-driven action behavior, nothing sentimental about it. Most don't even meet their offspring. They don't attach emotionally to one another.

Building on the neural machinery of these simpler creatures, we then, as mammals, learned to care for our young and form relationships with one another. Love entered the world. And then we humans, and, I believe, a few other nonhuman animals, were asked not only to connect meaningfully with one another but to actually adopt their perspectives; mentalizing and empathy joined the roster of social capabilities. This development was huge and occurred at lightning speed for humans, the most adept at this skill. We've barely had a moment, geologically speaking, to adjust to this new demand.

In short, the capacity for mindful and emotional connections with others developed from profound, biologically determined and unconscious self-involvement. In a certain sense, we go through this process with every interaction. We understand other people's actions by reference to our own bodies. We understand their thoughts and feelings in terms of our own thoughts and feelings. We constantly reference our own experience and knowledge in order to understand the minds and bodies of others. This order of things makes sense because self was all we had to start with. So we shouldn't be too hard on poor Emma, or on ourselves, for finding it difficult at times to escape our own desires, thoughts, and plans. We come by this bias honestly.

Yet, exactly *how* we use ourselves to understand others has generated a lively controversy in the mind-brain sciences. There are two schools of thought about how we accomplish the extraordinary feat of knowing other minds. These are known respectively as theory-theory and simulation theory. Theory-theory proposes that we understand the mental states of others by figuring out—that is, forming theories about—others' thoughts and feelings based on our familiarity with our own minds and observations of human behavior. That is to say, understanding another person's state of mind begins with knowledge of the thoughts and feelings that are associated with social signals. So if we see a friend laughing, we marshal what we know about the meaning of laughter from our knowledge and experience, options that include a response to something funny and an expression of embarrassment, and we put this together with contextual clues to figure out why she's laughing. We don't do this consciously; we don't need to because lightning-quick subliminal thought comes easily to the human mind-brain. In neurological terms, theory-theory is a top-down kind of processing because it posits that understanding the meaning and context of a social signal (such as laughter) depends on the higher brain structures that make meaning out of experiences.

The other explanation of mindreading is simulation theory, which maintains that we understand what others are thinking and feeling by actually simulating their internal states at lower, usually subcortical, levels of processing. We interpret the content of these simulations at higher cognitive levels (although this process is still subliminal because we remain unaware of our brain's activity) and then project our simulations back to the targets of our observations. This is a bottom-up process because it moves from lower, subcortical, levels of processing to higher, cortical levels. According to simulation theory, we run the program on ourselves and then apply it to those we observe.

For instance, if you see someone laughing, the subcortical neural areas that generate laughter in your own brain activate to some degree, although you don't necessarily laugh. You understand the other person's laughter by actually simulating her experience, and then you separate out the simulation and project it to where it belongs, back to the person you're observing. Simulation depends on what is called a "perception-action" model: We perceive and simulate, often involving our bodies as well as our brains, in order to makes sense of our perceptions of other people.

As you know, for Emma to empathize with Miss Bates, she must first understand her thoughts and feelings. According to theory-theory, Emma draws on what she knows about being elderly and downwardly mobile—Mr. Knightley has given her a vivid picture—to figure out Miss Bates's state of mind. She doesn't need to think this through because even potentially conscious thought can take place so swiftly that we ignore it. Simulation theory offers a different account: Emma, for a moment, actually becomes poor and old and then projects the feelings she experiences back to the target, Miss Bates. She becomes Miss Bates in order to understand Miss Bates.

Take another example. The other day I received a solicitation from a charity that funds operations to restore sight to blind children and I decided to contribute because I empathized. A short survey of your mail table will show that charity solicitations are clearly written to elicit empathy. But in order to take the perspective of these children, I first needed to understand their feelings. According to theory-theory, I drew on my experience and knowledge to figure out what it would be like to be a blind child whose sight might be restored by an operation and realized how such a child must feel, both about being incapacitated and getting surgery that would give him sight. A calculation induced my knowledge of the blind child's internal state. But simulation theory suggests that for however brief and subliminal a moment, I felt what it is like to be a blind child who can suddenly see. From that visceral knowledge, I became consciously aware of the thoughts and feelings that would be likely in this situation.

One important source of validation for simulation theory came from the dramatic discovery of mirror neurons, a eureka moment of the kind that makes science the stuff of legend and narrative. In the 1980s, in a lab in Parma, Italy, directed by Giacomo Rizzolatti, scientists were studying a brain area in macaque monkeys known as F5, a part of the premotor cortex, the area responsible for planning and implementing actions. Area F5 contains millions of neurons concerned with hand movements such as grasping, tearing, and, most important in terms of survival, bringing objects to the mouth, which primates (ourselves included) do in order to eat. The neuroscientist Vittorio Gallese was in the lab one day when the monkeys were resting between experiments. He grasped an object—he doesn't remember what it was, but let's say a banana—and heard an unexpected beep from a computer that was connected to a surgically implanted electrode in one of the monkey's brains. The beeping indicated that the monkey had grasped an object. But the animal hadn't moved; she'd simply observed Gallese reaching and grasping.

This wasn't a fluke. These distinctive macaque neurons, now dubbed "mirror neurons," routinely activated as the monkeys watched the scientists reach for and grasp objects. Rizzolatti's lab confirmed that the essential property of mirror neurons is that they fire with the observation as well as the performance of a given action. They have subsequently been found in the human brain as well.

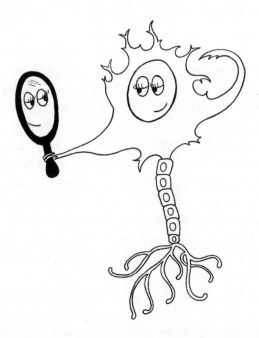

While scientists can't plant electrodes in human brains for purposes of experimentation because this is considered unethical, one study using epileptic patients who already had electrodes implanted for purposes of surgery, confirmed the existence of these copycat brain cells in humans. This suggests that our brains need to behave as if we're acting in order to understand the actions of others. Here was evidence that supported simulation theory, evidence that we run the program on ourselves to understand what's going on in the minds of others. I'm putting my money on simulation theory as opposed to theory-theory.

If explaining how we know that someone is reaching for a banana was exciting, the possibility of explaining how we understand feelings and motives had scientists out on the proverbial limb, a dangerous place for an ape, especially a human one pledged to follow rigorous protocols before reaching conclusions. As of 2014, the existence of mirror neurons in humans had been established solely for the motor system, which governs actions, such as grasping. Nevertheless, the possibility that mirror neurons might explain both simple and complicated forms of mindreading was just too tempting, and soon books and articles were appearing linking these copycat brain cells to very high-order processes such as empathy. Then again, this isn't so unusual because books about the mind-brain are often written in the subjunctive, the tense of "maybe" rather than "it is so."

But we don't need to pinpoint actual mirror neurons to observe the existence of neural mirroring, which provides strong support for simulation theory. Other kinds of neurons also appear to mirror. Jean Decety, a neuroscientist who studies empathy extensively, conducting his own experiments and reviewing those of other scientists, concludes that we understand emotion through neural mirroring. For instance, one study using fMRI (which tells us which areas of the brain are active) showed that when participants were asked to observe or imitate facial expressions of various emotions, increased activity was observed in the areas responsible for producing those emotions as well as in areas corresponding to the representation of faces.

Another example: Neuroscientist Tania Singer and her colleagues recruited male-female couples who watched one another receive shocks. The woman was in an fMRI scanner, but by the use of mirrors she could see when a shock was administered to her partner's hand. Brain areas involved in the processing of pain (the pain matrix areas) activated both for her own and her partner's pain. The neural mir-roring of pain is likely the most frequently studied instance of neural mirroring. Well-documented instances of neural mirroring have also shown that the insula, a cortical structure, is active in both the experi-ence and recognition of disgust.

In addition, nonneurological support for simulation theory has existed for decades. One of the earliest of these trials demonstrated that the muscle groups for grasping activate (as seen in twitching) in humans when they watch someone else grasping. It's significant that only the specific muscles needed for grasping, and not other muscles in roughly the same region, show activity. That muscles twitch in response to observation strongly suggests that mirroring takes place neurally as well as bodily. Further research indicates that simulation also takes place for actions involving the mouth and feet, not just the hands. And with respect to the social mind-brain, emotional conta-gion and emotional resonance involve replicating emotions (affect), feeling what someone else is feeling. Recall that these processes are subconscious and subcortical, so that it makes sense to think that they can be conveyed viscerally and immediately through simula-tion. The automatic mirroring of emotion is an implicit assumption of much of attachment theory, which is certainly widely accepted and noncontroversial.

Whatever the explanatory reach of the mirror neuron system, there's no doubt about the ubiquity of mirroring for our species. In an elegant formulation, Gallese (the scientist who discovered mirror neurons) coined the phrase "shared manifold hypothesis," which acknowledges the significance of mirroring to the human psyche at various levels. We recognize ourselves as beings who live within a larger community, including the community of humanity as a whole, because we resemble one another—we mirror—in essential ways. In fact, we tend to feel affinity and cohesion with others who are like us (the downside of this concerns the negative feelings for those who are different).

And whatever the order of neural events that produces empathy, an empathic response is a mirroring response, even at the level of neurons. This means that even if empathy and other forms of emo-tion sharing such as resonance and contagion don't begin as neural simulation, they end up as such since the production of similar feelings must involve similar neural activation. Emma knows what Miss Bates feels because she feels those feelings herself. So whether Emma relies on simulation theory, theory-theory, or a combination of the two, she eventually replicates Miss Bates's feelings in her own mind-brain.

And we mirror in a very obvious way through the facial and bodily imitation that accompanies emotional resonance and other more cognitive ways of mindreading. Next time you're having a meaningful conversation with someone, notice body language. Chances are you'll both be mimicking one another's body posture and facial expressions. People who take others' perspectives easily tend to frequently imitate others in this way. This is one way in which mirroring indicates to the "target" that his feelings are being understood, for adults as well as babies.

Mirroring demonstrates that the boundaries between people are much blurrier than we've often thought, not nearly as separate as our Anglo-European culture, with its hearty embrace of individualism, has often asserted. With few exceptions (such as Spinoza) Western philosophy from Plato to the Existentialists has taken human isolation for granted. But this way of looking at things is gradually eroding. A century-plus of psychology, including contemporary neuroscience, tells us that we're connected cognitively, emotionally, and bodily, in ways undreamt of in our philosophies.

The downside is that a lack of clear boundaries between our own and other minds can lead to the kinds of mentalizing errors Emma commits, as well as to various types of contagion and unsought influence. But confusion is the price we pay for connection. And it's the price we pay for love—true love—a bond grounded in an intimate knowledge of another person's mind and heart.

Emma and Mr. Knightley know one another all too well. This allows Mr. Knightley to anticipate Emma's schemes, which she'd much rather keep to herself. And Emma realizes that despite Mr. Knightley's role as benevolent patron of the community, the one who looks out for other people's interests, he might well have some interests of his own. That's why she worries about his marrying Jane Fairfax or (horrors!) Harriet.

Jealousy provides each of them with the occasion for recognizing that their relationship has a romantic dimension that had likely been masked by habit and, perhaps, by a sense that a romance between them might be inappropriate. Although marriages between older men and much younger women weren't unusual in Austen's day, Mr. Knightley isn't just old enough to be Emma's father (although a very young father) but has actually seen her grow up. In *Emma*, such long-standing closeness and familiarity fosters their bond and secures their love for one another. For Emma and Mr. Knightley, marriage means coming home.

ELEVEN

Crimes of the Heartless: Empathy Disorders, Part One

've suggested that one reason that so many people love Austen is that, like Shakespeare, she "holds the mirror up to nature," portraying a broad range of human feelings that we all recognize: happiness, excitement, anger, embarrassment, fear, and, above all, love. And so we feel empathy from Austen herself, the sense that she takes our perspective cognitively and emotionally; we have the feeling of "feeling felt."[*] Unlike Shakespeare, however, Austen doesn't display an equally broad range of human behavior: She avoids the atrocities that our kind are all too capable of committing. I can read Austen at bedtime without fear of nightmares because I know I'll encounter a relatively safe world.

Yet, while Austen doesn't portray the worst of human *behavior*, she nevertheless gives us the sense that she's encompassed the grim side of human *nature*. She achieves this Shakespearean inclusiveness by

---

[*]   Siegel, *The Developing Mind*, 176.

gesturing toward dangers that don't actually happen, leaving it to her readers to imagine tragic outcomes and gory details and to feel relieved that these haven't happened. We recognize the potential for trauma with a capital "T," but are then returned to the comfort of the sheltered world we presumably share with her characters.

Emma does this particularly well. Take Miss Bates. As an aging single woman without employment or resources, a bleak and impoverished future looms on the horizon for her. We can imagine her losing her home, living in a poorhouse where conditions are harsh, or in a cottage without a warm fire or enough to eat, comforts she's used to. Or she might have to become a poor relation in a home where she's resented and disrespected. It's hard to say which of these options is worse, for emotional pain can be just as hard to bear as a lack of creature comforts. Fortunately, our Miss Bates can depend on the kindness of neighbors to assure her an old age with dignity and ease.

We can paint the same kind of bleak future for Jane Fairfax, should she be forced to work as a governess, a position akin to that of a poor relation but with even greater potential for exploitation. But Jane too is rescued by Austen's plot, marrying the wealthy Frank Churchill. These averted futures invoke the sad stories of many others not so fortunate, of real and fictional people who lurk beyond the boundaries of Austen's pages.

Harriet's encounter with the gypsies performs a similar literary vanishing act. Harriet is walking alone along country roads when she encounters a band of gypsies who ask for money, which she gives. But this isn't enough; as the narrator tells us, "her terror and her purse were too tempting, and she was followed, or rather surrounded by the whole gang, demanding more." The threat of rape is the unspoken danger here, a threat conveyed with symbolism. You don't have to be a Freudian to see that the purse can be associated with female genitals. The "more" that the gang demands might simply be more money, but the thinly veiled demand is for more than money.

Frank Churchill comes to the rescue, which, of course, prompts Emma to think of a match between them. We're safely back in the sheltered world of romantic comedy, but again, we've caught a glimpse of the very real threats that lie beyond its borders. This is brilliant on Austen's part—she lets us glimpse true evil because it's important to an understanding of human nature, but she keeps us safe from witnessing its consequences.

Austen's technique of invoking terror only to return us to the comfortable world of provincial, middle-class England is of course writ large in *Northanger Abbey*. Catherine Morland, the novel's main character (or "heroine" as Austen somewhat ironically calls her), is so heavily influenced by her reading of Gothic horror novels that she becomes convinced that her host, General Tilney, has either murdered his wife or is keeping her prisoner in a secluded part of his home. The Tilney residence is a former abbey, the perfect setting for a Gothic scenario. Catherine discovers her mistake—there's no madwoman in the attic—which is enough to make her blush heartily in private. But to her dismay, Henry Tilney, the general's son and the man she loves, guesses her folly when he finds her lurking in the corridors of the unused wings of the abbey, looking for evidence. He scolds her for having such ludicrous thoughts:

> If I understand you rightly, you had formed a surmise of such horror as I have hardly words to—Dear Miss Morland, consider the dreadful nature of the suspicions you have entertained. What have you been judging from? Remember the country and the age in which we live. Remember that we are English: that we are Christians. Consult your own understanding, your own sense of the probable, your own observation of what is passing around you—Does our education prepare us for such atrocities? Do our laws connive at them? Could they be perpetrated without being known, in a country like this, where social and literary intercourse is on such a footing; where every man is surrounded by a neighbourhood of voluntary spies, and where roads and newspapers lay every thing open? Dearest Miss Morland, what ideas have you been admitting?

Henry says what we know (or come to know) as readers of Austen's fiction: We'll encounter a safe and predictable world in her pages, a world in which people by and large get what they deserve and where people are, by and large, shielded and safe.

Catherine's humiliation conveys a familiar moral, usually directed at women in the novels of the period: Don't give free reign to the imagination because imagination often misleads us. Better to trust in reason. Such was the creed of Samuel Johnson, one of Austen's much-admired literary predecessors.

But *Northanger Abbey*'s other observation is the more important and original one, which, apart from Austen's superb writing, gives this novel an edge over most other literary assaults on the dangers of the imagination: The character traits that make a man capable of murdering his wife or imprisoning her in his attic enable people to commit all manner of cruelties, large and small. When the general summarily dismisses Catherine from his home upon discovering she's not an heiress, sending her on a full day's journey by public coach without money or a servant, Catherine herself comes to realize this truth: "[I]n suspecting General Tilney of either murdering or shutting up his wife, she had scarcely sinned against his character, or magnified his cruelty."

Catherine is correct about "the banality of evil," to use the apt expression of twentieth-century philosopher Hannah Arendt. For evil is indeed what Austen is considering here as well as in other novels, and this includes both passive sins of omission on the part of a society that doesn't take care of its vulnerable members, as well as actual crimes such as rape and murder, flashed before our eyes as potentialities. Austen brilliantly realizes that evil is not only a moral problem, but a psychological one as well: In her view, evil is the failure or absence of empathy. All of Austen's novels focus to some extent on whether or not people are able to take the perspective of others, emotionally as well as cognitively. While not all her characters with limited abilities for mentalizing are bad (think of Mr. Woodhouse), her "evil" people are self-centered people, and such selfishness involves, above all, an inability or a refusal to empathize with others.

SUBJECTS VS. OBJECTS

Neuroscientist Simon Baron-Cohen also takes the view that a deficit of empathy is the core characteristic of evil, supporting his findings with a knowledge of the mind-brain that was obviously unavailable to Austen. In his view, experiencing empathy doesn't necessarily lead to helping actions, and the absence of empathy doesn't always result in dire consequences, but a lack of empathy is the essential quality shared by all who hurt others.

This is because such a lack allows people to view others as inanimate objects rather than as living beings. Empathy, which involves feeling and thinking from another person's perspective, is what makes people real—alive—to us. If you don't grasp other people's emotions in this intuitive, personal way, if you don't take their perspective both emotionally and cognitively, they'll remain "unreal" to you; you might know intellectually that they have thoughts and feelings, but you won't live that knowledge, feeling it in your bones and, hopefully, expressing it in your behavior. At this point, people, and other living creatures, become equivalent to objects.

And so we're capable of evil, of hurting or destroying others, only when we deny or fail to perceive the feelings of those who are the targets of our malice; they become the "objects" of our cruelty in more than one sense. The Golden Rule, seen as the ground of moral action in many religions and traditions, acknowledges this insight with its famous mandate to take a third-person perspective: "Do unto others as you would have others do unto you." If you put yourself in the place of another, you'll only practice behavior that you'd be willing to endure yourself. Once you identify with someone in this way, it becomes difficult, if not impossible, to inflict pain.

Of course, very few of us can be empathetic, truly conscious of other minds and hearts, all of the time. Emma is basically a good, kind person, but her empathy is definitely off-line when she insults Miss Bates. Nevertheless, within the parameters of such normal fluctuations, people possess empathy to greater and lesser degrees, with some people falling in the high-empathy and some in the low-empathy range. Baron-Cohen has formulated an empathy spectrum and a questionnaire to measure the extent of a person's capacity for empathy, their "empathy quotient." He has devised a simplified version of the empathy quotient scale, which has seven settings instead of the eighty-one of the EQ questionnaire: from zero (zero empathy) to six (highly empathetic). Like the EQ, this measures the "Empathizing Mechanism," the degree to which a person is capable of empathy.

Let's say we evaluated characters in *Emma* using the simpler Empathizing Mechanism scale. Mr. Knightley would likely receive the highest score, a Level 6, because he's one of those "individuals with remarkable empathy who are continually focused on other people's feelings, and go out of their way to check on these and to be supportive." Emma would score well on the test, but would place at Level 5, "not constantly thinking about others' feelings [but] others are nevertheless on their radar a lot of the time."* The Eltons would place in the lower ranges of the scale. Most characters, and indeed most people, would place within the middle range. (For the statistically minded among you, this creates a bell curve.)

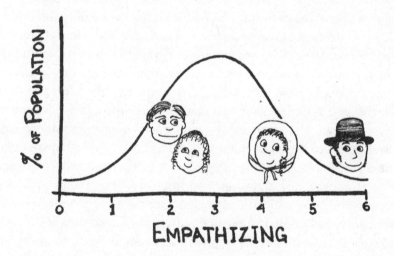

However, some fictional people, just like some real people, are unable to feel empathy. They have what Baron-Cohen characterizes as empathy disorders. These people divide into two basic types, those who do harm, who are capable of evil (he calls these "zero negative"), and those who lack empathy but are benign ("zero positive"). Zero positive refers to

---

*   Simon Baron-Cohen, *The Science of Evil: On Empathy and the Origins of Cruelty*, (New York: Basic Books, 2011), 28.

autistic people, while zero negative refers to those who suffer from what are called "Cluster B personality disorders" in the *Diagnostic and Statistical Manual of Mental Disorders, 5th Edition* (*DSM-5*), the diagnostic bible of the mind-brain sciences in the United States.

While all personality disorders are characterized by blunted affect and severe deficits in the ability to relate to others—a defective social mind-brain—in Baron-Cohen's view, lack of empathy is the defining feature of the Cluster B disorders. These are borderline personality disorder (BPD); antisocial personality disorder (APD), also called sociopathy and psychopathy; and narcissistic personality disorder (NPD). In the individual descriptions of these disorders, *DSM-5* either states explicitly or implies that lack of empathy is a characteristic. In the trait-based "experimental" chapter on personality disorders, which is included in a section on emerging measures and models, but which will likely replace the current syndrome-based version, empathy is listed as one of the defining criteria for all the personality disorders.

Like so many of our social capacities and temperamental characteristics, the features that characterize personality disorders, including empathy, are on a continuum with ordinary personality traits. A person might be cold and deficient in empathy, like Mr. Elton, but lack the severe impairment that characterizes the Cluster B personality disorders. The Empathy Quotient questionnaire usually reveals this difference, if people answer honestly, that is—sociopaths and psychopaths are prone to lie. Disorders are distinguished from traits by their consistency, duration, and intensity—the extent to which they are enduring and inflexible character patterns of inner experience and behavior that differ markedly from cultural expectations, and which create distress or impair functioning in one or more areas: social, occupational, emotional or cognititive.

All of Austen's characters who are diagnosable with empathy disorders demonstrate such consistency and degree of impairment. They exhibit the defining characteristics of their disorders over a long period of time, and they're compromised both cognitively and emotionally. Those characters who are just insensitive or who have questionable morals lack this consistency and severity of symptoms.

Cluster B personality disorders (zero-negative empathy disorders) are disorders of the attachment system. (It's likely that most

personality disorders fit this category.) Borderline and narcissistic personality disorders involve insecure attachment, while antisocial personality
disorder (psychopathy or sociopathy) means a person doesn't attach at
all. In addition to zero empathy, people afflicted with these disorders
also have poor powers of mentalization and self-regulation, with the
exception of a certain kind of ASD (high Machiavellian—see below),
in which case these powers are learned using top-down, cognitive
processes. Healthy intimacy, mentalizing, and emotional regulation
are precisely the functions that the attachment system builds according
to the theorists on attachment considered in earlier chapters: Bowlby
and Ainsworth (close relationships), Fonagy (mentalization), and
Schore (regulation).

Those who possess a secure attachment style have a "good-enough"
capacity with regard to each of these functions. For this reason, Baron-
Cohen characterizes secure attachment as "an internal pot of gold,"*
which gives a person the ability to deal with adversity and setbacks,
and to form intimate, affectionate, trusting relationships with others.
People with severely deficient attachment experiences usually lack this
characterological wealth; they're bankrupt socially and emotionally.

AN "EDGY DISORDER": BORDERLINE PERSONALITY DISORDER

Borderline personality disorder (BPD) got its name (first used in 1938)
from twentieth-century psychiatrists in the United States who believed
the condition was on the border between neurosis and psychosis—
between impairments in functioning and actual delusions. While it's
true that a person with BPD has a severely distorted view of relationships, and so of reality, BPD is no longer considered a psychosis. But it's
nevertheless an "edgy," volatile disorder, characterized by insecurity,
impulsivity, and a severe deficit in powers of self-regulation.

These traits lead to a pattern of instability in relationships. With
those close to them, people with BPD oscillate between idealizing and
devaluing, loving and hating; they might be affectionate one moment
and enraged the next. Uncontrollable rages characterize the condition.

---

*   Simon Baron-Cohen, *The Science of Evil*, 75.

Confidence might alternate with feelings of worthlessness, although such confidence is likely to be grandiose—inflated and unrealistic. People with the disorder tend to engage in risky behavior.

James Masterson, a psychiatrist who specialized in Cluster B disorders, accounts for the origins of BPD with a theory that draws on the work of mind-brain scientists we've met already: Bowlby, Mahler, Winnicott, Siegel, Schore, Fonagy, and Baron-Cohen. Keep in mind that the Cluster B disorders are disorders of the attachment system, and so the deficits that lead to insecure attachment contribute to these conditions.

The caregiver of the child who develops BPD consistently puts their own need for support, comfort, and love above those of the child, often beginning in infancy. This behavior is pathological in that it exceeds, in intensity or consistency, the ordinary solipsism, coldness, or preoccupation that produce regular insecure attachment. Love and support are offered only when behavior conforms to the caregiver's wishes—wishes that are often subconscious, but destructive nevertheless. With BPD, the caregiver's primary wish is to keep the child "enmeshed," psychologically fused with the caregiver.

We all need to individuate, to develop our own distinctive personalities, desires, and feelings, which might well differ from those of our caregivers and, later in life, close others. We're an interdependent species, but we also need autonomy, an important building block of individuation, and the work of "growing up" consists largely of finding balance between closeness and individuation, dependence and independence. In BPD, the child's drive toward autonomy in infancy and childhood—attempts at what is called "self-activation"—is punished with the withdrawal of support and love on the part of the caregiver. The adult with BPD has therefore learned to associate independence with abandonment, which means that their attempts at healthy separation from others whom they are close to, or the autonomy of such close others, brings on a sense of sadness and emptiness, even despair; this is known as "abandonment depression." Safety consists in staying enmeshed.

Successful individuation leads to what is known as the "real self." In addition to individuation, development in ways that are distinct and fulfilling, the real self encompasses a sense of security, a reflective capacity, and self-control, the hallmarks of secure attachment. (Of course the strength of these traits will vary among individuals while still remaining within a normal range, and insecure attachment does not indicate pathology.) Because in BPD the individual's real self isn't recognized or validated—the child didn't receive adequate attunement or mirroring from the caregiver, the heart of such validation—the child fails to develop a strong ToM (to be able to mentalize). Without seeing oneself from a third-person perspective, reflected in the validation of one's real self, one can't take that perspective with others. Furthermore, the child develops a "false self," one that conforms to the (often subconscious) wishes of the caregiver for the child, the retention of traits approved by the caregiver. People with BPD feel emotionally empty much of the time, as if their feelings are absent or unreal, which makes sense, since they learned to deny important aspects of themselves to maintain the love of the caregiver. (This is also true of those with narcissistic personality disorder.)

Another way to view this BPD dynamic is that the child, and later the adult, "splits" her idea of herself and of her caregiver into two polarized parts: good child and good caregiver on the one hand, bad child and bad caregiver on the other. The bad parts are the ones that wish to separate, either through attempts to develop a distinctive identity on the part of the child, or through rejection on the part of the caregiver, which is the consequence of such attempts. Subconsciously, autonomy is associated with the bad child part of the split, the naughty one who'll be punished with abandonment by the bad caregiver. Defenses are built up that keep them clinging to the false self because activating the real self comes at a terrible price. (Actually, people afflicted with BPD rarely attempt to activate the real self without substantial therapeutic help because it is so difficult and painful to do so.) People with BPD learn a procedural schema that consists of the "borderline triad": Self-activation leads to abandonment depression, which leads to defenses that prevent the activation of the real self.

People with BPD dread and fear rejection, which enrages them, and is associated with the bad, rejecting caregiver and the abandonment

---

*   D. W. Winnicott invented the terms *real self* and *false self*, which are widely used in
     psychotherapeutic theory.

depression. They never got the chance to integrate autonomy and closeness into a healthy combination, the golden mean in which the two coexist, and so they either idealize or devalue people, alternating between extremes according to how they fall within this dualistic, split world. People closely associated with those with the disorder, such as spouses or children, therefore become identified with this evil-person part, and the terrible pain rejection brings, whenever they "separate," however unreasonable that feeling might be. That's why people with this disorder can become enraged if they feel that someone they consider close fails to display adequate devotion. They tend to be "paranoid" in the colloquial sense of the word, finding rejection and abandonment where it doesn't exist. The person with BPD needs to be continuously fused with someone, emotionally and psychologically, as they were with the caregiver. This often takes the form of unquestioning devotion on the part of others. BPD can be thought of as anxious-ambivalent attachment on steroids.

ON THE EDGE WITH LADY SUSAN

Lady Susan, an early novella of Austen's that's sometimes considered a major work, features a main character whom we can diagnose with BPD, the eponymous Lady Susan herself. We can see the fear of abandonment depression driving Lady Susan through her fury at those who resist her charms. She needs not only devoted friends, but absolute disciples. But of course, she has *only* disciples since her devotees aren't genuine friends in any true sense of the word. They provide adulation rather than support and understanding, and she provides nothing in return except the privilege of allowing them to worship her. Even her confidante, Mrs. Johnson, functions more as an adoring audience for Lady Susan's exploits than as a friend.

When the novel begins, the recently widowed Lady Susan is about to visit her brother-in-law, Mr. Vernon. She's been staying at the home of her friends the Manwarings, where she caused no end of trouble. She found Mr. Manwaring entertaining and attractive, and to the great distress of his wife, the feeling was mutual. Austen strongly hints that they had an affair (she couldn't state this outright). Lady

Susan flaunts her power over the husband in the wife's own home, with zero empathy for how much pain this causes. Eventually, when the situation at the Manwarings becomes too hot to handle, Lady Susan decides to accept her brother-in-law Mr. Vernon's standing invitation to visit. A beautiful woman who trades on her charm, Lady Susan never pays her own way.

Lady Susan has other motives in addition to wanting a free ride. She's determined to make Sir Reginald de Courcy, Mrs. Vernon's brother, fall in love with her. This is partly because she wants to remarry to secure an income. In this, she's not so different from many other of Austen's characters since marriage was often the only respectable way of procuring financial security for women of the middle and upper classes. Although marriages of convenience such as that of Charlotte Lucas and Mr. Collins in *Pride and Prejudice* might make those with more refined sensibilities and greater opportunities (like Elizabeth Bennet) a bit squeamish, such behavior was not usually as positively heartless and manipulative in Lady Susan's mode. Charlotte and Mr. Collins understand the deal they're making, and neither has unrealistic expectations.

But for Lady Susan, this pragmatic motive takes a back seat to her compulsive and constant need for homage, which she seeks in intimate, or potentially intimate, relationships—typical borderline behavior. Lady Susan primarily targets men, usually successfully, but her hunger for reassurance also prompts her to try to win over those women who aren't competitors. In addition to her striking beauty and seductive manner, which most (heterosexual) men find irresistible, her charm is so intoxicating that even women fall for her lies. Mrs. Vernon feels this allure and has to summon her will—all of her cognitive, executive powers that tell her what Lady Susan is really like—to resist falling under Lady Susan's spell. As she writes to her brother, Sir Reginald (who will shortly fall in love with Lady Susan), "Her address to me was so gentle, frank, and even affectionate, that if I had not known how much she has always disliked me for marrying Mr. Vernon, and that we had never met before, I should have imagined her an attached friend . . . If her manners have so great an influence on my resentful heart, you may guess how much more strongly they operate on Mr. Vernon's generous temper."

Attraction and power are inextricably linked in Lady Susan's mind, so that she finds fulfillment in dominating and manipulating others through her charms; this way, she can keep people enslaved, and keep herself "safe," immune from abandonment. She plans to seduce her brother-in-law, Sir Reginald, into marriage, while his horrified family looks on, powerless to intervene. While Lady Susan thrills to the prospect of humiliating the entire de Courcy family (Mrs. Vernon's family of origin) by snatching the heir and his fortune, she has a special grudge against Sir Reginald, who dislikes and distrusts her—with good reason. By daring to disapprove of her in the past, he has made himself her particular target. In psychotherapeutic terms, by resisting Lady Susan, Reginald evokes the limits to her power that might lead her to face the emptiness of the abandonment depression, the emptiness that would engulf her if she ever failed in her attempts to control others.

Lady Susan's other plan is to force her daughter, Frederica, to marry against her will. She has in mind a wealthy but ridiculous man, a fop, who actually finds Lady Susan much more attractive than her daughter. Arranged marriages, like marriages of convenience, were not unheard of in Austen's day, but these occurred mainly within the aristocracy. It was generally thought that young people should be allowed to decide whom they would marry, within reason; a parent's consent was still a necessary moral, if not legal, prerequisite.

Lady Susan ignores such norms. She wants to disburden herself of responsibility for the girl, thereby ridding herself of the female competition posed by a beautiful daughter, and, even more delightful, torture her daughter in the process. After all, Frederica has dared to protest against the marriage, to separate her own feelings and tastes from those of her mother. For this, for committing the "sin" of individuation, Frederica must be punished—subjugated and made to suffer.

Displaying the lack of empathy characteristic of the disorder, Lady Susan treats Frederica like an object, an object that she no longer wants to have to care for. To further her plans and prevent Frederica from finding allies, Lady Susan tells everyone that her daughter is a stubborn, worthless girl, unteachable and incorrigible. But Frederica is actually a decent, lovely young woman who's terrified of her oppressive mother and desperate to escape a marriage she finds repugnant.

When Frederica asks Sir Reginald's help in averting the marriage her mother has planned for her, Lady Susan's borderline rage emerges. The domain of intimate personal relationships is precisely where she's most likely to be triggered. Sir Reginald is sympathetic to Frederica, and Lady Susan can't bear this challenge to her domination, which suggests the possibility that Sir Reginald isn't completely under her sway (fused with her). She angrily confronts Sir Reginald, and she's so obnoxious that he determines to break with her and to leave his sister's house for the remainder of her visit. But Lady Susan soon regains her equilibrium and repairs her relationship with Sir Reginald so thoroughly that, to the horror of the rest of the Vernon and de Courcy families, they become engaged.

Lady Susan uses all her charm and strategy to repair this breach, and when she succeeds, she confesses to her friend Mrs. Johnson,

> Oh how delightful it was, to watch the variations of his countenance while I spoke, to see the struggle between returning tenderness and the remains of displeasure. There is something agreeable in feelings so easily worked on. Not that I would envy him their possession, nor would for the world have such myself, but they are very convenient when one wishes to influence the passion of another.

Lady Susan's lack of feeling, frankly and proudly admitted, suggests that empathy disorders can lead to all manner of evil, large and small. I won't spoil the ending in case you haven't read this wonderful novella (or seen the excellent movie that was made of it, *Love & Friendship*), but this indeed is Austen's world. A gesture toward tragedies that might have been will suffice.

THE SOCIOPATH NEXT DOOR: MEET MR. ELLIOT

The second Cluster B disorder I'll consider is called antisocial personality disorder (APD), also known as psychopathy and sociopathy. People afflicted with APD routinely disregard the feelings and violate the rights of others. They fail to conform to social norms, in many cases, by committing crimes. They can be irritable, aggressive, and impulsive, behaving with total disregard for their own safety as well as the safety of others.

APD appears to originate in early, chronic, and prolonged neglect or abuse. If we characterize it in terms of the attachment disorders, it's an extreme case of reactive attachment disorder, the inability to attach to anyone. Not only do the afflicted fail to establish attachments to others, they are also relatively indifferent to human connection. (This isn't true of those with BPD and NPD, who might lack empathy but care very much about their relationships.) Those with the dangerous version of APD are capable of viewing murder as a minor infraction or appropriate response to frustration. The psychiatrist Bruce D. Perry recounts asking a prisoner why he had killed two adolescent girls and raped their dead bodies. The answer, "We started talking and they invited me up to their apartment to fool around. Then when they got me up there, they changed their minds. It pissed me off." [*]

People with APD are frequently motivated by the need to dominate. Some find pleasure at seeing others suffer. But whether or not they have a taste for sadism, they display muted or absent emotional responses, especially with regard to positive, prosocial, benevolent emotions. They're generally willing to do whatever it takes to get what they want. Treating others like objects, they ride roughshod through people's lives.

While APD is characterized by flaws in emotion-processing systems, the disorder appears to divide into more and less controlled versions. Some people with the condition can't contain their impulses, and they lash out at others violently and with little provocation; the dysregulatory aspects of the condition prevail in these people. People with this type of APD are often jailed for serious crimes. No one in Austen's novels fits this profile.

Some people with APD are coldly manipulative, conning other people into giving them what they want. They might still wish to harm or dominate others, but they often, although not always, have better powers of self-regulation than their impulsive, often violent counterparts. To make matters worse, they can be charming, which

---

[*]   Bruce D. Perry, *The Boy Who Was Raised as a Dog*, (New York: Basic Books, 2006), 103.

makes them dangerous; it's often difficult to know that someone has this form of APD until the damage has been done. It's likely that different forms of APD correlate with different irregularities in brain structure and circuitry, but little is known about this at the moment.

DSM-5, doesn't note these differences among those with the disorder, a flaw that might well be rectified in future editions of the *DSM*. I'm going to make the distinction by using a term was offered by the psychiatrist Hervey M. Cleckley (1903–1984), "high Machiavellians," "high machs" for short, to describe the type of socially adept person who has the disorder. The manipulative individual with antisocial personality disorder does indeed fit the profile of the perfect politician described in Machiavelli's *The Prince*, a treatise on how to succeed in politics by being strategic, devious, and deceitful. Austen's characters with APD have the regulated, manipulative version of this syndrome. But remember, whatever form the disorder takes, whether violence or manipulation or deceit is inflicted on others, lack of empathy predominates.

Mr. Elliot in *Persuasion* is a high mach, as heartless as Lady Susan, but much more successful at concealing his malevolence. He is the charming cousin of Anne Elliot (the heroine); he is also heir to the Elliot title and fortune—currently possessed by Anne's father, Sir Walter Elliot—which descends through the male line. Ten years earlier, when Anne had been away at boarding school, Mr. Elliot had been in constant touch with her family, raising hopes of a marriage between himself and Anne's older sister, Elizabeth. He suddenly abandoned this connection without explanation. He rekindles his relationship with the family once more when he meets them at Bath, paying particular attention to Anne, whom he finds very attractive.

While Anne is gratified by her handsome cousin's admiration, with her usual sharpness she senses that something isn't quite right: "There was never any burst of feeling, any warmth of indignation or delight, at the evil or good of others. This, to Anne, was a decided imperfection. . . . She felt that she could so much more depend upon the sincerity of those who said a careless or a hasty thing, than of those whose presence of mind never varied, whose tongue never slipped." Anne, who's an exquisitely accurate judge of character, picks up on the artificial nature of Mr. Elliot's emotional expressions. Mr. Elliot can't leave anything to spontaneity, for he must work to produce the outward expression of feelings that he's incapable of experiencing, feelings that come naturally to people with unimpaired emotional systems.

Anne learns the truth about Mr. Elliot's character from her friend, Mrs. Smith, a former schoolmate who's fallen on hard times. Mrs. Smith is in Bath to "take the waters" (bathe in the warm springs) for her declining health, but she's so impoverished that she can barely afford the minimal medical care that she needs. Her husband has recently died, leaving her with difficult financial and legal problems, which, we learn, are principally due to Mr. Elliot's behavior. When Mrs. Smith decides to reveal Mr. Elliot's true character to Anne, she prefaces her information with a general description that indeed diagnoses him as a person with APD:

> Mr. Elliot is a man without heart or conscience; a designing, wary, cold- blooded being, who thinks only of himself; who, for his own interest or ease, would be guilty of any cruelty, or any treachery, that could be perpetrated without risk of his general character. He has no feeling for others. Those whom he has been the chief cause of leading into ruin, he can neglect and desert without the smallest compunction. He is totally beyond the reach of any sentiment of justice or compassion.

Mrs. Smith then offers proof of the callousness of Mr. Elliot's actions while also shedding light on his strange behavior toward Anne's family. Mrs. Smith knows all about him because when Mr. Elliot was young and relatively poor, the Smiths generously welcomed him into their home. Mrs. Smith in fact became his confidante and supporter.

According to Mrs. Smith, Mr. Elliot's one goal at that time was to get rich through marriage. A match with Anne's sister Elizabeth would have satisfied his desire for wealth, but as the husband of Elizabeth, he would have been accountable for his whereabouts and behavior. He would have been forced to assume a respectable lifestyle far more often than suited his tastes, which tended to run toward the sordid and the low. Mrs. Smith has no information about Mr. Elliot's recently deceased wife because she was too inferior, likely in moral as well as socioeconomic terms, for a woman of Mrs. Smith's standing to associate with. And Mrs. Smith is neither rich nor titled. (Alas, Austen is not above all the snobbery of her time.)

Mrs. Smith further reveals that Mr. Elliot held Anne's entire family in contempt, proving this with a letter in which he boasts of having gotten rid of Sir Elliot and Elizabeth: "I have got rid of Sir Walter and Miss. They are gone back to Kellynch . . ." So little did he value the nobility of which Sir Walter is so proud that he boasts, "[I]f baronetcies were salable," he would have sold his "for fifty pounds, arms and motto, name and livery included."

In the intervening years, however, Mr. Elliot has learned to value the good things that come with a noble title, and this accounts for his wish to reestablish a connection with Anne's branch of the family. In particular, he fears that Sir Walter (Anne's father) will marry Mrs. Clay, a lawyer's daughter who is pursuing him, and that this marriage might produce a boy, who would of course inherit the baronetcy and the wealth that goes with it. Mr. Elliot hopes to prevent this, so he stays close to the family to watch Mrs. Clay and find a way to thwart her schemes, should this become necessary. In addition, contrary to his usual taste in women of a lower class, he is smitten with Anne—I won't say "in love" because he is incapable of this, but he does find her attractive. With lesser urgency than he feels to watch Sir Walter, he stays around to woo Anne.

Mrs. Smith has also matured and come to alter her values, although this has taken her in a different direction than Mr. Elliot's. Were she to meet with attitudes like Mr. Elliot's today, her response would be quite different from what it had been in her youth, when "they were all a gay set." However, her wisdom has come at a price. Mr. Elliot led her late husband into ruinous financial ventures, and although he has the means to repair some of the damage by helping her to reclaim some property in the West Indies that still belongs to her, he refuses to help, ignoring her repeated requests. Mrs. Smith has hoped, with Anne's engagement to Mr. Elliot, to have an advocate who would effect some material change in her circumstances. When she learns the truth about Anne's feelings, she has instead a good friend who'll listen to her troubles, and the relief of finally telling them.

DOING WHAT COMES UNNATURALLY

Mr. Elliot possesses strong powers of self-control that enable him to project a front of respectability when he encounters the Elliots in Bath. Of course, all of us on occasion encounter situations in which it's necessary to call upon willpower in order to avoid inappropriately expressing our true thoughts; this is an important aspect of emotional regulation. But for high machs, this is a continuous process, a necessary evil, because self-control is crucial to being able to manipulate others; high machs are consummate actors.

Nevertheless, Mr. Elliot shares the fundamental dysregulation that's a feature of his disorder, although he's learned to keep it in check (indeed, most high machs do this). Although Mr. Elliot never loses his cool during the time he reconnects with Anne's branch of the family (as Anne observes, nothing about him is ever impulsive), his past reveals that such powers of tightly wound restraint have not come naturally.

Mrs. Smith tells Anne that in the days when they were close, Mr. Elliot led a riotous life, succumbing thoughtlessly to his impulses and living only to fulfill his cravings of the moment. He cared nothing for the future or what anyone thought of him. Mr. Elliot's changing values, in particular his desire to inherit the baronetcy, have given rise to different modes of behavior. He's certainly not a better man, just one who's learned to defer lesser gratifications in pursuit of greater ones. Perhaps his craving for domination got the better of his less sophisticated yearnings—the money and status that come with a title afford plenty of opportunities for gratification at the expense and humiliation of others.

Another talent that Mr. Elliot and all high machs acquire is the capacity for ToM, which includes being able to infer what others are feeling, despite their lack of full-blown empathy—they have cognitive but not affective empathy. In fact, their ability to manipulate others depends on a strong and accurate ToM; you can't con someone into doing what you want if you can't predict their behavior, and you have to be able to read thoughts and feelings in order to predict correctly. But high machs don't develop the ability to read emotions by recognizing emotions automatically at bodily and subcortical levels and then translating them into conscious perceptions. They lack an internal reference point for reading emotions. They learn to decode emotional expression from what they know about how people behave. They learn that certain expressions lead to certain behaviors; for instance, when someone smiles at you, they're being friendly and are more likely to grant you a favor.

This process might become more or less automatic, entering procedural memory through repeated experiences of deliberate analysis. But it would nevertheless always be an acquired talent rather than a visceral response, and therefore less consistently accurate than normal modes of reading feelings. So high machs would be liable to make mistakes in predicting others' reactions or behavior when they failed to perceive feelings accurately.

An analogy: Think of a very well-trained blind person making his way through an unfamiliar part of town with a walking stick. He'll rely on senses other than vision, and on the action of the cane, in order to know how to proceed. He might become very accomplished at navigating his way around, but he'll likely still be at a disadvantage compared to a sighted person. And if he does become nearly as proficient as a sighted person, this happens through alternative senses. Ditto for our high mach, who reads emotions well most of the time.

Because Mr. Elliot lacks such intuitive knowledge of many common emotional responses, he sometimes miscalculates the effects of his behavior. For instance, he compliments Anne by observing that she's "too modest for the world in general to be aware of half her accomplishments, and too highly accomplished for modesty to be natural in any other woman." He insists that his observations are not mere flattery, but that he's had a longer acquaintance with her "disposition, accomplishments, and manner" than she's aware of. Anne realizes that they must have a mutual acquaintance and tries to get Mr. Elliot to reveal who this person is. He defers the answer to another meeting.

Anne doesn't have long to wonder, for the next day, when Mrs. Smith realizes that Anne doesn't have strong feelings for Mr. Elliot, she reveals that she's the common acquaintance, and she also tells Anne the truth about his character. If Mr. Elliot had possessed any sense of how a person of integrity would react to hearing about his behavior toward the Smiths in the past, and of his neglect of Mrs. Smith's pleas for aid in the present, he would have steered as far away from the topic of Mrs. Smith as possible. But on the contrary, by dropping hints of a common acquaintance, he invites Anne to discover the truth. He obviously doesn't have a clue about how knowledge of his behavior would affect Anne. He lacks the social intelligence to understand that she'd feel indignation on her friend's behalf.

While Mr. Elliot doesn't win Anne's heart, this isn't because Anne discovers his true character. Marrying Anne was never his main objective. Above all, he wants to secure his inheritance, and in that area, he does triumph, diverting Mrs. Clay by running off with her himself. Given his taste for women who don't hail from upper-class circles, he's likely to be much happier with Mrs. Clay than he would have been with Anne anyway. The narrator suggests that Mrs. Clay might ultimately manipulate Mr. Elliot into marrying her so that she too will enjoy the perks of belonging to the elite. Not bad for a country lawyer's daughter. Blessed with the ability to get others to give her what she wants, Mrs. Clay might indeed be the highest of the high machs in Austen's work. Perhaps someone who writes novels based on Austen's books will tell her story.

EMPATHY AND MORALITY: SOME CLARIFICATION

In *Emma*, Mr. Knightley scolds Emma for her lack of empathy, but he might just as well have blamed her for a breach of ethics or decorum. Her behavior is certainly open to criticism on these grounds. It's not much of a stretch to say that Emma breaks the Fifth Commandment, "Honor thy father and thy mother," since Miss Bates was one of the mother figures in Emma's childhood, as Mr. Knightley points out. And young ladies were not supposed to insult their elders, or anyone else for that matter, especially in Emma's public, flagrant mode. But Mr. Knightley focuses on Emma's lack of empathy rather than her breaking of the rules, and this prompts her to do the right thing.

Austen suggests here and elsewhere that empathy is an effective and important source of morality, far more important than abstract principle. Like much of Austen's thinking, this observation agrees with the philosophy of her near contemporary, David Hume, who argued that empathy, or sympathy as he called it, was the ground of ethical behavior. This view radically challenged prevailing notions about ethics that were central to Western civilization. Christian thought has traditionally suggested that morality stemmed from reason, the God-like quality in human nature that distinguishes us from all other animals. Secular philosophy of the Enlightenment was in accord, as was much of the literature and philosophy of the Classical world, ancient Rome and Greece (remember Plato's charioteer from Chapter Two).

Many mind-brain scientists today agree with Hume and Austen that empathy and morality are connected. Others call the connection into question. Because empathy is such a critical aspect of social intelligence—our most thorough access to one another's minds and hearts—it's worth looking, if only briefly, at claims about the scope and limits of this capability.

To begin with—quite literally to begin with—empathy is the source of morality in evolutionary terms. Frans de Waal, an ethologist and psychologist whose work also addresses anthropology and philosophy, fought for decades to get this view accepted among scientists. He struggled against a dominant ideology that he calls "veneer theory." This is the belief that humans are basically nasty and brutish, and that morality is merely a thin veneer over our despicable natures (another traditional idea, expressed eloquently by the seventeenth-century philosopher Thomas Hobbes). Whatever good we have comes from our capacity for reason, our ability to formulate moral codes that enable human beings to live together without destroying one another. De Waal disagrees vigorously.

De Waal counters that morality originated with our emotions and visceral reactions—with our empathy for one another, which we see in less developed forms in other mammals: "We started out with moral sentiments and intuitions, which is also where we find the greatest continuity with other primates. Rather than having developed morality from scratch through rational reflection, we received a huge push in the rear from our background as social animals."[*] De Waal readily admits that he is "a firm believer in David Hume's position that reason is the slave of the passions."

---

* Frans de Waal, *The Bonobo and the Atheist* (New York: W. W. Norton & Company, 2013), 17.

Primatologists working in the field with the great apes (including de Waal) have reported countless instances of caring, generosity, and altruism among our close cousins. But if these claims were to be taken seriously by the scientific community, they had to be shown in the lab rather than observed in the field. De Waal and his team designed an experiment that did just this, demonstrating the presence of empathy in chimpanzees.

Two chimps, Peony and Rita, were the subjects in this experiment. Peony was asked to pick from a bucket full of red and green tokens. No matter which color she chose, Peony would be rewarded with a treat. But if she picked a green token, Rita would also receive a reward. After a while, Peony began to select the green tokens two out of three times, ensuring that Rita also got rewarded.

The same behavior was seen in other chimp pairs in the same situation. But if a chimp was alone and asked to choose, she wouldn't distinguish between the colors, choosing randomly. In addition, in the two-chimp scenario, when the chooser picked the wrong color, the deprived neighbor would often protest, hooting or begging. But intimidation wasn't a successful strategy; it actually prompted the choosing chimp to pick the red, "selfish," tokens. It's hard not to think that this was spite. And dominant chimps, who had the least to fear, were the most generous. Noblesse oblige.

The chimps weren't acting on principle, thinking that, for instance, it's fair to share your treats, as we tell our children. Not even a chimp or bonobo is going to act for the greater good as a result of moral reasoning; they really don't have the brainpower for that. That the chimps understood that their partners wanted rewards and were sad not to get them—that they empathized—is the only explanation that makes sense.

This experiment therefore provides strong evidence for the claim that empathy is the source of morality in evolutionary terms because chimps are near to us on the evolutionary ladder; they share ninety-eight percent of our DNA, their brains resemble our own, and they have levels of cognitive intelligence comparable to young children in many respects. I think it's likely that chimps are able to mentalize and therefore that the fortunate chimps in the protocol understood that their neighbors felt deprived. But even in nonhuman animals who very likely can't think at these higher levels, such as rats, emotional resonance (affective empathy) appears to lead to prosocial actions.

Another support for viewing empathy as an important building block of morality comes from the way we actually make moral choices much of the time. In day-to-day life, instances of fairness, virtue, kindness, and cooperation don't come from abstract principles, but from feelings. Affective empathy and the desire to help have been ingrained in our nervous systems.[*] Charles Darwin, who believed that morality stemmed from empathy and was found in other nonhuman animals, wrote of altruism, "Such actions . . . appear to be the simple result of the greater strength of the social or maternal instincts than that of any other instinct or motive; for they are performed too instantaneously for reflection, or for pleasure or pain to be felt at the time."[**] Reason has little to do with our benevolent impulses much of the time.

When Frank Churchill rescues Harriet from the gypsies, he doesn't stop to think of his obligation as a gentleman to rescue a damsel in distress. He just acts, impelled by feelings that are deeply bred in the

---

[*]   Dacher Keltner, *Born to Be Good: The Science of a Meaningful Life* (New York: W.W. Norton & Company, 2009), 50.

[**]   Charles Darwin, *The Descent of Man* (New York: Penguin, 2004), 134.

bone. You can bet that Emma does charity work out of compassion that's grounded in empathy, her understanding of, and resonance with, the sufferings of the impoverished. That's because Emma never succeeds at anything she decides to do on principle, such as cultivating her accomplishments. Emma has to feel that something's important, or she fails to act.

Nevertheless, for humans, doing the right thing doesn't require empathy. We can be impelled by forces other than empathy to perform good deeds. The existence of competing, allegedly better, motives for benevolence is indeed one of the arguments against viewing empathy as a precursor to moral action. For instance, Emma might have been kind to Miss Bates because she wanted to look good in Mr. Knightley's eyes, and so have been motivated by entirely selfish reasons. Or she might have been inspired by guilt rather than compassion, and so acted out of a sense of obligation to others that nevertheless had little to do with empathy. Or she might have wanted to behave appropriately, which meant that her kindness stemmed from the desire to conform to accepted behavior and moral codes rather than fellow feeling. Or perhaps she was guided by reason, the knowledge of right and wrong; it was wrong to insult Miss Bates and right to atone for this by effortful benevolence. These are the grounds on which Mr. Knightley does *not* scold Emma. Psychologist Paul Bloom argues that moral reason, the last of these alternative motives, is a much more reliable foundation for good works than empathy. And so we're back to Enlightenment thought about morality, similar arguments to the ones Hume and Austen opposed.

Or take Mrs. Elton, who decides to connect Jane Fairfax with an excellent prospect for employment as a governess. This appears to be a benevolent, helpful project, since it's likely that Jane will be compelled to support herself, and a job as a governess with a good family is the best that she can hope for. But Mrs. Elton isn't motivated by empathy, and in fact it's Mrs. Elton's insensitivity—her lack of empathy—that prevents her from seeing that Jane doesn't want her help. At our most generous, we might say that Mrs. Elton acts on principle, on the assumption that finding Jane a job is the right thing to do. Or that she acts out of concern for Jane. (Of course, knowing Mrs. Elton, many of us suspect that she is taking this task upon herself as a way of declaring her own importance as a patron rather than because she truly wishes to help Jane.)

Just as we can be inspired to do the right thing by motives other than empathy, a lack of empathy doesn't always lead to cruelty, aggression, self-centeredness, or any other of the negative traits that characterize personality disorders, nor does it always lead to evil. Baron-Cohen describes those who behave in antisocial or immoral ways as possessing zero-negative empathy, but he also has another empathy disorder category, zero positive. This applies to autistic people, who often lack the ability to empathize or mentalize. Like those who have personality disorders, autistic people have severe deficits in social intelligence when compared to neurotypicals. But they don't harm others. Empathy is one factor among many that determines a person's moral nature and behavior.

It's also possible to empathize and deliberately suppress or act against the feelings that arise from empathy. When Harriet comes to Emma to tell about Robert Martin's proposal, Emma very likely empathizes with Harriet in the technical sense, apprehending Harriet's excitement both cognitively and emotionally. But she acts against her empathy because she has other plans for Harriet. She understands Harriet's disappointment but reasons that the better life that will follow from her schemes will ultimately compensate Harriet for any distress she feels at the moment.

A more sinister example is seen in the famous experiments in obedience to authority conducted by Stanley Milgram in the 1960s. A researcher in a white lab coat (which signals authority) instructed participants to continue to push a button that gave electric shocks to fellow participants, even though they were aware that these shocks were painful and were escalating in intensity. Most subjects were willing to do so despite the protests and suffering of their co-participants. Don't worry about the person who received the shock; he was actually a part of Milgram's team, and the shocks weren't real. But *do* worry about a species capable of doing this. Most rhesus monkeys will refrain from pressing a lever that gives them food if the lever simultaneously shocks another monkey. They're willing to starve to death.

Some mind-brain scientists argue that empathy can actually do more harm than good. For instance, since empathy offers a window into vulnerabilities, it can tell you how best to hurt someone. But this applies to cognitive empathy, not full-scale empathy, which includes emotional resonance; cognitive empathy means *knowing* about some-one's feelings rather than sharing them. But even when we act on full-fledged empathy, feeling as well as thinking from someone else's point of view, the results can be less than admirable.

Even though empathy can inspire moral action, it is often limited in its scope. The closer we are to someone, or the more closely they resemble us, the more likely we are to empathize with them. Mr. and Mrs. Elton lack empathy for Harriet because they perceive her as belonging to the "out" group, not of their class or kind. Mr. Elton feels no compunctions about adding to her humiliation with a caustic remark when she stands alone and neglected at a ball. Racism, sexism, and all the other instances of unjust discrimination depend on this bias, on the failure of empathy to activate for people whom one group has designated as different and other.

This tendency to look out for our own also means that we often fail to empathize with, or care about, those who are distant in terms of geography as well as relationship—out of sight, out of mind, as the saying goes. We also tend to feel empathy for individuals, which makes caring about the suffering of populations, however distressed, a challenge. This is known as the "identifiable victim effect," described by economist Thomas Schelling:

> Let a six-year-old girl with brown hair need thousands of dol-lars for an operation that will prolong her life until Christmas, and the post office will be swamped with nickels and dimes to save her. But let it be reported that without a sales tax the hospital facilities of Massachusetts will deteriorate and cause a barely perceptible increase in preventable deaths—not many will drop a tear or reach for their checkbooks.

Fundraisers for charities understand this. Think of how many of the appeals you receive contain stories about individuals that make their plight and their humanity real to us.

As humans, we have the cognitive ability to overcome the bias in favor of our own, those who are like us or close to us. We're capable of enlarging what philosopher Peter Singer calls "the circle of care," the reach of the help and protection that we're willing to give to others. We often call on reason in order to do this. This is what institutions like the United Nations and the World Court, grounded in principle, attempt to do. Legal measures such as the Geneva Conventions that guarantee humane treatment for prisoners of war, and statements like the Universal Declaration of Human Rights similarly attest to our powers of moral reasoning. But these instances of our humanity haven't significantly decreased the *inhumanity* we humans display in so many places and on so many levels, usually to those who are different or outsiders. The difficulty we have in extending compassion and justice to all, even in countries where such principles are supposed to prevail, shows how hard it is to act solely on principle. Indeed, our principles often follow our feelings (reason is the slave of the passions), so that it becomes right in our minds to discriminate against—even exterminate—a given population.

Which brings us back to evil. Feeling empathy doesn't guarantee goodness or compassion, but the absence of empathy makes it far easier to harm others. Although people sometimes act against their feelings of empathy because they believe that it's the right thing to do, this doesn't mean they find it easy. Far more often, people who harm others lack empathy, or turn off their empathy, in order to be able to hurt others. But even then, feelings of identification and the recognition of another person's humanity can take place subliminally. Veterans who suffer from PTSD often feel the aftereffects of having committed atrocities alien to their natural capacity for empathy.

We can also call on empathy itself rather than moral principle to enlarge our circle of care. We're certainly capable of feeling genuine empathy for others who are distant or different from us, although we often fail to do so. As with all empathy, this requires paying attention—really thinking, for instance, about the distress of those others, even if their identities differ from our own and even if they're halfway around the world.

Many mind-brain scientists agree that empathy is connected to morality even if it isn't an absolute precondition for it, nor a guarantee that those who empathize will do the right thing. This view matches with what we see throughout Austen's work. Austen's claims for the value of empathy aren't quite as strong as Hume's; they're closer to Baron-Cohen's thinking. Her point isn't that empathy necessarily leads to good works—although this is frequently the case in her novels—but rather that an absence of empathy enables a person to hurt others. Just as important, if you're going to act in ways that benefit or help someone else, you must be able to take their perspective, at least to some degree. In Austen's view, empathy might not be a panacea for the selfishness and callousness that we're all too prone to as a species, but it's nevertheless at the moral center of our lives.

Our mind-brains evolved when we lived in small groups, and they're still meant to function in that kind of environment. In the small hunter-gatherer communities that survive today, human nature appears to much greater advantage. Empathy and care are abundant, and people live good, although simple, lives. Almost everyone contributes to the survival and well-being of the community. But this isn't difficult in a group in which everyone more or less knows everyone else.

In Austen's novels, where characters inhabit a world with private property and hierarchies of status and power, a world that was quickly becoming our own, people generally create their circles of care by opting out of the competition for wealth and glory. Austen's heroines and heroes are fortunate enough to be able to do so, and they do as much good as they can within the reach of their influence. Some readers view this as a depressing retreat from responsibility, a refusal to work on the structural problems generating injustice and poverty. Mr. Knightley might ensure the well-being of his parish poor, but without structural solutions to poverty, such well-being is only guaranteed for his lifetime.

While I wouldn't be as judgmental about Austen as some, they're right that we do need solutions that don't depend on the kindness of strangers. But these solutions are hard to come by because global caring of the kind needed in large societies is extremely difficult for our species to embrace, as we clearly see from the world news. Empathy might be a poor foundation for moral action, but I'm not convinced that we are, on the whole, capable of a better one.

One problem might well be that the people who tend to rise to power aren't interested in extending our circles of care. Austen certainly thought this the case, which is why a retreat from the larger world appears to her to be a good option for her characters. She likely agreed with Voltaire, who wrote: "We must cultivate our garden." This is the moral of *Candide*, which Austen is sure to have read. What this means in the context of Voltaire's novel is that the world is a terrible place where horrendous things happen and where the least ethical people are in charge. The best we can do is retreat to our own spheres of caring and action and do the good we can do at this local level.

Even so, while Austen showed that a retreat from the world was a good option for her characters, she didn't mean to suggest they should disengage from civic duties. We don't see the public lives of her male characters, but as noblemen (Darcy), clergymen (Edmund), and landed gentry (Mr. Knightley), they certainly participate in public affairs. And while her couples live in the country, far from the poverty-stricken slums of London and the rising industrial towns of the north, their surrounding communities provide opportunities for helping others. Mr. Knightley helps and advises the farmer, Robert Martin, and Emma tends to the poor. This is personal help rather than societal change, but if Robert Martin does well, his family will be financially secure and perhaps even upwardly mobile; there's a famous saying that it takes three generations to make a gentleman. Living in the country might afford a more sheltered life, but it doesn't necessarily mean sticking your head in the sand. In Austen's view, if you're going to build a better world with better values, you have to start small, and at home, with families and communities. People need to think locally, and maybe, if we're lucky, we'll eventually act responsibly, ethically, and globally.

TWELVE

Crimes of the Heartless: Empathy Disorders, Part Two

One of Austen's major insights about human nature is that people are, as a rule, self-centered. This usually accounts for the moral deficiencies, as well as mistakes in perception and judgment, on the part of Austen's fictional people. It's their primary comic-tragic flaw. And so, even though her novels feature characters like Elizabeth and Emma who conquer such deficiencies to find the good within others, and within themselves, Austen isn't optimistic about the moral aptitude of most people. A multitude of characters with narcissistic tendencies inhabit Austen's pages.

Yet above and beyond garden-variety narcissism, there are two characters whose thoughts and behavior so far exceed the ordinary self-centeredness of human nature that they can be diagnosed with full-fledged narcissistic personality disorder (NPD): John Thorpe in *Northanger Abbey* and Sir Walter Elliot in *Persuasion*. Since personality disorders are on a continuum with personality traits, it's not surprising that people afflicted with NPD have much in common with those who are simply self-centered, even monstrously so. What makes these fictional people diagnosable is not their selfishness alone, shared by many, but a cluster of symptoms that have been seen to consistently lead to a particular set of impairments that are so pronounced that they render a person incapable of authentic and close relationships with others.

The *Diagnostic and Statistical Manual of Mental Disorders, 5th Edition* (*DSM-5*), the primary diagnostic tool of therapists and psychiatrists in the United States, describes NPD as "[a] pervasive pattern of grandiosity (in fantasy or behavior), need for admiration, and lack of empathy beginning by early adulthood and present in a variety of contexts."[*] This can lead to boasting; preoccupation with fantasies of unlimited success, power, brilliance, beauty, and so forth; the conviction that she or he is special and can only be understood by, or only associate with, other superior people; a need for excessive admiration; a sense of entitlement; a tendency to exploit others; envy; and arrogance.

Mind-brain scientists have complicated this diagnosis by noting that NPD can take different forms. For instance, neuroscientist Simon Baron-Cohen notes that some narcissists are very outgoing and want to be the center of attention. Others are withdrawn, but still have a sense of entitlement; they expect others to be respectful and compliant, but they lack awareness that they should reciprocate. Psychiatrist James Masterson suggests that there are two kinds of pathological narcissism, exhibitionist (the type described in *DSM-5* and above) and closet narcissism. Closet narcissists are still self-obsessed, but they are aware of their sense of deflation and emptiness. They experience the pain of imperfection, which is kept at bay by defenses among exhibitionist narcissists. Still another type of narcissist might be dangerous; it's been suggested that serial killers are narcissists. This likely describes Raskolnikov in Dostoyevsky's *Crime and Punishment*, who kills an old lady just to see what it feels like to kill. What greater sense of entitlement is there than to think that you have the right to take another person's life? The subtype that appears in Austen's novels is the outgoing, grandiose narcissist.

NPD shares features with BPD and APD. All three are empathy disorders. But the characteristics of these conditions nevertheless differ in many ways. People with NPD are generally not as violent as

---

[*]   American Psychological Association, *DSM-5*, 669.

dysregulated psychopaths (apart from those serial killers), nor are they as out of control as those with BPD. And unless they're very high functioning, they're much less subtle than high machs. With the grandiose, exhibitionist kind of NPD, obnoxious self-preoccupation and inflated sense of importance are there for all to see. In this sense, they're generally much less dangerous than people afflicted with the other empathy disorders; with most narcissists, you know what you're dealing with.

MIRROR, MIRROR ON THE WALL

Sir Walter Elliot of *Persuasion* might be Austen's most famous narcissist. The novel opens with the narrator's biting description of Sir Walter's absorption in his favorite book, the *Baronetage*, a dictionary of England's baronets that was periodically updated. The "page at which the favorite volume always opened" is the entry about himself. This is a stunning symbol of the narcissist's stunted circle of awareness: With all the narratives of history and fiction available in the library of a gentleman's country estate, Sir Walter focuses on a small dictionary entry that gives his rank and the dates of notable life events, such as his marriage and the birth of his children.

This image of Sir Walter staring at this description of himself evokes the well-known myth of Narcissus (from Ovid's *Metamorphoses*) who fell in love with his own reflection in a lake and drowned trying to embrace the image. More literal mirrors abound in Sir Walter's house, for Sir Walter is just as obsessed with his looks as with his status. When Admiral Croft rents Kellynch Hall from the Elliots, the only change in furnishings he makes is to take down some of the mirrors.

Other characters are well aware of Sir Walter's narcissism and know they must appeal to it if they're going to get him to agree to anything. The high mach manipulates others, but narcissists like Sir Walter can easily be the targets rather than the perpetrators of manipulation since they're so vulnerable to flattery. When it's clear that Sir Walter needs to rent his estate in order to pay his debts, his lawyer, Mr. Shepherd, appeals to his vanity. He tells Sir Walter that this is a sound course of action because in his financial circumstances, he couldn't maintain his lifestyle in a manner that accorded with the "ancient dignity" due to his position and his estate. That Sir Walter has a moral obligation to pay his debts and preserve his inheritance for his children has no place in Mr. Shepherd's reasoning. The lawyer also reassures Sir Walter that moving elsewhere will not compromise the baronet in any way because Sir Walter will set the tone wherever he goes: "In any other place [other than Kellynch], Sir Walter . . . would be looked up to, as regulating the modes of life, in whatever way he might choose to model his household."

Narcissists need to feel that everything associated with them is the best; their grandiosity extends to their "possessions," including other people. This need is one path to the distortion of reality we often see in this disorder. When Sir Walter and his equally narcissistic daughter Elizabeth proudly display their rented rooms at Bath, Anne isn't surprised that her father and sister can be happy with such an obvious descent in status and lifestyle from their estate at Kellynch, because she knows they they'll gild the lily, no matter how wilted. But she nevertheless "must sigh that her father should feel no degradation in his change; should see nothing to regret in the duties and dignity of the resident land-holder; should find so much to be vain of in the littlenesses of a town."

This field of distortion often encompasses those associated with narcissists, or those whom they like, because these people also have to be the best. Narcissists idealize those they're attracted to, just as they exaggerate the value of their own traits, talents, and possessions. As Sir Walter's liking for his lawyer's daughter Mrs. Clay increases, he begins to see her differently, observing that her freckles are much diminished. We can bet the family fortune that Mrs. Clay has no fewer freckles than she had when Sir Walter first met her. Sir Walter's fancy for Mrs. Clay demonstrates that narcissists, like high machs and those who suffer from other forms of APD, can be attracted to others. But they don't really care in any genuine sense about anyone but themselves. People with NPD have zero empathy, so they view other people as objects. Some of these "objects" are more alluring than others, or redound to their glory; others can be denigrated or ignored.

Anne Elliot's treatment by her father and sister Elizabeth shows zero empathy in action. Sir Walter is openly scornful and dismissive of Anne. He not only ignores her needs and wishes (indeed, he's oblivious to them), but he also fails to offer common kindness. And although his favorite daughter, Elizabeth, who also has the disorder, is significantly older than Anne, Sir Walter doesn't worry that she might have passed her prime marriageable years; it's Anne who's treated like the poor spinster, tolerated and exploited because she has nowhere else to go. We can guess that Anne was far too unlike Sir Walter, and far too unwilling to flatter him unduly, to be included in his charmed circle of narcissism (the scenario of three sisters and an old narcissist is reminiscent of *King Lear*; perhaps Austen had this play in mind). Nevertheless, Sir Walter's cruelty stems from obtuseness rather than an active desire to inflict pain. People with NPD are unable to take the perspective of others, but they don't, in general, actively seek to harm others.

The inability to mentalize accounts for much of the bizarre and counterproductive behavior of people with NPD, as well as their slender grasp of reality. They tend to alienate people because, unable to read minds, they can't understand how their behavior affects others. Mindreading is not only compromised but also avoided because it might be dangerous to know what people really think. Lack of a ToM functions as a very effective defense mechanism that keeps people with NPD from having to face the fact that they're not perfect, not the best at everything. (They know this deep down, but more of this in a moment.) Most defense mechanisms involve distorting reality for purposes of self-protection, but for those with NPD, this is a continual mandate: They must maintain an unrealistic, grandiose conception of themselves and all those associated with them.

Sir Walter certainly views the world through a distorted lens if he can believe that rented rooms at Bath are as impressive as a well-managed gentleman's country estate (not to mention his complete failure to recognize Anne's worth). But the character Austen uses to explore the narcissist's distortions most fully, especially in the context of relationships, is John Thorpe in *Northanger Abbey*. John, a bumbling fool who fits the diagnostic criteria for NPD, is a friend of Catherine's (the heroine's) brother. He falls for Catherine, who wants nothing to do with him.

As you might recall from Chapter Ten, a lack of a ToM often involves psychic equivalence, the inability to take the context of mind into account. People who think in psychic-equivalence mode might think that what others think and say *must* be true, or attribute their own thoughts and beliefs to others; both deficits stem from their inability to perceive how feelings and motives, their own and those of other people, might influence perceptions. You need to be conscious of minds as minds, one hallmark of a reflective capacity, to understand this. We see these tendencies, respectively, in Mr. Woodhouse and Miss Bates. Miss Bates hears Emma's insult as truth rather than the misguided witticism of a haughty and out-of-sorts young woman, and Mr. Woodhouse thinks everyone enjoys a dish of thin gruel. Psychic-equivalence mode translates into very low social intelligence, and so, as we see with these two, a distorted take on reality. Likewise, John projects his own thoughts and wishes onto others to such an extent, and expresses views of events that are so clearly inaccurate, that he appears to have a slim grasp of reality. John reshapes the world to give him the adulation he so desperately needs.

On one occasion, John asks Catherine to accompany him on an outing to Bristol on a day that she has made a date with the Tilneys (Henry Tilney, the man she likes, and his sister Eleanor) to go on a country walk. John comes to Catherine's lodgings to collect her, and when she reminds him of her prior engagement, he says that he saw Henry and Eleanor driving away in a carriage and overheard Henry say that they were going to a destination sufficiently far away to make an afternoon walk with Catherine out of the question.

Catherine believes John and assumes that Henry and Eleanor have forgotten the appointment. But when she and John drive past the Tilneys, who are walking in the direction of Catherine's lodgings, she realizes that John hasn't told the truth. John defends himself by saying that he must have seen a man who looked exactly like Henry, and he refuses to stop the carriage to let Catherine go to her friends. While NPD isn't usually characterized by violence, this scene conjures the violence that zero empathy makes possible. As noted with respect to Emma's embarrassing carriage ride with Mr. Elton, Austen's contemporary readers would have recognized the possibility of rape and abduction associated with a woman's imprisonment in a carriage from the bestseller *Clarissa* by Samuel Richardson, one of Austen's favorite authors.

Catherine reschedules the walk, and John again tries to prevent her from accompanying the Tilneys in order to go on yet another outing. He's jealous, but rather than admit this vulnerability to himself, he acts out his envy and disappointment. At first, he tries to persuade Catherine to break her appointment. When she stands her ground, he actually goes round to the Tilneys and tells them that Catherine can't go with them because she has a prior appointment with *him*. Catherine is furious and quickly goes to see her friends and sets things right.

John's distortions of the truth account not only for minor mishaps but they also explain the major misunderstanding of the novel. When John still has hopes that Catherine will become his wife, he boasts to General Tilney, Henry's father, that Catherine will inherit a considerable fortune. At this point, John still considers her part of his charmed circle, and so she *must* be wealthy, or so the narcissistic logic goes, since all that belongs to a narcissist must be the best. Acting on this information, the general graciously invites Catherine to stay at Northanger Abbey because he would love for his son to marry an heiress.

But when John meets the general in town during this visit, and John is "under the influence of exactly opposite feelings" and "irritated by Catherine's refusal" of his friendship, which has become obvious even to John himself, he exaggerates the meagerness of Catherine's financial prospects. At this point, John has lost all hope for a marriage with Catherine, as well as of a match between his sister Isabella and Catherine's brother James. Catherine now no longer belongs to him in any way. And so she enters the narcissist's devalued world of outcast others, of those who have nothing to do with *me* and are therefore worthless. And even worse, he has bad feelings, which also spur him on. After John tells the general that Catherine is not an heiress, the general sends her packing without protection or money for her long journey home.

Well, you might ask, in these instances, is John lying or does he believe what he says? Is he delusional, or just highly manipulative? This is unanswerable. Austen, who usually has no compunctions about eavesdropping on the minds of her characters, doesn't say.

Nevertheless, Austen strongly hints that John does indeed believe his own lies. Early on in the novel, John takes Catherine for a ride, during which he contradicts himself from moment to moment. With the goal of boasting about the superiority of his own carriage, he tells Catherine that her brother's carriage is unsafe: "It is the most devilish little rickety business I ever beheld!—Thank God! we have got a better. I would not be bound to go two miles in it for fifty pounds." Putting others down to elevate oneself is a frequent tactic of people with NPD. When Catherine naturally becomes alarmed for the safety of her brother, John reverses himself: "Oh, curse it the carriage is safe enough, if a man knows how to drive it; a thing of that sort in good hands will last above twenty years after it is fairly worn out. Lord bless you! I would undertake for five pounds to drive it to York and back again, without losing a nail." For the curious among you, the distance from Bath to York is 186.52 miles, a significantly farther stretch than the two miles of the first statement.

Anyone a bit more sophisticated than Catherine would have seen through John's contradictions and his boasts, such as his claim that his horse is capable of covering fifty miles a day, or that he had paid too much for his carriage because he pitied the man who was selling it, another untruth. That John can't remember or avoid contradictions suggests that he's trapped in psychic-equivalence mode, unable to see beyond the wishes of the moment, and constantly deluding himself in order to ward off untenable truths such as that he was duped by a salesman, and that Catherine would rather be with the Tilneys than with him. You can bet the Elliot estate that Mr. Elliot wouldn't have been caught contradicting himself. High machs keep track of their lies.

Whether or not John is unable to distinguish desire from reality, or he deliberately lies, his behavior reveals a complete lack of the ability to mentalize. And so he has no idea of how he comes across to other people, of the effects of his statements and actions. How could John possibly think that Catherine would be pleased that he had canceled her appointment with her friends behind her back? Even if she preferred to accompany John rather than the Tilneys (she doesn't!), she's certain to resent someone's tampering with her schedule surreptitiously. In *Emma*, Mr. Knightley tells Emma, "I have blamed you and lectured you, and you have borne it as no other woman in England would have borne it." But scold as he might, Mr. Knightley never takes it upon himself to actually interfere with Emma's plans. Not only does he realize how inappropriate that would be, but he also knows that such interference would be a nearly unforgivable mark of disrespect.

John, mindblind as he is, can't understand this, or how, more generally, that his behavior drives Catherine away, exactly the opposite of what he means to do. Rather than canceling her appointments, Mr. Elliot, or any other high mach, would have let Catherine go with the Tilneys and found another time to see her. Mr. Elliot would have been so charming that Catherine, who at this point is very naïve and not yet totally in love with Henry, might have begun to find this charismatic older man attractive. Thankfully, she has her own novel, safe from the predatory "high mach-inations" of a Mr. Elliot.

But in case we forget that fully functioning and well-meaning people are subject to blips of narcissism, that very rarely do we entirely get over ourselves, Austen includes a scene showing that Catherine can be almost as insensitive and dull as John. While still in Bath, she visits John's sister and is looking forward to dining with Eleanor Tilney later in the day. John approaches her in the parlor before she leaves the Thorpe's lodgings, and he all but declares his love. He goes so far as to ask if he can pay his respects to her parents, a strong indication of his intentions, even to a girl as naïve as Catherine.

This is one of John's best moments (even if Austen can't resist telling us that he forces a "foolish laugh"), and we see that he genuinely cares for Catherine to the limited degree that he can care for anyone. But she misses the point entirely. Absorbed as she is in her own feelings and desires, which include her love for Henry and her wish to be close to Eleanor, Catherine fails to understand John's feelings and rebuffs him in a manner almost as insensitive as his own.

We also need to remember that a little bit of "narcissism" is a good thing. Actually, when narcissism is good, we no longer call it narcissism but rather, healthy self-esteem, a positive self-image based on a realistic assessment of our capabilities and accomplishments. Paradoxically, this is precisely what the narcissist lacks.

ORIGINS OF NPD

I'm going to turn to attachment theorists once again for a psychological account of how NPD develops. According to psychiatrist James Masterson, the conditions that foster NPD likely begin in the second year of life, and they result from the actions of a self-involved caregiver, perhaps one who herself has NPD. Like forms of insecure attachment and the other empathy disorders, NPD results primarily from the caregiver's failure to provide emotional resonance (attunement) and mirroring, the core behaviors that lead to secure attachment, the ability to regulate emotions, and the capacity for mentalization. This lack of attunement likely begins when the child is ten months old at the earliest, because during roughly the first year of life, a child is incapable of the complex thoughts and behaviors that evoke the failure of attunement on the part of narcissistic caregivers.

In fact, during these early months, if caregiving is "good enough" and not abusive or neglectful, all infants, and not just those who'll develop NPD, have a grandiose sense of self because in general, their wishes are fulfilled by others. This allows the infant to feel that she's an all-powerful being who controls her environment; she usually gets what she wants, and so she has little sense of her own limits or imperfections. But this halcyon state of affairs can't last.

The malattunement that leads to NPD develops when the child begins to participate to a greater extent in the world outside the nursery, and with people other than her primary caregivers. As she ventures out into the world, which means exploring on her own (even if this is only a few feet away from the caregiver), she discovers that she's not grandiose, that she's indeed a very little person, not very powerful, who doesn't always get her way. She feels frustration, fear, and loneliness on these early forays into autonomy. This is known as deflation, and she needs to return to her caregiver, her secure base, for refueling. Here's where the problem begins.

The danger of narcissism enters when the caregiver not only fails to resonate with the child's deflated state, but reflects the disappointed grandiosity instead. This might happen despite the best of intentions. Let's say that the toddler sees a toy he wants to play with and another child picks it up first. Instead of telling the toddler that he must wait his turn, or share, the caregiver says, "You should have had that toy. You're better than everyone else and deserve to get what you want." While this is an exaggerated example—although probably not unrealistic treatment for the only son in an eighteenth-century English aristocratic family!—this is the basic pattern. Or a toddler learning to walk might fall down and begin to cry. Instead of acknowledging the baby's distress, the caregiver tells the child he's all right and is doing a great job walking. An older child might come to the caregiver upset because he lost a ball game. Instead of saying, "I know how you feel, losing is difficult," the caregiver says something along the lines of "You just had an off day. I know you're the best player." Or "Maybe the others cheated." Or "You're smaller than everyone else. In another year, no one will be able to beat you."

When the caregiver fails to mirror the deflated state and mirrors the grandiose self instead, the child learns that he's loved and approved only to the extent that he's successful. This kind of response also prevents the child from developing the necessary coping tools, the procedural schemas, for dealing with deflation—with failure and shame. By mirroring and soothing the child after painful experiences, including the ones she necessarily engenders through socialization, a "good enough" caregiver teaches the toddler to control his impulses and to regulate his negative deflation when he encounters difficulties.

The child eventually internalizes the capacity for self-comfort. In short, he learns that disappointments are a part of life, that you can survive them, and that they don't mean you're incompetent or unlovable. This is precisely what people with NPD have failed to learn.

A similar process of malattunement occurs in regard to the child's wishes, dreams, goals, and even his personality. A narcissistic caregiver views the child as an extension of himself. This is true to some extent of all who associate with a person who has NPD, since they must be superior in order to affirm his sense of superiority. But a child functions as an extension in other ways as well. He's often asked to fulfill the caregiver's fantasies and dreams, to be what the caregiver would really like him to be. If the child's desires and temperament don't match those of the narcissistic caregiver, disapproval will be expressed, often subtly, through tone or facial expression. The child of a narcissistic parent learns that her own wishes and ways of being don't count compared to those of the caregiver. The child who develops NPD feels he's nothing but the sum of those accomplishments that please the caregiver, while the child with a healthy sense of self (a "real self") learns that he has inherent and inalienable worth that doesn't depend on what he does or doesn't achieve.

As a result of the caregiver's need for narcissistic affirmation on the part of the child, seen in the child's superiority (*Everything of mine is the best*) and in the projection of her own wishes onto this young person, the child develops a false self, as in BPD. For the person with NPD, the false self takes the form of the grandiose self, the perfect being who fulfills the caregiver's fantasies and therefore affirms the caregiver's superiority. (After all, this child is one of her possessions.) The child learns that love and approval depend on maintaining this false self, and that activation of the real self, which includes the child's realistic appraisal of his accomplishments and knowledge of his own desires, threatens the withdrawal of love and so the ensuing abandonment depression. For the person with NPD, abandonment depression includes feelings of envy as well as feelings of rejection, shame, and worthlessness. The false self protects the child from experiencing these painful effects. As with BPD, the true self remains repressed because whenever the child, and later the adult, self-activates, which means accessing this true self, the abandonment depression also activates.

Abandonment depression can also result when the systems that keep grandiosity in place break down, as in a divorce or the loss of a job.

We all have ideal images of what we would like to be and achieve: This is what psychotherapists call the "ego ideal." But most of us are able treat such standards as goals toward which we strive, and we're capable of forgiving and accepting ourselves when we fall short. A healthy outlook means that our ideals are likely to be realistic to begin with, even if lofty: We don't think, *I'm going to be the best ballplayer in the world*, but rather, *I can't be the best ballplayer in the world, but I can become a good ballplayer.* (Perhaps you're old enough to remember the concept of "personal best," a bit of common sense addressed to a narcissistic culture.) Accepting an imperfect self and having realistic expectations are important tools for surviving and processing short-comings and disappointments. But the person with NPD lacks these emotional tools and feels obligated to be perfect. The alternative is too dreadful: a sense of shame and worthlessness and the abandonment depression that makes him feel unfit to be loved.

Some people with NPD, or narcissistic traits, tend to oscillate between grandiosity and shame, or to feel shame most of the time (this applies to Masterson's closet narcissists). Others maintain the narcissistic grandiose false self by finding ways to devalue those who challenge their inflated self-image, surrounding themselves with those who confirm their superiority, and denying realities that don't support their grandiosity. We never see Sir Walter or John suffering shame, but we certainly see the lengths to which they go to maintain the false self. Sir Walter surrounds himself with flatterers, devalues (Lear-like) the one daughter who's honest with him, and fails to note the marks of his own aging as well as the abundance of Mrs. Clay's freckles. John's false self is even more deluded, and if he doesn't have the wealth and standing to attract flatterers, he at least associates with those who tolerate his inconsistencies and boastfulness. Just as Sir Walter rejects Anne, John devalues Catherine once he realizes she's not interested in him.

But despite the hard work of maintaining defenses, the person with NPD lacks a stable and authentic sense of self-esteem and never really feels good enough, deep down. The search for constant validation of the grandiose self serves to ward off his knowledge of his imperfections and the depression this would bring. But subconsciously, or when defenses falter, the narcissist realizes he's not absolutely fabulous, that his caregiver's reassurance was hollow, that there were kids who actually did play a better ball game than he did, or who were smarter, or more handsome, or who had talents that he didn't have.

When emotions and knowledge are dissociated to this extent, they usually find a way to cause trouble. Because people with NPD can't recognize their fears and must live the life of the grandiose self, they often feel empty, unfulfilled, and inauthentic (as with BPD), the consequence of living a lie and having a false self. Moreover, a person with NPD can never find genuine support—true attunement and resonance—because he has dissociated from the very feelings that he needs to share with others for refueling: vulnerability and shame. He can't take the risk of having a real self, which would acknowledge such feelings. And so he avoids true intimacy, which would mean revealing an authentic self in a relationship, a self he can't allow to emerge. Intimacy also carries the danger that his "fraud" will be discovered, the knowledge that he's not perfect, and he will then be rejected. The state of crisis in which he constantly lives, often unknowingly, leaves him without the psychological resources to give in return, to be a true friend. He desperately needs people, but no one can get too close.

We get some important clues in *Northanger Abbey* about John's childhood that hint at why he developed NPD. His mother, Mrs. Thorpe, has an inflated, grandiose view of all her children, as we learn in her conversation with Mrs. Allen, the family friend who invited Catherine to accompany her to Bath. The narrator tells us, "Mrs. Thorpe, however, had one great advantage as a talker over Mrs. Allen . . . and when she expatiated on the talents of her sons, and the beauty of her daughters,—when she related their different situations . . . and [that] all of them [were] more beloved and respected in their different stations than any three beings ever were, Mrs. Allen had no similar information to give."

Mrs. Thorpe's behavior toward John shows that she repeatedly validates his grandiose view of himself, not least by tolerating everything he says, no matter how rude or outrageous. It isn't much of a stretch to imagine her failures of resonance and her narcissistic expectations throughout John's life.

THE FAULT LIES IN OUR STARS? GENES? ENVIRONMENT? MORALS?

We're a species that likes to find fault. It goes with the territory of moral reason and advanced cognitive intelligence. Finding fault is a version of perceiving cause and effect, a capacity we share with many nonhuman animals. It confers a terrific advantage in the struggle for survival. If you understand cause and effect, you can predict events and avoid dangers (*If I enter that lion's den, I'll probably be killed*) and seek benefits (*That grove is lush, so there will probably be ripe fruits for me to eat*). Among nonhuman animals with significant social intelligence, such as the great apes, the perception of cause and effect often acts as a deterrent: *If I steal the dominant chimp's bananas, I'm sure to be beaten up because that's what usually happens*. Humans take this a step further to internalize rules of right and wrong, and many feel guilt as well as fear at the prospect of wrongdoing. In a basic sense, cause and effect is the foundation of law and ethics, necessary for civil society.

But above and beyond these pragmatic benefits, a sense of cause and effect makes us feel safe, and this response might be specific to humans. If you can find a reason that something bad happens, or something good, you feel more in control. You might say to yourself, "That person got colon cancer because of a poor diet but if I eat well, that won't happen to me." And speaking of cancer, John Green's title for his novel about teens with cancer, *The Fault in Our Stars* (quoted in my subheading above), makes the point that sometimes bad things happen and no one's to blame, except the stars—bad luck or, if you're a believer, some kind of astrological determination. The important point here is that there isn't a person or some other entity responsible for the tragic plight of Green's characters.

We can say the same about most instances of cancer. Let's bracket known risk factors such as smoking and polluted areas where carcinogenic elements can be traced to the actions of a specific person or corporation. (If you're living in the U.S. in 2017, these are legally the same.) Cancer begins because something goes wrong with the functioning of cells. We don't blame or punish anyone. We understand that there might be causal factors such as pollutants, or diet, or genetics, but we accept that we aren't going to hold someone responsible. It's nobody's fault.

Many would say that cancer is evil, personifying this frightening disease. But what about literal evil, harm committed by one person against an innocent victim? Is someone who takes a life for no good reason evil? To put this another way, is he to blame? As a consultant on a criminal case, psychiatrist Bruce D. Perry clearly charted the abusive developmental history that enabled a young man to murder two teenage girls, and he writes about this in a wonderful book about childhood trauma, *The Boy Who Was Raised as a Dog*. But despite the fact that the perpetrator was also a victim, he was legally responsible for his actions.

Most readers will probably agree with the courts in this case, but the answer isn't always so clear. The legal finding of insanity dictates that someone who commits a crime without understanding what they're doing isn't responsible for his actions; he isn't to blame. We're willing to say that, in both a legal and moral context, this person isn't at fault because there's something wrong with his brain. But our prisons are full of people with APD who've committed murders and other heinous crimes. They understand what they've done, although their attitude is different from that of most people. And there is indeed something wrong with their brains. The brain of Perry's subject was terribly damaged.

We can actually refer to areas likely to be damaged or underdeveloped in people with empathy disorders. Neuroscientist Simon Baron-Cohen has identified an empathy circuit within the brain, a loop of ten brain areas with multiple interconnections that are instrumental in generating empathy. Together, these areas control perspective taking, emotional response, emotional expression, and emotional regulation; this last is crucial to empathy and to all positive social connections. Lo and behold, our old friends, the amygdala and the orbitofrontal cortex (OFC) appear on this circuit, contributing in various ways to the experience of empathy. For instance, the OFC activates when a person sees a needle going into another's hand, and the amygdala prompts us to attend to people's eyes, which are key in registering emotional expression.

Many studies show compromised empathy circuit areas specifically with regard to Cluster B disorders. For instance, abnormalities of the OFC have been found in the brains of those who exhibit violent and aggressive behavior, characteristic of some forms of APD. This makes sense since the OFC is the braking structure that shuts down the emergency/stress system, which tells a person he's in danger and should fight. If you can't quiet your anger over a slight, you're likely to react with aggression beyond what a situation calls for. Studies have also revealed reductions in the volume of the entire brain of people with APD, and especially in the temporal lobes, where many areas of the empathy circuit are located, and in the frontal lobes, which mediate logic and planning (especially the dorsolateral prefrontal cortex and the ventromedial prefrontal cortex, which often includes a part of the OFC). One patient developed APD traits as a result of damage to the OFC caused by a tumor.

Neurological studies also reveal abnormalities in people with BPD and NPD. One study showed that in subjects with BPD, negative emotion evokes decreased prefrontal activation (logic and planning) and increased amygdala activation (stress and aggression) as compared with the brains of subjects who don't have this condition. This indicates both greater negative affect and a reduced ability to regulate such affect. Imaging studies investigating the brains of those with NPD compared with healthy control subjects have shown that people with NPD have less gray matter (brain volume) in the areas along the empathy circuit, including the OFC. Also compared with normal control subjects, people diagnosed with NPD have lower activation in the right anterior insula during tasks designed to evoke empathy; this area is on the empathy circuit.

Bear in mind that although studies tend to explore one condition at a time, their findings are relevant to personality disorders other than the one under consideration in any given study because these disorders tend to have many traits in common. This is true to such a great extent that the authors of *DSM-5* considered including a general trait-based category called "Personality Disorders," rather than a listing of specific disorders, separate from one another. The writing committee couldn't agree to do this, and so the trait-based categorization of the personality disorders appears as an appendix, with the understanding that the next *DSM* might well revise the section in accord with a trait-based approach. I think this will happen because defining personality disorders as one condition in which impairments don't necessarily follow specific categories makes sense. Also in line with the tendency to focus on the common denominators of personality disorders, neuroscientists Jean Decety and Yoshiya Moriguchi suggest that interventions that address empathy deficits will likely be useful across a wide array of different clinical conditions, including the Cluster B (empathy) disorders and autism. This is supported by a study that found that when people with psychopathy were asked to deliberately feel the emotions demonstrated in a video clip, brain scans showed increased activity in brain areas associated with empathy, although these people didn't spontaneously respond in this way. As noted in a previous chapter, Fonagy has formulated a treatment that addresses BPD by encouraging the development of mentalization.

As you know, the environment, especially interactions with primary caregivers, develops the social brain, and a person certainly can't be held responsible for the environment into which he's born. We've seen repeatedly that interactions determine attachment styles and personalities to a great extent. They also determine pathology, not only in the rather complex ways seen in the Cluster B disorders, but in the simple correlation between neglect and reactive detachment disorder seen in so many orphanages where babies weren't given the chance to bond with particular caregivers.

The findings on the interaction of genes with attachment experiences are impressive with respect to APD. One study that looked at gene-environment interaction in the development of antisocial personality traits found that abused boys who carried a mutated version of a particular gene were more likely to engage in bullying, violence, cruelty, and other antisocial behaviors that fit the profile for APD than those who didn't have this version of the gene. This gene determines how much of the neurochemical monoamine oxidase-A (or MAOA) is produced; low levels of MAOA have been linked to aggression.

However, the tendency to antisocial behavior, including violence and cruelty, was more likely only when those who possessed the gene had also suffered childhood abuse (neglect or maltreatment). Of the fifty-five men studied, low MAOA levels alone did not produce a greater likelihood of developing antisocial behaviors. Abusive or inadequate caregiving was necessary to elicit the potential effects of the gene. Men who came from homes with "good enough" caregiving didn't have an increased risk of developing these negative traits. This finding was corroborated by another study that found that teenagers who possessed this gene but had a secure attachment style (as teens) were able to successfully regulate aggression.

The more we know about the mind-brain, the more difficult it gets to distinguish psychological-neurological factors from moral ones. Why isn't a person whose brain is damaged because of genetics or an abusive environment just as worthy of exoneration, and forgiveness, as the person who literally doesn't realize what he's doing? The person with APD is mindblind in moral terms, unable to feel that his actions are monstrous. His case is certainly different to that of someone capable of feeling empathy and guilt who ignores or suppresses such feelings—signals that tell us to do the right thing. When we punish people with APD, we're drawing a line in the sand between criminals and victims.

This might appear to be a contemporary problem, but I believe that Austen, prescient and ahead of her time in her astuteness about people, saw this difficulty as well. To begin with, she appears to be aware that some people have abnormalities in thinking and feeling. Take Mr. Woodhouse, for instance, whose capacity to take the perspective of others is clearly limited. When a deficit is harmless, as in this case, Austen treats the character as a beloved eccentric, a course followed for the most part by the fictional people in her pages. And when limitations clearly wreak havoc, as in Mr. Elliot's treatment of Mrs. Smith, she isn't inclined to be charitable.

But what about someone like John Thorpe, whose behavior certainly puts others in uncomfortable predicaments? He certainly isn't as malevolent as Mr. Elliot. And unlike Mr. Elliot, he is himself constantly victimized by petty indignities such as buying inferior merchandise because the seller appeals to his need to have the best. Thorpe is a bumbling fool rather than a clever villain. And a bumbling fool suits Austen's exploration of the ethical question as to whether people with malfunctioning mind-brains should be held accountable for their behavior. This is a question that we have yet to answer.

Austen was moralistic and created a moralistic fictional world. But because she had a sense that some people have cognitive and emotional limitations that account for their behavior, she faced the same ethical difficulty we face today in determining whether those with damaged mind-brains should be treated as criminals or victims. I believe that she articulates the difficulty in her characterization of John Thorpe. Austen can afford to investigate the finer points of assigning blame to a character whose evil has limits because she's dealing with minor infractions rather than outright and cruel crimes. John's lies might have placed Catherine in danger (the long ride home without an escort or money), but this wasn't an outcome he could have anticipated. Conversely, Mr. Elliot understands the difficulties he creates for Mrs. Smith. Note also that Mr. Elliot's behavior leads him to break with the ideal world of Austen's provincial communities at the end of the novel, and although he chooses his banishment, he's excluded from the circle nevertheless. John gets no such banishment. He doesn't get the girl in the end, but he never really had a chance of that to begin with.

Earlier, I noted a quirk on Austen's part, that she doesn't tell us whether John believes his lies or not, although this defies her usual tendency to clarity with her readers. I think that leaving this issue ambiguous is her solution to the dilemma posed by damaged people who nevertheless damage others. It's a clever move on Austen's part. If John were truly delusional, he'd be exonerated to some extent. And Austen believes that people should be held responsible for their actions, so she doesn't want to excuse him. But she also understands that there's something very wrong with him. She wants to hold him responsible for his actions, but also say he's not to blame. So Austen wisely leaves it up to her readers to judge. Or *not* to judge, as the case may be.

Before leaving these empathy disorders, I'd like to return to the mirror as a symbol of narcissism. Unlike Sir Walter, John isn't obsessed with his looks, and mirrors aren't symbolically significant in his story. *Northanger Abbey* is one of Austen's earliest complete novels, and perhaps early in her career Austen purposely veered away from using the mirror as a symbol of narcissism because she thought it was a cliché. Everyone in Austen's day who was educated, even if they hadn't gone beyond primary (elementary) school, would have known the story of

Narcissus; the famous poet John Dryden had translated Ovid's *Meta-morphoses* into English from Latin, and the myth of Narcissus is one of that work's most popular and enduring stories. It's still familiar, even today. But by the time Austen came to write *Persuasion*, her last completed novel, she understood that this familiar icon, the mirror as an emblem of narcissism, could convey meanings beyond the obvious. The mirror was a perfect symbol for embodying several different aspects of the pathology of narcissism, and not merely the self-love that distinguishes the disorder.

The narcissist looks into the world but sees only himself—either through projections of his own psyche (as in idealizing others) or in the confirmation of grandiosity that he extracts from others. He's always looking in the mirror in one way or another, seeing himself when he looks outward. In addition, the physical properties of mirrors as surface rather than depth renders them an apt symbol of the narcissist's psychological limitations; he's doomed to live with surfaces in emotional and social terms, entering into relationships that lack depth and that never truly connect him to others. And this is ultimately a lonely existence, for even when you see others in the mirror standing next to you, you don't see real people. Sir Walter never sees Anne for who she truly is, nor even his favorite daughter Elizabeth.

Sir Walter is fortunate in being surrounded by tolerant people, like Lady Russell, who is kind and devoted out of loyalty to the Elliot family and respect for Sir Walter's position, as well as those who jolly him along in order to manage him, like Mr. Shepherd (Sir Walter's lawyer) and Mrs. Clay. Sir Walter's daughters also shield him from the truth: Anne is too respectful to challenge her father. Mary, the youngest daughter, too self-absorbed. And Elizabeth and Sir Walter are complicit in bolstering one another's grandiosity. Although Sir Walter likely possesses the inner emptiness of the person with NPD, he's well protected from ever having to confront the abandonment depression. Perhaps as he ages, his changing looks will bring on a crisis that he can no longer avoid. Or perhaps his defenses are so strong that he'll never be forced to confront his real self, not even in the mirror. He lives a diminished life, but he might well be protected from ever discovering this lack.

Poor John Thorpe isn't so lucky. He's not in a position, financially or socially, to command confirmation of his grandiosity from any but his own family. His friends tolerate him because they're good-natured. But I have a feeling that Thorpe's failure to win Catherine's heart will be one in a series of disappointments that will be painful. If he's lucky, this will prompt a transformation that leads to a better life, as with Darcy. But given what we know of him, this is highly unlikely. If only John had been born a century later, when such checks to his grandiose self-image might have brought him to the newly created analyst's couch.

EPILOGUE

'No One So Proper, So Capable'

've saved the best for last. The best heroine that is. Anne Elliot of *Persuasion* is Austen's most brilliant character in terms of social intelligence. She has the most developed sense of empathy—an exquisitely astute reflective capacity and an unerring sense of attunement. Beyond this ability to understand other people and herself, she is able to use her mindreading skills to act with wisdom and compassion.

We have special access to the thought processes that comprise these abilities. Austen is famous for doing some mindreading of her own, "eavesdropping" on the thoughts of her characters. Literary scholars have observed that she accomplishes this feat through a narrative technique called "free indirect discourse," known as FID—literary scholars as well as mind-brain scientists can use acronyms! If Austen wasn't the first author to use this technique, as many believe, she certainly perfected it. Free indirect discourse means that the narrator reports the thoughts of a character (who of course thinks in the first person, as "I") from a third-person perspective so that the two identities merge rhetorically. You can often hear the character's voice through the narrator's report, even though the narrator is writing in the third person.

Here's an example that shows this especially well; the narrator tells us Lady Russell's opinion of Anne's engagement to Wentworth:

> Anne Elliot, with all her claims of birth, beauty, and mind, to throw herself away at nineteen; involve herself at nineteen in an engagement with a young man, who had nothing to recommend him, and no hopes of attaining affluence, but in the chances of a most uncertain profession, and no connections to secure even his farther rise in that profession; would be, indeed, a throwing away, which she grieved to think of! Anne Elliot, so young; known to so few, to be snatched off by a stranger without alliance or fortune; or rather sunk by him into a state of most wearing, anxious, youth-killing dependence! It must not be, if by any fair interference of friendship, any representations from one who had almost a mother's love, and mother's rights, it would be prevented.

In this vehement account of Lady Russell's feelings, which include fear, indignation, and determination, you can hear her voice coming through in the choice of words and sentence structure. The narrator would never take this view or express herself in this way. Yet, it is clearly the narrator who is speaking ("which *she* grieved to think of"), not Lady Russell. FID has a lot in common with empathy because both involve an outsider (third person) thinking and feeling from the perspective of another person (first person). It's fitting that Austen developed a narrative technique—a form—that is the equivalent of empathy—a perceptual mode—in novels that revolve around the topic of social intelligence.

Using FID frequently, the narrator shows us that Anne analyzes her own thoughts and feelings, and those of others, in greater detail and with greater astuteness and accuracy than any of Austen's other heroines. Even those who are socially astute most of the time tend to see the broad outlines rather than the fine lines of character and action. Fanny knows that Edmund is in love with Mary, Elinor understands that Marianne has been floored by trauma and depression, Elizabeth realizes that she's been mistaken and learns to know herself. Ditto for Emma and Marianne.

But Anne has an active, searching, and analytical wisdom, as well as an intense awareness of the weaknesses that the human mind is heir to. *Persuasion* almost makes social intelligence into a spectator sport, tracing the scope of Anne's extraordinary thinking, the source of her superlative social skills. Anne constantly deals with difficult people who have conflicting agendas, perceptions, and desires, handling situations with unparalleled judgment and tact.

Well might we wonder how Anne could emerge from the same family that produced the other Elliots, including those with personality disorders: her father, Sir Walter (NPD) and her cousin, Mr. Elliot (APD). Austen might have sacrificed psychological realism for the demands of plot, character, and theme, a rare decision on her part. Or maybe Anne was the only one who had sustained contact with her mother for reasons having to do with eighteenth-century child-rearing practices. Temperament certainly intersects with the environment to produce personality, but we must admit that the gap in social intelligence is huge between Anne and the rest of her family.

Persuasion not only has the "best" heroine, but it is the most romantic of Austen's tales. (This reader weeps with joy at the ending, every time!) Anne Elliot had become engaged to Captain Wentworth eight years ago. She was nineteen at the time, and Wentworth was an unknown quantity. Their love was solid—they had true knowledge of one another's minds and a sense of being on the same wavelength. Anne's father, Sir Walter Elliot, thought the match was beneath her, but his opinion weighed little with Anne, even at that young age. However, her deceased mother's best friend, Lady Russell (quoted above), persuaded Anne to think that the engagement was wrong, and after "a few months of exquisite felicity," Anne ended it.

We are told this history in a flashback in the fourth chapter. When the novel begins, Anne has been immured in the country for the past eight years, living with her simply dreadful father and his equal in narcissism, her older sister Elizabeth. Her married sister Mary lives nearby, and although also very self-centered, at least Mary values Anne's company for the support and help Anne so freely gives. And of course, Anne is still close to her mentor, Lady Russell. But, as Lady Russell knows all too well, Anne is wasted where she is. Anne should be the wife of a man who deserves her, and associating with people who appreciate her.

All of this changes when the Elliots must rent out their country estate to pay their debts because of Sir Walter and Elizabeth's extravagance. Anne stays first with Mary in the village of Uppercross; then with Lady Russell, closer to Kellynch, her family's estate; and finally with her father and sister, who have rented rooms (an apartment) in Bath. In the course of events, she acquires new friends, gets closer to old friends, makes herself beloved and useful, and, in the end, is reunited with Wentworth. (Yes, that's a collective sigh you just heard from all of Austen's most romantic readers.)

But let's return to Anne's capacity for empathy—in a technical sense—for inferring what people are thinking, and resonating with them emotionally. The person we see her mindreading in this special way much of the time is Wentworth. To begin with, Anne understands that Wentworth has not forgiven her for rejecting him, and that his coolness to her stems from anger rather than apathy. At a gathering early on in his reappearance in her life (his sister and her husband have rented the Elliot estate), he discusses the succession of ships he has captained, addressing his reminiscences to his two admirers in particular, Louisa and Henrietta Musgrove, Anne's young relatives (by marriage). Anne knows that he's thinking of her as he speaks of the past: "Anne felt the utter impossibility, from her knowledge of his mind, that he could be unvisited by remembrance any more than herself. There must be the same immediate association of thought, though she was very far from conceiving it to be of equal pain." In this, she's correct. Wentworth doesn't feel equal pain, not because it isn't there, but because he has defenses against it. More of that presently.

Anne has confirmation of her insights about Wentworth's continued anger when she overhears him talking to Louisa on a walk (she is unseen behind a hedgerow and can't help but hear). Wentworth discusses the value of firmness, of character, of not yielding to "persuasion" as Anne had done, saying, "If Louisa Musgrove would be happy in her November of life, she will cherish her present powers of mind." (It's harsh to think that Wentworth might consider Anne to be in the November of life at age twenty-nine, but he has noticed that she looks drawn and generally faded.) Yet even though Anne feels hopeless about a future with Wentworth, and believes he might be becoming attached to Louisa, she sees "there had been just that degree of feeling and curiosity about her in his manner [when Louisa mentions her], which must give her extreme agitation." Why agitation? Because it shows he's not apathetic to her. He has shown other marks of consideration that convey the same sentiment.

Anne knows Wentworth better than he knows himself. Everyone in Anne's circle, including Wentworth, thinks that he's going to propose to one of the Musgrove sisters. While they try to predict who will be his bride, Anne "could not but think, as far as she might dare to judge from memory and experience, that Captain Wentworth was not in love with either of them." Her fear, a legitimate one, is that the situation "might, probably must, end with love with some." And if this is one or both of the sisters, there's potential for great unhappiness for all parties involved. When Wentworth finally does know his own mind—that he doesn't want to marry Louisa and that he does want to marry Anne—he realizes that to abandon Louisa after having led her on would indeed be dishonorable; he would rather make the mistake of his life in marrying Louisa than impeach his honor. Wentworth leaves Lyme, where Louisa is recovering from her concussion, and a short time later, she and Captain Benwick become engaged. A lucky escape!

After Anne realizes that Wentworth might still have positive feelings for her, that at the very least he's forgiven her, it takes a while for her to figure out that he loves her. But this isn't because of a lack of astuteness; circumstances make it difficult for her to speak to him or observe him long enough to understand his feelings. When she encounters him in Bath (she doesn't know that he has come to seek her out), she sees that he's "not comfortable" talking to her and that he gives her "a momentary look of arch significance" when he mentions Louisa. She also sees he's "changed." But she doesn't yet have sufficient information to realize that the change consists of his having realized he still loves her.

It's only when they get to talk at some length, precious moments snatched before a concert begins, that Wentworth says enough for Anne to understand that "he had a heart returning to her." He doesn't speak of his feelings overtly, but simply observes that his friend Benwick had chosen unwisely in engaging himself to Louisa because she isn't smart or intellectual enough to be a true companion for "a reading man," and of course, Anne knows Wentworth is a reader. Even more important, he says that Benwick ought not to have gotten over the death of his fiancée so quickly because "[a] man does not recover from such a devotion of the heart to such a woman!—He ought not—he does not." Of course, she understands that he's speaking of himself. And when Anne sees evidence that same night that Wentworth is jealous of Mr. Elliot, who has indeed been paying attention to his cousin in pointed ways, she understands that Wentworth loves her, that he has never stopped loving her. And so Anne is thrilled but not surprised when he confesses this love. She's been reading Wentworth all along.

But it isn't just in her understanding of Wentworth that we see Anne's social capability. She accurately assesses everyone around her. To begin with, she deals with her own family as well as anyone could, even enabling Mary to behave herself better than she ordinarily would. Considering the Musgrove sisters, Anne realizes that neither Louisa nor Henrietta truly loves Wentworth: "They were more in love with him [than he was with either of them]; yet there it was not love. It was a little fever of admiration." And Anne is able to empathize with the sorrows of a young man everyone seems to have forgotten in the rush of feverish admiration for Wentworth (on the part of all the Musgroves, not just the sisters): poor Charles Hayter, whom Henrietta had been all but engaged to marry before Wentworth's arrival. Anne "had a delicacy which must be pained by any lightness of conduct in a well-meaning young woman, and a heart to sympathize with the sufferings it occasioned." But Anne knows that it's better to cause such suffering sooner rather than later, and that Henrietta should call the engagement off if she doesn't love him.

And there's Captain Benwick. Everyone believes that he will mourn the early passing of his fiancée for a long time to come. When he becomes engaged, Wentworth isn't the only one who's surprised and disappointed in Benwick, although thankful that this engagement clears him of any obligation to Louisa. Captain Harville, the deceased young lady's brother, is grieved and upset at this turn of events. But Anne understood early on that Captain Benwick would soon attach himself to another woman, despite his tragic loss.

And of course, Anne finds Mr. Elliot untrustworthy while everyone else in the Elliot-Musgrove circle accepts his reform at face value. They believe it's natural, right, and proper that Mr. Elliot should be in touch with Sir Walter and his family, since he is the heir to the title of Baronet and the Elliot estate. As in *Pride and Prejudice*, the estate has been entailed to descend through the male line. Sir Walter and Elizabeth are so blinded by their narcissism that they also believe Mr. Elliot is angling for a match with Elizabeth. Of course, they're very wrong; it's Anne he likes, and who intrigued him even before he learned she was an Elliot.

Lady Russell agrees with the prevailing view of Mr. Elliot, although with more common sense than Sir Walter and Elizabeth. She clearly sees that Mr. Elliot finds Anne attractive, and fervently hopes for a match between them. How fitting that Anne should become Lady Elliot, taking her dear deceased mother's place and restoring Kellynch to its moral as well as financial glory. Even Anne finds this tempting: "The idea of becoming what her mother had been; of having the precious name of 'Lady Elliot' first revived in herself, of being restored to Kellynch, calling it her home again, her home for ever, was a charm she could not immediately resist."

In addition, Anne has been flattered by her handsome cousin and is grateful to him for the attention. Mr. Elliot first noticed Anne when he passed by her twice at Lyme, where she was with the Musgroves on the fateful outing that ended in Louisa's fall. Both times his interest clearly showed that she had made a strong impression on him. And she becomes even prettier afterward, for even more than the fresh air and the company, which have done a lot to restore Anne's faded "bloom," Mr. Elliot's interest has a beneficial effect on her looks and her spirits. She has felt herself to be not only isolated but "on the shelf" for eight long years, and suddenly she realizes all isn't necessarily over for her. She actually connects her improved appearance with her cousin's attentions.

But despite these moments of temptation and gratitude, Anne knows that she won't be Mr. Elliot's wife. And it isn't just that she's still emotionally attached to Wentworth. To begin with, she distrusts him on account of the past, his conduct of eight years ago when he disrespected and broke with her father. She thinks there must be more in Mr. Elliot's reestablishing contact than simple goodwill. (At first, she wonders if perhaps he really does like Elizabeth, but as she later learns from Mrs. Smith, he's there to prevent Sir Walter from marrying Mrs. Clay because a son would inherit the title and property.) Although Mr. Elliot now speaks and behaves with perfect propriety, and seems to be good-natured, Anne suspects his sincerity. She wonders, "who could answer for the true sentiments of a clever, cautious, man, grown old enough to appreciate a fair character? How could it ever be ascertained that his mind was truly cleansed?" The present influences her as much as the past. As aforementioned, Anne detects a lack of warmth and spontaneity in Mr. Elliot that signals danger to her. Wishful thinking clouds Lady Russell's judgment, as is the case with so many of Austen's fictional people, but Anne keeps her wits about her.

One potential benefit of social intelligence is the capacity for leadership. I've focused on empathy and its concomitant qualities throughout *Jane on the Brain*, and leadership isn't necessarily a consequence of such skills. But a good theory of mind is a prerequisite for leadership in many cases. This was certainly true for our early human ancestors. Recall that among chimpanzees, excellent social skills are important to achieving and maintaining high rank within the troupe. Looking around me at those in leadership positions today and in the recent past, I can't help but conclude that the lack of such a prerequisite among humans is one of the less laudable ways we've managed to transcend our evolutionary heritage. Bullies and dictators don't rise to the top among our great-ape cousins, but they're rife in human societies. Be that as it may, social intelligence is certainly important for ethical, compassionate leadership.

We see that Anne is just such a natural leader. Although she's devalued by her family at home, everyone in both Musgrove households (that includes her sister Mary's household) recognizes Anne's superior capabilities. Indeed, they're in the habit of confiding in her and appealing to her to arbitrate disputes, or agree with their points of view. People sense her capability, and they turn to her for guidance.

Anne wishes there were a little less involvement of such kind, but she handles it well, finding solutions when possible, and listening attentively and validating feelings (although not always agreeing with what someone has to say) when solutions are unavailable: She's

especially skillful with Mary. For instance, Mary continually feels
she's unwell when she doesn't receive sufficient attention (she too has
narcissistic traits), especially from her husband, Charles. But Anne
knows how to jolly her along, and after a few minutes in Anne's company, Mary is completely recovered. A drawback to such skills—all
the Musgroves recognize them, and so they're continually asking Anne
to make Mary see reason.

While not eager to put herself forward, Anne quickly takes charge
when others around her falter. We see this early on, when Mary's
older son has a fall and dislocates his collar bone. Austen doesn't
make a fuss about this but tells us that "Anne had every thing to do
at once—the apothecary* to send for—the father to have pursued and
informed—the mother to support and keep from hysterics—the ser-
vants to control—the youngest child to banish, and the poor suffering
one to attend and soothe."

Of course, this incident foreshadows Anne's management of the crisis
at Lyme. When Louisa insists on jumping off a high ledge (the Cobb)
into Captain Wentworth's arms, she miscalculates the distance and
falls, hitting her head. Everyone on this pleasure party panics: Mary
and Henrietta faint and have hysterics while the men—Wentworth,
Charles Musgrove, and Captain Benwick—freeze. Wentworth then
calls out for help, clueless about what to do. It is Anne who acts, telling
Charles and Benwick, who have caught the fainting Henrietta, to go
to Wentworth, who is holding Louisa, to rub her temples and offer
her smelling salts (Anne has these on hand) to see if these can revive
her. She then sends Benwick for the apothecary. When the party is
discussing who will stay to care for Louisa (still unconscious, she has
been moved to the Harvilles' home), it is initially decided that Anne
will be the one, until Mary makes such a fuss that Anne changes places
with her. Wentworth's opinion speaks for all: "[N]o one so proper, so
capable as Anne."

If Anne knows when to act, she also knows when to refrain. There's
nothing she can do to make things better for herself at home, living
with such emotionally and ethically stunted people. She very occasionally tries to intervene to save them from their foolishness. But most of

---

*   Apothecaries were medical practitioners as well as pharmacists in Austen's day.

the time she's a prisoner of circumstances, sequestered in an environment where she's forced into passivity and her talents are wasted. Her friendship with Lady Russell and her usefulness at Uppercross offer some relief, but they certainly don't provide a full and satisfying life. Anne languishes, and it's not surprising that when Wentworth first sees her again, he finds her altered beyond his knowledge [recognition], or at least that's what he says to Mary. However, we should take this with a grain of salt because he's still very angry at her and likely glad to see that she has languished.

Yet, despite the neglect and devaluing that would have eaten away at the assurance of many in her situation, Anne retains an unassailable and realistic sense of self-esteem. She knows Louisa and Henrietta are far happier than she is, but "she would not have given up her own more elegant and cultivated mind for all their enjoyments; and envied them nothing but that seemingly perfect good understanding and agreement together, that good-humoured mutual affection, of which she had known so little herself with either of her sisters." As always, Anne wisely knows what to value.

As this assessment of her own mind demonstrates, Anne doesn't just possess the ability to understand what people are thinking and feeling, which is the basis for her prodigious social intelligence, but she also thinks about thinking—what people think about, how they think, the quality of their minds. Many people do this intuitively, but Anne actually reflects on the process. Take her perception of Mr. Elliot. Her understanding of the ways minds work enables her alone to distrust him while all around her are falling for the glitz—the fantasy of a contrite, reformed man who will behave as Sir Walter's devoted heir ought to do. (Actually, the irony is that he does behave like Sir Walter's heir—heir to his extraordinary solipsism and lack of empathy as well as his estate!) In order to do so, she must understand that a lack of spontaneous emotional expression indicates that something is wrong. She must further understand that the expression of emotion escapes control, that social signals as well as what people say convey authenticity and sincerity.

One of her most important insights is an observation we see in all of Austen's novels, usually on the part of the narrator, or left implicit: that people's desires skew their perceptions. Perhaps it's Anne's awareness of this bias that enables her to escape its pitfalls. If you understand the tendency to solipsism, you can work on attentively taking other perspectives. Anne's awareness of this human failing is an important building block of her social capabilities as well as her wisdom, for understanding that people are cognitively and emotionally self-centered gives her an advantage in dealing with them. Of course, all mindreading confers an advantage; if you can understand what someone is thinking, you can respond appropriately. But if you can grasp someone's overall patterns of thought, the forms their solipsism will take, you can formulate overall strategies for dealing—and coping—with them.

Several passages in *Persuasion* stress the ubiquity of solipsism—the tendency to take our own perspectives for granted, and so to believe they are shared and valued by others. Such limitations signal a lack empathy in a technical sense, the inability to take other perspectives cognitively and emotionally. One of these passages is in the voice of the narrator, which means it is the narrator's perception rather than Anne's. This is important because the narrator in *Persuasion* is reliable, one whose views we trust. Anne's observations are frequently validated by according with the narrator's.

The narrator's observation comprises a rather famous passage about perception. Anne and Lady Russell have spent Christmas with the Musgroves, amid a level of noise that both have found nerve-racking. Anne wonders that the Musgroves aren't bothered by it, considering the anxious time they've had with Louisa. But Mrs. Musgrove observes that "after all she had gone through, nothing was so likely to do her good as a little quiet cheerfulness at home." Lady Russell's views are even stronger than Anne's: "'I hope I shall remember, in future,' said Lady Russell, as soon as they were reseated in the carriage, ' not to call at Uppercross in the Christmas holidays.'" The narrator comments,

Every body has their taste in noises as well as in other matters and sounds are quite innoxious, or most distressing, by their sort rather than their quantity. When Lady Russell, not long afterwards, was entering Bath on a wet afternoon, and driving through the long course of streets from the Old Bridge to Camden Place, amidst the dash of other carriages, the heavy rumble of carts and drays, the bawling of newsmen, muffin-men, and milkmen, and the ceaseless clink of pattens, she made no complaint. No, these were noises which belonged to the winter pleasures; her spirits rose under their influence; and, like Mrs. Musgrove, she was feeling, though not saying, that after being long in the country, nothing could be so good for her as a little quiet cheerfulness.

What I find so extraordinary about this paragraph is the insight that feelings influence not only thoughts about other people and our evaluations of experience, but our very sensory perceptions. The larger implication is that if desires and tastes can influence pure sense perception, then of course they influence what we think about, what we deem important, and how we assess people and situations around us. This isn't an unusual insight today, although it took until midway through the twentieth century for us to figure this out, but empiricism, the idea that all knowledge comes from sensory experience, and that such experiences are therefore trustworthy, was a dominant Enlightenment idea. Even Hume, who understood the power of emotion, didn't extend its sway to simple sensory perception; Hume was an empiricist.

Persuasion makes a point of showing that Anne, like the narrator (and Austen, of course!) similarly reflects on this cognitive bias. When it is decided that the Elliots will rent out Kellynch, everyone connected with the household is full of the subject. Sir Walter and Elizabeth worry about maintaining their dignity, of living in a style that broadcasts their superior rank and fortune, the latter, of course, greatly diminished, while Anne mourns leaving her beloved home, especially in autumn, the peak of the countryside's beauty. Sir Walter and Elizabeth assume everyone must be interested in their affairs. (In fact, their lawyer tells them they need not advertise the rental because people will just hear about it. One wonders what Mr. Shepherd actually did to get the word out!) But Anne knows better. Here is another passage worth citing at length:

Anne had not wanted this visit to Uppercross, to learn that a removal from one set of people to another, though at a distance of only three miles, will often include a total change of conversation, opinion, and idea. She had never been staying there before, without being struck by it, or without wishing that other Elliots could have her advantage in seeing how unknown, or unconsidered there, were the affairs which at Kellynch Hall were treated as of such general publicity and pervading interest; yet, with all this experience, she believed she must now submit to feel that another lesson, in the art of knowing our own nothingness beyond our own circle, was become necessary for her; for certainly, coming as she did, with a heart full of the subject which had been completely occupying both houses in Kellynch for many weeks, she had expected rather more curiosity and sympathy than she found [at Uppercross] . . . She acknowledged it to be very fitting, that every little social commonwealth should dictate its own matters of discourse; and hoped, ere long, to become a not unworthy member of the one she was now transplanted into. With the prospect of spending at least two months at Uppercross, it was highly incumbent on her to clothe her imagination, her memory, and all her ideas in as much of Uppercross as possible.

The passage is pure Anne. She understands that the focus at Uppercross will be different from that at Kellynch. And even further, Anne takes it as a lesson for herself about the necessity of blending in and entering into the life and concerns of those she'll be living among. This won't affect her behavior, because the way she's treated at Uppercross, as a combination of mediator, wise elder, and therapist, suggests that she's acted on this lesson many a time in past visits. But by figuring out even more about the limitations and the failures in empathy to which even well-meaning, benevolent people are all too vulnerable, Anne adds to her stock of knowledge about human nature.

Anne's social intelligence doesn't manifest itself only in her dealings with others, but in her own life as well. Of all Austen's heroines, Anne is the only one who doesn't need to learn a lesson in the course of the novel, whose maturity and acumen are as good as it gets for an imperfect species such as our own. That Marianne, Elizabeth, and

Emma have dramatic increases in self-knowledge is evident in their respective novels. The others heroines are impeccable most of the time, but not quite up to Anne's standard. In *Sense and Sensibility*, Elinor learns that she's been too closed and guarded with her beloved sister, a rare but important lapse for this fictional person. Fanny is nearly perfect, but not as feisty or confident as Anne; a realistic sense of self-esteem is an important aspect of social intelligence. And so, *Mansfield Park* is largely about Fanny's coming into her own. But at nineteen (Fanny's age when her novel begins), Anne is already there. The one who must learn a lesson in *Persuasion* is Wentworth, who might well say, along with Elizabeth, "I never knew myself." He must learn that what he's mistaken for indifference is really anger, pain, and love; he must learn to know his own mind and heart. And he must learn "to distinguish between the steadiness of principle and the obstinacy of self-will, between the darings of heedlessness and the resolution of a collected mind."

This distinction (made with FID voicing Anne's thoughts), refers to Wentworth's judgment of her for ending their engagement. For eight long years, Wentworth believed that this was the result of Anne's infirm, persuadable character. But of course he was wrong. Anne gave up the engagement because she believed it was the right thing to do. Lady Russell pointed out its dangers: Wentworth was a nobody in the Navy, without important connections and without an assured future. But Anne backs down not for fears of her own future, but out of concern for Wentworth: "Had she not imagined herself consulting his good, even more than her own, she could hardly have given him up." Even though loneliness and a terribly circumscribed life follow from this decision, Anne doesn't regret it, not even after she is reunited with Wentworth.

No other character in Austen's fiction is so closely identified with Austen as Anne. To begin with, they share the same ethics and values. Other fictional people might at times express opinions that are clearly Austen's, but in *Persuasion*, Anne unfailingly speaks for Austen. Let's add a third "character," the narrator, who, it is generally agreed, expresses Austen's views and whose opinions also match Anne's. These convergences make Anne a figure for the author, as literary critics say.

Indeed, on the topic of the novel's central event, the broken engage-ment, Anne, the narrator, and Austen agree: Anne was right to break the engagement on Lady Russell's advice, but such advice was wrong.

There's another shift here from Austen's other novels: In no other novel does a heroine believe that it would have been right to marry in such uncertain circumstances. In no other novel is love elevated so greatly above other concerns. We see one disaster that ensues from the marriage of a woman of good family with a naval officer in the Price household in *Mansfield Park*. Marianne of *Sense and Sensibility* thinks that love in a cottage will suffice, but her idea of a cottage is more like a mansion. How can we account for Austen's change of mind and heart, expressed through her heroine?

Austen wrote *Persuasion* while she was ill, and it's likely that in the course of her writing, she knew she would not get better. This might well account for *Persuasion*'s elegiac tone and shift in emphasis. The novel begins in autumn, Anne's favorite season, and at that point Anne appears to be in the autumn of her own life, although the happy ending will grant her "a second spring." Austen, at forty, likely felt that she too was in the autumn of her life, although she wasn't granted a similar recovery. As she lay ill, perhaps her priorities shifted somewhat. She had insisted on a balance between prudence and passion in her earlier novels, and this is still the case in *Persuasion*, although the weight of the terms has shifted. Anne believes she did the right thing by ending the engagement, but even so, "she felt that were any young person, in similar circumstances, to apply to her for counsel, they would never receive any of such certain immediate wretchedness, such uncertain future good. She was persuaded that under every disadvantage of dis-approbation at home, and every anxiety attending his profession, all their probable fears, delays and disappointments, she should yet have been a happier woman in maintaining the engagement, than she had been in the sacrifice of it."

In this reflection of Anne's, and throughout her story, *Persuasion* shows the value of love, as well as our intense need to love and be loved, and this applies even to the most secure among us. If you can enjoy a *perfect* (in the old sense of "whole") love with a partner, one that unites intimacy, friendship, and passion, you've discov-ered one of the greatest treasures this earthly life has to offer. It won't do to sacrifice your morals or your honor in the pursuit of personal happiness, but neither should you let pride or prejudice (and indeed, Wentworth forms a prejudice against Anne) or even excessive prudence interfere with your happiness.

Austen herself might have come close to finding Anne's happy ending in her own life. Biographer Jon Spence in *Becoming Jane Austen* suggests that Austen was romantically involved with a handsome young man, Thomas Lefroy, and that they wished to marry but had to refrain because of economic circumstances. The movie of the same title embellishes this episode, actually showing that the lovers began to elope. Jane backed out when she thought of what this would mean for Lefroy's family, who were all depending on him to provide an income. Burdened with a wife, it might well have been difficult for him to complete his law studies and start his career. That this flirtation with Lefroy (which Austen alludes to in her letters) indicated serious feelings on Austen's part is somewhat speculative, as Spence admits. And the film is pure fiction; there's no evidence that Austen ever thought of running off with someone. Perhaps Austen told all in her letters, much more than we know at any rate, but her sister, Cassandra, burned them after Austen's death to protect her privacy. But it's possible that Austen gave Anne the happy ending she didn't have.

While the same values and (possibly) a shared story identify Austen and Anne, it is in their thinking process that their convergence is most significant. Social neuroscience has been aptly defined as the science of "people thinking about thinking people." I've noted that this characterizes Anne, and of course it's spot-on about Austen. Portraying the attributes of the human mind with such extraordinary accuracy means that Austen frequently thought about people: what they want, what they need to have a sense of well-being, ways in which they're good and bad, ways in which they're strong and weak, how they perceive and how they react—all in the context of their relationships with one another. And of course, as you know, understanding people requires empathy, the highest form of social intelligence, possessed in abundance by both Austen and Anne.

Empathy. It's the moral behind every one of Austen's novels, the heart of the matter. Everyone wants a happy ending with a brilliant marriage, and likely Austen wanted this for herself as well. She didn't find the kind of intimate partnership she generously accorded her heroines, but she had many other kinds of love in her life: the love of a devoted sister, parents, aunts, cousins, nieces, nephews, friends. True love—authentic and mutual love—in all kinds of different relationships usually means understanding and resonating with someone else. It means seeing and feeling from another perspective. Walking a mile in someone else's shoes, as the saying goes.

I've suggested that we sense Austen's empathy for her readers through stories and fictional people that reflect our own feelings and desires as well as those of people we know. And not just the good ones. Austen can palpably convey the evil in Mr. Elliot as easily as she enables us to feel Darcy's awkwardness. Through her fictional people, these brainchildren of a brilliant mind, we sense empathy—resonance and understanding. Reading Austen's novels, we have the feeling of "feeling felt." Austen's ability to create compelling narratives and her extraordinary, witty style have earned her a reputation as one of England's greatest novelists. But I believe that empathy accounts for her tremendous popularity, for that sense of connection with her that's so very personal for so many of Austen's readers. I believe that in what she likely thought would be her last words, the story she tells in *Persuasion*, she wanted to leave us with a heroine who possessed her most precious ability, who shared the empathy that characterizes her writing.

In addition to a shift in emphasis and mood, we might notice another difference in *Persuasion*: Anne and her beloved Wentworth are the only Austen couple who don't end up living on property in the countryside. Given the almost continuous warfare that England sustained in the eighteenth century, Austen likely believed that a brilliant young officer like Wentworth would be seeing action again before too long. And so it's likely that Anne will end up leading an itinerant life much like that of Mrs. Croft, Captain Wentworth's sister.*

---

* In truth, the Napoleonic Wars ended in 1815 (with a treaty signed on November 20), and England was officially at peace for a significant period of time thereafter; the next major war was World War I, which England entered in 1914. Austen began writing *Persuasion* on August 8, 1815. However, we can still assume that Wentworth would be posted to different naval bases, even if he didn't fight in any large-scale wars. England might have enjoyed peace with other first-world powers, but the military fought local battles as England accrued an empire by conquering other lands.

By marrying an officer in the Navy, and moving about to be with him, Anne will touch many more lives than she would have done living on a country estate, even if she'd been the most charitable and conscientious patroness of those within her purview. We see how those who seek an authentic connection with her, such as Benwick, Harville, and, of course, Wentworth, benefit from having done so. Even those who can't appreciate her wisdom are better for inviting her into their lives. Mary is always better for Anne's company.

Just as many of us are better for Austen's company. It has yet to be proved whether or not reading fiction makes you more empathetic, with arguments on both sides of the question. It has been demonstrated that reading activates brain areas that would activate for the same situations in real life, which suggests that if you read about feelings, you're likely to feel them yourself to some degree. Most novels force us to take the perspective of other characters cognitively by relating to the world from their point of view. So it's likely we resonate with the feelings of fictional people and take their perspective. This is just to assert what every novel reader knows, that people tend to empathize when they read—otherwise, why would we care so deeply about characters, and why would we get so immersed in their stories? But do we take this capacity out into in the real world? And if so, does it make us more compassionate, better people?

As you can guess, I'm inclined to say that it does. But in any case, there's another connection between character and characters that might lead us to good works: learning by example. When we read, we don't distinguish between real and fictional people, and some of us continue to blur the boundaries well after having put the book aside. And so, just as we model ourselves on real people, we're subject to modeling ourselves on fictional people. We might not consciously say, "What would Anne do in this situation?" but for many readers, the question and the answer ripple through the cognitive unconscious, exerting subliminal influence. And some of us really do ask the question, and knowingly look to fictional people for ways to live in the real world.

In any case, the empathy we feel on identifying with characters can be comforting and validating. Perhaps reading about Marianne won't cure your broken heart, but you'll at least have the solace of company and the knowledge that there's a way back. Maybe reading about Anne won't make you a better person all the time, but you'll have a model of tact, compassion, understanding, and empathy to draw upon. Fictional worlds and fictional people give us procedural schemas for becoming our best selves.

And so, just as Austen sent her last, best heroine beyond the confines of the landed estate to work her magic within a wider sphere, she sent her books out into the world. In this sense, Anne is also a figure for the author, enacting in her person what Austen did in her books: touching hearts, minds, and lives. Both women are fit for the task. As Wentworth says, "[N]o one so proper, so capable as Anne." And as her readers have known, in many times and many places, no one so proper, so capable as Jane Austen.

SOURCES

A NOTE ON SOURCES

With the abundance of information being generated about the mind-brain, anyone who writes on the topic must pick and choose among resources. I will list the books, articles, and other media that I've found to be particularly relevant to the topic at hand for each chapter. In many of the sources I cite, you can usually find dozens of references to a given topic. To use the metaphor originated by the twelfth-century ecclesiastic, Bernard of Chartres, whatever I've learned about the mind-brain, it has been by standing on the shoulders of giants.

The book that imbues all my thinking in *Jane on the Brain* is Daniel Siegel's *The Developing Mind*, originally published in 2001. This book inspired my study of the mind-brain, which eventually led to my career as a therapist. Dr. Siegel has recently updated and expanded material for the second edition. See Daniel Siegel, *The Developing Mind, Second Edition: How Relationships and the Brain Interact to Shape Who We Are* (New York, The Guilford Press: 2015).

For my basic account of neuroscience—brain anatomy and function—I've relied on Michael S. Gazzaniga, Richard B. Ivry, and George R. Mangun, *Cognitive Neuroscience: The Biology of the Mind, Fourth Edition* (New York: W. W. Norton & Company, 2013).

I will cite appropriate chapters from these two books in the sources for individual chapters.

I include the sources most relevant to the discussion at the end of each chapter. There is a significant amount of overlap in this material. For instance, books cited for chapters on the emotions are likely to be relevant to other chapters, although I don't necessarily duplicate the citation.

The following books are useful introductions to social intelligence, the mind-brain, and Jane Austen's life and times.

Ackerman, Diane. *An Alchemy of Mind: The Marvel and Mystery of the Brain*. New York: Scribner, 2004.

Adkins, Roy and Leslie Adkins. *Jane Austen's England: Daily Life in the Georgian and Regency Periods*. New York: Penguin, 2014.

Carter, Rita. *Mapping the Mind*, Revised Updated Edition. Chapel Hill: University of North Carolina Press, 2010.

———. *The Human Brain*. London, New York: Dorling Kindersley, 2014.

Davidoff, Leonore. *The Best Circles*. London: The Ebury Press, 1986.

Goleman, Daniel. *Emotional Intelligence: Why It Can Matter More than IQ*. New York: Random House, 2005.

———. *Social Intelligence: The New Science of Social Relationships*. New York: Random House, 2007.

Klingel, Joan Ray. *Jane Austen for Dummies*. Hoboken, N.J.: Wiley. 2006.

O'Shea, Michael. *The Brain: A Very Short Introduction*. Very Short Introductions. Oxford, England: Oxford University Press, 2005.

Siegel, Daniel. *Pocket Guide to Interpersonal Biology: An Integrative Handbook of the Mind*. Norton Interpersonal Neurobiology. New York: W. W. Norton & Company, 2012.

Spence, Jon. *Becoming Jane Austen*. New York: Continuum, 2007.

Ratey, John J. *A User's Guide to the Brain: Perception, Attention, and the Four Theaters of the Brain*. New York: Vintage, 2002.

Tomalin, Claire. *Jane Austen: A Life*. New York: Vintage, 2007.

Pinel, John P. J. and Maggie Edwards. *A Colorful Introduction to the Anatomy of the Human Brain: A Brain and Psychology Coloring Book*, 2nd Edition. London: Pearson, 2007.

Pool, Daniel. *What Jane Austen Ate and Charles Dickens Knew: From Fox-Hunting to Whist—the Facts of Daily Life in Nineteenth-Century England*. New York: Touchstone, 1994.

CHAPTER ONE: PRECIOUS FEELINGS

Barret, Lisa Feldman. "Are Emotions Natural Kinds?" *Perspectives on Psychological Science* 1, no. 1 (2006): 28–58.

———. *How Emotions Are Made: The Secret Life of the Brain*. New York: Houghton Mifflin Harcourt, 2017.

Braitman, Laurel. *Animal Madness: How Anxious Dogs, Compulsive Parrots, and Elephants in Recovery Help Us Understand Ourselves*. New York: Simon & Schuster, 2014.

Damasio, Antonio. *Looking for Spinoza: Joy, Sorrow, and the Feeling Brain*. New York: Harcourt, 2003.

De Gelder, Beatrice, "Uncanny Sight in the Blind," *Scientific American* 302 (2010): 60–65.

De Gelder, Beatrice, Jean Vrooman, and Larry Weiskrantz. "Non-Conscious Recognition of Affect in the Absence of Striate Cortex." *Neuroreport* 10, no. 18 (1999): 3759–3763.

De Waal, Frans. *Are We Smart Enough to Know How Smart Animals Are?* New York: W. W. Norton & Company, 2017.

Ekman, Paul. *Emotion in the Human Face.* Palo Alto, Calif.: Malor Books, 2015.

Evans, Dylan. *Emotions: A Very Short Introduction.* Very Short Introductions Series. New York: Oxford University Press, 2010.

Fox, Elaine. *Emotion Science: Cognitive and Neuroscientific Approaches to Understanding Human Emotions.* London: Palgrave Macmillan, 2008.

Gazzaniga, Michael S., Richard B. Ivry, and George R. Mangun. "Emotion." In *Cognitive Neuroscience: The Biology of Mind*, 424–467. New York: W. W. Norton & Company, 2013.

LeDoux, Joseph. *The Emotional Brain: The Mysterious Underpinnings of Emotional Life.* New York: Simon & Schuster, 1998.

Gazzaniga, Michael S., Richard B. Ivry, and George R. Mangun. "Emotion." In *Cognitive Neuroscience: The Biology of Mind*, 424–467. New York: W. W. Norton & Company, 2013.

Hobaiter, Catherine and Richard W. Byrne. "The Gestural Repertoire of the Wild Chimpanzee." *Animal Cognition* 14, no. 5 (2011): 745–767.

Keltner, Dacher, Keith Oatley, and Jennifer M. Jenkins. *Understanding Emotions.* New York: Wiley, 2013.

Lamb, Susan. *Bringing Travel Home to England: Tourism, Gender, and Imaginative Literature.* Newark, Del.: University of Delaware Press, 2009.

LeDoux, Joseph. *The Emotional Brain: The Mysterious Underpinnings of Emotional Life.* New York: Simon & Schuster, 1998.

Lewis, C. S. *The Discarded Image.* Canto Classic Series. Cambridge, England: Cambridge University Press, 2012.

McCrae, Robert R. and Paul T. Costa, Jr. "Personality Trait Structure as a Human Universal." *American Psychologist* 52 (1997): 509–516.

Panksepp, Jaak. *Affective Neuroscience: The Foundation of Human and Animal Emotions.* New York: Oxford University Press, 1998.

———, and Douglas Watt. "What is Basic About Basic Emotions? Lasting Lessons from Affective Neuroscience." *Emotion Review* 3, no. 4 (2011): 1–10.

———, and Lucy Biven. *The Archaeology of Mind: Neuroevolutionary Origins of Human Emotions.* Norton Series on Interpersonal Neurobiology. New York: W. W. Norton & Company, 2012.

Pentland, Alex. *Honest Signals: How They Shape Our World.* Cambridge, Mass.: MIT Press, 2010.

Prinz, Jesse. "Which Emotions Are Basic?" In *Emotion, Evolution, and Rationality*, edited by Dylan Evans and Pierre Cruse, 69–88. New York: Oxford University Press, 2004.

Rolls, Edmund T. *Emotions Explained.* New York: Oxford University Press, 2005.

Siegel, Daniel "Emotion." In *The Developing Mind, Second Edition: How Relationships and the Brain Interact to Shape Who We Are*, 146–185. New York: The Guilford Press, 2012.

Trull, Timothy J. and Thomas A. Widiger. "Dimensional Models of Personality: The Five-Factor Model and the DSM-5." *Dialogues in Clinical Neuroscience* 15, no. 2 (2013): 135–46.

CHAPTER TWO: *PRIDE AND PREJUDICE* AND BRAINS

Barrett, Louise. *Beyond the Brain: How Body and Environment Shape Animal and Human Minds*. Princeton, N.J.: Princeton University Press, 2015.

Cozolino, Louis. "Focus on the Amygdala." In *The Neuroscience of Human Relationships: Attachment and the Developing Social Brain*, 164–168. New York: W. W. Norton & Company, 2006.

Edelman, Shimon. *Computing the Mind*. New York: Oxford University Press, 2008.

Gage, Fred H. "Neurogenesis in the Adult Brain." *Journal of Neuroscience* 22, no.3 (2002): 612–613.

Gazzaniga, Michael S., Richard B. Ivry, and George R. Mangun. "Sensation and Perception." In *Cognitive Neuroscience: The Biology of Mind*, 162–217. New York: W. W. Norton & Company, 2013.

———, Richard B. Ivry, and George R. Mangun. "Structure and Function of the Nervous System." In *Cognitive Neuroscience: The Biology of Mind*, 22–69. New York: W. W. Norton & Company, 2013.

Hobaiter, Catherine and Richard W. Byrne. "The Meanings of Chimpanzee Gestures." *Current Biology* 24, no. 14 (2014): 1596–1600. "Infinite Monkey Theorem." *WhatIs.com?* http://whatis.techtarget.com/definition/Infinite-Monkey-Theorem. Retrieved August 4, 2017.

Kelso, Scott J. A. *Dynamic Patterns: The Self-Organization of Brain and Behavior*. Cambridge, Mass.: MIT Press, 1995.

Lakoff, George and Mark Johnson. *Philosophy in the Flesh*. New York: Basic Books, 1999.

LeDoux, Joseph. *Synaptic Self: How Our Brains Become Who We Are*. New York: Penguin, 2003.

Mayer, Emeran. *The Mind-Gut Connection: How the Hidden Conversation Within Our Bodies Impacts Our Mood, Our Choices, and Our Overall Health*. New York: Harper Wave, 2016.

Mehl-Madrona, Lewis. *Healing the Mind Through the Power of Story: The Promise of Narrative Psychiatry*. Rochester, Vt.: Bear and Company, 2010.

"Monkeys at Typewriters 'close to reproducing Shakespeare.'" *The Telegraph*. http://www.telegraph.co.uk/technology/news/8789894/Monkeys-at-typewriters-close-to-reproducing-Shakespeare.html. Retrieved August 4, 2017.

Montgomery, Arlene. *Neurobiology Essentials for Clinicians: What Every Therapist Needs to Know*. New York: W. W. Norton & Company, 2013.

Rolls, Edmund T. and McCabe, Ciara. "Enhanced Affective Brain Representations of Chocolate in Cravers Vs. Non-Cravers." *European Journal of Neuroscience* 26 (2007): 1067–1076.

Shaw, Peter Knox. *Jane Austen and the Enlightenment*. Cambridge, England: Cambridge University Press, 2009.

Siegel, Daniel. "Integration" In *The Developing Mind, Second Edition: How Relation-ships and the Brain Interact to Shape Who We Are,* 336–377. New York: The Guilford Press, 2012.

———. "States of Mind: Cohesion Subjective Experience, and Complex Systems." In *The Developing Mind, Second Edition: How Relationships and the Brain Interact to Shape Who We Are,* 186–218. New York: The Guilford Press, 2012.

———. *Mind: A Journey to the Heart of Being Human.* New York: W. W. Norton & Company, 2016.

Swanson, Larry W. *Brain Architecture: Understanding the Basic Plan.* Oxford, England: Oxford University Press, 2011.

Thelan, Esther. "Dynamic Systems Theory and the Complexity of Change." *Psychoanalytic Dialogues* 15, no. 2. (2005): 255–283.

University of Pennsylvania. "Young Children Have Grammar and Chimpanzees Don't." *Science Daily.* April 10, 2013. www.sciencedaily.com/releases/2013/04/130410131327.htm. Retrieved August 4, 2017.

Varela, Francisco J., Evan Thompson, and Eleanor Rosch. *The Embodied Mind and Human Experience,* 2nd ed. (Cambridge, Mass.: MIT Press, 2017).

CHAPTER THREE: THE SENSE OF SENSIBILITY

Adolphs, Ralph, Daniel Tranel, Hanna Damasio, and Antonio R. Damasio. "Fear and the Human Amygdala." *Journal of Neuroscience* 15, no. 9 (1995): 5879–5891.

Carter, Sid and Marcia Smith Pasqualini. "Stronger Autonomic Response Accompanies Better Learning: A Test of Damasio's Somatic Marker Hypothesis." *Cognition and Emotion* 18, no. 7 (2010): 901–911.

Craske, Michelle G. *Cognitive Behavioral Therapy.* Theories of Psychotherapy. Washington, D.C.: American Psychological Association (2010).

Damasio, Antonio. *Descartes' Error: Emotion, Reason, and the Human Brain.* Reprint ed. New York: Penguin, 2005. First published 1995 by Harper Perennial.

———. *Looking for Spinoza: Joy, Sorrow, and the Feeling Brain.* New York: Harvest, 2003.

———. *Self Comes to Mind: Constructing the Conscious Brain.* New York: Pantheon Books, 2010.

Duncan, Seth and Lisa Feldman Barrett. "Affect is a Form of Cognition: A Neurobiological Analysis." *Cognition and Emotion* 21, no. 6 (2007): 1184–1211.

Feinstein, Justin S., Colin Buzza, Rene Hurlemann, Robin L. Follmer, Nader S. Dahdaleh, William H. Coryell, Michael Welsh, Daniel Tranel, and John A. Wemmie. "Fear and Panic in Humans with Bilateral Amygdala Damage." *Nature Neuroscience* 16 no. 3 (2013): 270–272.

———, Ralph Adolphs, Antonio Damasio, and Daniel Tranel. "The Human Amygdala and the Induction and Experience of Fear." *Current Biology* 21, no. 1 (2011): 34–38.

Gläscher, Jan, Ralph Adolphs, Hanna Damasio, Antoine Bechara, David Rudrauf, Matthew Calamia, Lynn K. Paul and Daniel Tranel. "Lesion Mapping of Cognitive Control and Value-Based Decision Making in the Prefrontal Cortex." *PNAS* 109, no. 36 (2012): 14681–14686.

Hatfield, Elaine, Richard L. Rapson, and Yen-Chi L. Le. "Emotional Contagion and Empathy" In *The Social Neuroscience of Empathy*, eds. Jean Decety and William Ickes, 19–30. Cambridge, Mass.: MIT Press, 2009.

Hennenlotter, Andreas, Christian Dresel, Florian Castrop, Andres O. Ceballo-Baumann, Afra M. Wohlschläger, and Bernhard Haslinger. "The Link Between Facial Feedback and Neural Activity within Central Circuitries of Emotion—New Insights from Botulinum Toxin-Induced Denervation of Frown Muscles," *Cerebral Cortex* 19, no. 3 (2008): 537–42.

Hume, David. *A Treatise of Human Nature*. New York: Penguin, 1985.

Knox-Shaw, Peter. *Jane Austen and the Enlightenment*. Cambridge, England: Cambridge University Press: 2009.

Kramer, Peter. *Against Depression*. New York: Penguin, 2006.

Noonan, M. P., N. Kolling, M. W. Walton, and M.F.S. Rushworth. "Re-Evaluating the Role of the Orbitofrontal Cortex in Reward and Reinforcement." *European Journal of Neuroscience* 35 (2012): 997–1010.

Phelps, Elizabeth. "Emotion and Cognition: Insights from the Study of the Human Amygdala." *Annual Review of Psychology* 57 (2006): 27–53.

Porges, Stephen W. "The Polyvagal Perspective." *Biological Psychology* 74 (2007): 116–143.

———. *The Polyvagal Theory: Neurophysiological Foundations of Emotions, Attachment, and Self-Regulation*. New York: W. W. Norton & Company, 2011.

Reimann, Martin and Bechara, Antoine. "The Somatic Marker Hypothesis as a Neurological Theory of Decision-Making: Review, Conceptual Comparisons, and Future Neuroeconomics Research." *Journal of Economic Psychology* 31, no. 5 (2010): 767–776.

Sapolsky, Robert M. Why Zebras Don't Get Ulcers. 3rd ed. New York: Holt Paperbacks, 2004.

Schaik, Carel P. and Judith M. Burkart. "Social Learning and Evolution: The Cultural Intelligence Hypothesis." *Philosophical Transactions of the Royal Society B* 366, no. 1567 (2011): 1008–1016.

Shaw, Peter Knox. *Jane Austen and the Enlightenment*. Cambridge, Mass.: Cambridge University Press, 2009.

Siegel, Daniel. "Emotion." In *The Developing Mind, Second Edition: How Relationships and the Brain Interact to Shape Who We Are*, 146–185. New York: The Guilford Press, 2012.

Spezio, Michael L., Po-Yin Samuel Huang, Fulvia Castelli, and Ralph Adolphs. "Amygdala Damage Impairs Eye Contact During Conversations with Real People. *Journal of Neuroscience* 11, no 15 (2007): 3994–3997.

Tomasello, Michael. *A Natural History of Human Morality*. Cambridge, Mass.: Harvard University Press, 2014.

CHAPTER FOUR: I NEVER KNEW MYSELF

Bazan, Ariane, Howard Shevrin, Linda A. W. Brakel, and Michael Snodgrass. "Motivations and Emotions Contribute to a Rational Unconscious Dynamics: Evidence and Conceptualization." *Cortex* 43 (2007): 1104–1105.

Cary, Benedict. "H.M., and Unforgettable Amnesiac, Dies at 82." *New York Times*, December 4, 2008. http://www.nytimes.com/2008/12/05/us/05hm.html.

Cherry, Colin E. "Some Experiments on the Recognition of Speech, with One and Two Ears." *Journal of the Acoustical Society of America*, 25, no. 5 (1953): 975–979.

Corkin, Suzanne. *Permanent Present Tense: The Unforgettable Life of the Amnesic Patient, H. M.* New York: Basic Books, 2013.

Damasio, Antonio. *Descartes' Error: Emotion, Reason, and the Human Brain.* Reprint ed. New York: Penguin, 2005. First published 1995 by Harper Perennial.

———. *Self Comes to Mind: Construction the Conscious Brain.* New York: Pantheon Books, 2010.

Dunn, Barnaby D., Tim Dalgleish and Andrew D. Lawrence. "The Somatic Marker Hypothesis: A Critical Evaluation." *Neuroscience and Biobehavioral Reviews* 39. (2006): 239–271.

Fink, Bruce. *A Clinical Introduction to Freud: Techniques for Everyday Practice.* New York: W. W. Norton & Company, 2017.

Gazzaniga, Michael S. "The Split Brain in Man." *Scientific American* 217, no.2 (1967): 24–29.

———. "The Split Brain Revisited." *Scientific American* (2002): 27–31.

———, Richard B. Ivry, and George R. Mangun ."Hemispheric Specialization." In *Cognitive Neuroscience: The Biology of Mind*, 120–159 . New York: W. W. Norton & Company, 2013.

———, Richard B. Ivry, and George R. Mangun. "Memory." In *Cognitive Neuroscience: The Biology of Mind*, 378–418. New York: W. W. Norton & Company, 2013.

Gigerenzer, Gerd. *Gut Feelings: The Intelligence of the Unconscious.* New York: Penguin, 2007.

Herman, Judith. *Trauma and Recovery: The Aftermath of Violence.* New York: Basic Books, 2015.

Hornstein, G. A. "The Return of the Repressed: Psychology's Problematic Relations with Psychoanalysis, 1909–1960." *American Psychologist* 47, no. 2 (1992): 254–263.

"Information for Health Care Professionals: Corpus Callosotomy." *Epilepsy Foundation.* http://www.epilepsy.com/information/professionals/ diagnosis-treatment/surgery/corpus-callosotomy

Kahn, Michael. *Basic Freud: Psychoanalytic Thought for the Twenty-First Century.* New York: Basic Books, 2002.

Kihlstrom, J. F. "The Cognitive Unconsious." *Science* 237, no. 4821 (1987): 1445–52.

————, Terrence M. Barnhardt, and Douglas J. Tataryn. "The Psychological Unconscious: Found, Lost, and Regained." *American Psychologist* 47, no. 6 (1992): 788.

LeDoux, Joseph E., Donald H. Wilson, and Michael S. Gazzaniga. "A Divided Mind: Observations of the Conscious Properties of the Separated Hemispheres." *Annals of Neurology* 2, no. 5 (1977): 417–421.

McKay, Ryan, Robyn Langdon, and Max Coltheart. "'Sleights of Mind': Delusions, Defences, and Self-Deception." *Cognitive Neuropsychiatry* 10, no. 4 (2005): 305–326.

———— and Mike Anderson. "Reconciling Psychodynamic and Neurological Perspectives on Denial." *Cortex* 43 (2007).

Milner, Brenda. "The Effect of Hippocampal Lesions on Recent Memory." *Transactions of the American Neurological Association* (1956–7): 42–48.

————. "Brenda Milner." In *The History of Neuroscience in Autobiography Vol. 2*. ed. Larry R. Squire, 278–305. New York: Academic Press, 1998.

Mlodinow, Leonard. *Subliminal: How Your Unconscious Mind Rules Your Behavior.* New York: Pantheon, 2012.

Pribram, Karl. "Freud Through the Centuries." *Cortex* 43 (2007): 1108–1110.

Prinz, Jessie. *Gut Reactions: A Perceptual Theory of Emotion.* Oxford, England: Oxford University Press, 2004.

Schore, Allan N. "The Right Brain Implicit Self Lies at the Core of Psychoanalysis." In *The Science of the Art of Psychotherapy*, 118–151. New York: W. W. Norton & Company, 2012.

Siegel, Daniel "Memory." In *The Developing Mind, Second Edition: How Relationships and the Brain Interact to Shape Who We Are*, 46–90. New York: The Guilford Press, 2012.

Skinner, B. F. *Walden Two.* New York: Macmillan, 1968.

Tamietto, Marco and Beatrice de Gelder. "Neural Bases of the Non-Conscious Perception of Emotional Signals." *Nature Reviews Neuroscience* 11 (2010): 697–709.

Turnbull, Oliver H. and Mark Solms. "Awareness, Desire, and False Beliefs: Freud in the Light of Modern Neuropsychology." *Cortex* 43, no. 8 (2007): 1083–1090.

Winkielman, Piotr, and Kent C. Berridge. "Unconscious Emotion." *Current Directions in Psychological Science* (2004): 120–123.

————, Kent C. Berridge, and Julia L. Wilbarger "Unconscious Affective Reactions to Masked Happy Versus Angry Faces Influence Consumption Behavior and Judgments of Value." *Personality and Social Psychology Bulletin* 31, no. 1 (2005): 121–135.

CHAPTER FIVE: CHANGING YOUR MIND

Andrews, Paul W. and J. Anderson Thompson. "The Bright Side of Being Blue: Depression as an Adaptation for Analyzing Complex Problems." *Psychological Review* 116, no. 3 (2009): 620–654.

Banks, Sarah J., Kamryn T. Eddy, Mike Angstadt, Pradeep J. Nathan, and
     K. Luan Phan. "Amygdala-Frontal Connectivity During Emotional
     Regulation." *Social Cognitive and Affective Neuroscience* 2, no. 4 (2007):
     303–312.
Cozolino, Louis. *The Neuroscience of Psychotherapy: Healing the Social Brain*. 3rd
     ed. Norton Series on Neurobiology. New York: W. W. Norton & Company,
     2017.
———. *Why Therapy Works: Using Our Minds to Change Our Brains*. Norton Series
     on Neurobiology New York: W. W. Norton & Company, 2015.
Fosha, Diane. *The Transforming Power of Affect: A Model for Accelerated Change*.
     New York: Basic Books, 2000.
Ernst, Aurélie and Jonas Frisén. "Adult Neurogenesis in Humans: Common and
     Unique Traits in Mammals." *PLoS Biology*, 13, no. 1 (2015): e1002045.
Gross, Charles G. "Neurogenesis in the Adult Brain: Death of a Dogma." *Nature
     Reviews Neuroscience* 1, no. 1 (2000): 67–73.
Gross, James J. "Emotional Regulation: Conceptual and Empirical Foundations."
     In *Handbook of Emotion Regulation*. 2nd ed., ed. James J. Gross, 3–20. New
     York: The Guilford Press, 2015.
Herman, Judith. *Trauma and Recovery: The Aftermath of Violence—From Domestic
     Abuse to Political Terror*. New York: Basic Books, 2015, 133.
Jacobs, B. L., H. Van Praag, and F. H. Gage. "Adult Brain Neurogenesis and
     Psychiatry: A Novel Theory of Depression." *Molecular Psychiatry* 5, no. 3
     (2000): 262–269.
Kandel, Eric. "Eric Kandel." In *The History of Neuroscience in Autobiography*, vol.
     9, eds. Thomas D. Albright and Larry R. Squire, 166–219. New York: The
     Society for Neuroscience, 2016.
———. *In Search of Memory: The Emergence of a New Science of Mind*. New York: W.
     W. Norton & Company, 2007.
———. "Psychotherapy and the Single Synapse." *New England Journal of Medicine*
     301, no. 19 (1979): 1028–1037.
Lau, Beth. "Optimism and Pessimism: Approaching *Sense and Sensibility*
     Through Cognitive Therapy," *Persuasions: The Jane Austen Journal* 33
     (2011): 40–52.
Mehl-Madrona, Lewis. *Healing the Mind Through the Power of Story: The Promise of
     Narrative Psychiatry*. Rochester, Vt.: Bear and Company, 2010.
Shapiro, Francine and Margot Silk Forrest. *EMDR: The Breakthrough Therapy
     for Overcoming Anxiety, Stress, and Trauma*, Updated ed. New York: Basic
     Books, 2016.
Van der Kolk, Bessel. *The Body Keeps the Score: Brain, Mind, and Body in the Healing
     of Trauma*. New York: Penguin, 2015.
Wachtel, Paul L. *Therapeutic Communication: Knowing What to Say When*. New
     York: The Guilford Press. 2011
Wallen, David J. *Attachment in Psychotherapy*. New York: The Guilford Press, 2007.

CHAPTER SIX: THE MAP OF LOVE

Bartels, Andreas and Semir Zeki. "The Neural Basis of Romantic Love." *NeuroReport* 11, no. 17 (2000): 3829–3833.

—— and Semir Zeki. "The Neural Correlatetes of Maternal and Romantic Love." *NeuroImage* 21 (2004): 1155–1166.

Berridge, Kent C. "The Debate Over Dopamine's Role in Reward: The Case for Incentive Salience." *Psychopharmacology* 191 (2007): 391–431.

Buchheim, Anna, Markus Heinrichs, Carol George, Dan Pokorny, Eva Koops, Peter Henningsen, Mary-Frances O'Connor, and Harald Gündel. "Oxytocin Enhances the Experience of Attachment Security." *Psychoneuroendocrinology* 34, no. 9 (2009): 1417–1472.

Burnham, T. C., J. Flynn Chapman, P. B. Gray, M. H. McIntyre, S. F. Lipson, and P. T. Ellison. "Men in Committed Romantic Relationships Have Lower Testosterone." *Hormones and Behavior* 44, no. 2 (2003): 119–22.

Fisher, Helen. *Anatomy of Love: A Natural History of Mating, Marriage, and Why We Stray, Completely Revised and Updated with a New Introduction.* New York: W. W. Norton & Company, 2016.

——. *Why We Love: The Nature and Chemistry of Romantic Love.* New York: Holt Paperbacks, 2005.

——, Arthur Aron, and Lucy L. Brown. "Romantic Love: An fMRI Study of a Neural Mechanism for Mate Choice." *The Journal of Comparative Neurology* 493 (2005): 58–62.

Gray, Peter B., Sonya M. Kahlenberg, Emily S. Barrett, Susan F. Lipson, and Peter T. Ellison. "Marriage and Fatherhood Are Associated with Lower Testosterone in Males." *Evolution and Human Behavior* 23 (2002): 193–201.

Handlin, Linda, Eva Hydbring-Sandberg, Anne Nilsson, Mikael Ejdebäck, Anna Jansson, and Kerstin Uvnäs-Moberg. "Short-Term Interaction Between Dogs and Their Owners: Effects on Oxytocin, Cortisol, Insulin and Heart Rate—An Exploratory Study." *Anthrozoös* 24, no. 3 (2011): 301–315.

Hefferman, Marie E. and R. Chris Fraley. "How Early Experiences Shape Attraction, Partner Preferences, and Attachment Dynamics." In *Bases of Adult Attachment*, ed. Vivian Zayas and Cindy Hazan, 107–128. New York: Springer, 2015.

Heinrichs, Markus, Bernadette von Dawans, and Gregor Domes. "Oxytocin, Vasopressin, and Human Social Behavior." *Frontiers in Neuroendocrinology* 30 (2009): 548–557.

—— and Gregor Domes. "Neuropeptides and Social Behaviour: Effects of Oxytocin and Vasopressin in Humans." *Progress in Brain Research* 170 (2008): 337–350.

Hogan, Patrick Colm. *The Mind and Its Stories: Narrative Universals and Human Emotion.* Cambridge, England: Cambridge University Press, 2009.

Horstman, Judith. *The Scientific American Book of Love, Sex, and the Brain: The Neuroscience of How, When, Why, and Who We Love.* New York: Jossey-Bass, 2012.

Leyton, Marco. "The Neurobiology of Desire: Dopamine and the Regulation of Mood and Motivational States in Humans." In *Pleasures of the Brain,* eds. Morten L. Kringelback and Kent C. Berridge, 222–243. Oxford, England: Oxford University Press, 2010.

Komisaruk, Barry R., Beverly Whipple, and Carlos Beyer. "Sexual Pleasure." In *Pleasures of the Brain*, eds. Morten L. Kringelback and Kent C. Berridge, 169–177. Oxford, England: Oxford University Press, 2010.

McMurran, Mary Helen. *The Spread of Novels: Translation and Prose Fiction in the Eighteenth Century.* Princeton, N.J.: Princeton University Press, 2009.

Nagasawa, Miho, Shouhei Mitsui, Hiori En, Nobuyo Ohtani, Yasuo Sakuma, Tatsushi Onaka, Kazutaka Mogi, and Takefumi Kikusui. "Oxytocin-Gaze Positive Loop and the Coevolution of Human-Dog Bonds." *Science* 348, no. 6232 (2015): 333–336.

Olff, Miranda, Jessie L. Frilling, Laura D. Kubzansky, Bekh Bradley, Mark A. Ellenbogen, Christopher Cordoso, Jennifer A. Bartz, Jason R. Yee, and Mirjam van Zuiden. "The Role of Oxytocin in Social Bonding, Stress Regulation and Mental Health: An Update on the Moderating Effects of Context and Interindividual Differences." *Psychoneuroendocrinology* 38, no. 9 (2013): 1883–94.

Panksepp, Jaak. *Affective Neuroscience: The Foundation of Human and Animal Emotions.* Series in Affective Neuroscience. Oxford, England: Oxford University Press, 2004.

Ryan, Christopher and Cacilda Jethá. *Sex At Dawn: The Prehistoric Origins of Modern Sexuality.* New York: HarperCollins, 2010.

Salamone, John D. "Functions of Mesolimbic Dopamine: Changing Concepts and Shifting Paradigms." *Psychopharmacology* 191, no. 3 (2007): 389–389.

Song, Hongwen, Zhiling Zou, Juan Kou, Liu Yang, Lizhuang Yang, Anna Zilverstand, Federico d'Oleire Uquillas, and Xiaochu Zhang. "Love-Related Changes in the Brain: A Resting-State Functional Magnetic Resonance Imaging Study." *Frontiers in Human Neuroscience* (2015): https://doi.org/103389/fnhum.2015.00071.

Scudéry, Madeleine de. *Clélie: Histoire Romaine,* ed. Delphine Denis. 1654–60. Paris: Gallimard, 2006.

Tallis, Frank. *Love Sick: Love as a Mental Illness.* New York: Thunder's Mouth Press, 2004.

Young, Larry, and Brian Alexander. *The Chemistry Between Us: Love, Sex, and the Science of Attraction.* New York: Penguin, 2012.

Young, Larry J. and Zuoxin Wang. "The Neurobiology of Pair Bonding." *Nature Neuroscience* 7, no. 10 (2004): 1048–1054.

CHAPTER SEVEN: TIES THAT BOND

Ainsworth, Mary D. Salter, Mary C. Blehar, Everett Waters, and Sally N. Wall. *Patterns of Attachment: A Psychological Study of the Strange Situation.* Abingdon (England): Psychology Press and Routledge Classic Editions, 2015. First published 1978 by Lawrence Earlbaum Associates.

Atzil, Shir, Talma Hendler, and Ruth Feldman. "Specifying the Neurobiological Basis of Human Attachment: Brain, Hormones, and Behavior in Synchronous and Intrusive Mothers." *Neuropsychopharmacology* 36 (2011): 2603–2615.

Bowlby, John. *A Secure Base: Parent-Child Attachment and Healthy Human Development.* New York: Basic Books, 1988.

———. *Attachment and Loss,* Three Volume Set. New York: Basic Books, 1969.

———, Margery Fry, and Mary D. Salter (Ainsworth). *Child Care and the Growth of Love.* London: Pelican, 1953.

Bowlby, Rachel. *A Child of One's Own: Parental Stories.* Oxford, England: Oxford University Press, 2013.

Bretherton, Inge. "The Origins of Attachment Theory: John Bowlby and Mary Ainsworth." *Developmental Psychology* 28 (1992): 759–775.

Buchheim, Anna, Markus Heinrichs, Carol George, Dan Pokorny, Eva Koops, Peter Henningsen, Mary-Frances O'Connor, and Harald Gündel. "Oxytocin Enhances the Experience of Attachment Security." *Psychoneuroendocrinology* 34 (2009): 1417–1422.

Cozolino, Louis. *The Neuroscience of Human Relationships: Attachment and the Developing Social Brain,* 2nd Edition. New York: W. W. Norton & Company, 2014.

Duschinsky, Robbie. "The Emergence of the Disorganized/Disoriented (D) Attachment Classification, 1979–1982." *History of Psychology* 18, no. 1 (2015): 32–46.

Edelman, Shimon. *Computing the Mind.* New York: Oxford University Press, 2008.

Feeney, Judith A. and Patricia Noller. "Attachment Style as a Predictor of Adult Romantic Relationships." *Journal of Personality and Social Psychology* 58, no. 2 (1991): 281–291.

Francis, Richard C. *Epigenetics: How Environment Shapes Our Genes.* New York: W. W. Norton & Company, 2012.

Heinrichs, Markus, Bernadette von Dawans and Gregor Domes. "Oxytocin, Vasopressin, and Human Social Behavior." *Frontiers in Neuroendocrinology* 30 (2009): 548–557.

Hesse, Erik. "The Adult Attachment Interview: Protocol, Method of Analysis and Empirical Studies: 1985–2015." In *Handbook of Attachment: Theory, Research, and Clinical Applications* 3rd ed., eds. Jude Cassidy and Phillip R. Shaver, 553–597. New York: The Guilford Press, 2016.

Holmes, Jeremy. *The Search for the Secure Base: Attachment Theory and Psychotherapy.* Sussex, England: Brunner-Routledge, 2001.

Hrdy, Sarah Blaffer. *Mothers and Others: The Evolutionary Origins of Mutual Understanding.* Cambridge, Mass.: The Belknap Press, 2011.

Joiner, Thomas. *Why People Die by Suicide.* Cambridge, Mass.: Harvard University Press, 2007.

Levine, Amir and Rachel Heller. *Attached: The New Science of Adult Attachment and How It Can Help You Find—And Keep—Love.* New York: TarcherPerigree, 2012.

Lewis, Thomas, Fari Amini, and Richard Lannon. *A General Theory of Love.* New York: Vintage Books, 2000.

Mahler, Margaret, Fred Pine, and Anni Bergman. *The Psychological Birth of the Human Infant: Symbiosis and Individuation.* New York: Basic Books, 1975.

Main, M. and Judith Solomon. "Discovery of a New Insecure-Disorganized/Disoriented Attachment Pattern." In *Affective Development in Infancy*, edited by M. Yogman and T. B. Brazelton, 95–124. New York: Ablex, 1986.

Mikulincer, Mario and Phillip R. Shaver. *Attachment in Adulthood: Structure, Dynamics, and Change.* New York: The Guilford Press, 2007.

Moriceau, Stephanie and Regina M. Sullivan. "Neurobiology of Infant Attachment." *Wiley InterScience.* (2005): DOI 10.1002/dev.20093

Ridley, Matt. *Nature Via Nurture: Genes, Experience, and What Makes Us Human.* New York: HarperCollins, 2003.

Salter, Mary D. and John Bowlby. "An Ethological Approach to Personality Development." *American Psychologist* 46, no. 4 (1991): 331–341.

Shah, Prachi E., Peter Fonagy, and Lane Strathearn. "Is Attachment Transmitted Across Generations? The Plot Thickens." *Clinical Child Psychology and Psychiatry* 15, no. 3 (2010): 329–345.

Sapolsky, Robert. "A Gene for Nothing." In *Monkeyluv: And Other Essays on Our Lives as Animals,* 13–27. New York: Scribner, 2005.

Siegel, Daniel. "Attachment." In *The Developing Mind, Second Edition: How Relationships and the Brain Interact to Shape Who We Are*, 91–145. New York: The Guilford Press, 2012.

Vaughn, Brian E., Kelly K. Bost, and Mainus H. Ijzendoorn, "Attachment and Temperament as Intersecting Developmental Products and Interacting Developmental Contexts Throughout Infancy and Childhood." In *Handbook of Attachment: Theory, Research, and Clinical Applications Third Edition*, eds. Jude Cassidy and Phillip R. Shaver. New York: The Guilford Press, 2016.

Verhage, Marije L., Carlo Schuengel, Sheri Madigan, R. M. Fearon, Mirjam Oosterman Pacsco, Rosalinda Cassibba, Marian Bakermans-Kranenburg, and Marinus H. Ijzendoorn. "Narrowing the Transmission Gap: A Synthesis of Three Decades of Research on Intergenerational Transmission of Attachment." *Psychological Bulletin* 142, no. 4 (2016): 337–366.

Wallin, David J. *Attachment in Psychotherapy, Reprint Edition.* New York: The Guilford Press, 2007/2014.

Winnicott, D. W. "Part One: Papers on Development." In *The Maturational Processes and the Facilitating Environment: Studies in the Theory of Emotional Development*, 15–105. London: The Hogarth Press and the Institute of Psycho-Analysis, 1965.

Zeifman, Debra M. and Cindy Hazan. "Pair Bonds as Attachments: Mounting Evidence in Support of Bowlby's Hypothesis." In *Handbook of Attachment: Theory, Research, and Clinical Applications Third Edition*, edited by Jude Cassidy and Phillip R. Shaver, 416–434. New York: The Guilford Press, 2016.

CHAPTER EIGHT: GROWING REGULATION

Atzil, Shir, Talma Hendler, and Ruth Feldman. "Specifying the Neurobiological Basis of Human Attachment: Brains, Hormones and Behavior in Synchronous and Intrusive Mothers." *Neuropsychopharmacology* 36, no. 13 (2011): 2603–2616.

Bath, Howard I. "Calming Together: The Pathway to Self-Control." *Reclaiming Children and Youth* 16, no. 4 (2008): 44–46.

Cacioppo, John T. and William Patrick. *Loneliness: Human Nature and the Need for Social Connection.* New York: W. W. Norton & Company, 2008.

Diamond, Lisa M. and Lisa G. Aspinwall. "Emotion Regulation Across the Life Span: An Integrative Perspective Emphasizing Self-Regulation, Positive Affect, and Dyadic Processes." *Motivation and Emotion* 27, no. 2 (2003): 125–156.

Fredrickson, Barbara L. "The Role of Positive Emotions in Positive Psychology: The Broaden-and-Build Theory of Positive Emotions." *American Psychologist* 56, no. 3 (2001): 218–226.

———. "What Good Are Positive Emotions?" *Review of General Psychology* 2, no. 3 (1998): 300–319.

Heinrichs, Markus, Thomas Baumgartner, Clemens Kirschbaum, and Ulrike Ehlert. "Social Support and Oxytocin Interact to Suppress Cortisol and Subjective Responses to Psychosocial Stress." *Biological Psychiatry* 54 (2003): 1389–1398.

Kidd, Tara, Mark Hamer, and Andrew Steptoe. "Examining the Association Between Adult Attachment Style and Cortisol Responses to Acute Stress." *Psychoneuroendocrinology* 36 (2011): 771–779.

Mikulincer, Mario and Phillip R. Shaver. "Adult Attachment and Emotion Regulation." In *Handbook of Attachment: Theory, Research, and Clinical Applications Third Edition*, edited by Jude Cassidy and Phillip R. Shaver, 507–533. New York: The Guilford Press, 2016.

Neumann, Inga D. "The Advantage of Social Living: Brain Neuropeptides Mediate the Beneficial Consequences of Sex and Motherhood." *Frontiers in Neuroendocrinology* 30 (2009): 483–496.

Siegel, Daniel "Interpersonal Connection." In *The Developing Mind, Second Edition: How Relationships and the Brain Interact to Shape Who We Are*, 307–335. New York: The Guilford Press, 2012.

Ogden, Pat, Kekuni Minton, and Clare Pain. "Chapter 3: Attachment: The Role of the Body in Dyadic Regulation." In *Trauma and the Body: A Sensorimotor Approach to Psychotherapy*, 41–64. New York: W. W. Norton & Company, 2006.

Quirin, Markus, Julius Kuhl, and Rainer Düsing. "Oxytocin Buffers Cortisol Responses to Stress in Individuals with Impaired Emotion Regulation Abilities." *Psychoneuroendocrinology* 36, no. 6 (2011); 898–904.

Shapiro, Janet R. and Jeffrey S. Applegate. "Cognitive Neuroscience, Neurobiology and Affect Regulation: Implications for Clinical Social Work." *Clinical Social Work Journal* 28, no. 1 (2000): 9–21.

Sapolsky, Robert M. *Why Zebras Don't Get Ulcers*. New York: Holt Paperbacks, 2004.

Schore, Allan N. *Affect Regulation and the Origin of the Self: The Neurobiology of Emotional Development*. Mahwah, New Jersey: Lawrence Erlbaum Associates, 1994.

———. *The Allan Schore Reader: Setting the Course of Development*, ed. Eva Rass. New York: Routledge, 2017.

Taylor, Shelley E., Laura Cousino Klein, Brian P. Lewis, Tara L. Gruenewald, Regan A. R. Gurung, and John A. Updegraff. *Biobehavioral Responses to Stress in Females: Tend-and-Befriend, Not Fight-or-Flight*. Psychological Review 107, no. 3 (2000): 411–429.

———. *The Tending Instinct: How Nurturing is Essential to Who We Are and How We Live*. New York: Times Books, 2002.

CHAPTER NINE: EMPATHIC EMMA

Baron-Cohen, Simon. *Mindblindness: An Essay on Autism and Theory of Mind*. Cambridge, Mass.: The MIT Press, 1995.

———. *The Essential Difference: The Truth About the Male and Female Brain*. New York: Basic Books, 2003.

Batson, Daniel C. "These Things Called Empathy: Eight Related but Distinct Phenomena." In *The Social Neuroscience of Empathy*, eds. Jean Decety and William Ickes, 5–15. Cambridge, Mass.: MIT Press, 2009.

Butler, Marilyn. *Jane Austen and the War of Ideas*. Oxford, England: Clarendon Press, 1988.

Decety, Jean and Claus Lamm. "Human Empathy Through the Lens of Social Neuroscience." *The Scientific World Journal* 6 (2011): 1146–1163.

——— and Meghan Meyer, "From Emotion Resonance to Empathic Understanding: A Social Developmental Neuroscience Account." *Development and Psychopathology* 20 (2008): 1053–1080.

——— and Philip L. Jackson. "The Functional Architecture of Human Empathy." *Behavioral and Cognitive Neuroscience Reviews 3*, no.2 (2004): 71–100.

Deresiewicz, William. *A Jane Austen Education: How Six Novels Taught Me About Love, Friendship, and the Things That Really Matter*. New York: Penguin, 2012.

Eisenberg, Nancy and Natalie D. Eggum. "Empathic Responding: Sympathy and Personal Distress." In *The Social Neuroscience of Empathy*, eds. Jean Decety and William Ickes, 71–84. Cambridge, Mass.: MIT Press, 2009.

Eliot, Lise. *Pink Brain, Blue Brain: How Small Differences Grow Into Troublesome Gaps—And What We Can Do About It*. Wilmington, Mass.: Mariner Books, 2010.

Fine, Cordelia. *Delusions of Gender: How Our Minds, Society, & Neuorsexism Create Difference*. New York: W. W. Norton & Company, 2009.

———. *Testosterone Rex: Myths of Sex, Science, and Society*. New York: W. W. Norton & Company, 2017.

Gallese, Vittorio. "The 'Shared Manifold' Hypothesis: From Mirror Neurons to Empathy." *Journal of Consciousness Studies* 8, no. 5–7 (2001): 333–50.

Hare, Brian. "Survival of the Friendliest: Homo Sapiens Evolved via Selection for Prosociality." *Annual Review of Psychology* 68 (2017): 155–186.

Harris, Jocelyn. "Satire, Celebrity, and Politics in Jane Austen." *Transits: Literature Thought & Culture, 1650-1850.* Lewisburg, Penn.: Bucknell University Press, 2017.

Hrdy, Sarah Blaffer. *Mothers and Others: The Evolutionary Origins of Mutual Understanding.* Cambridge, Mass.: The Belknap Press, 2011.

Johnson, Claudia L. *Jane Austen: Women, Politics, and the Novel.* Chicago: University of Chicago Press, 1990.

Kelly, Helena. *Jane Austen, The Secret Radical.* New York: Knopf, 2017.

Morelli, Sylvia A. and Matthew D. Lieberman. "The Role of Automaticity and Attention in Neural Processes Underlying Empathy for Happiness, Sadness, and Anxiety." *Frontiers in Human Neuroscience* 7 (2013): doi:10.3389/fnhum.2013.00160

McGlamery, Mary Elizabeth, Steven E. Ball, Tracy B. Henley, and Megan Besozzi. "Theory of Mind, Attention, and Executive Function in Kindergarten Boys." *Emotional and Behavioural Difficulties* 12, no. 1 (2007): 29–47.

Preston, Stephanie D. and Frans B. M. De Waal. "Empathy: Its Ultimate and Proximate Bases." *Brain and Behavioral Sciences* 25, no. 1 (2002): 1–20.

Shamay-Tsoory, Simone G., Judith Aharon-Peretz and Daniella Perry. "Two Systems for Empathy: A Double Dissociation Between Emotional and Cognitive Empathy in Inferior Frontal Gyrus Versus Ventromedial Prefrontal Lesions." *Brain* 132, no. 3 (2009): 617–627.

Singer, Peter. *The Expanding Circle: Ethics, Evolution, and Moral Progress.* Princeton, N.J.: Princeton University Press, 2011.

Singer, Tania and Claus Lamm. "The Social Neuroscience of Empathy" *The Year in Cognitive Neuroscience 2009: Annals of the New York Academy of Sciences* (2009): 81–96.

Williams, Raymond. *The Country and the City.* Oxford, England: Oxford University Press, 1975.

CHAPTER TEN: MENTALIZING AND REALITY

Aichhorn, Markus, Josef Perner, Benjamin Weiss, Martin Kronbichler, Wolfgang Staffen, and Gunther Ladurner. "Temporo-Parietal Junction Activity in Theory-of-Mind Tasks: Falseness, Beliefs, or Attention." *Journal of Cognitive Neuroscience* 21, no. 6 (2008): 1179–1192.

Astington, Janet Wilde and Jodie A. Baird. "Representational Development and False-Belief Understanding." In *Why Language Matters for Theory of Mind,* eds. Janet Wilde Astington and Jodie A. Baird (Oxford, England: Oxford University Press, 2005).

Baron-Cohen, Simon. *The Science of Evil: On Empathy and the Origins of Cruelty.* New York: Basic Books, 2011.

Carr, Laurie, Marco Iacoboni, Marie Charlotte Dubeau, John C. Mazziotta, and Gian Luigi Lenzi. "Neural Mechanisms of Empathy in Humans: A Relay from Neural Systems for Imitation to Limbic Areas." *Proceedings of the National Academy of Sciences of the United States of America* 100, no. 9 (2003): 5497–5502.

Decety, Jean. "To What Extent is the Experience of Empathy Mediated by Shared Neural Circuits?" *Emotion Review* 2, no. 3 (2010): 204–207.

––––––– and Thierry Chaminade. "When the Self Represents the Other: A New Cognitive Neuroscience View on Psychological Identification." *Consciousness and Cognition* 12, no. 4 (2003): 577–596.

––––––– and Claus Lamm. "Human Empathy Through the Lens of Social Neuroscience." *The Scientific World Journal* 6 (2011): 1146–1163.

Dow, Gillian and Katie Halsey. "Jane Austen's Reading: The Chawton Years." *Persuasions* 30, no.2 (2010): http://www.jasna.org/persuasions/on-line/vol30no2/dow-halsey.html.

Ferrari, P. F. and G. Rizzolatti. "Mirror Neuron Research: The Past and the Future." *Philosophical Transactions of the Royal Society B*, 364, no. 1644 (2014): 2030169.

Fonagy, Peter, Gyorgy Gergely, Elliot Jurist, and Mary Targe. *Affect Regulation, Mentalization, and the Development of the Self.* New York: Other Press, 2005.

Goldman, Alvin I. *Simulating Minds: The Philosophy, Psychology, and Neuroscience of Mindreading.* Oxford, England: Oxford University Press, 2008.

Gopnik Alison and Janet W. Astington. "Children's Understanding of Representational Change and Its Relation to the Understanding of False Belief and the Appearance-Reality Distinction." *Child Development* 59, no. 1 (1988): 26–37.

Grossman, Klaus E., Karin Grossman, and Everett Waters, eds. *Attachment from Infancy to Adulthood: The Major Longitudinal Studies,* New York: The Guilford Press, 2006.

Kidd, Tara, Mark Hamer, and Andrew Steptoe. "Examining the Association Between Adult Attachment Style and Cortisol Responses to Acute Stress." *Psychoneuroendocrinology* 36, no. 6 (2011): 771–779.

Keysers, Christian and Valeria Gazzola. "Social Neuroscience: Mirror Neurons Recorded in Humans." *Current Biology* 20, no. 8 (2010): R353–R354.

Iacoboni, Marco. *Mirroring People: The Science of Empathy and How We Connect with Others.* New York: Picador, 2009.

–––––––, Istvan Molnar-Szakacs, Vittorio Gallese, Giovanni Buccino, John C. Mazziotta, and Giacomo Rizzolatti. "Grasping the Intentions of Others with One's Own Mirror Neuron System." *PLoS biology* 3, no. 3 (2005): https://doi.org/10.1371/journal.pbio.0030079.

Keysers, Christian. *The Empathic Brain: How the Discovery of Mirror Neurons Changes Our Understanding of Human Nature.* New York: Social Brain Press, 2011.

––––––– and Galeria Gazzola. "Social Neuroscience: Mirror Neurons Recorded in Humans. *Current Biology* 20, no. 8 (2010): doi: 10.1016/j.cub.2010.03.013.

Marcus, Gary. *Kluge: The Haphazard Construction of the Human Mind*. New York: Houghton Mifflin, 2008.

Preston, Stephanie D. and Frans B. M. De Waal. "Empathy: Its Ultimate and Proximate Bases." *Brain and Behavioral Sciences* 25, no. 1 (2002): 1–20.

Repacholi, B. M. and A. Gopnik. "Early Reasoning About Desires: Evidence from 14-18-Months-Olds" *Developmental Psychology* 33 (1997): 12–21.

Rizzolatti, Giacomo and Leonardo Fogassi. "The Mirror Mechanism: Recent Findings and Perspectives." *Philosophical Transactions of the Royal Society B*, 364, no. 1644 (2014): 20130420. http://rstb.royalsocietypublishing.org/.

——— and Corrado Sinigaglia. *Mirrors in the Brain: How Our Minds Share Actions, Emotions, and Experience*. Oxford, England: Oxford University Press, 2008.

Saxe, R. and N. Kanwisher. "People Thinking About People: The Role of the Temporo-Parietal Junction in 'Theory of Mind.'" *NeuroImage* 19 (2003): 1835–1842.

Stern, Daniel N. *The Interpersonal World of the Infant: A View from Psychoanalysis and Developmental Psychology*. New York: Basic Books, 2000.

Wicker, Bruno, Christian Keysers, Jane Plailly, Jean-Pierre Royet, Vittorio Gallese, and Giacomo Rizzolatti. "Both of Us Disgusted in My Insula: The Common Neural Basis of Seeing and Feeling Disgust." *Neuron* 40 (2003): 655–664.

Winnicott, D. W. *Playing and Reality*. London: Tavistock Publications Ltd., 1971/ Routledge Classics. New York: Routledge, 2005.

CHAPTER ELEVEN: SOURCES CRIMES OF THE HEARTLESS, PART ONE

American Psychiatric Association. *Diagnostic and Statistical of Mental Disorders*, 5th Edition (*DSM-5*). American Psychiatric Publishing, 2013.

Baron-Cohen, Simon. *The Science of Evil: On Empathy and the Origins of Cruelty*. New York: Basic Books, 2011.

Bartal, Inbal Ben-Ami, Jean Decety, and Peggy Mason. "Empathy and Pro-Social Behavior in Rats." *Science* 334, no. 6061 (2011): 1427–1430.

Beatty, Margot T. "Early Development of Personality Disorders—Mother-Infant Dyadic Formation of the Infant Mind: The Psychological Dialectic." In *The Personality Disorders Through the Lens of Attachment Theory and the Neurobiologic Development of the Self: A Clinical Integration*, ed. James F. Masterson, 19–60. Phoenix: Zeig, Tucker & Theisen, 2005.

Blair, R.J.R. "Psychopathy, Frustration, and Reactive Aggression: The Role of Ventromedial Prefrontal Cortex." *British Journal of Psychology* 101 (2010): 383–399.

———. "The Amygdala and Ventromedial Prefrontal Cortex in Morality and Psychopathy." *Trends in Cognitive Sciences* 11, no. 9 (2007): 337–392.

Bloom, Paul. "Empathy and Its Discontents." *Trends in Cognitive Sciences* 21, no. 1 (2017): 24–31.

De Waal, Frans. *Are We Smart Enough to Know How Smart Animals Are?* New York: W. W. Norton & Company, 2017.

———. *Primates and Philosophers: How Morality Evolved.* Princeton Science Library. Princeton, N.J.: Princeton University Press, 2009.

———. *The Bonobo and the Atheist: In Search of Humanism Among the Primates.* New York: W. W. Norton & Company, 2014.

Echols, Stephanie and Joshua Correll. "It's More than Skin Deep: Empathy and Helping Behavior Across Social Groups." In *Empathy: From Bench to Bedside*, ed. Jean Decety, 55–71. Cambridge, Mass.: MIT Press, 2012.

Fonagy, Peter and Anthony Bateman. "Attachment, Mentalization and Borderline Personality Disorder." *European Psychotherapy* 8, no. 1 (2008): 35–47.

Keltner, Dacher. *Born to Be Good: The Science of a Meaningful Life.* New York: W. W. Norton & Company, 2009.

———, Jason Marsh, and Jeremy Adam Smith, eds. "Part One: The Scientific Roots of Human Goodness." *The Compassionate Instinct: The Science of Human Goodness*, 5–93. New York: W. W. Norton & Company, 2010.

Kiehl, Kent A. *The Psychopath Whisperer: The Science of Those Without Conscience.* New York: Crown, 2014.

Levy, Kenneth N., Benjamin N. Johnson, Tracy L. Clouthier, Wesley J. Scala, and Christina M. Temes. "An Attachment Theoretical Framework for Personality Disorders." *Canadian Psychology* 56, no. 2 (2015): 197–207.

Masserman, Jules H., Stanley Wechkin, and William Terris. "'Altruistic' Behavior in Rhesus Monkeys." *The American Journal of Psychiatry* 121 (1964): 584–585.

Masterson, James F. "Integrating Attachment and Object Relations Theories and the Neurobiologic Development of the Self." In *The Personality Disorders Through the Lens of Attachment Theory and the Neurobiologic Development of the Self: A Clinical Integration*, ed. James F. Masterson, 1–18. Phoenix: Zeig, Tucker & Theisen, 2005.

———. *The Narcissistic and Borderline Disorders: An Integrated Developmental Approach.* New York: Taylor and Francis Group, 1981.

———. *The Personality Disorders.* Phoenix: Zeig, Tucker & Theisen, 2000.

Meffert, Harma, Valeria Gazzola, Johan A. den Boer, Arnold A. Bartels, and Christian Keysers. "Reduced Spontaneous but Relatively Normal Vicarious Representations in Psychopathy." *Brain: A Journal of Neurology* 136 (2013): 2550–2562.

Milgram, Stanley. *Obedience to Authority.* New York: Harper Perennial Modern Classics; Perennial Books, 2009.

Perry, Bruce D. *Born for Love: Why Empathy is Essential—And Endangered.* New York: William Morrow, 2010.

———, and Maia Szalavitz. *The Boy Who Was Raised as a Dog and Other Stories from a Child Psychiatrist's Notebook.* New York: Basic Books, 2017.

Schelling, T. C. "The Life You Save May Be Your Own. In *Problems in Public Expenditure Analysis*, ed. S. B. Chase, 127–162. Washington: The Brookings Institution, 1968.

Ugazio, Giuseppe, Jasminka Majdandzic, and Claus Lamm, "Are Empathy and Morality Linked? Evidence from Moral Psychology, Social and Decision Neuroscience, and Philosophy." In *Empathy and Morality,* ed. Heidi H. Maibom, 155–171. New York: Oxford University Press, 2014.

Winnicott, D. W. "Ego Distortion in Terms of True and False Self." In *The Maturational Process and the Facilitating Environment*, 140–157. New York: International Universities Press, 1965.

CHAPTER TWELVE: CRIMES OF THE HEARTLESS: EMPATHY DISORDERS, PART TWO

American Psychiatric Association. *Diagnostic and Statistical of Mental Disorders*, 5th Edition (*DSM-5*). American Psychiatric Publishing, 2013.

Baron-Cohen, Simon. *The Science of Evil: On Empathy and the Origins of Cruelty.* New York: Basic Books, 2011.

Beatty, Margot T. "Early Development of Personality Disorders—Mother-Infant Dyadic Formation of the Infant Mind: The Psychological Dialectic." In *The Personality Disorders Through the Lens of Attachment Theory and the Neurobiologic Development of the Self: A Clinical Integration*, ed. James F. Masterson, 19–60. Phoenix: Zeig, Tucker & Theisen, 2005.

Campbell, Keith W. and Joshua D. Miller, eds. *The Handbook of Narcissism and Narcissistic Personality Disorder: Theoretical Approaches, Empirical Findings, and Treatments.* New York: Wiley, 2011.

Levy, Kenneth N., Benjamin N. Johnson, Tracy L. Clouthier, Wesley J. Scala, and Christina M. Temes. "An Attachment Theoretical Framework for Personality Disorders." *Canadian Psychology* 56, no. 2 (2015): 197–207.

Decety, Jean and Yoshiya Moriguchi. "The Empathic Brain and its Dysfunction in Psychiatric Populations: Implications for Intervention Across Different Clinical Conditions." *BioPsychoSocial Medicine: The Journal of the Japanese Society of Psychosomatic Medicine* 1, no. 22 (2007): DOI: 10.1186/1751-0759-1-22.

Knight, Zelda G. "Some Thoughts on the Psychological Roots of the Behavior of the Serial Killers as Narcissists: An Object Relations Approach." *Social Behavior and Personality: An International Journal* 34, no. 10 (2006).

Masterson, James F. "Integrating Attachment and Object Relations Theories and the Neurobiologic Development of the Self. In *The Personality Disorders Through the Lens of Attachment Theory and the Neurobiologic Development of the Self: A Clinical Integration*, ed. James F. Masterson, 1–18. Phoenix: Zeig, Tucker & Theisen, 2005.

———. *The Emerging Self: A Developmental, Self, and Object Relations Approach to the Treatment of the Closet Narcissistic Disorder of the Self.* Philadelphia: Bruner Mazel, 1993.

———. *The Narcissistic and Borderline Disorders: An Integrated Developmental Approach.* New York: Taylor and Francis Group, 1981.

———. *The Personality Disorders.* Phoenix: Zeig, Tucker & Theisen, 2000.

Winnicott, D. W. "Ego Distortion in Terms of True and False Self." In *The Maturational Process and the Facilitating Environment*, 140–157. New York: International Universities Press.

EPILOGUE

Bal, P. Matthijs and Martijn Veltkamp. "How Does Reading Influence Empathy? An Experimental Investigation on the Role of Emotional Transportation." *PLoS ONE* 8, no. 1 (2013): e5534. https://doi.org/10.1371/journal.pone.0055341.

Bal, Mieke. "Levels of Narration." In *Introduction to Narratology,* 48–74. Toronto: University of Toronto Press, 2009.

Boulenger, Veronique, Olaf Hauk, and Friedemann Pulvermüller. "Grasping Ideas with the Motor System in Idiom Comprehension." *Cerebral Cortex* 19, no. 8 (2009): 1905–1914.

Goldman, Corrie. "This is Your Brain on Jane Austen, and Stanford Researchers Are Taking Notes." *Stanford University News.* September 7, 2012. Retrieved August 26, 2017. http://news.stanford.edu/news/2012/september/austen-reading-fmri-090712.html

González, Julio, Alfonso Barros-Loscertales, Friedemann Pulvermüller, Vanessa Meseguer, Ana Sanjuán, Vicente Belloch, and Cesar Avila. "Reading Cinnamon Activates Olfactory Brain Regions." *NeuroImage* 32, no. 2 (2006): 906–912.

Hernadi, Paul. "Dual Perspective: Free Indirect Discourse and Related Techniques." *Comparative Literature* 24, no. 1 (1972): 32–43.

Keen, Susan. *Empathy and the Novel.* Oxford, England: Oxford University Press, 2010.

Kidd, David Comer and Emanuele Castano. "Reading Literary Fiction Improves Theory of Mind." *Science* 342 (2013): 377–380.

Palmer, Alan. *Fictional Minds, Frontiers of Narrative.* Lincoln: University of Nebraska Press, 2008.

Paul, Annie Murphy. "Your Brain on Fiction." *New York Times* (March 17, 2012). http://www.nytimes.com/2012/03/18/opinion/sunday/the-neuroscience-of-your-brain-on-fiction.html.

Zunshine, Lisa. "Why Jane Austen Was Different and Why We May Need Cognitive Science to See It." *Style* 41, no. 3 (2007): 275–298.

ACKNOWLEDGMENTS

The moral of *Jane on the Brain*, insofar as one exists, is that no one goes it alone, and I have many people to thank for helping me write. My husband Paul Sawyer provided unconditional love, feedback, and support, giving me the "holding environment," as Winnicott put it, in which to work. My daughters Jocelyn Sawyer and Maggie Sawyer read countless extracts of my work in progress; their comments were unerringly thoughtful and helpful. Maggie accompanied me on my midlife career change, studying the mind-brain sciences along with me. Jocelyn's illustrations are sure to "instruct and delight" readers, advice from the Classical poet Horace that Austen surely knew. Sonia Covington's love and friendship have been invaluable.

Michael Chen read draft after draft of *Jane on the Brain*, helping me to find the voice and style appropriate to what I had to say. I'm grateful to Daniel Matusiewicz for our many conversations about the mind-brain, which have been as informative as any of the books I read or classes I took. Yona Zeldis McDonough and Paul Cody, dear friends of long duration, as well as inspired novelists, contributed essential help and advice on many aspects of writing and publishing. Barbara Ganzel was my go-to person for neuroscience, as was Jane Mendle for psychology—they are pals as well. Shimon Edelman, my first teacher as I ventured into a new discipline, has remained a chum, and my favorite person to argue with.

Anke Hoffstaetter, Kimberly Wheeler, and Micaela Corazón have demonstrated social intelligence in action through their generosity and wisdom. Alison Case, graduate-school classmate, gifted novelist, and English professor, has been the best of friends throughout the years. I'm indebted to Steven Cornelius and Aidan Chambliss for their willingness not only to lend support in various ways, but also to forgive me for disappearing for long periods into the "writing cave." Lisa Sundquist, Michael Alvich, Lee-Ellen Marvin, and Maude Rith created a supportive work environment as I segued into a new career. I'm grateful to my friends from academia, Molly Hite, Eric Cheyfitz, Stuart Davis, and Cynthia Chase for their continued friendship and loyalty, even though I left the fold. Tracy Hamler Carrick and Jennifer Janke gave much-appreciated encouragement, especially as I was completing this project. My cohorts at Binghamton, many of whom were also changing careers, remain close to my heart. And of course, my ballet buddies at the Ballet Center of Ithaca kept me sane in mind and healthy in body.

Jessica Case, my editor, has been outstanding: creative, helpful, attentive, tolerant—and she has Austen's treasured quality, empathy. I'm grateful to Laura Wood, my agent, for having confidence in my project, the vital ingredient for turning a collection of words into a book. Shayna Sobol, my copyeditor, has the patience of a saint; I know I can't spell. I'm thrilled with the book's appearance, "loveliness itself" as Mrs. Weston says of Emma (Jane would also be thrilled!): My thanks to Maria Fernandez for the text layout and to FaceOut Studio for the cover.

My parents, Vicki and Iz Singer, provided "secure attachment," the greatest gift a parent can give a child. *Jane on the Brain* is dedicated to them.

INDEX